CELESTIAL FIRE

A Naval Aviator's...

Spiritual Odyssey

Larry James Stevens

SOUL TALK UNLIMITED

Pahrump, Nevada

Celestial Fire
A Naval Aviator's Spiritual Odyssey

Larry James Stevens

Published by:
Soul Talk Unlimited, LLC
Post Office Box 6611
Pahrump, NV 89041

Orders and contact personnel at: www.soulmanlarry.com

The non-attributed and "Soul Man Truisms," by Larry James Stevens
Cover art-layout, by Robert Thompson and Lee Saldivar: Level3VisualArts.com
Interior formatting assistance, by Paul Lloyd Warner: www.plw.org
"Than Son Nhut takeoff" sketch, by Robert Thompson
"Great Balls of Fire and little Green Men" art, by Gae "Gaby" Hirsh
"Integrated Self " and "How We See" sketches (Fig. 1, 2), by Dr. Louis Nitti, Jr.
Sioux Indian art, by Paul Surber
Soul Talk and SoulMan logos, by "Design Diva" Ivy Hover: PoizenIdeas.com
Cover and text printing, by Malloy Inc. ~ Ann Arbor, MI (www.malloy.com)

ISBN, print ed.   0-9765577-0-3

First printing 2005
Printed in the United States of America

1. Inspirational Self-Help
2. Practical Spirituality
3. Holographic Psychology
4. Philosophy

Library of Congress Control Number: 2005900600
Standard Address Number (SAN):   2 5 6 – 4 1 8 1

What the EXPERTS say about *Celestial Fire:*

♥ ♥ ♥ ♥ ♥ ♥ ♥ ♥ ♥ ♥ ♥ ♥ ♥ ♥ ♥ ♥ ♥ ♥

"Rarely do I see *any* presentation, let alone a comprehensive life-guide, with zero criticism and 100% acknowledgment. Larry is an *Inspired Learner* and *Inspired Learning Facilitator*™. I *guarantee* his book will inspire YOU."
— **Peter Reding, Founder of the "Foundation for Inspired Learning"** (www.InspiredLearning.org).

"Larry was a brave man during the Vietnam War, but he's even braver to so intimately share his inner quest for wholeness and harmony. *This man's personal journey is a* **wake-up call to the many of us still sleeping.**"
— **Paul Von Ward, Interdisciplinary Cosmologist and author of *Our Solarian Legacy;* and *God, Genes, and Consciousness*** (www.vonward.com).

"Larry James Stevens is a Spiritual Will Rogers. With intelligence, humor, and sensitivity, he goes the extra quantum to bring expanded meaning and purpose to the bookends of agony and ecstasy. Larry is one of the very few qualified to use ALL levels of HP in his spiritual coaching practice."
— **Dr. James P. Pottenger, former protégé of Science of Mind Founder, Ernest Holmes, and the developer of Holographic Psychology™.**

"*Celestial Fire* ignites the *fire in the belly* of each one of us, and fans that inner empowerment flame into levels of awareness previously reserved only for the world's most advanced thinkers. Utilizing his playful but incredibly practical guide to the ultimate in potential, one's life journey becomes vastly simplified and miraculously enhanced."
— **Bill Bauman, Ph.D., Bill Bauman Seminars, author of *Oz Power: How to Click Your Heels and Take Charge of Your Life*** (www.BillBauman.net).

"In *Celestial Fire* Larry takes you with him on the flight of your life…emotionally and Spiritually. In so doing, he helps you find your master key to a life free of victimhood and un-forgiveness."
— **Colin Tipping, author of *Radical Forgiveness - Making Room for the Miracle*** (www.RadicalForgiveness.com).

"Larry James Stevens is the real thing…a writer, teacher, and Spiritual mentor who comes from heart with his every word and deed. His book is a GIANT bear hug, full of great questions, observations, and inspirations. While the perfect co-pilot to have on any Celestial flight, Larry wants to bestow the power and wisdom to take flight all on your own…how wonderful is that?"
— **Raphael Cushnir, author of *Unconditional Bliss,* and *Setting Your Heart on Fire*** (www.LivingtheQuestions.org).

"After 20 yrs. in metaphysics, I'd no idea a book could reveal so much about ME."
— **Vicki Worthington, professional editor (www.thepencilworks.com).**

"Larry has written a *fascinating* mix of extraordinary personal experience and metaphysical wisdom that's sure to appeal to both the seasoned Spiritual seeker *and* the newly curious."
— **Dr. Ron Scolastico, transpersonal psychologist and author of *Doorway to the Soul*—among several others (www.RonScolastico.com).**

"Dear Larry…you are a very happy Divine Soul on this Divine planet. You are showing the true light from your Divine heart. Enjoy your divinity and please share with other Divine Souls of this universe."
— **Yogi Ramesh, Hollywood's "Guru to the Stars" (www.UniversalYoga.org).**

"The **Power Prologue** was thrilling and so well written…I can hardly wait to read the whole thing!!! Good on ya, Larry!"
— **Tahdi Blackstone; Southwest Regional Community Coordinator for the Institute of Noetic Sciences.**

"**WOW!** What a read in just Chapter One! You had me wanting more and going back to reread some of the gems…several times. What a powerful start to a book!"
— **Rev. Joan Scimeca, BSL, J.D. RSciM; RS minister and CA attorney.**

"Larry's message is stirringly inspirational, and so very empowering…a smorgasbord for the Soul."
— **Margrit Spear, PhD/MFT; author of *Life Changing Explosion of Consciousness - Introduction to Holographic Psychology* (www.SimplyJoy.com).**

"No pie-in-the-sky offering, Larry delivers potent options for succeeding in today's highly complex world, as well as practical ways to get in direct contact with one's own inner Spiritual Source. A must read for any SSR!"
— **Dr. Louis Nitti, Jr., Psychology Professor, "Serious Spiritual Researcher," and author of *Discovering the Inner Writer - The Zen Method of Creative Writing*.**

"*Celestial Fire* is a dramatic and continual series of *burning bush* experiences…I'm finally seeing the light!"
— **Rev. Darrell Gudmundson, P.Eng, RScP, author of *Maxi-Mind & Turn the World On its Head*.**

"*Celestial Fire* is a rare opportunity for the many of us who have not as yet found our center. Following Larry through his *dark night of the Soul*, into an empowering and joyous awakening, is an emotional experience of the highest order…**especially for the analytical skeptic.**"
— **Celeste Kelley, Writer, Internet Talk Show Producer, Director, and former Host for WSRADIO.COM's *"Good Heavens! ASK THE STARS."***

"Dear Larry, I value your response and appreciate very much your willingness to share your opinion; I hope you will do so more frequently."
— **Rev. Edward Viljoen, Founder of NewThoughtMinisters Chat Group on Yahoo, and co-author of *Seeing Good at Work* (www.cslsr.org).**

"My goodness, Larry, I had no idea you were such a cut-up—funny!"
— **Rev. Carolyn Claiborne (www.spiritualmidwife.com).**

Table of Contents

BOOK TWO

DEDICATION

♥ ♥ ♥

To the multitude of Susans that have provided so much love and support throughout my life... especially my beloved former wife, Suzanne. Had she and the entire Politi family not gifted me with five glorious years of unconditional love, acceptance, and devoted encouragement, the empowering message herein would exist only in potential. Although we've had no direct contact since 1976, both Suzanne and her father, Angel Author and Love/Life-Master, Leo Politi, remain *demonstrated* examples that help light my way. I am grateful beyond words. I invite you to read (Appendix) my tribute to Leo, who made his glorious transition in 1996. This is for YOU Leo. In my heart you shall forever remain...*father-in-love*.

To my mother, June, and stepmother, Ruth, who both chose to wait at least until this book was published before riding into the sunset to join my inventive father in a *spectacular* castle he has no doubt prepared...your *non-judgment* day is at hand.

To my wonderfully gifted, guided, and beloved Sister, Wendy...who was a witness to, and participant of, much of it.

About the Author

Larry James Stevens grew up in the foothills of Studio City, California, as the son of an inventive genius who introduced him to multiple ways of perceiving any sensed experience...rather than only *reacting* to input and opportunities. Thomas A. Stevens, a trouble-shooting expert in experimental aircraft design/flight-test work for Kelly Johnson and Lockheed Aircraft's "Skunk Works," in Burbank, California, had a favorite saying: "What you don't have in your *head,* son, you must have in your *feet* or your *pocketbook.*"

Emulating his father's interest in aviation, Larry completed an intensive 20-month U.S. Navy flight training program, receiving his Commission as Ensign and the coveted *Wings of Gold* on the 5th of May, 1965. During the next three plus years, while repetitively flying into and from the many South Vietnamese airfields, Larry survived several *paranormal-like* interventions. While life-extending, these multiple encounters defied rational explanation. Larry soon began a thirty-year quest to uncover the mysteries of the extraordinary, including a stint as a reserve UFO investigator for APRO. In 1998, Larry was invited to join an avant-garde, NT research discipline, (Holographic Psychology™), which studies Spiritual DNA and multifarious components of the human personality matrix. Larry additionally volunteers as an independent Community Coordinator (NorCo IONS) for the Institute of Noetic Sciences (www.noetics.org).

Blending an open-ended (non-dogmatic) scientific and Spiritual perspective, Larry, a *quantum heart-shift facilitator* and Spiritual Coach, dedicates his life to the purpose of helping others wake up to their *preexisting* wholeness and potential. "Heaven on Earth exists now," says Larry. *"Acceptance-by-degree* is our vehicle to unlimited love, inclusive harmony, and joyous abundance."

ACKNOWLEDGMENTS

♥   ♥   ♥

In addition to thanking those on my "experts" list (opening pages), a special acknowledgment to all who have, unwittingly or otherwise, interacted with my often intense energy...especially during the more *self-absorbed* years. You are a vital part of this creation. Writing a book of this genre is a monumental undertaking...no less than launching any small business. Significant therapists and educators, like Terry Nash and Bettye Binder, crossed my path exactly when needed.

Editors: Award-winning poet and script editor, Nancy Berg, read through my rough manuscript, twice...each time presenting me with comprehensive critiques on what was needed to meet literary standards. Still driven to do the work myself, it took another five years to complete. Nancy wrote a time-line sample, which is part of the Office-Place Scenario in Chapter Six. Later, Laura Paxton (laurapaxton.com) provided brilliant reorganization of the material. Metaphysical specialist Vicki Worthington (thepencilworks.com) supplied the critical, intuitive finish editing. "Awesome Lady," Gayla Gary (icanproofread.com), supplied *awesome* proof reading. The multi-gifted Paul Lloyd Warner (www.plw.org) helped with final touches. Talented illustrator, Robert Thompson, intuitively plugged into my descriptive narration to recreate the incredible cockpit scene and basic cover art. He also produced the "escape" drawing in Chapter 13. Lee Saldivar (level3visualarts.com) did the cover layout, spine art, and other cover improvements...and improved on *reality* with his Author's photos. Friends and readers of complete drafts gifted me with valuable feedback: Bobbi Judy, Rev. Joan Scimeca, and award-winning author Raphael Cushnir (livingthequestions.org). Clark McCann, my *best-friend* from childhood, a professional writer himself, took time to help his buddy. Psychology Prof. and former cartoonist, Dr. Lou Nitti, Jr., provided Figure 1 and 2 sketches. Design Diva Ivy Hover (poizenideas.com) produced my logo and website. Ron and Susan Scolastico, plus Eternal *wisdom of the "Guides,"* are *very* present. New Thought *mega-leaders* Christian Sorensen, Dennis Jones, Les & Audrey Turner, furthered the cause, as did Irving Braverman (Chap. 15). Beloved Science of Spirit researchers, "BIG Brother" James Pottenger (Foreword) and Margrit Spear (simplyjoy.com) supplied the structure (Holographic Psychology™) that explains *preexisting potential* and transcendent awareness. To you special ones, and so many more...this part of our co-creation contract is complete.

FOREWORD

♥　　　♥　　　♥

Some call me an NDE survivor, but I say "thrive-or." After morgue personnel noted some slight motion, surreal events led to my rebirth and an eventual parent-son relationship with Ernest and Fenwick Holmes...Founders of the "Science of Mind" philosophy. Until Larry James Stevens came *rocketing* into my world with a zest for life I've rarely seen, I'd never shared the full details of my miraculous *resurrection*. Larry's childlike enthusiasm and appreciation, especially for a *mystery*, was difficult to resist. At that time, I focused on the transpersonal-level study of human potential, entrusted to me by Ernest. But Larry reminded me of the inspirational power of a gallant story...especially when *written-off* ones rally against all odds (Chapter 16). Having already sampled his bountiful storytelling, I was sold.

After witnessing or verifying his many years of psychological and ministerial study, service to others, and an incredible resume of personal growth work...all combined with thirty years of "miracles" research, I not only ordained Larry as a New Thought minister in 1998, I immediately invited him to join our Science of Spirit research team. Today, he is one of the very few qualified to effectively represent all levels of our multi-sensory, avant-garde teaching and ongoing research at LACCRS. Blending science with spirituality, Rev. Larry focuses on facilitating the actualizing of human potential; more specifically, the relationship between human freewill (choice) and the transcendent or *collective unconscious* influences.

Larry's fevered prodding immeasurably enhanced Holographic Psychology's look into Spiritual DNA, reality levels, and LOCATION of Comprehension. Helping us see the significant shifts within shifts, "Acceptance by Degree"—a transcendent replacement for cause and effect—was largely developed through his probative insight; as was "ASR" (Advanced Second Reality, Ch. 3). On the entertaining side: Larry's humorous *Will Rogers* manner of expressing not only titillates but inspires multiple ways of perceiving environmental data. Observing this facilitative dynamic led me to enhance our organization's *giggle-power* model as a method to release stress, activate endorphins, and reestablish creative free-flow. While reading his more poignant stories, I found myself running the gamut of human thought and feeling. Enjoying great delight and harmony in his current pathway, Larry's curiosity and enthusiasm *afterburner* (pilot jargon) remains fully lit. Should this Whirling Dervish come to *your* venue, I suggest you climb aboard or *duck & cover*.

BOOK: *Celestial Fire* is about the grandest vision of the greatest relationship of which you've ever conceived. And just when you think you're done, and can stretch no more, Larry supplies *another* booster rocket. As we're told in the Power Prologue (don't skip it), this IS a LOVE STORY of the highest order...one YOU can emulate by following this facilitator's laser-clear guidelines.

Instructed by book gurus to separate the memoir and flying stories from the empowerment teachings, Larry said "NO WAY!" I am therefore delighted to introduce an incredible chronicling of human Spirit. Authentically comprehensive, and psychologically sound, the first 10 chapters of this TWO-BOOK life-guide charmingly entertain while providing a practical explanation for how we, as humans, function—a virtual smorgasbord for Secular Humanists and other rational, cognitive, take-responsibility types. Great benefits inure to those looking to more effectively replace lack, limitation, and all forms of expressed unworthiness, with unlimited creativity and abundance.

The second portion of this *way-showing* extravaganza demonstrates Larry's intuitive, visceral, sacred connection, by whisking us away into delight, conjecture, and the magical realm of the paradoxical. Once there, Larry continues weaving his seductive web of imagination and possibilities. So much so that the so-called "paranormal" assumes a plethora of uniquely inspired forms, and the whimsical becomes a rationally minded, heart-centered person's *nectar of the gods*. While all his stories are riveting and thought provoking, Larry's flying experiences reign supreme—not just for their sensationalism, but for what they say about our synergism and divinity.

The summarizing portions masterfully synthesize the relationship between involution and evolution. Larry goes the extra quantum to bring expanded meaning and purpose to the bookends of agony and ecstasy. Balanced realism like this comes only from one who's walked both Dante's Inferno *and* the flowering field of dreams.

This *SoulMan's* inclusionary torah blasts through barriers that have enslaved humans for thousands of years. Not the timid person's sandbox, but if you'll stay *Celestial Fire's* victim-busting course, you will claim *Heaven on Earth*...and do so in style!

~ ~ ~

Dr. James Paxton Pottenger: Founder of LACCRS (1961), the Dodona Human-Potential and Science of Spirit Research Center, and pioneering developer of Holographic (*multi-sensory*) Psychology.

Group Attunement Invocation

♥   ♥   ♥

In this moment–both in and beyond space and time–we open ourselves completely…to all that is good…to perfection…to love.

We open in the wish to be of service to one another, and to all ones seeking health, liberation, connection, and truth.

We attune to the collective energy of our mutual guiding ones–whatever we choose to call them–as we stand believing in peace, harmony, joy, goodness, wholeness, creativity, and…

LOVE

The author's modified version of an attunement invocation used by Dr. Ron Scolastico.

DISCLAIMER

♥   ♥   ♥

The transformational journey of Larry James Stevens is personal to him. Many of the exercises mentioned within the text are typical of the processes that helped shift the author to new levels of personal awareness and spiritual growth. It must be understood, however, that Larry James Stevens is not a doctor or a therapist and does not prescribe or dispense medical advice. He does not recommend the use of any technique or process for physical or medical purposes—either directly or indirectly. The intent of the author and publisher is to offer an educational alternative, for self-help purposes only. The author and publisher cannot guarantee that all or any information or processes provided within this book will result in identical outcomes for a divergent readership.

Everything within these pages (except direct quotes) represents the author's own subjective opinion. Although Larry James Stevens is intimately familiar with the facilitative works of: transpersonal psychologist, author, and transcendent medium, Dr. Ron Scolastico; and Dr. James Pottenger, 1961 Founder of LACCRS and the Dodona Center for Human Development (where Holographic Psychology™ was developed); the author does not speak for these two gentlemen, or any other individual or entity endorsed or mentioned within this book. Certain story-line names have been changed to respect privacy.

BOOK ONE

Power Quotations

♥   ♥   ♥

No one sets aside the old ways to seek the new, until they *personally* feel the need for it.

The author's modified version of an old adage.

For those who *will,* the Universe leads; for those who *won't,* the Universe drags.

From a wise seer of Ancient Rome.

POWER PROLOGUE

♥   ♥   ♥

Flying over a desolate section of the Pacific Ocean, one ominous night, my DC-6 transport crew and I fought to stay airborne during a blinding electrical storm. In route to Wake Island, with classified and exceedingly dangerous cargo, we suddenly encountered an energy phenomenon so horrifying and bewildering that its reportage was rejected by investigative personnel attached to Navy squadron, VR-21.

At that very instant of abject terror, believing I was about to meet my maker, stunned aviator senses recorded an instantaneous life review.

Some months later, at cruising altitude during another stormy, but otherwise boring night flight in the Pacific Rim, the flight engineer hee-hawed as I attempted to clean a coffee spill off my khaki uniform. While mutually enjoying this moment of gregarious merriment, the aircraft and both its cockpit occupants were abruptly blinded. With no auto pilot, instruments, or visual reference of any kind, my chances of keeping a 100,000-pound aircraft in the air were slim.

Pushing through the sensory overload, one thought dominated: *"Pilot skills — alone — are not going to save us."*

In another harrowing encounter: Subic Bay, Philippines, was crowded with anchored ships from the Seventh Fleet. A large-class destroyer filled the cockpit window as our fully loaded plane inched its way through 150 feet of altitude — having just completed its takeoff run from NAS Cubi Point. Then, without warning, the impossible happened; life as we *previously* knew it, ceased to exist.

There's more. It was the monsoon season and I was flying left seat for a less-than-optimum, Visual Omni Range (VOR) instrument-approach and jungle landing at Cam Ranh Bay airfield. Touch-down on a narrow, recently-constructed and very slippery metal-mat landing surface, which Flight Ops was calling a runway, would be especially tricky. On short-final, *my hair suddenly stood on end*. With no visual reference or NOTAMS (notices to airmen) from the control tower, I sensed we were in extreme danger. Lacking sufficient time to explain my sudden *knowing* to the co-pilot or flight engineer, I prepared for a short-field landing procedure. Unbeknownst to any of us, this rarely used action would prove critical in the saving of aircraft and crew. *What was the source of my internal alarm?*

These and other extraordinary circumstances during the Vietnam War seemed well beyond any human capability or rational interpretation. And many more years of stumbling into the right places at the right times, left me with more questions than answers. Had this life-saving synchronicity been wasted on a self-indulgent character like me?

My relentless, agnostic-based pursuit of the extraordinary, while not as yet confirming Divine Intervention, did lead to a wondrous and all-encompassing human potential. I uncovered short-cut methods to quickly heal, release, and replace underlying feelings of lack and unworthiness—in both my life and the lives of others— *without* changing one's external environment. As a human-potential coach, I was steadfastly holding to the belief that personal growth facilitations could be proven and presented in a psychologically sound, non-esoteric (secular) manner. Approximately thirty years after having survived several inexplicable paranormal-like flying encounters in Vietnam, my empirically-based self-empowerment project took a major hit. While entering a signaled intersection in Escondido, California, I found myself awash in such knowledge, light, and protective influences, I had to instantly redefine who and what we—as humans—are.

Escondido Intervention

After eight exhaustive weeks providing restorative assistance to my two most significant Escondido-based relatives, I experienced a phenomenon that—hard as I tried—*could not be explained away by coincidence.* Traveling southbound on Rose Street, approaching Washington Avenue, I had driven the same route—stepmother to mother—dozens of times, juggling my time between both, as necessary, to help them recover from their respective crises. My intention, as usual, was to proceed through this signaled intersection to E. Valley Parkway, the street my mother (June) lived on, where I would then turn east. While approaching the green light, thinking positively about the good family work I had accomplished and my desire to return home to Las Vegas, *an invisible but extremely strong energy force took command of my actions.* Startled, I fought to counter the quick, unconscious movement of my right leg, but could not overcome the command to brake. "What's happening—why am I having this panic stop?" flashed through my mind. No words adequately explain what it feels like to observe and experience some purposeful force taking temporary custody of one's physical actions. Perhaps stroke or seizure victims experience similar feelings during an incapacitating attack. At this moment in time, more in awe than shock, I uncharacteristically accepted the forced braking action with a curious type of calm.

Just then, from my left, a Lincoln® Town Car blasted through the red light at approximately 50 miles-per-hour—way over the posted limit. With the intersection blind from the east, I had no visual or other conscious warning of approaching vehicles. After blissfully sailing through the red light, the driver finally slammed on his brakes and screeched to a stop. A huge man, the motorist appeared disoriented and possibly under the influence of some debilitating substance. I will always remember his stoically transfixed expression. Afterwards, thinking of him reminded me of those barely animated ghouls featured in the horror movie, *Invasion of the Body Snatchers.*® This eerie encounter prodded me to consider the possibility of *myself* becoming a disembodied voice, crying in the darkness, should I continue disavowing the remainder of my own internal woundedness.

After a five-second delay, the red-light-busting motorist spun his wheels in rapid departure. As I slowly cleared the far side of the intersection, I caught the transfixed eye of the one witness to this eerie scene. In a light-colored sedan, she had been waiting properly in the eastbound lane. The witness had a perfect view of both vehicles as they made their respective approaches, but now *she* seemed to be in shock. Both her telepathic communication and facial movements asked, "How did you know? You should have been killed!" As I nodded acknowledgment of her bewildered expression, I silently questioned, "Why me?" Had my self-image been in a little better shape, the more supportive side of my personality might have quickly countered with, "Why *not* me?"

I noted later that other than our party crasher and the one perplexed witness, this normally busy intersection remained empty during the entire ordeal.

Reflection

So, approximately thirty years after completing my military tour of duty, I am gifted (or cursed) with another extraordinary, life-saving intervention. The answers and explanations that I, as a dedicated researcher, had been relentlessly seeking—not only for myself but for all humankind—were about to be revealed.

Spirit to Larry

The physical reality of my close call finally hit me. With trembling torso and legs of rubber, I pulled over to the curb. Parked along the eastern side of Washington City Park, slowly regaining control of my physical senses, I noticed children joyously running and playing in the park—oblivious to the lifesaving event that had just occurred.

My years in professional aviation provided me with knowledge of relative closure velocities. Had I maintained a consistent rate of speed, my intended *Body Snatcher* would have broad-sided me in what accident investigators call the "Kill Zone."

Realizing my physical life had just been saved by some intervening force, or guidance, located beyond my conscious awareness, an intense goose-bump-producing shiver went through me. Looking toward the paranormal or metaphysical realm to explain my miraculous delivery, I wondered: was this another example of Divine intervention? If so, what was the source? Souls, Spirit Guides, Guardian Angels, the God Force itself? At that particular juncture, the specific nature or label of my deliverance—although of interest—was not my primary focus.

While still euphorically rapturous and grateful, I spontaneously went with my feelings and declared, through copious tears of relief and joy: "*Thank you, thank you, thank you! Human existence must have more significance than I realized, and you—whomever or whatever you are—want me and perhaps others to realize a greater appreciation for life's gifted opportunities.*"

I joked nervously about recognizing an attention-getting 2x4 blow to the head. I continued my verbalizing: "*I will make you* [speaking to the unidentified force] *a commitment. For at least the next 30 days, my time is completely yours. As of this moment, my personal agenda is on hold. I will follow every insight, hint, intuition, gut instinct and directed impulse. As best I can, I will place my analytical self on 'observer-mode' until the 30-days are over. Only then will I try to logically scrutinize what all of it (my observations) has meant.*"

I was setting out on a course discontinued at age 12½—after suffering some emotionally devastating circumstances. Once again I would entrust many of my daily choices to *intuitive* thoughts and feelings. I would not think about it—just DO it and BE it...within reason, of course. Making this emotional commitment filled me with euphoric feelings of peace, confidence, and excited anticipation. I had not the slightest concern that these intervening forces, although still not clearly identified (to my mind), would lead me to any harm. How could I possibly be guarded about my safety after what had just happened? I was on BONUS PLAY!

Let the Odyssey Begin

After a semi-futile attempt to explain my Escondido intersection encounter, I said a temporary goodbye to my confounded relatives. From the very beginning of my purposeful journey I felt the continual presence of guiding influences. The condensed schedule would have overwhelmed the best travel agent or personal secretary on the planet. In spite of the self-empowering nature of every event and encounter, all beneficial activities were spontaneously generated. Difficult to explain, but I spent most of this gifted month in a kind of giddy daze—neither here nor there, but *everywhere* simultaneously. The itinerary, so gloriously executed and personally satisfying, felt like winning a Megabucks jackpot. Taking a break from my predominant focus on analytical, self-absorbency, I was being handsomely rewarded. It was as if some shepherding force concluded: "OK team, we've got one month before his visceral door closes—again. Let's cram in everything Stevens can handle!"

Odyssey Inventory

Those thirty days and nights proved to be essential, integral, synergistic components to my never-ending discovery quest:

- **How and why are we here on Earth—what is the full purpose to our physical lives?**

- **How can we heal our internal pain, emotional fear, and feelings of unworthiness?**

- **What are the secrets to achieving deeply connected love and fruitful Earthly abundance?**

- **What is the truth about God, Souls and Soul-mates, devils, and our Eternal nature?**

On a beautiful mountain top in Malibu, California, the blitz of insight and connected healing reached its pinnacle during a retreat hosted by a very special duo—Ron and Susan Scolastico. As my odyssey would have it, one spot opened up and I got in on short notice.

Note: I never actually met Dr. Ron Scolastico until October 1996, but had benefited from his transpersonal "medium" work via two telephone consults in 1993. Years earlier, I read how Edgar Cayce, the "Sleeping Prophet," effectively used the telephone to conduct detailed consultations or "readings." I had researched Mind Dynamics™—a spin-off of Silva® Mind Control. Being favorably disposed, remote viewing did not seem particularly unusual or limiting. After spending many years questing for knowledge, fueled by several paranormal-like intervention experiences, I took my answers any way I could get them.

During my second evening at the majestic Malibu retreat, I had an even-more awe-inspiring contact with the same forces that intervened in Escondido. At a moment of surrendering release, I was bathed in a euphoric, but temporarily debilitating jolt of penetrating cosmic energy. Some describe this union as "Kundalini" energy combined with Samadhi self-realization. [*"Samadhi" is Hindu for a state of mystical contemplation where distinctions disappear between the little self and the Soul, or BIG Self*].

My incapacitating, yet energizing experience, felt like holding onto live electrical wires, but without any pain, unpleasantness, or shorting to ground. I awoke to the firm realization that *we all possess the power to recreate or change the significance of any portion of our life experience.*

This manual contains potent healing techniques and empowering insights from my concentrated Spiritual intensive. The Escondido experience and aftermath helped me finally realize that intervening forces had, in fact, been present before—during my flying days in Vietnam. Originally discounted, my previous encounters with aviation-related phenomena were thought to be exceptional *blind* luck. I now understand the true design of both my childhood *and* Navy experiences. These two experiential groupings of events combined to form precursory Spiritual seeds. Once planted, they awaited further cultivation—when and if I should awaken to their higher significance.

My true account shows how a rough-and-ready, but emotionally dysfunctional aviation warrior, finally found peace, harmony, joy, goodness, and love. A love story of the *highest* order—with its significance not limited to the eclectic transformation of one individual—your benefit will evolve from a willingness to embrace the wondrously empowering discoveries unearthed along the way. These findings, once internalized, can potentially provide you a joyous and universally-connected life once thought obtainable only in the Great Beyond—if at all. *Heaven on Earth* is an idea whose time has come…and now comes again.

Today, as a Quantum Heart-Shift Facilitator, Spiritual Coach, and seeker of all-inclusive truth, I hypothesize that an inner Spiritual DNA code provides love-based, intuitive encouragement…by which many feel prodded. My research team theorizes that this underlying element rests at the very core of a person's personality matrix. As such, it helps establish one's inner motivation to actualize both creative and sometimes challenging life circumstances. Our continuing supposition: Spiritual DNA contains a Celestial blueprint, specifically created for every manifested human expression.

If you're not happy about what you are doing and feeling in life, you may be reacting to fear-based, ego-mind conditioning, rather than responding to love-based, *Soul-heart* choices. You'll likely continue this modus operandi until sufficiently motivated to replace non-serving thoughts, feelings, and associated actions with more beneficial options. Rather than being dead in the water, as *shift happens,* you'll benefit from learning the vital role that inner beliefs play in your subjective experience and quality of life.

When the Mystery Began

I named this book for the most remarkable of my Naval Aviation energy encounters (Chapter Thirteen). The larger significance of unexplainable phenomena did not fully penetrate my conscious awareness until the Escondido intervention and its aftermath. Everything you will read resulted from many years spent piecing together the often-puzzling circumstances surrounding our human existence.

Have you ever been plagued with doubts about God, Souls, salvation, devils—the what, why, where, and how of both our Earth-bound *and* cosmic selves? When you asked probative questions of rigid authority types, were your serious queries interpreted as hedonistic preoccupation, or a lack of faith, sincerity and loyalty? Do you long for deeper, more profound feelings of connection and love? If your answers range between *yes* and *occasionally,* travel with me, now, as I share a rational, empowering message from an omnipotent, collective source.

Is there a universally conscious power base irrevocably interwoven within our Being? Assuming that an intrinsic, creative force exists, does it unconditionally support us even with all our temporarily expressing human warts and hangnails? I offer answers of peace, harmony, goodness, joy, connective acceptance, and love—resulting from my tenacious search—to sincere persons hungering for a dogma and superstition-FREE union.

If you—like most—have experienced inner feelings of lack or unworthiness, set those concerns aside for the moment. Consider how *self-diminishing thoughts or feelings are just temporarily distorted thoughts and feelings—NOT truths.* This message not only welcomes healthy skepticism, it encourages it. I promise you will not have to take anything, herein, on *blind* faith. This Spiritual handbook illustrates psychologically sound concepts and principles—revealing them as practical, testable, fully provable facets of everyday life. Although some may interpret my fervor and passion as being a bit too spirited, rest assured there will be no attempt to *clone* your thinking or suggest adherence to any religious belief or doctrine—to the contrary. This is a book about our true place in a magnificent Universe of unconditional love and all-inclusive synchronicity. This orientation does not preclude open-minded individuals from experiencing this message from a religious perspective, however. For those so inclined, consider my restorative, inspiring stories and narratives as recounted testimony. As this book reveals its twenty-first century empowerment options, know that their incorporation is best achieved by ones not content to simply *dream* a life of wishful ascension, but to live it.

More than just material for happy-hour or party conversation, this inspired offering presents a practical *plan of action*—an Eagle Flight. Although not a requirement, consider the benefits of opening to a loving expansion of your thinking, self-image, and habit patterns. We will step into what many consider treacherous—even forbidden—waters. More than once I found myself in the proverbial swamp with hungry crocodiles as escorts. Although snacked on from time to time, I eventually learned to swim with energy-draining reptilians *without* becoming their main course. Regardless of any psychological bogs, quagmires, or other personal obstacles you may be encountering, I will show you simple and permanent ways to replace those labyrinths of fear and uncertainty through a joyous exploration of the inner Spirit.

Objectives

As my journey companion you will acquire:

- **Practical, meaningful understandings of human behavior, and how beliefs are formed and changed.**
- **Instructional ways to dramatically improve your relationships (both human and Divine).**
- **Demonstrations of how ordinary events in your life can lead to profound healing, deeper discernment, and cosmic connection.**
- **An all-inclusive, commonsense solution to the great Evolutionism-Creationism debate.**
- **Innate proof that we are immortal, universally-connected Beings...and never alone.**

The INTRODUCTION that follows provides a significant foundation for everything you will learn and experience throughout this book.

To all my truth-seeking brethren and sistern, I affirm the following: "I can't promise anyone an instant rose garden. But, these pages *will* show you the location of all the sun, soil, seed, and support nutriments needed to create your own paradise on Earth. We will think, reason, laugh, and cry. Together, we'll say goodbye to feelings of loneliness, heartache, worthlessness, and isolation. And HELLO to joy, peace, harmony, goodness, love, creativity, and FUN!"

sketch by Lou Nitti Jr.

THE INTEGRATED SELF

Figure 1

POWER INTRODUCTION

Lift Off

♥   ♥   ♥

Your time has come to begin a grand transformation. That you find this life-guide in your hands is no coincidence. Vaguely put, your very best friend wanted you to have it. Just for FUN, let's reveal the identity of that most special *amigo* a little later.

You are about to embark on a marvelous journey — an adventure of wondrous enlightenment — which will provide you specific tools to empower yourself as never before. You, much like the rest of us, have been driving nails with a rock. Wouldn't you rather have a hammer?

We have been working hard on Earth, but not with total efficiency. *Activity does not guarantee accomplishment.* Regardless of current results, you deserve these forged gifts to ease your burden and provide insights to the full purpose of your life. If you so choose, you may now trade in that old, suffering *victimhood* curriculum in favor of the Earth adventure intended for graduate students. It's time to reclaim that *stuff* we keep giving away — our personal power — and learn to chart our own course...captain our own ship, in life. Through activation of your preexisting potential, your complete array of Terra-specific gifts, talents, and abilities can be joyfully retrieved. We — as Souls — have already provided our human selves the potential to successfully master every challenge and creative opportunity that crosses our vibrant paths. As a Human Being, expressing under an *amnesiac veil* that temporarily limits full conscious awareness, our five-sensory detectors — by themselves — are insufficient to rediscover (remember) the key to personal salvation and mastery of the Earth pathway. But not to worry...you'll soon learn to develop your *omni-sensory* ability, thereby releasing yourself from mental (psychological) and emotional bondage and limitation. Let a fellow

Soul traveler show you how to break those shackles that enslaved humanity for many millennia.

As a Navy pilot flying in Vietnam, I had no clue about any of what I share with you in this manual, nor could I explain my extreme and continuing good fortune. In one dramatic life-extending event after another I egotistically referred to exceptional good luck as my personal rite of passage. Eventually, I was to realize how ignorant I had been.

For the pilots or other less-patient readers that require the instant gratification of flying stories, or the rushing toward *cosmic contact,* before I offer foundational evidence of miracles and your preexisting potential, proceed to BOOK II (Chapter Eleven) after this Introduction — or even now, if that serves you. Although the intensity of your experience may not measure up to those who do their precursory homework, *and* you'll miss the skills and knowledge of how to maximize relationships and prosperity, I promise nothing harmful will befall you should you make the instant-gratification choice. Some — mostly right-brainers [see "Left-Brain/Right-Brain" under "Tools for the Developing Mind"] — don't care to be *burdened* with the knowledge of why or how *shift happens.* For the more discriminating and preserving, the **real** empowerment message that emerged from my relentless search continues from here.

Transformational Overview

This guidebook shows you how to determine whether your current belief-system serves you, and if not, how to change it. BOOK I contains a tri-level (interdisciplinary) explanation of how we — as uniquely manifested Human Beings — function. Chapter Two clearly delineates the "First Reality" system of perception, which limits our fullest human expression, and explains why the majority of us live in a state of psychological slavery to our inner beliefs. To truly begin the liberation process, it's vital you learn to harness the power of Chapter Three's "Second Reality" — the advent of true choice-making. Chapter Five then turns our mutual Spiritual odyssey toward the transcendent-connective realm, or "Third Reality." Examples of "three-realities" knowledge, provided by the new, empowering philosophical-based science of Holographic Psychology™, help ones to not only cope but thrive in life's often-difficult circumstances.

I demonstrate how reality levels determine both the severity and quality of:

❶ **Grief processing;**

❷ **Our views of both justice and forgiveness;**

❸ **Our concepts of right and wrong;**

❹ **Interpersonal and transpersonal relationships;**

❺ **Diverse states of being; located everywhere between separation and oneness.**

In BOOK II I share my own personal experiences with the paranormal—including many *near-fatal* encounters—in order to answer the question of whether miracles exist, and in what form(s) they manifest. I offer my detailed accounting of "Celestial Fire," before summarizing my multi-hemisphere analysis of what is often referred to as *Divine Intervention*.

Before we build up a full head of steam, I provide more preparatory background and further explain my role as a Quantum Heart-Shift (Spiritual-journey) Facilitator. But first, defining new terms will help structure the actualizing of your *full* potential, and provide the foundation for the "who are you and why are you here?" question.

Tools for the Developing Mind

Part of the process I use proves quite different from other self-help guides. Not limited to one-dimensional views of human conduct—such as behavioristic-based pathology, or other cause-and-effect determinants—we take our 21st Century lead from the ever-expanding fields of psychology, philosophy, anthropology, and linguistics. This gives us a heightened, pragmatic awareness of the shaping factors in human thinking, feeling, and action. To keep our enlightenment possibilities practical for everyday life, our foundational structure is provided by the limitless, all-inclusive principles of Holographic Psychology (HP) and its cornerstone, "Location of Comprehension (LOC)."

This introduction basically defines these new psychological and philosophical theorems—and their respective payoffs—in a moment. Through narrative example and illustrative dialogue, ensuing chapters list even more benefits. With technical delineation held to a minimum, we examine and learn effective uses of our instinctive, right-brain gifts. With the blended combination of logic and guided/directed intuition, a powerful transformation is not only possible, but likely. Recipients of this message potentially enjoy significant savings in time and money with any needed counseling or healing processes—but with pathology chasing either greatly reduced or eliminated.

I use the latest findings from HP to categorize behavior and personal empowerment from a three- and even a four-dimensional (cosmic) overview. From a holographic perspective, you'll find that *our world—for all practical purposes—is subjective reality based purely on mirrored projections of our own beliefs, habit patterns, and self-image.* Subjective-based interpretations starkly contrast with the objective, fact-based reality most persons believe is definitively determined through empirical study.

After learning the true source of your own behavior and how to change both it, *and* your world, all from within, you'll find changes to the environmental playing field provide neither prerequisite, nor solution. Discovering your options and how to access higher consciousness levels provide you a new set of positively expressed perceptions. Finding your individually selected motivational component, as part of your human personality matrix, shows you how Spiritual DNA (see Glossary) determines impetus for discovery and change. During these various processes, you may experience shifts, or *bursts,* of conscious awakening. You'll soon realize how and why these shifts occur and how your new level of awareness benefits not only yourself, but your loved ones and the world, as well. Personal empowerment will be obvious to all who cross your majestic path.

I will be referencing the leading-edge work of human-potential and Science of Spirit researcher, Dr. James P. Pottenger. A former protégé of Science-of-Mind founder Ernest Holmes, and the developer of Holographic Psychology, Dr. Pottenger confirms: "All substantive mental/emotional change—and the corresponding improvement in quality of life—is solely an internal process. It can be fully and harmoniously achieved without any obvious or intentional manipulation to a subject individual's external environment. *It is in our subconscious belief-system, and its transcendent connection, that all real, permanent change takes place.*"

Affirmations

Positive declarations verbalized and interpreted solely within the conscious mind, although quite positive in their own right, create very little lasting benefit. When an affirmation is not accepted by one's underlying belief-system, permanent modifications in behavior are unlikely to manifest.

I've Been There

Some—perhaps many—reading these words are distraught, perhaps even terrorized by fears of war, incapacitation, abandonment, loss of love, unworthiness, or tormenting hopelessness about the world and their place in it. Even if you think everything is basically OK, take a quiet moment, now, to sense whether the *complete* fullness of life is passing you by.

In this book I give you the road map and psychological tool kit I wished for myself, thirty years ago. The Universe answered my prayer the same way it does for others. Presented with a shopping list of challenges that helped me look in the right direction(s), my wounded heart and negative self-image were healed through the facilitation provided by often-difficult circumstances. Pain, an excellent feedback diagnostic, definitely motivates us. But *beneficial change does not require torturous circumstances*...unless we insist. Ask yourself this: *"Is this sandbox I'm creating, the one I wish to play in?"*

Are you open to consider whether predetermined Spiritual components could be guiding your learning, growing, and awakening opportunities? "If so," you might inquire, "how does said Guidance square with predestination; the concept of a foreordained lifetime?" Great question...and one I intend to answer, in stages. Before I received even a fraction of the illumed gifts of guidance and insight, I first had to feel worthy of them. Perhaps *you* have figured out the Universe gives us what we need to complete our life's curriculum. What our pleasure-seeking, pain-avoiding selves ask for, or want, is generally not the same.

In defining terminology, let's begin with the premise that all language, metaphorically or symbolically, represents its user's current reality; whether in presentation or interpretation. New phrases and jargon become progressively clearer as we demonstrate meaning via storyline example.

Left-Brain/Right-Brain [see figure 1 – last page of Prologue]

Basic to our communications, I will often refer to "left-brain" and "right-brain" or "left-right-hemisphere" thinking and feeling. Most have heard these *symbolic* terms before—perhaps even used them on occasion—without any clear understanding or agreement on their meanings. Using this definition as an all-inclusive model for

"Brain/Mind," visualize *Brain* (left hemisphere) as the hardware, and *Mind* (right hemisphere) as the software. This dualistic view — postulated by the father of modern philosophy, Rene Descartes — serves us until we are ready to transcend space and time to explore the more synchronous vision (Oneness) of Baruch Spinoza, and, this may surprise you...*Plato*. Although mainstream philosophy considers the revered Greek to be the father of dualism, SOS research theorizes that Plato was describing, in his "Allegory of the Cave," overlapping levels or stages of *waking-up* teleology — not separating disunion.

For our purposes here, let us say that left-brained thinking revolves around analytical examination and orderly detailed problem solving. In our left brain, referred to as "head" or male energy, we break down the *whole* into the sum of its parts. Television or computer hardware repair exemplifies learned behavior motivated primarily by five-sensory, tab-A into slot-B, procedural, left-brain use. Let us agree that right-brain or female energy orientation represents our unregulated, multi-sensory, creative nature, or *heart*. While right-brain focused, our thoughts lightly drift without structure or censure — as in lucid dreaming, attunements, or so-called altered-states of consciousness.

To summarize: we define analytical *thinking* as primarily a rational, five-sensory, left-hemisphere, language-based, *nuts-and-bolts* activity. We define artistic, free-flow, intuitive sensing, channeling, and unregulated feeling as omni-sensory, right-hemisphere-dominated facilitation. As they are not mutually exclusive, we use a degree of both hemispheres — often not equally — during everyday activities. Our mind (Soul-software) uses our human brain as the hardware to *animate* us while here on Earth. With nothing "official" in these definitional examples, they are not intended to perfectly adhere to established physiological or esoteric protocol.

Our definitional model is mostly reversed (right for left) for the eight- to nine percent of natural left-handers. Physiologically speaking, a left-hander's hemisphere indications prove more complex, varied, and much less predictable. Almost all right-handers show left-brain dominance, with natural left-handers generally right-brain dominant. However, to the consternation of neurological researchers, many lefties (my mother included) are left-brain dominant also.

Although it may appear so in my presentations, defaming reductionist views, or the scientific method (generally limited to five-sensory data), is not my intention. Even with a multi-sensory blind spot — or because of it — conventional science has served us well.

Consider, however, that *simultaneous integration of both heart* **and** *head afford the maximum in empowerment options and awakening potential.* This is the way of the Spiritual Warrior. With an appropriately grounded paradigm as our new guide, the Spiritually disenfranchised have a limitless, dogma-free medium to explore their *Infinite Inner.* That medium is the Science of Spirit, or in the secular world, Holographic Psychology™.

Following is a very brief explanation of relevant terms. For those wishing a more detailed *word* explanation, see APPENDIX - GLOSSARY. For others (right-brainers), you may gain a larger, more useful grasp of term significance through upcoming illustrations.

And now...for the more inquiring minds:

❶ **Holographic Psychology™ (HP).** *An all-inclusive study and delineated structure explaining the human/Soul mind and the involutionary-evolutionary process that brought us to this unprecedented threshold of remembering [to use Plato's term].* HP uses three distinct levels of comprehension, which embody individual dynamics and related world views: ① Behavioral (first-level understanding); ② Humanistic (second-level understanding); and ③ Transpersonal (third-level understanding). All three stages directly relate to perspective, behavior, and the resulting quality of life—whether dealing with human challenge or creative expression.

One of the greatest benefits of Holographic Psychology: for perhaps the very first time in human history (although the great mystics *intuited* what I share here) we have a science, or theory, defining human behavior that does *not* throw the baby out with the bath water. HP, an *all-inclusive* facilitation, fully embraces all elements of past human behavior, experience, and scientific study, without labeling behaviorism, humanism, or transpersonal perspectives (or any other view) as wrong, bad, or obsolete.

This (our) inclusive participation leads us on a path of consciousness rediscovery, prodding us to *remember* both observer and observed as **one** (Third Reality). Michael Talbot, author of *The Holographic Universe*, terms human experience "omnijective" (rather than *objective* or *subjective*), relating it to tantric (Hindu) "maya," an illusionary dream state.

❷ **Spiritual DNA.** *The human-life blueprint created by higher-source intelligence.* Spiritual DNA—in collaboration with its genetic-based partner—determines general Earth themes, or curricula, for the respective individual.

❸ **Self-image.** *An individual's subconscious mental image that validates his or her belief-system.* An essential part of the decision-making process, self-image forms the basis of an individual's self-acceptance, or state of being, projected to the world. Chapter Two covers self-image in detail.

❹ **Subjectiveness.** *Communication based on our current level of understanding.* The assumed knowledge of the individual's conscious awareness, as separate from the object world, is where we, as Human Beings, interpret data with the resources available to us at the time.

❺ **Truth.** *What we feel in the very core of our being.* Truth is perceived by the Soul-mind as functional wisdom, converted to a system of values fathomable within a Human Being. More on the significance of truth, in Chapter One.

❻ **Dualism.** *A belief in the division of body, mind, Spirit, and the environment.* Dualism exists until one awakens to the reality that he or she, rather than external factors, is (psychologically) evaluating and creating respective world views. Dualism will have more meaning and significance after we explore: ① our human history of suffering and victimization, and ② transcendent realms not limited by space and time (Third Reality).

❼ **SELF vs. self.** *Our Soul- or Universal-Mind existence (Big Self) vs. our human personality matrix* and our view of the operating system we believe solely determines our choices and behavior (little self). Upon reflection, we awaken to advanced levels of comprehension (SELF) and discover in stages that dualistically oriented perceptions are temporary, but intended, illusions.

❽ **Attunement.** *A so-called Altered-State process of directed subconscious contemplation.* In most metaphysical arenas, "attunement" is simply a synonym for conventional meditation. Here, it's a vehicle to bypass some portions of the conscious mind for the purpose of obtaining clarity of thought...with a *specific* objective.

❾ **Location of Comprehension (LOC).** *An emancipating principle of reflection that represents the apex of Holographic psychology.* The very few cosmologists and Spiritual facilitators that know of it, consider Location of Comprehension the definitive quantum leap in human psychological evolution. Paradigm shifts in understanding begin to arise in Second Reality awareness. LOC provides freedom to referee (what Wayne Dyer and Ken Wilber call *witnessing*) one's own thoughts, feelings, and actions, while enjoying—for the first time— true and complete options in the decision-making process. *LOCATION is the master key to authentic inner power and omnisensory perception.*

⑩ **Cloning.** In this psychological context, cloning is the attempt to make over another in a compatible image. Through this outer, belief-system manipulation, one hopes to achieve an elusive comfort zone without turning within for change. A belief in externally caused life conditions is a fundamental First Reality illusion (limitation).

Other than from the great masters and mystics of past times of Earth, or perhaps our ever-present internalized "Guiding Ones," we have not generally been told that what we humans give meaning to, is *psychologically* based. Slave mindsets of previous civilizations were so environmentally oriented that individuals—with rare exception— were incapable of reflective thought. Realizing the subjectivity of language provides new-paradigm, conflict-free liberation and unprecedented empowerment. Neutral observation frees us from those rigid, canonized, person-diminishing dogmas perpetuated by ignorant and self-serving slave masters; i.e. "if you don't do this or that, you will burn in hell."

We no longer need to make the other person or group wrong, in order to make choices that serve ourselves. LOC awareness transcends (makes moot) negatively judgmental comparatives about *anything*—including religion. In place of moralistic and separating judgment comes appreciation and acknowledgment of life's unique and varied expressions, and a great confidence in the *involutionary* (intelligent design) process contained within experiential life.

When accepted that all language is metaphor, and interpretation therefore subjective opinion, there's suddenly plenty of room for differing sentiments without the need for defensiveness or external wrestling over definitions. How many millions of people have suffered torturous deaths and other forms of teeth gnashing by battling over the meaning, significance, and ultimate labeling of God? LOC eliminates the fear of external authorities, as beneficiaries can no longer be psychologically manipulated by outside influences— unwittingly or otherwise.

Should these introductory definitions seem a little too technical, *or a little too abstract,* release your concern. **Bottom line**: *Mastering intuitive realizations, ably facilitated by Holographic Psychology, represents* *a quantum leap in human understanding, while also eliminating boundaries that have been enslaving humans for many thousands of years.* We (you and I), together, can break those remaining shackles that bind—right here, right now! To all the "Rip Van Winkle" types out there, this is your wake-up call.

> What comes to me intuitively: We are guided—never forced—to follow our Soul's preference. If, however, we humans get too far afield on the negative side of the ledger, we generally create a lot of pain and suffering for ourselves that may not have been part of the original game plan. Nothing *conventionally* scientific in the above—just reporting what's coming to me through the expanded realms. One advantage of *not* being a scientific, five-sensory reductionist: I don't have to hold back any of the good and juicy parts from you!

I supply definitions primarily for those inquisitive minds motivated to prod for the deeper, intellectual understanding of how things work. Although I present many summarized explanations and descriptive narratives, cognitive shifts are actually more of an intuitive, *feeling* process. For us touchy-feely right-brainers, the role-playing dialogue and illustrative stories provide more clarity.

My Role

To outline my role in our journey together, I feel it important to establish something—especially with my agnostic-based brethren/sistern—before we take any leaps into the *elsewhere* areas. Even during my most arrogant and deluded years, I never saw myself as a person of especially remarkable gifts. I'm not a Seer, Sage, Guru, Svengali, or Messiah—just a reasonably observant, very curious guy that's often been actively (sometimes passively) participating in extraordinary events and circumstances. Afterwards, it did not take a rocket scientist to follow the bread crumbs—especially by one as Spiritually hungry as I.

I use contemplative attunements as a method to clarify thought, feeling, and experiential meaning. Although I'm having FUN with the "Soul-Man/Soul-Woman" integration, I do not present myself as an independent voice of God, Souls, Angels, or the Eternal Forces. Consider *this SoulMan* your guide for a wonderful adventure of Spirit. And before we kick in the *afterburner,* know that we all visualize or imagine God and various other entities—both now and during our glorious transition—according to our own beliefs. I find the energy of Souls, Spiritual Guides, and Angels, even if *expressed* differently, meaningful for me. These metaphors symbolize the ONENESS of our existence. Use the labels that personally serve you. I won't spoil your FUN by suggesting that it's all the same stuff—at least not for now.

Review Disclaimer. As well as not being a Guru, Svengali, or Messiah, I'm neither a medical doctor nor a licensed therapist. All material in this book is for educational and self-help purposes, only. Today, I no longer sense any clear lines of demarcation between wisdom inspired by a mentoring one, or connecting insight that may be originating from the *Collective Ether*. I show this psychological blending and filtering of past and present experiential knowledge, which metaphysicians often call "Akashic Accessing," as a process common to all. We avail ourselves of it through directed focus (attunement). The way we philosophically and psychologically interpret information and process human experience are products of our underlying belief-system and self-image. This subjective elucidation directly determines our well-being and quality of life. *If you want to do and experience differently, you must believe differently.*

Any ardent observer knows that individually channeled thought, from an expanded focus (beyond the ego-dominated mind), can and normally should have some parallel—even congruency. Research psychologists, beginning with Carl G. Jung, define this parallel as *synchronicity*. Experts disagree—depending on their level of consciousness—on whether synchronistic mentalities are empirically provable, parapsychological in origin, coincidental, or intrinsically innate. If a little romanticism resides within you, see if you can open to a fifth possibility...a perspective that suggests what we are about to share is both natural *and* positively magical! Consider waiting until after we've explored and embraced the influential nature of Spiritual DNA, before you presume to know the answer.

Even if I so desired, I know of no way to prevent overlap, or repetition, of presented thoughts, feelings, and concepts. If you sense any similarity between these teachings and other inspiring or uplifting guidance...rejoice over the intended reaffirming of your emerging awareness! At the same time, don't overlook those portions that emotionally push your internal buttons. This *shake-up* may help you expand beyond that comfort zone you're currently stuck in.

I have done my best—coming from heart as much as head—to offer my transpersonal reality as an option for others. Although *I'm* presenting these empowerment concepts, hold a picture in your mind that ultimately *you are your own meaning maker.* Once fully open to this realization, you'll no longer need this guide or any other guide to achieve mastery over your respective Earth curriculum. Assisting others to make their own direct link achieves my highest life purpose. You'll be the final judge whether a life expressing from all-inclusive synchronicity answers your prayers for limitless love, abundance, and FUN.

It's All Good

My intentions do not involve bashing, smashing, or trashing any organization or person. Many fine, caring, dedicated volunteers and staff members work in various organized religions or philanthropic groups that serve many. I sincerely salute them for their service. My expressed purpose is to facilitate an open, honest, no-holds-barred communication. Authoritarian-based *master/slave* relationships have been a consistent theme throughout human history. Understanding the motivations behind this mutually agreed-upon (level) posturing can expedite liberation. Shifts in realization provide the awakening individual more coping options, as well as the thriving FUN of self-directed purposefulness. It will also allow the more controlling elements, which have been mirroring our unworthiness and lack issues, to shift to more creative endeavors.

Presenting this message will inevitably ruffle some belief-system feathers. If you feel an inner button pushed with *anything* you ever see, read, or hear (experience), you have the potential choice of turning (mentally and emotionally) within to peel back the layers of your personal *onion.* Awaken to the true cause of your discomfort (ego-based fear) with anyone expressing an opinion different from yours. My purpose, as a quantum heart-shift facilitator, is to help make you aware of choices and potential consequences commonly associated with various perspectives of thinking and feeling; not to judge or tell ones how they *should* think, feel, or act.

Although I feel very connected and guided in what I present here, only you can decide if the message serves a practical function. I both laughed and cried, without censure, during several developing sections. The uplifting clarity of these teachings gifted me enormously. I joyfully accepted those periods where it felt as if I were taking cosmic dictation. I am confident a great number of you have experienced similarly guided events. If not...don't worry; "we" are here to help you achieve that wonderfully loving connection. My part is to capture, as best I can, the transformational catharsis experienced not only with this writing, but during the Earth-world events that—linearly speaking—came before and will come after. I have attempted to tie behavioral example and principle together in practical ways, with hopes that this format can end self-created victimization and much of the worldwide suffering from psychological slavery. You will be shown (or reminded) that *terrorist or other negative activities, unless you choose to make them so, do **not** determine your security and life quality.*

Special Message for the Spiritually Disenfranchised

Have you, like myself, experienced some challenge with the orthodox depiction of a judgmental, controlling, and conditionally-loving type of god that exists dualistically separate from yourself? Do Western fear-based concepts like *Original Sin,* Eastern philosophies such as *Karmic Debt,* or any other teaching or theory suggesting humans are born with cosmic encumbrances, leave you less than satisfied? If so, perhaps you will finally have something of a Spiritual nature that speaks to you. Through INCLUSIVITY, there's a protective way to live harmoniously with all belief systems—including the more rigid and extreme ones. Together, beginning in Chapter One, we unearth the larger truth...***God Does Not Give Exclusives.***

The labels you use to describe your highest love-based self, or "higher power," are not important...unless you *believe* that are. More significant is the preexisting potential, already within, that optionally provides for any life you can conceive of and believe in. Evidence of this inherent, but often dormant, capability will be forthcoming; but pause a moment, now, to notice the subtle amplification of your appreciation for the power of belief. Although it will increase in intensity with every word consumed, your transformation has already begun.

As a *"recovering"* left-brainer, I know that many analytical types need a logical foundation before intuitively leaping to where humans have rarely gone before. For you wonderfully sensitive love entities, *not* lacking in creative input, this book provides meaningful structure and replacement practice for *practical* compartmentalizing of intuitive thought and feeling. For those who desire only a *warm feeling* from their self-help material, I have a loving suggestion. Save your time and money by treating yourself to a hot bath. *For those who seriously experience comprehensive reading to completion, this Spiritual guide provides its beneficiaries the mastering potential to create bastions of unprecedented beauty and dramatic accomplishment.*

Since the evolving archetype of expanded awareness can not be identified solely through intellectual analysis, paradigm shifts must be emotionally felt and experienced in one's core mindfulness. Certain triggering experiences and encounters, such as what we do here, can help facilitate our shifts. And remember...there are no coincidences.

Beneficial results require three important contributions from you.

❶ An **OPEN MIND**. While reading, you may occasionally feel like putting up mental and emotional walls. You may encounter teachings and options contrary to your cultural or world beliefs, or feel the desire to stop and intellectually analyze (that's *you*, my kindred left-brainers) and dissect the information as we go along. A need to analyze to the exclusion of all else, rather than trust any visceral feelings, often involves a subconscious defense mechanism triggered by buried personal fears or issues. Either that or you have bought into conventional psychology's position: the unreliability of intuition. For years, a fear-based defense posture held me back from accessing the expanded realms.

I suggest you sail past all forms of distraction or stoppages for now. Send your keen, critical mind to the background, as a temporary observer. Accepting negative suggestions (chatter) from your subconscious mind about alleged imperfections, especially during this initial breakthrough period, will clearly not serve you. You can—and left-brainers will—later scrutinize the larger significance of it all.

❷ The second requirement: **PATIENCE**. I support you in denying yourself the common human desire for instant gratification. BOOK I provides the groundwork necessary to effectively integrate the all-inclusive teachings and inspiration that follow. To arrive where you are now has taken you all these years. You can either dedicate a few focused hours in the pursuit of a more desirable location, or wait and hope that "Scottie" arrives in time to beam you up.

As life tests our ability to expand beyond exploratory, left-brain intellect, intuitive, multi-sensory observation becomes more accessible. Achieving deeper, emotional, right-brain (subconscious) connections, best facilitates Trinity (mind, body, Spirit) healing and the acceptance of beneficial replacement. Realizing and practicing the enclosed concepts will enhance and ensure your inherent intuitive abilities. In lieu of exposure to a daily banquet of mental junk food, you'll receive healthy, positive, love-based nourishment from your

Soul (Universal Energy) during this Spiritual exercise. Open to it—embrace it. You deserve unlimited love in your life now.

❸ The third requirement: the **COURAGE TO TAKE ACTION** on what you determine is appropriate replacement for non-serving beliefs. Complacent procrastination is often the final fear-based obstacle in implementing what cosmology physicist Dr. Gary Zukav calls, "Authentic Inner Power."

This may be a lot to take in during one, concentrated introduction. When required, I can be as persistent and methodical as a lumbering elephant. Like my tusked brethren, I am loyal, tenacious, and never forget my commitments. As this communication may be vital to your health and well being, I promise to keep coming at you from several perspectives until confident I've solidly covered the fundamentals. NOTE: During the following exercise, if your animalistic, protective self screams to fight or flee, this might indicate a vitally important area to your psychological health and empowerment. I will show you how to better differentiate between legitimate physical threats and psychologically based (Memorex) illusion.

Quiet! Humans at Play

In this moment, mute your external world a bit by taking in some deep, cleansing breaths. Relax your body and mind. Best results occur with focus and being totally in the moment. As you relax, relaax, relaaaax, let some blessedly supportive, Spiritual energy flow into you from the Universe that loves you. Intended as heart *and* head communication, experience the flow of what is being shared by *feeling* it. By allowing emotions to emerge, without censure or edit, you *defang* the resisting energy and open yourself to a wondrous transformation.

Strive to keep focused on the subject material. But if something in these lessons triggers a past-memory recall, and you sense a cathartic opportunity, by all means go with it. Releasing, then replacing, useless mental and emotional garbage is most desired, and quite necessary for participation in graduate-level studies of connection and love. Remember, we're not here just to impart intellectual understanding. After any temporary diversion, bring yourself back to where you left off. Except for those special and very beneficial deviations, try to stay the course. Your benefits will become clearer as you progress. I will be here to celebrate your healing and enlightenment breakthrough(s). Although facing submerged, fear-based thoughts and feelings takes mettle, the transition will be much easier than you may think. I will help you to *de-claw* your inner shadow through the intimate sharing of my own trial and recognition process. Note that I did not say "error."

Many of us have psychologically created giant *monsters* with fangs, out of mental *pussycats*. Our innermost emotional fears, when acknowledged and processed, reveal themselves as nothing more than user-friendly self-diagnostics. This view starkly contrasts with the multi-horned monster many believe to be lurking behind the door of psychological fear and emotional pain.

Spirituality for Agnostics

One of my primary objectives: *to locate and define powerful success principles that work* regardless *of a person's belief in God, Souls, or Spiritual afterlife.* In spite of worldwide dogmatic and cultural posturing to the contrary, the Eternal Forces do not require allegiance in order to provide gifts, talents, and abilities that enable humans to maximize quality of life in the here and now. I used to drive nails with a rock until I found *my* hammer. Although I still occasionally strike a thumb with the sparkling new hammer, it's a pure joy to know I am finally finished with that crusty, old rock. I assure you, any useful implement that I intuitively uncovered can be found in your Spiritual tool kit, as well.

Permission to engage FUN is hereby granted

Regardless of my previous issues with unforthcoming groups and agenda-based moral authorities, it is never my intention to disparage any individual or group—but to guffaw at life, itself. I finally figured out that life was meant to be FUN.

With great sensitivity for persons that currently reside, or have resided, in mental institutions, I suspect the balance of us would be extremely miserable—either secluded away in a lonely cabin like the Mad Bomber, bouncing off the walls of some rubber room, or institutionally whacked out on *happy-drugs*—if not for the ability to see at least some semblance of amusement in our human difficulties. Who among us would not wish to trade in the moth-eaten *Life Sucks* hat for a colorfully flamboyant *Life is FUN* sombrero? You've already bought your ticket. Why not enjoy the ride?

Although life transformation is fairly weighty stuff, we humans have a tonic to balance temporary stress—humor and laughter. Whether a smile, chuckle, or one of those deep, belly-explosions of joy, humorous merriment and buffoonery touch our Spirit. Somehow, things don't look so somber and relationships don't feel so distant, after a good laugh. As serious as the releasing, replacing, and healing of non-serving beliefs and issues are to our well-being and quality of life, the willingness to not take ourselves too seriously, wonderfully adjuncts any personal-development process. You will notice that I often poke fun at Earth and its inhabitants. I will not always be politically correct. Laughing at the paradoxes of life — as well as myself — has gotten me through some rough periods. I'll wager this is true for you, as well.

You will also be introduced to "Caustic James" (CJ), the part of my personality that, during stressful episodes, provides much-needed comic relief. As we proceed, CJ will occasionally throw in his 'two-cents' worth.

As you've probably noted, I sometimes say *we*, instead of *I*, when introducing defining principles or other subject material. Intuitively and inherently I believe this message both originates from and is shared by *us* — the Collective Universal Consciousness which manifests human personalities and Souls. In spite of what humans often feel, we are truly not isolated, or alone. Imagine, if you can, a *vertical* perspective (non-linear) where "past" and "future" are intended illusions — limited to a space-time orientation. From our intrinsic, multi-sensory, Third Reality existence, *only* the current moment exists. Proof, you ask? Select a memory from the past, or any envisioning of the future. Now, to another person, try to describe these events or imaginings without discussing them in the present. Rather difficult, is it not? It's not "Memorex" figments you need concern yourself with. Although we — as humans — live under many illusions, Earth experience is as *real* as you choose.

At this very moment, awakening energy is being accelerated within every fiber of your Being. Guiding forces (universal energy, or God, if you prefer) are with us as we share this interaction and associated message of peace, harmony, joy, goodness, creativity, wisdom, and LOVE. Embrace this opportunistic union by opening yourself completely. Bring forth your questions, doubts, and passion to understand the full meaning of life and your place in it. If you can accept this gift of facilitation, *consciousness ascension* may be upon you.

As we go through this guidebook, and assist actualizing your full, human potential, you may be inclined to ask; *"Where in the heck is Stevens getting all this stuff from?"* This question takes the entire book to answer. Although they may seem distant, separate, and mysterious, higher truths reside much closer than you realize. You'll likely be required to step out of that amnesiac comfort zone and enter a state of temporary confusion, as a prelude to realization. Thinking of a question? If so, *the answer is already within you.*

Now that we have the preliminaries out of the way...**LET'S ROCK!**

CHAPTER ONE

God Does Not Give Exclusives
Question Everything

♥   ♥   ♥

If you skipped the Power Prologue and Introduction, I *strongly* recommend you read them prior to continuing. The Prologue and Intro set the stage for all you will experience herein.

Christmas 1949

The church pastor noticed the often-mischievous seven-year-old boy staring up at a wall-to-wall engraving recently installed in the church foyer. The pastor walked up, patiently stood beside the lad and said quietly, "Good morning son." "Good morning pastor," replied the youngster as he focused on the black, marbleized plaque listing hundreds of names. "What is this?" asked the boy innocently. "Well, son, this plaque lists all the people from this general geographical area that died in the service," replied the cleric. They stood together for a few more moments, soberly gazing at the large remembrance. Then the boy turned to the pastor and asked plaintively, "Which one, sir — the 8:30 or 10:30 service?"

Although not original, the preceding story typifies my own innocent childhood shenanigans. My uninhibited curiosity and unguarded expressions did not exactly endear me to those in the religious arena of my childhood. Perhaps I was just a *little* impetuous.

My pre-adolescent self could not comprehend why, but something in me stubbornly kept refusing to accept *status quo*. This, in spite of continual reminders that life would be a lot simpler if I swallowed those early religious teachings without question or comment. Even after experiencing a bitter parental divorce, combined with another adolescent trauma — which you'll read about — I continued the prodding in my quest to understand higher truths.

The Questioning Begins

With these thoughts preoccupying my young mind, I questioned the authority figures of my day—whenever I had the opportunity—about their interpretations of the following themes.

- **Ritualized presentations.**
- **Virgin births.**
- **Evolution versus Creationism.**
- **Fear-based edicts such as immortal or original sin, sanctified guilt, karmic debt.**
- **Anything purported to be a commandment from God.**

During my somewhat sporadic access to clergy, I always received the same rhetorical answer to my prodding: "Larry, you must learn to have faith and accept these proclamations as truth, because God works in mysterious ways." Lacking more complete and synchronous answers, my frustration over orthodoxy's position that *one can never know why God does what HE does*, continued.

As a maturing child, I was generally polite, having been taught to respect elders. Civility also minimized the severity of the reprimands that were a repetitive consequence of my relentless interrogation of those in authority; a behavior I seemed unable to resist. I would often rebut those *blind-faith* axioms with a childlike version of, "Well ma'am/sir, could it be that the reason the 'ways' are so mysterious is simply because we don't understand them yet?" Responses from the various clergy-persons were swift, predictable, and for me...annoyingly consistent. Having had their fill of this unyielding irritant; ministerial faces turned red, dismissive eyes glazed over, and ear canals filled with wax. Then they terminated my questioning with stern admonishments and a swift expulsion for my inventive impetuousness.

Somehow surviving to adulthood without a broken nose, I remained undeterred in my agnostic-based pursuit of rational, practical explanations for humanity's heterogeneous beliefs. Not unwilling to embrace a more expansive, but rational reality, my questions repetitively centered on the fixed definitions espoused by rigid, non-inclusive theologies. My inner-core Belief-Center refused to buy into the generally accepted, orthodox, Supreme Being.

While earnestly engaged in my Spiritual journey, I still asked myself and others, "How can I open my heart and accept a cosmic overseer that expresses manipulative, wrathful, judgmental, or conditionally-loving sentiments…essentially a threatening, force insisting that persons do things ITS way or else?" Even as an ignorant young sprout, my inner sense knew all the preceding attributes as exclusively human. Before becoming a believer, or recognizing any deity or potential as *"Supreme" or "Almighty,"* I wanted to see a few more credentials.

The Relentless Detective

The empowering message shared, herein, resulted from the Spiritual Odyssey that evolved after the "Miracle in Escondido" [See Prologue]. Like many of you intuitively prodded toward these words, I have been internally driven to question, test, and share all that you read and experience here. With this impulse so strong, I eventually quit asking "why me?" and agreed to simply honor the progression. The results of that decision continue to astound me. This writing could not have been produced—as is—without tapping into some form of expanded Consciousness or "Universal Mind." Consider that this is how the process works for us *all*. First, we get our ego-personality in sync by healing and releasing our inner, fear-based issues. Next, we replace that incessant, self-diminishing background mind chatter that often preoccupies us. Then, a relatively simple process directs one's intuitive inflow. As we continue, I attempt to facilitate your own direct connection.

Absolute Truth versus Subjective Interpretation

In a moment, I list the filtering criteria that I use to process all input— talk, writing, or empowerment message; I am always skeptical when I hear someone espouse that they have *the word* or absolute truth. Dogen (1200-1253), the Spiritual master and founder of the Zen school of Buddhism, said: *"If you can not find truth right where you are, where else do you expect to find it?"* A further examination of truth's relative nature serves us.

From a practical standpoint, "truth" is what we personally believe it to be at any given moment—always subject to change, unless we remain closed to expansion and change. In other words, our ego-mind *subjectively* interprets current truths, even in the most obvious and pragmatic circumstances. Truth is never *absolute* (frozen) unless one resists growth, discovery, and expansion of consciousness. In times past, for example, virtually everyone believed the world was flat. In time, humanity eventually awakened to a larger reality—except for a few holdouts. Even today some believe planet Earth to be flat, with five sides. Have you heard of the "Flat Earth" Society? Others can show you cursory proof that the first Astronaut crew never went to the Moon. Their data suggests (from their unique perspective) that at a minimum, the first Apollo mission was a Hollywood-manufactured hoax. Taken out of context, as they have, in my opinion, this particular group's *evidence* actually looks convincing.

While easy to dismiss *fringe* belief-systems, should all truths espoused by minority groups be considered threatening or suspect? Or just the ones with which we don't personally agree? Authoritarians of the past quickly dispatched any expressions that might make waves for their hierarchy. Should portions of my unconventional teaching seem personally prepared for you... welcome to *another* minority group.

In general, truth changes when an individual's belief-system changes. Messengers of new ideas, concepts, and realities encounter resistance because their teachings generally fly in the face of status quo. If a researcher wishes to attract serious consideration by the masses, he or she must supply volumes of *empirical* evidence proving such insightful and expanded theories. In past times of Earth, hierarchies even refused to accept incontestable proof. Scientists consider Galileo Galilei (1564-1642), the brilliant Italian inventor, astronomer, and physicist, the creator of the scientific method of empirical observation. The response Galileo received, at age 70, when he finally published his astronomical findings, proved less than receptive. Galileo conclusively revealed the Earth as neither the center of the Universe, nor the center of the Solar System. Point of fact, he simply confirmed mathematical descriptions published in 1543 by Nicolaus Copernicus, a distinguished Polish intellectual. Even so, Galileo's declaration was labeled blasphemous, because in 1619 the Catholic church—still the preemptive authority—decreed Copernicus' world view forevermore prohibited from consideration or mention.

To be a leading-edge scientist in those days required great courage. The esteemed Galileo, forced to recant after threatened with the infamous RACK, remained under house arrest until he passed—in spite of a governing Pope that adored him. Even after the repudiation, Church administrators were so fearful of Galileo's findings that they refused to look through his telescope!

Rather than accept what I say, here, on face value, I support you in thoroughly testing the presented concepts and facilitative techniques. Determine, for yourself, whether the empowerment options offered serve you in a practical way.

O. J. (OJ), the Facilitator

To further advance my point that all evaluations are subjectively interpreted, let me review the most widely publicized investigation of its time—the O. J. Simpson murder trial in Los Angeles, California. I hear your collective moans, but bear with me for a moment.

Scientific DNA, obtained from blood, semen, saliva, or other body fluids, is accepted in the scientific community as near-absolute personal identification. During the OJ criminal trial, the jury discounted the DNA evidence. In polls taken from members of the general public who reported they watched the presentation of the evidence—in its entirety—approximately 85 percent of African Americans thought OJ innocent of the charges, while approximately the same percentage of Caucasian Americans believed him guilty.

Evidence is what we believe it to be at the moment. We base our conclusions primarily on our underlying beliefs, conditioned through cultural programming and self-experience, reinforced by habit. For individuals to hold true to their previous convictions—even in the face of incontrovertible and contrary testimony—is not unusual. Polls taken *after* Simpson's civil trial conviction showed substantial shifts toward more proportional percentages, although a racial disparity still remained. Here we have the same world, same regurgitated evidence, but a large difference in the opinionated interpretation of the same data.

A great temptation exists to opt for the right/wrong judging scenario in these and similar situations; we find righteous comparison so much easier than taking responsibility for our subjective, belief-linked (biased) opinions. We create massive stress and suffering with our validating need to be proven right. When we pause long enough to witness the self-immersed judge and executioner within, other *ways of knowing* come to mind.

In the aftermath of the investigation and trial, two differing perspectives developed. Many people—perhaps the majority—believe the OJ criminal trial represents one of the greatest travesties of our justice system. They conclude that a wealthy man, with popularity and influence, beat a murder rap. A multitude of others, with a more expanded, all-inclusive viewpoint, agree the murders were a tragic event—as all murders are—but, for their purposes, this gross iniquity actually turned into a *blessing in disguise*.

During the criminal proceedings, monetary donations to domestic-abuse agencies doubled. Then these same agencies enjoyed another many-fold increase after the not-guilty verdict. Offers for domestic-abuse volunteer services experienced a similar upsurge. Offerings of space, support facilities, volunteer hours, and money, greatly alleviated preexisting needs for additional shelters for battered family members. Mr. Simpson, unbeknownst to him, took domestic abuse out of the closet and placed it under a public microscope. The civil trial gave another, but less gargantuan supply boost to the domestic-support charities. The result: hundreds—perhaps thousands—of persons have been or will be helped because mistreated family members now feel encouraged to come forward. Most social workers would quietly acknowledge the sudden burst of resources as a byproduct of the publicity generated by the O. J. Simpson case—mostly from the outrage associated with the criminal trial's *not-guilty* finding.

Here we have the same world, same reportage of the tragedy, but a totally different perception of its significance. Denise Brown, sister of murder-victim Nicole Brown Simpson, began heading up one of the support organizations—determined that her sister's sacrifice not be in vain. So, was the OJ verdict only a travesty of justice, or also a blessing to the many spousal-abuse victims in dire situations? Which perspective (belief) is correct? Doesn't it seem immaterial to focus on the issue of right-and-wrong judgment? Instead, let us focus on choices and the consequences of those choices...and our interpretation of the *facts* as subjectively derived opinion. As we move toward a muti-sensory interpretation of events, circumstances, and beliefs, the hypercritical "either-ors" begin to fade. In their place comes the realization that *all* perceptions have their function in experiential life.

We *do* need a degree of mutual compromise and structure (rules) to help us function efficiently in a crowded world. If not for GO lights, we'd find it virtually impossible to drive safely through any large city. If individuals from all walks of life healed their underlying issues of unworthiness and negative self-image, what would result? Could humanity emerge from all that self-absorbency and awaken to a reality without war, conflict, and ongoing feelings of separateness? If we collectively developed an unconditional love for all life on Earth, similar to what a normal, healthy, mother feels for her children, would we be as quick to moralistically judge others or to selfishly plunder our planet?

Bottom line (1). Do your current beliefs serve you? If so, rejoice. If not, you may be ready for that belief-system makeover. Once you ask those deeply probative questions of your core mindfulness (heart), and not just the ego-self (head), you may stop your fearful distortion of answers. Although wonderful to be sensitive and desiring of peace, balance, and love in the world, I now realize my job is not to decide the agendas of others. We can lead by example, however. The need to manipulate a mature adult of sound mind, especially when we are emotionally charged, points to our *own* fear and corresponding issues to work through. We learn and awaken through self-experience, not by being browbeaten or cajoled by our well-intentioned friends and family members. Actual, life-threatening attacks, of course, denote self-defense exceptions.

Dominating the material world may scratch the itch, but will never cure the rash. If you desire codependent anxiety, unhappiness, estrangement, depression, and mental/physical dis-ease, then trying to clone the belief-system of another is definitely the way to go. I am not addressing you from any theoretical pillar. I now appreciate the difficulty of appropriately interacting with those whom we are emotionally involved. When *their* pain becomes *our* pain, how do we *not* feel vulnerable?

If you're ready to release remnants of the old-paradigm reactive compulsions and associated suffering, I'll share my secret to deepening one's intimate connections while still maintaining personal boundaries — and this from a former warrior, no less. Consider our time together to be an abridged and less-strenuous version of the "Last Samurai." It helps if you've seen the movie.

Beginning from that previously-referred-to turning point, age 12½, I created a lonely, isolated existence for myself until I saw how estrangement was of my own doing. *We ultimately obtain our highest quality of life by courageously embracing the **current** moment with all the intensity and passion we can muster* — not by stashing unresolved fears in the psychological cellar. Consider the following criteria prior to any internal makeovers.

SoulMan's Criteria for Belief-System Upgrades:

❶ **Is the message or process positive and uplifting?** I do not personally benefit from doomsday predictions, or Armageddon edicts, while attempting personal growth.

❷ **Is the message/process designed to be independently self empowering?** Or do I depend on repeated visits to the guru, sage, preacher, evangelist, or shrink? Am I expected to routinely check in for booster shots of the conditional *ether juice,* to keep negative evil influences at bay?

I look for a tool I can take with me relatively soon—to use independently from that time forward. The feel-good rah-rah sessions, providing a temporary outer-motivational high followed by an inner emotional crash when the *smelling salts* dissipate, are usually entertaining and I enjoy them. I just don't label them "personal development." **Note:** I now delight in rah-rah sessions because I no longer depend on outer-originated stimulation or fixes. Being empowered from within makes you immune to *withdrawal* crashes.

❸ **Is the message/process love-based, or fear-based?** Am I being told that if I don't *believe,* I'm destined to burn in hell—or shiver in purgatory? Does the proffered material offer an assortment of cosmic beasts or energy traps to guard against with protective crosses, silver bullets, garlic, bay leaves, white light, silver cords, etc? Or is the presentation fully positive and supportive?

❹ **Is the message/process consistent in its theme?** Or does it vacillate between unconditional love and guardian angels on one hand, hellfire and brimstone on the other? Again, this classic *Carrot-and-the-Stick* motivational technique can be a FUN night out—especially if they have good music—but it's definitely in the *entertainment* category for me.

❺ **Does the message/process stand alone?** Or does it depend on the personality, charisma, or personal reputation of the speaker, writer, or facilitator? I expand on this criterion because it represents perhaps the number-one source of outer-oriented, Spiritually delivered influence. Outer forms of inspirational stimulation can lead to emotional crashes and, on rare occasions, even death. *Readers: **this one is serious.***

Message vs. the Messenger

Difficulties occur when one transfers his or her original focus on the proclaiming message, to an eventual worshipping of the human messenger. History indicates that Buddha, Jesus, and other masters found adoration a frustrating byproduct of their facilitation. I refer to their human personalities, possibly vulnerable to frustration prior to full enlightenment. A true master prefers that his or her *teachings* become a source of independent liberation.

Other than a few apostles and perhaps a small handful of followers, I believe it unlikely that any assembly understood the *oneness* and *inclusivity* that Jesus promoted with words like, "The kingdom of God is *within*—the Father and I are ONE," etc. If we can believe the surely distorted records of second and third-party testimony credited to Peter, John, Mark, Luke, and especially the more learned Paul, few—if any—of Jesus' closest followers even approached a deep understanding of his synchronistic message until after the emancipating emissary was gone. Much of the cognitive challenge resulted from the prevailing slave mindset of that time period. Believing the external environment responsible for even the tiniest morsel of physical and emotional sustenance, the locals felt that Jesus must touch them or perform a healing on them before they could leave their tormenting living conditions behind. Belief in outer causes continues today, but blessedly in ever-decreasing numbers.

Throughout the ages, intensified awe and reverence for *mystical* masters generally prevented followers from comprehending transformational messages. Like a thirst-quenching spring located just around the next bend, most perished without realizing the mechanism for both their salvation and delivery rested fully within themselves, all along.

Qumran

With the retrieval of the Dead Sea Scrolls from the Essene settlement in Qumran, some believe we now access additional pre- and early Christian writings (such as the Aramaic presentation of Job and the Gospel of Thomas), and many Gnostic-based references. The Gnostics believed in the *spirit within* and thought Jesus a messenger for the truth of Gnosis, which directly conflicted with the new Christians that saw Jesus as a separate and distinct incarnation of God.

Humanity continues to debate the significance of the many-times translated and surely distorted words of the Mystics, Essenes, Gnostics, and monumental facilitators like Jesus and Buddha. Consider that the universal, love-based desire of these prophets was for humankind to understand that *each of us is our own meaning maker, while still being an intimate and irrevocable part of the Collective Mind, or God.*

Toxic Adoration

The main distortion and potential danger, as I see it: Many thousands, probably millions, identify with the personality and charisma of the messenger. Some names like James Bakker, Jimmy Swaggart, and Jim Jones come to mind. [Whoops! My middle name is James—thanks Mom!] This threesome's followers' intense faith and feelings of personal connection effectively canonized these *James* Boys. The subsequent behavior of this evangelistic triad devastated their followers when these boys—like the rest of us—proved less than perfect-acting Human Beings. Many felt such despair that they reported to friends and family that *all* was lost. Afterwards, many took a short trip to the toxic *punch bowl*—figuratively and literally.

So, the question is: What happened to the beautiful and uplifting metaphors that fired the spirit and caused many people to feel truly understood by these men? In another example of the baby thrown out with the bath water, followers placed emphasis on the messenger rather than the message (outer orientation vs. inner actualization), thus losing most or all the potentially liberating benefits, when these men "fell" from grace. Instead of allowing the reformational words of love and wisdom to transform one's inner Core of Being, many chose adulation and blind obedience. This can easily happen when we divest ourselves of an independent self-image and our inner-protective garbage filters.

Inspirational words and teachings from the great masters (we subjectively decide if they are great) have stood the test of time—even if not available in pure form—because they continue to inspire us, regardless of how conveyed. Perhaps the words and teachings of past mystics have a deeper significance today, in part, because we're no longer distracted by magnetic personalities that evoked so much worship in their day. Consider, also, that enhanced appreciation reflects in humanity's gradually evolving consciousness.

In summary, instead of investing large amounts of energy determining whether an individual messenger is true to his or her own teaching, I suggest you ask yourself: "Does the message, itself, serve me?" If it does, rejoice and incorporate it into your belief-system. Go about your way just as if you received it from a two-thousand-year-old scroll or incunabulum. What difference does it make where, or from whom, you received assistance? Decide that you deserve gifts and accept them from the Universe that loves you. Empowering bestowments, upon acceptance, are yours forever; with benefits undeterred by outside influences.

Wisdom has Strange Bedfellows

Some of the most fierce conquerors and despots from human history—many known for inflicting mayhem and death—left us with documented quotations that most persons consider powerfully uplifting and insightful. I could share some of these "pearls" with a gathering of eager recipients and they would most likely love them. If I were, then, to disclose that the adored passages originated from any of our most despised list of historical tyrants, those same beneficiaries would immediately and strenuously disavow any previous benefit, regardless how uplifted they may have been initially. This acceptance and repudiating process is, of course, all psychological.

Decide what is inspirational and truthful for your self/Self, rather than relying on so-called experts or society's judgment. Anything the *wizards* of the world supply represents their own subjective interpretation of reality, not an absolute or concrete truth. Unless your chosen experts have awakened to Second Reality (see Chapter Three), they will likely identify their diagnosis as the complete answer and consider all other opinions flawed.

How many of us have been reluctant to get a second opinion on a medical, or other, issue, even though intuitively nudged from within to do so? Most of us avoid questioning or confronting authority — doctors as an example — because we feel unequal or afraid of upsetting the practitioners. If we shrink from individual accountability out of concern that others might then fail to give us their best, might we be giving away personal power and our right to self-determination? If any medical person becomes agitated because you respectfully request a second "look-see," maybe his or her fear-based reaction is an internal issue for that physician to resolve...not a reason for you to abdicate responsibility for your own welfare. While one thing to respect the years of education and training that any skilled practitioner brings forth; it's something else to turn all decisions about your care over to another because they have impressive initials before or after their name. A holistic alternative to the conventional surgical procedure or toxic treatment might serve you better — or not. How can you learn about your options while confined to the opinion of just one expert? Specialists are naturally predisposed, subconsciously or otherwise, toward their own modality, which they may very well consider to be near absolute.

Think about the now widely accepted directive, "Second *Opinion*." Doesn't this term indicate that the *first* diagnosis must have also been an opinion? Otherwise we would be calling the follow-up a "secondary *conclusion*," would we not? Do you really want to go under the knife, or on some toxic drug, based solely on one person or group's *estimation* of what's needed? Probative questioning and second opinions prove relevant whether we address mind, body, *or* Spiritual matters.

The Power of Intuition

If you choose to trust it, you possess an inner-intuitive diagnostic ability more inclusive than any physical symptom one could possibly observe. Conventional (behavioristic) psychology says you should not trust intuition because it's not reliable. For important decisions, I use second sight (gut instinct) as a guiding influence. Once I assemble the informed opinions and have my updated list of options, I contemplate (meditate) and summarize using a blend of cognitive and visceral input. While still remaining open to last-minute updates, I make my purposeful determination by logical conclusion and intuitive *feel*-ing.

Consider researching the Internet or local library for information and leads. By availing yourself of all applicable resources, *and* asking every relevant question you can think of, you will feel more in control—even during a health crisis. When using skilled professionals to help determine the best course of action, try expanding your focus beyond the worshipping of metaphorical "totem poles" (the outer authority). Realize that *you* (the inner authority) are the ultimate determiner regarding your own life. Doctors, as well as other authority figures, are of God—just as are you. But being human, experts are not beyond "stage" awakening and the need for experiential practice. That said, I greatly respect medical practitioners for being wonderfully motivated professionals providing often-critical and much-needed services.

Self-empowering choices include looking at *all* services as available tools to use for your own enlightenment and healing. The tools, themselves, don't heal you—*you heal yourself.* If we can learn to believe in something more expansive than *blind* faith, or the unquestioned acceptance of the expertise of others, we can move beyond fear of the unknown. Making this shift will leave you feeling much less vulnerable and helpless during everyday life.

Writing and publishing experts tell me that, to ensure my credibility with you—the reader—I must continually quote *authority* sources from sacred and secular fields of study. You, I am told, are not open to new thoughts or ideas unless delivered by those particular mediums. So, once again, I chose to fly in the face of conventional teaching and challenge you to *decide for yourself* whether insights shared within these pages serve you. I invite you to feel the messages in your core mindfulness and accept or reject them through an *internal assessment.* Consider how blindly accepting subjective opinion from me, or any other "ex-spurt," affects your self-esteem.

Many principles expressed, herein, are not limited to analytical conclusions or Earth-bound resources. Some were intuitively delivered to me through an expansive realization of inherent perfection within personal struggle, during the counseling of others, meditative attunements, or even now, as I write. Concepts offered as therapeutic examples of what served me and others, may, or may not, benefit you at this time. Without *right or wrong* to determine, only the consequences of choosing—or not—remain. As a self-expert, you possess all the innate gifts, talents, and abilities to make the best call. After emphatically deciding you are worthy of self-determination, you can open your suitcase of guiding gifts and take charge of your life.

It's the message, not the messenger that serves us unconditionally. Inner-actualizing, instead of outer-fixating, permanently provides immunity from most negatives. Once we "get it" that we are our own meaning-maker, life becomes much less complicated and a lot more FUN.

Consider the following: *Terrorists cannot exist without persons responding (reacting) to threats of terror.* Before you write this statement off as outrageously simplistic, feel the significance of the following information.

Co-Creator or Victim? I recently read a responding letter from a Jewish man, living in Israel, who—during an interview—intently explained his perspective to westerners. When asked why Israelis continue to frequent restaurants and open-air assemblies while terrorist bombers run amuck, this was his paraphrased answer. *We do what we need...to defend ourselves, but we refuse to be cowering victims, regardless of the amount of carnage. We try to keep the cost of freedom in perspective. In the United States, as an example, more people die every month on your nation's highways than we have lost (in totality) to suicide bombings. Do you plan to give up your liberating automobiles because of the risks associated with freedom?*

This wise and passionate man then concluded his short, but effective, soliloquy. *We have not, as yet, discovered a diplomatic solution to the differing philosophies, beliefs, and wants of our neighbors; but we continue to go about the business of living and loving while trying to do so. To do otherwise is to have the emotions of hate, anxiety, and fear* [rather than love, peace, and joy] *rule us.*

Blind Faith not a Requirement—TEST Everything

The fundamentals presented, herein, are fully testable. They work more powerfully without blind faith or a belief in any dualistic (separate), outside power or force. Thinking about and then acknowledging our feelings, not just reacting to stimuli, provide the opportunity to reclaim personal power.

Although my initial orientation will likely interest Secular Humanists and others uncomfortable with esoteric, cosmic-like persuasions, my facilitation is not limited to secular values (see Third Reality). Later segments in this book provide more on the creative, healing power of non-conditional faith and prayer.

We have the entire book to further explain and demonstrate your new empowerment tools. For now, know that once you incorporate these bedrock principles, including but not limited to the all-inclusive science of Holographic Psychology™, you will be among the first on Earth to benefit from their awesome significance.

Bottom Line (2). *The potential to end conflict and war, not only in our own relationships but throughout the planet, is now available to us;* a **bold** statement—to be sure. When we finally have a World society of individuals expressing *inclusivity*, rather than the judgmental control-and-manipulate exclusivity that creates so much resistance, differing perspectives and beliefs will no longer threaten anyone.

Through life transformation I've discovered a fierce, love-starved, generally ineffective *warrior* persona no longer serves me. With the rare exception of a physical-defense situation, I've exchanged my bear gun for a bear hug. I still have a gun, but I no longer sleep with it under my pillow. As we proceed, *you* decide whether making love is more fun than making war.

Some erroneously believe that to love others and ourselves weakens our desire for self-preservation. To the contrary; loving your self/Self gives you an expanded, connecting perspective that provides an empowering and joyous life experience, even during fearful and challenging periods. *Victimization is a state of mind and heart—not the result of the human condition.*

Practical Freedom in a Non-Free World

I plan to intimately acquaint you with the dynamics that free us from what often appears to be a non-free world. What my left-brained, analytical self brings to the table is the steadfast desire to make all of this *practical* for the *here and now*. There will be no purely philosophical or feel-good hyperbole presented. Any principle that did not prove its worth in sound, psychological presence—when manifested in everyday human life—did not make the cut.

I know how it feels to be alone in a crowded room. No stranger to frustration, heartache, even desperation—believing no one on the planet understood my inner turmoil—I, too, experienced intimate feelings of helplessness and powerlessness. I will never suggest any insight or process, no matter how apparently profound or life transforming, unless I proved it beneficial in my own life and in the lives of others under my observation. Although we each have our own perspectives and preferences, certain love-based axioms—once integrated—are the *master key* to maintaining a unique and magnificent human life. I will show you how to see past the "amnesiac veil," to sense and experience some of the expanded nature of the holographic universe. With empowerment principles incorporated into our Being, we are suddenly heroes and heroines to all we touch. If you bring an open mind with you on our continued journey, I'm confident I can help you find the door to a liberated and fulfilled existence. Sensing even a small portion of this implied opportunity suggests you are fully capable of manifesting the expanded and more joyous part of life that Soul intended.

If disheartened by the negativity and mayhem often expressed in the world, or if you feel overwhelmed by life's challenges—or both—take heart. These teachings show you how to reach deep within yourself to grasp that still-smoldering glimmer of childhood vision, to *reclaim that rainbow of inner spirit.* Together, using this celestial, joy-juice-generating message as our guide, we recapture your internal essence and energized confidence. My fondest wish and determined goal: for a co-facilitated, Spiritually-symbolic, love-unlimited orchestra, with more and more of us playing—in concert—the fear-free masterpiece within us all along.

With humanity's current opportunities constantly birthing from the evolutionary ashes created by thousands of years of human suffering, humankind has more than paid its subservience dues. Today, we have more expansive mediums to explain where and how behavior originates. In spite of terrorist activities and technological weapons suggesting the contrary, we live on the very cusp of a quantum shift in group consciousness. This shift will result in greater understanding of both the Science of Mind *and* Spirit. You are reading these words because Spirit intends that the preexisting tools for an expansive shift-change be made clear to you. Perhaps you've noticed the increased number of empowerment facilitators present today?

There is nothing more powerful than an idea whose time has come...and is accepted by you NOW.

In order to fully manifest our next grandest vision, we must internalize the relationship between levels of consciousness and the *appearance* of reality. This teaching includes methods for periodic, current-moment centering, for you to reflectively witness your behavior and fuller potential before resuming the forward march to greatness.

If you're ready to step it up a notch, let us begin the serious process of tapping into that unlimited potential. Left-brainers will greatly benefit from an understanding of "stage-shift" or "level" awareness contained within the next two to three chapters. For right-brainers, the illustrative stories will hopefully entertain while demonstrating the empowerment principles under review.

CHAPTER TWO

First Reality

♥   ♥   ♥

Childhood Boogie Monsters. As a young lad, I was *terrified* of the freestanding bottled-water machine in our hallway. That living thing gurgled menacingly every time I tried to sneak out of my bed to go to the bathroom. For an agonizingly long period of my childhood, I took the potentially humiliating gamble of becoming a bed-wetter, rather than risk capture by the imagined water beast. Today I understand how adult fears of the misunderstood, or unknown, can feel just as terrifying as the sound of releasing air bubbles to an unaware child. Our challenge is to heal our localized human darkness while also releasing any fear of big-league *cosmic* shadow. This allows the full engagement of a liberated, loving, and creative life during the short time we have on Earth. The details of my multifarious experiences demonstrate that we are not alone during *any* phase of our lives—especially those scary bump-in-the-night moments. To really get this, however, I had to first de-fang my self-created demons.

The Forbidden Planet

One of the most liberating messages I awakened to is that there are absolutely no beasts waiting to eat us—other than those we psychologically create in the recesses of our own mind. Readers my age, or older, surely remember the futuristic, late 1950's science-fiction movie called, "The Forbidden Planet." You might watch for it on cable television, or rent the video.

To review my interpretation of this relevant tale, an expedition of human interstellar explorers revisited an Earth-like planet allegedly abandoned by an ancient race of intellectually superior Beings, called the Kreil. Upon arrival, the amazed crew found the sole survivor of a long-lost scientific exploration, along with his curious and vivacious daughter—Altaira. This is the movie that introduced the Herculean

"Robbie the Robot," which later popularized the TV series, "Lost in Space."

Altaira's father, a brilliant but whimsical and eccentric scientist (Morbius, played by Walter Pidgeon), had lost faith in the future of humanity. So, he — with a few other scientific hopefuls — traversed the dark, limitless vacuum of space, to find a new habitat capable of supporting his plan for a new Eden.

By all appearances, the Forbidden Planet seemed a marvel of both alien (Kreil) technological innovation and natural beauty, not the least of which was Morbius' innocent but somewhat pretentious daughter, charmingly played by Anne Francis. Totally liberated, unspoiled, and raised with unconditional love and acceptance, Altaira had been encouraged to be both curious and respectful of all life forms. Apparently free of any emotional/psychological bogs or reservations, Altaira pursued her planetary curiosity with an intensity rivaling the indigenous Kreil technology. However, her lack of interactions with any other Human Beings placed major portions of Altaira's philosophy in the theoretical category. As you might imagine, plenty of male volunteers stepped forward from the space crew to assist with her missing practical experience. The list included a young Leslie Nielson playing the role of Commander Adams — the crew's valiant captain.

I recall, from my first theater viewing, how we moviegoers were ready to book passage on the next space barge leaving for the Forbidden Planet. Shortly after that dreamy thought of living in such a perfect paradise, here came the Eden Monster. I observed the audience all nodding their heads with the realization that paradise found was now lost and, sure enough, it *was* too good to be true. I chastised myself for letting my guard down, being so easily manipulated. How could I have been so gullible to believe a perfect place like this could exist? As our wishful human gathering watched this cinematic fairyland unfold, I was convinced most others felt as I did. My distorted belief was that Human Beings did not deserve a perfect paradise or Heaven, unless it came at the price of a monster continually nipping at their heels.

Wait! Here comes the real lesson. Materializing for the first time in nineteen years, the invisible-energy monster began attacking the perimeter defenses around the space vessel. This particular energy force had wiped out all the other members of the scientific expedition — except for Dr. Morbius, his wife (who died from natural causes), and their infant daughter.

The Battle Resumes. For every attempt at increasing the strength of the defense barriers, there was an equal and opposite response from the insidious monster. When Altaira declares her love for Commander Adams and expresses her intention to return to Earth, the monster suddenly forces their (she, Adams, and Morbius) retreat to the scientist's inner sanctum — an impenetrable fortress designed to resist any conceivable foe. Safely inside, while congratulating themselves on their newfound security, a renewed and vengeful monster starts pounding on the once-impervious entryway. When the barrier weakens, the good doctor, so busy resisting (therefore attracting) his moment with the Grim Reaper, fails to appreciate the vast beauty that surrounds him.

Monster From the id

Just as all seemed lost, with the day of reckoning at hand, an awareness of the Eden beast's true origin emerged...tap, tap, tapping on their chamber door. This was the monster the brilliant scientist subconsciously tried to evade by leaving Earth. He distortedly believed that evil — and therefore all conflict — existed exclusively in the outer environment. By simply changing and creating a new perfect *outer*, he (mistakenly) felt any future pain and suffering for himself and his beloved family thus avoided. *Finding solace by retreating from life's ever-relentless challenges proves futile.*

Morbius finally understood how this potentially lethal creation came — in fact — from his own depraved mind. Faced with imminent destruction, Morbius turned within to confront his human-created shadow. By facing the black, inky cloud of self-absorbed unworthiness, the contrite scientist embraced his subconscious fears.

At that very instant, Morbius saw how he'd invested his entire adult life futilely attempting to manipulate and control the outer environment, believing this the appropriate way to defeat inner challenges. With his personal demon acknowledged, all its power and hold over him, including the perceived threat to the innocent daughter and space crew, began to withdraw. The self-created attack halted a little too late to save the remorseful doctor's *physical* life, however.

Conclusion. What a great metaphorical example of how subconscious beliefs run the show! By turning within, we more effectively determine whether our old tapes currently serve us. *Like our woeful scientist, we either go within, or we go without.*

Only Love in the Cosmos

As a warrior in Vietnam, I believed that, to live, I must slay the fire-breathing dragons craving *their* day of retribution. As we open ourselves to higher levels of consciousness, our internal demons take a day off—eventually retiring altogether. This revelation does not circumvent the reality that sometimes our physical lives may be threatened. Our nature provides automatic preservation reflexes for swift lifesaving responses. Human Beings—as a species—would not have survived, thus far, without an inherent ability to escape the *Sabertooth Tigers* of the past. Ancient skills included basic reflex action, intellect, socialized cooperation, and the early beginnings of those intuitive talents and capabilities currently under discussion. Almost entirely instinctive and very primitive, conscious-awareness levels of early Human Beings resided in what Holographic Psychology™ calls "pre-First Reality," with little or no capability to understand moralistic differences between right and wrong. But then...shift happened!

First Reality

Based in behaviorism, First Reality expresses a predictable response following a controlled stimulus. This level revolves around observed, learned behavior and operant conditioning, which in most childhood cultures represents the limit of our basic education. In the absence of any other conscious imperatives, it's "monkeys see...monkeys do."

Robotomorphic Education

In widely accepted educational systems within the United States and other countries, young children are treated as isolated, empty vessels needing rigid conditioning. If our teaching elders possessed a greater reflective, encompassing capability, might our children (instead) be revered as largely uncorrupted, pure-channel, omniscient Beings, intimately interwoven within the cosmic framework? From that more-expansive and reverential view, *all* would be treated as "Indigo" (especially aware) children. Much of today's world, however, robotically conditions students to believe that material considerations limit individual potential. *Authority* refers to this as the "placing of realistic boundaries."

Material-world programming can slow, but not permanently stop, the magnificently uninhibited dream (life blueprint) that lives forever within a person's Spiritual DNA. The reactive world of First Reality consciousness, firmly centered in five-sensory materialism, relates to both the environment and one's self. Without clear and purposeful introspection, we generally believe we are viewing (defining) an objective reality. Mastery of the first level proves essential to successful manipulation of the physical world, including but not limited to our animalistic survival instincts. This focus, in its primal form, embodied the predominant—if not exclusive—realm of those ancient humans who spent every waking moment just trying to stay alive.

Many material benefits reside within First Reality. In current periods, this level led to our brilliantly devised technology. Limitation becomes conspicuous when behavioristic practitioners decree that *all* human conduct (and therefore change) comes at the behest of the environment. The "If I follow the given instructions, I will arrive at the correct answer" mindset works just fine when learning to drive an automobile, or program a computer. And, as stated, pre- First Reality reflexes definitely serve us during survival-based, fight-or-flight situations. First Reality perspectives, by definition, do not include personal responsibility for thoughts, feelings, or even actions. Instead, this awareness level assigns negative events—or perceptions of such—to someone else: boss, spouse, children, parents, work-mate, government, terrorists, etc. Quick to blame environmental circumstances—such as the condition of their vehicle, or the weather—individuals expressing from First Reality easily justify their lack of performance. *Possessors* have an automatic and predictable defensive reaction when confronted or challenged. Similarly, fate, superstition and luck determine a *good* day, month, or life—in First Reality.

Human history reflects that turning within for personal responsibility and vested change—with rare exception—is a very recent manifestation. Even with the development of early psychology, almost everything emotionally unsettling or *wrong* with an individual was believed inherently pathological, behavioristic in origin (secular beliefs), or the devil's work (sacred belief). Blame for *devilish* influences peaked approximately 1000 A.D. With the heyday of Freudian behaviorism from the late 1920s to the middle-to-late 1950s, many assigned outside environmental factors the cause of practically all emotional difficulties. This previously exclusive paradigm was upstaged with the advent of humanistic (1960) and transpersonal (1969) principles.

Green Beans, Anyone?

CAUTION: For the protection of yourself and others nearby, I recommend you not be eating anything during the reading of this prescribed attempt at behavioral programming.

In the late 1940s and early 50s, I was a young, rapidly growing preadolescent who absolutely hated green beans. No amount of Jack & the Beanstalk stories, or bribes of ice cream or cookies, could shake my determination to avoid those leguminous pods. The family pediatrician, complete with impressive initials both before and after his name, ardently advocated the power of reverse psychology. He gave my frustrated, but ever-hopeful, mother the definitive solution to this crisis of taste. He instructed her to feed me nothing other than the dreaded green beans until I learned to accept them eagerly. The good doctor believed that hunger would eventually supercede my psychological resistance and...*abracadabra*..."bring on them beans!" He assured my skeptical mother that if she followed this sure-fire behavioristic model, I would beg for second helpings in no time.

In spite of Dad's silent head shaking, my mother's strenuous browbeating got us to the second bean-fest evening, where I was, once again, forced to cram those waxy tubers down a resisting throat. Although I consumed nothing but green beans over the previous two days, somehow I ingested an additional cup-and-a-half of the *devil's brew* during this second, agonizing dinner period. With an upset stomach, I invoked a reprieve and asked that I be allowed to go to my room. Spurred by our behaviorist guru, Mom relentlessly pursued the *Promised Land*. Through copious tears of torment, I tried one more spoonful. You know what came to dinner next. That final swallow triggered a domino effect of protesting gut, a heightened level of revulsion, and airborne green beans! I spewed forth a full cup-and-a-half of the gooey green mixture directly onto the kitchen table's red floral centerpiece! [*Now you understand the "no eating" precaution.*]

Filled with bittersweet embarrassment, but finally devoid of green beans, I was quickly dispatched. Wendy, my younger sister, tells me she had to suffer the ensuing parental bickering. My mischievous self would have found that quarrel both entertaining and restorative. A little legume *quid pro quo* would be exactly what I would have ordered for the *practicing* physician that conjured up this little brainstorm.

The upshot: not only did I not have to eat any more green beans, but both the ugly floral arrangement (sorry Mom) and the doctor's behavioral training book went into the rubbish bin. Much later, when

I could look at a green tuber without urgently running to the facilities, I discovered it was those canned, wax-coated beans that set those dominoes in motion.

For the more inquisitive: Yes, my green-bean gag reflex has thankfully abated (thanks for asking)—a *great* benefit when attempting to keep an attractive dinner companion in her chair. Eventually someone courageously introduced me to *fresh* green beans, and, now, I even consider Chinese pea pods a delicacy. In time, I forgave my mother for the green-bean fiasco, assisted no doubt by the fact that she had saved me from certain suffocation, a year or so earlier. It's a miracle so many of us make it to adulthood—even in the West.

To expand beyond the first level of comprehension, where behavioristic beliefs and associated programming reign supreme, ones (including experimenting parents) must awaken to the distinction between external/outer causal factors (stimulus-response) and subjective, inner evaluations. This paradigm shift differential requires an independent viewer, which Holographic Psychology calls the *"observer"* or *"neutral referee."* Avatar Masters refer to this transferal processing as "Belief Management." **First Reality beliefs, not the environment, are the number-one reason for a poor self-image and associated feelings of powerlessness and victimization.** First Reality perspectives drive the creation and acceptance of the muti-billion-dollar, symptom-treating, *pain-relief-in-a-bottle* industry.

The following fable illustrates the inherent limitations of living exclusively within a fear-based, First Reality Consciousness. What a wealth of additional opportunities for those who break through to Second Reality.

The Blind Fisherman

There once was a troubled person, of rigid negative thinking and uninspired beliefs, about to receive a great gift. His name was Thomas and he lived with his family on the barren outskirts of a small, Northern Province. His list of hardships included a lack of food to feed his ever-increasing brood. Thomas worked hard—but with less than fully inspired wisdom and creativity—to provide sustenance to his beloved ones. One day, while Thomas tended to his sparse vegetable garden, a stranger passed through his village with a catch of fresh fish—quite surprising, since there were no large bodies of water nearby.

The approaching stranger noticed Thomas' tattered children playing in a makeshift tree house and graciously offered them some fish. While painful for a prideful father to watch his *flesh and blood* eagerly accepting handouts, his conflicting emotions were tempered by the knowledge that his children were desperate for nourishment. Thomas decided to welcome the charity by inviting the benevolent stranger to dinner.

After the wonderfully shared feast and spirited conversation, the guest arose to excuse himself. Thomas and his appreciative family members promised to pray for his continued safe journey. They also voiced the wish that they could find some fish for themselves. The sympathetic benefactor responded by telling a somewhat doubtful Thomas about a previously hidden fresh-water lake within a day's journey. "The abundance of fish upon this unspoiled body of pristine water is so plentiful that you can virtually scoop up your bounty without artificial implements," the charismatic drifter reported. "With the very fertile soil for planting seed, you could potentially feed your family for a lifetime," he added. The saintly man suggested moving the homestead to the lush and available Eden, where most — if not all — the family's physical needs could easily be met. With appreciative hugs and final good-byes, the angelic provider bid adieu — never to be seen again.

Thomas concluded this Eden story too good to be true. He diminished its value when recounting what he surmised was a whimsical tale told by an entertaining vagabond. He asked Claire, his ever-hopeful spouse, "How can we possibly trust the word of a complete stranger?" Thomas emphasized how difficult the journey would be — only to be set up for another of life's many disappointments. In spite of Thomas' doubts as to the meal's origin, there was much merriment and heartened celebration. His family continued to eat their fill from the remainder of the cherished delicacy.

At the expressed urging of the children and the enthusiastic Claire, Thomas finally agreed to make the trek to the hidden valley. Always a farmer, Thomas lacked any specific knowledge of fishing. If the stranger's depiction were true, specialized skills would not be required for success. Undeterred by patriarchal reservations, all family members eagerly agreed to tend the garden, care for the animals, and complete the other seasonal chores while awaiting Thomas' return. Although not shared by her pessimistic husband,

Claire believed the stranger a Heaven-sent messenger arriving in response to her heartfelt prayers for a better life for their children.

With provisions for several days, including a special, baked treat scrounged together by his lovingly loyal and now-animated spouse, Thomas began his journey. He believed the hardships of life his due, and did not expect any relief. So far, life had responded with one challenge after another—for which Thomas had unwittingly requested.

Upon his arrival at the forested paradise, Thomas admitted it was, indeed, the most beautiful place he had ever seen. Extremely lush growth indicated the soil as fertile as promised. A tinge of hopeful elation entered the consciousness of this fearful provider, just moments before his heart sank in recriminating acceptance of his expected disappointment.

At the shoreline of the serene alpine lake, Thomas *cast* his gaze— for several long moments—over the lavish vista. But not one fish appeared. Thomas began to curse the oversized pond, the stranger, and mostly himself for having considered the validity of some fanciful tale told by a transiting drifter. Disheartened, Thomas returned home with his dispirited "I told you so" announcement, temporarily masking underlying feelings of humiliation and worthlessness.

After witnessing the light of hope and inspired creativity dimming in the eyes of his beloved family, Thomas could no longer hold back his shameful weeping. Attempting to console her anguished husband, the once-buoyant matriarch asserted that perhaps they had been foolish to dream of a better place and greater opportunity. Her young and impressionable children nodded in quiet acknowledgement. With heads hung low, and shoulders slumped, the young ones resigned themselves to their collective impoverishment. Returning to the meager lettuce garden, the family's vision of a lush and abundant paradise was soon forgotten.

Conclusion. Thomas and his family members made the same distorted choice that many of us duplicate in today's world. We often allow our childhood dreams to be replaced by the debilitating blindfold of tired acceptance and conformed complacency. As we observe from this fictional, but metaphorically significant tale, we do not find truth by simply going to the shore and casting our gaze upon the lake of life. The expanded reality: *all the love and abundance we could possibly imagine, both for us and those we care for, is here for the taking.* It requires courage, faith, and determination to *prod beneath the surface* of our manifesting opportunities.

Living a life by disavowing our gifts, talents, and abilities, is not much fun, is it? Unless firmly convinced this sad depiction is your assigned lot in life, let doubting Thomas' lesson prompt you to look beyond the five-sensory world for expanded truth and the all-inclusive treasure that awaits discovery. As you continue *true* north on your destined rendezvous with the Inner Spirit, use the message from the Blind Fisherman story as your motivational zenith. Or...you can turn everything over to the fate of lottery ticket purchases—your choice.

From this point forward, we use our probative abilities to examine cultural mores that often hold us in fearful subservience. Because belief-system toes invariably get stepped on, this may be a difficult process for some.

One of my strongest motivations for looking beyond the five-sensory world: my father's creative examples. The following remembrance illustrates the ways Dad continuously prodded and actualized his underlying potential.

Living with a Genius

When not working at Lockheed Aircraft, or on the ongoing construction and modifications of our ever-expanding abode, Dad normally reserved his fanaticism and remaining free time for his various gadgets and inventions. To my mother's consternation, Dad's mind was always scheming and configuring. He sketched and doodled around the border of the kitchen place mats until no white space remained. My father delighted in developing multiple projects in his specially built basement workshop. For a young boy, his laboratory was a Tinker-Toy and Erector-Set paradise.

Dad prided himself on being able to repair any mechanical or

electrical device...not always a benefit. I remember a time when Mom became furious over his putting off repairs to our broken television set. While missing all her favorite programs, Dad was down in the basement happily preoccupied with his latest brainstorm.

Larry & Sister Wendy on Go-Cart Test

He could not tolerate her paying someone else to do repair work, however. When Mom threatened to call Hollywood's most expensive television shop, Dad had the set on and operating by the following evening.

Saucer in the Hills

Our home became front-page news after the unceremonious unveiling of one of Dad's more spectacular inventions. He had designed a solid, 32-foot-diameter swimming-pool cover from scrap aluminum and magnesium—all discarded leftovers from Lockheed's infamous "Skunk Works." The silver disc—operating like a toilet-seat lid—attached by cable to an electric wench securely imbedded in the steep bank directly behind the cylindrical 30-foot swimming pool (that Dad also designed and built). While in the raised position, two retractable arms rigidly extended from the embankment to hold the main lid braces in place. When the pool was not in use, we simply reversed the wench and returned the elaborate cover to its full-down position. This pool-cover scheme actually took Dad longer to design and build than did the pool, itself. But the droppings from our constantly shedding forest of oak trees ceased their ferocious contamination. Dad's inventions saved me from some of the more arduous hillside chores.

The first day we raised the completed monument to my father's unyielding inventiveness, it was immediately noticed by hundreds—perhaps thousands—living throughout the San Fernando Valley. Calls came pouring into the Studio City and North Hollywood Police Stations—and, therefore, the media—suggesting a "Flying Saucer" crash-landed in the foothills. From a different angle, the massive disc apparently looked like a hole in the mountain.

A Los Angeles Times' news crew, not knowing the entrance to our private driveway, began hacking their way through the steep, prickly hillside foliage and thick underbrush that lay between our house and the winding roadway, below. My dad, tickled by this motivated display, sat back and patiently awaited their arrival.

Torn, bleeding, and exhausted, the journalistic entourage eventually reached their intended target. My inventor father, resplendent in the afterglow of having his brilliance recognized, held court. Standing proudly for the cameras, Dad answered questions and described the design details of his latest mechanical marvel. "Would you care to see my ultra-glide pontoon boat, super lightweight egg-shell travel trailer, or other innovations?" he asked. The offering of

cold beer, lemonade, and sterile dressings bought some extra time and conversation. But then the resilient reporters had to leave in time to both meet their deadlines *and* tend to their wounds. Some remembered the malevolent "Saucer in the Hills" longer than others, when the poison oak, which the determined surveyors had been so keen to dispatch, found tortuous access to their every nook, cranny, and orifice.

Learning to Think Outside the Box

Developing an appreciation for our own preexisting potential better prepares us to take advantage of manifesting opportunities. My father continually demonstrated the adage: "Opportunities are never lost; they simply pass on to someone else." Might this be the time to prepare yourself for those new treasures coming *your* way?

As force-fed youngsters, we more, or less, accept society's *facts of life,* with original beliefs a constant until we awaken to a higher reality. Unfortunately for both our parents and ourselves, we must first endure the teenage years where we *think* we have awakened to it all. Having survived that challenging time, some of us begin to chart our own course. In so doing, we also help lead others out of the darkness. When we realize just how subjective and arbitrary our interpretation of life's processes, we automatically shift to a more expanded view and become more focused on the *inclusive* nature of life. Unless determined to resist our wakeup call to the bitter end, we learn—in stages—to release those feelings of victimization and the need to fight to be right. As we discover that real, genuine power to change comes solely from within, we relax our need to control others or to blame outside circumstances for our condition in life. This potentially leads to the elimination of war and all forms of conflict. If—during this reading—you come to this same liberating conclusion, you might perhaps sense the significance inherent in a message of emancipation and all-inclusive synchronicity.

You no longer need to clone the thinking and behavior of others in distorted, futile attempts to reach an elusive comfort zone. Your newfound freedom includes the realization that emotional, mental, and Spiritual salvation is achievable only within your existing domain, not in any separate entity or force. As you'll increasingly discover, this newly actualized level of belief begins with Second Reality consciousness. I continue to review and discuss the various applications of the reality levels—and their relationship to quality of life—throughout this guidebook.

Karmic Debt and Other Punishments

The new paradigm reveals we do not live an obligatory lifetime to reconcile the sins of the father, nor as punishment for past-life transgressions. Consider that a temporarily independent ray of Universal Consciousness, which we term "Soul," has chosen to be here. The Soul does not view the world through the traditional animalistic perspective that all pain is *bad* and all pleasure *good*. The *right-and-wrong* judgment business is fodder for much of our current-day misery. I do not refer to defensive reflexes our animal nature provides for self-preservation. Protective instincts are not only appropriate, but essential for bodily survival. If about to be eaten by an African Lion, that's not the time for philosophical contemplation, meditative attunements, or love offerings—unless your gift is a Wildebeest carcass. I am emphasizing the *imagined beasts* we psychologically self-create through mental and emotional distortion. Our *creature* inventory includes warped judgments made during periods of marked fear, greed, and self-absorbency.

During those rare times when a lion happens to consume a human, this act of nature is not *bad* from the Soul perspective. It most certainly serves the lion and its pride. We human types, however, generally prefer to use our instincts and great intellect to avoid being lunch for carnivorous beasts.

Consider how often our intuitive abilities become desensitized through programmed conditioning. Limited to First Reality perspectives, we unknowingly offer ourselves as tasty main courses for bullies and assorted control freaks, which results in feelings of isolation and powerlessness. In victimization scenarios, those that readily prey on the unaware soon gobble up an individual's power. Lifeless victims then find themselves stuck in a repetitive feedback loop, believing that God, or some other external determinate, decreed they should suffer. You and I reenergize our powerful intuitive instincts, to cease being silage for the agenda of others. Once you heal and replace your major areas of unworthiness, fear-based energy vampires exit your world in swift retreat. That portion of your life curriculum will then be mostly—if not completely—concluded.

As we have been learning, Souls value *all* experiential life. Souls wish to enter the variety, intensity, and narrow concentrated focus that experiential human life contains. *Celestial benevolence is not a no-consequences license to plunder and rape, however.* We experience our free-will consequences in the here and now, *and* during our initial transition. Negative imbalances normally (except with mental illness) directly and reciprocally affect our well-being and quality of life. If we *practice* love, joy, and happiness, these same properties become our primary experience. Those consumed with worry, anxiety, or other fear-based preoccupations (like anger and revenge), rarely acknowledge the *"it happens unto you as you believe"* dynamic. Unresolved, large-scale negativity often sets up an archetypal group-soul pattern that—in time—comes full circle in its quest for healing and mastery. Again, do not to confuse this with Western concepts of celestial punishment, or Eastern beliefs in karmic debt.

Resolving underlying patterns of emotional fear and self-absorbed (separating) greed has always been a main theme of Earth school, ever since we—as humans—left the "Garden." This guide offers the foundational precept that we are *not* required to get sick first in order to appreciate health, and we do not *require* cause-and-effect influences to remember who and what we truly are. Cause-and-effect curriculum stands ready to step in, as needed. When we truly understand that suffering and feelings of unworthiness and separation denote a *level* of awareness not yet shifted to a larger, more expansive and empowering realization, we no longer require the more tortuous courses. For example: Are you open to consider a "good" passing being infinitely more joyous, in the so-called afterlife, than one where unresolved issues and traumatic negative-energy manifestations precede physical death? Well before our inevitable transition, benefits inure from realizing that we each create (subconsciously or otherwise) Heaven or hell, right here on Earth. At third-level conscious awareness, nothing is caused—what already exists is simply realized and accepted.

Be Right or be Free

When young and struggling to find an identity for myself, I often fought (debated) to prove others wrong. I subconsciously needed to feel righteous and secure in my newly formed beliefs. This typical response, part of the competitive, negatively conditioned, and culturally motivated First Reality world, is often the initial process in the *appearance* of achieving one's right of passage.

If we—as parents—could understand our adolescents' awakening processes and associated consciousness levels, we could avoid much of the *Hell-on-Earth* curriculum that adolescents often facilitate. Expressing from a First Reality perspective, *raising a teenager can only be described as an attempt to nail Jell-O to a tree.* Struggling and suffering are guaranteed if we have not yet shifted our perspectives. At the first level, we believe we *are* making objective, fact-based decisions. But Dr. Pottenger's human-potential research, as well as evidence from our own lives, conclusively demonstrate that we (in First Reality) actually respond to stimuli in subjectively conditioned ways. The good news: *we are evolving.* In past times of Earth, almost all humans spent their entire lives at the subordinate level. Very few *enlightened ones* walked the planet in those ancient periods. This orientation factored foremost in why so many humans were slaves. Even so-called slave *masters* operated in First Reality. They were just more forceful about it. Regardless of the domination perpetuated on the masses, the controlling elite still lived in constant fear. They obsessed over betrayal, or the fear of bigger, tougher bullies coming to town with swifter swords and hungrier armies.

True Source of Worldwide Negativity

The new paradigm opens us to consider all alleged negativity currently expressed on Earth as *human* created—in content or interpretation. Alleged negativity results from past and present choices (or reactions) made in greed-based selfishness and fear. An illustrative example: In the material world, humans create environmental challenges—such as pollution—by ignorant choices or self-absorbed overindulgence. This then translates into a fear of *lack,* a belief in scarcity, and the selfish desire for instant gratification. The resulting imbalance produces a potential focal point for us to gather around. All our choices—both serving and non-serving—including a symbolic *dark-night-of-the-soul* fire walk—helps initiate Spiritual DNA curriculum. The playing out of our so-called karmic or archetypal lessons eventually leads to harmonized healing and the beginnings of true joy, peace, love, and happiness. Experience manifests from our life curriculum, leading to ever-increasing stages of awareness and new, more expanded levels of experience. The cycle of creative and expressive life...a wonder to behold, is it not?

In First Reality we concern ourselves with the search for a better *pill* to eliminate pain, or a bigger *toy* to facilitate pleasure. At that level, we distortedly believe manipulation of material reality the exclusive formula for a successful, even if largely unfulfilled, life.

Can I safely conclude you would like to end your participation in humanity's recurring pattern of torment and feed-back-loop existence? OK, let's learn how to get productively engaged during our Earth adventure.

Relaxation and Altered States

When we take some regular moments to quiet our dominant Beta brainwave activity (normal left-brain ego awareness) and open to even a small portion of our expanded selves, the experience can be transforming and irrevocably life changing. Through quiet contemplation, or meditation, where we set aside everyday goals and challenges for a few moments, we often discover many new (to us) realms of existence. We *all* frequently slip in and out of Alpha states of consciousness—daydreaming or twilight sleep—just prior to drifting off or waking up. An excellent time to practice attunements—especially for beginners—is before fully awakening from a sleep period.

Do not be dissuaded by those who say you must have some special mantra or expert meditation technique to enter a simple Alpha State, or even the deeper Theta levels of consciousness. Just the process of basic relaxation and deep rhythmic breathing takes you there. This is why processes such as guided visualization, breath work, and other tools to access the subconscious mind, prove so effective. When we expand beyond the Beta mindset, we more easily reach our deeply centered *core level* where substantial replacement of non-serving thoughts and behavior takes place.

Let me emphasize: *believing in Souls, Cosmic Guides, God, or the "Collective," is not necessary for you to beneficially access the subconscious mind.* Once trained to implement this entry, the potential for success primarily depends on three factors.

- **Your motivation.**
- **The psychological dynamics in your psyche and their associated emotional impact(s).**
- **Your willingness to accept beneficial suggestions, especially from yourself.**

Self-Guided Visualization and Relaxation—a Simple Process

CAUTION! All processes in this book are for educational, self-help purposes only. If currently under the care of a psychological counselor or therapist, ask your caregiver whether you require professional supervision during any subconscious or altered-state work. If you suffer from intense depression, suicidal thoughts, or other debilitating or potentially dangerous mental/emotional pain or condition, please get professional help IMMEDIATELY. It may be crucial that you be stabilized for your current safety.

Meditation, for the vast majority, is a comfortable, relaxing, connecting process. I issue these warnings for the rare individual that may encounter some unexpected difficulty. Some of you have not previously experienced any intended subconscious-accessing work, or made any deliberate attempts at purposeful relaxation. For those in this category, be assured that your conscious mind—although somewhat in the background—is always with you and under your control during any relaxation or memory regression process. This is true whether you relax on your own or with a facilitator.

Relaxation is a mild form of hypnosis and *all* hypnosis is self-hypnosis. Some experts feel that facilitators should never use the word "hypnosis" because of the public's fear of being coerced into doing something embarrassing, dangerous, non-serving, or anything beyond their control. Rather than coddle any alleged insecurity, I suggest you not let metaphorical symbols (words) determine your experience. *All* senses are enhanced during meditative attunements. Your inner alarm bell brings you out of any altered state if you experience an overly fearful scenario. Trust your unconscious instincts to alert you to any (unlikely) danger and keep you safe.

Consider the mindset that psychologists and hypnotherapists refer to as "altered," is actually much closer to our *true* Soul presence. Letting go of your five-sensory preoccupation allows more ease of focus toward expanded realities. In spite of the Spiritual guidance (Infinite) with us always, I give you these additional options and precautions because many of you will begin this exercise at home with just this guidebook as your companion. *If you are a complete beginner to meditation, or self-guided visualization, consider group classroom environments as a supportive starting point.* The nice folks at your local new-age bookstore normally have information about beginning classes in meditation, relaxation, breath work, guided imagery, and other altered-state facilitations.

For those of you who wish to continue on with me, understand that even with heightened senses, your primary focus will not be the physical environment. Be sure to turn off your stove, steam iron, and coffeepot. Extinguish any unsafe candles or smoking materials. Eliminate the potential for anything untoward taking place while attempting to release yourself from the stress of constant focus on material world events. Something very near the surface of your conscious awareness—upon realization—might be startling. I want you prepared should any unexpected thought or feeling unceremoniously begin gushing forth with reckless abandon. Do not *expect* this to happen, as you begin slowly with sessions of basic relaxation combined with light, contemplative exploration. However, the possibility of extraordinary input potentially exists, even for beginners.

Experiencing spontaneous memory retrieval during altered-state (subconscious mind) access is possible even when not being prodded by a professional therapist. And can involve both pleasurable and/or traumatic memories. On rare occasions, remembered events may even materialize from the limitless ether—beyond space and time—and therefore have little or no Earthly explanation other than their personal import to you. Normally, these intuitive-type phenomena— which many metaphysicians believe to be Spiritually guided recall— represents a wonderful opportunity to heal and release past, perhaps previously submerged, issues and emotions. Short term, the rare memory may be confusing, scary, or seemingly threatening for a very few of you. If you experience anything beyond your basic comfort level, follow up your solo sessions with professional counseling assistance. If you experience emotional pain too much to bear on your own, that's the time to back off and call for supportive assistance.

Now that we have covered the primary precautions, let us quiet ourselves and try an exercise in relaxation and potential releasing of troubling issues. If you wish, there is no harm in just reading through this section for now. I strongly suggest you then make it a priority to practice this exercise on a regular basis. The foundation you establish, here, prepares you for the more-expansive healing and Spiritual connection facilitated in later segments. So, make the sometimes Herculean effort to set yourself free from ordinary outside distractions such as loud noises, children, telephones, pagers, pets, neighbors, etc. Put yourself in a comfortable sitting position so that you will be less likely to fall asleep. There's no threat of harm should you nod off; you will just wake up naturally. Falling asleep early in your relaxation means you have not directed the attunement process to its fullest potential and you probably have missed—for that session—some, or most, of the benefit this technique provides. However, you *will* benefit from a great nap—sometimes referred to as "power sleep."

Although experts disagree on how much input the subconscious mind effectively incorporates while in our regular sleep patterns, too much stimulation can be sleep depriving.

Let's begin. Close your eyes and take several deep breaths— through the nose if possible. Hold each of those life-giving breaths for several seconds. As you direct all tightness and stress to leave your body, release the air slowly through your mouth. Continue focusing on those extra-deep, still rhythmic breaths, while visualizing a peaceful location. Picture a babbling brook, a gentle waterfall, or ocean with seagulls soaring and squawking softly in the distance. Repeat the focused breath work until you feel deeply relaxed. Then, let your natural breathing take over.

On every inhalation, think the words and mental state of "at ease." On every exhalation, think "relaxed." Continue this for several minutes. Feel yourself going deeper and deeper. A sequence that works well is to begin your focus at the top of the head and gradually, with each exhalation, move down your body in sections. Equally effective is to start with your toes and mentally move up your body, finishing with your head or crown-energy chakra. (See the APPENDIX - GLOSSARY for a more detailed explanation of *chakras*.)

As you feel each part of your body relax, sense, see, feel, or imagine a narrow, descending laser beam of gold; a beam followed shortly by ribbon after ribbon of rainbow-colored light—all pouring into your crown chakra. Feel these sequential ribbons of light-energy bathe you with a calming, healing, and empowering force. See, feel, sense, or imagine them taking their turn in fully penetrating your body from the top of your head to the bottom of your feet. Mentally give thanks for all the teachers in your life, including your parenting ones. If you choose, mentally or verbally repeat a love affirmation at this point—such as the attunement prayer given at the very beginning of this book.

Upon reaching a comfortable depth of relaxation, take some time to just *BE*. Focusing on your breathing often helps to clear much of the physical world preoccupation and ego-mind chatter. Do not expect to eliminate all thoughts and feelings. A mental vacuum is not required to benefit from this exercise, or any altered-state process. If you feel your mind wandering into complex areas not serving you, just bring your focus back to the breathing procedure. Visualize, feel, or imagine oxygen flowing from your lungs as it nurtures all the cells of your body. Concentrate on the rhythmic flow of that oxygen and the redness of your own blood thereby created. Focus on your internal circulation…to deepen your process, while crowding out extraneous static. After some moments of feeling completely relaxed and *only* after you have practiced this basic induction several times and are fully comfortable with it, try asking for clarity and guidance in your life. I remind you that you are fully in control at all times. For those who experience anything more severe than the common uneasiness and stress often associated with venting and releasing troubling issues, I urge you, again, to seek a group environment or individual therapist where you can be better supported during healing sessions.

Assuming your experience is completely within your comfort zone, begin focusing on your emotional pain and negativity, with emphasis on the underlying source of its nutriment. Picture yourself mentally peeling back the layers of a symbolic onion. Courageously expose the underlying emotional fear that enables your negative feelings. This is a primary step in Second Reality consciousness emancipation. Acknowledgment, responsibility acceptance, release from blaming and bargaining, and a self-empowered belief in a new beginning can all follow a venting and forgiveness exercise. Remind yourself that self-diminishing thoughts and feelings are just temporary — not truths. Say to yourself:

"My core being can never be damaged or destroyed by any human experience, no matter how traumatic or vile. I can actually feel my personal demon-fears of unworthiness dissolve lovingly into my arms, as they are blessedly set free from their diagnostic imperative. I now feel the truth that those false manifestations of negative thought and feeling no longer have any hold over me. I take back my power with the renewed awareness — I am now reinstated as Captain of my own ship."

Experience the flow of the rainbow of light as it fills and heals those previously wounded areas. Say to your self/Self: *"The truth of me has **always** been magnificent and powerful!"* Choose to accept the evidence of that, *now*. Feel the joyous presence of loving Beings, a special force or deity, universal energy, or any higher Self you attune to, dancing in your heart. Open to the gift of joyful love. Continue to use angelic light energy to suture your psychological wounds. Rejoice in this monumental breakthrough! Give thanks to all entities and forces that assisted your healing and/or enlightenment. When you're ready, mentally count to five and return yourself to full conscious awareness. Have a sip of water or a piece of fruit to help ground you.

Unrealistic Expectations

Welcome back! If this was your first effort at self-directed meditation, I hope it was at least relaxing, if not therapeutic or enlightening. There is a tendency, especially with newcomers to meditation and self-guided visualizations, to give lots of left-brained thought to whether they do it correctly. Meditative attunement or contemplation is *not* something we do, but, rather, something we allow to be visited upon us. Meditation is an ego-transcendent focus. To meditate effectively, let the world *BE*, without comment or judgment (opinion) on your part. All egos aside, the world continues on and does just fine without our input.

A reminder: we are *not* attempting to stamp out the ego or make it our enemy. We...allow a gentle releasing of our physical world preoccupation. Lovingly direct your ego mind to an important observational role for the duration of any relaxation or attunement process. Your ego mind will have plenty of time to analyze, later.

For best results I suggest you also release all thoughts and concerns about the form your input may take. Some persons visualize, some auditorialize, some kinetically feel input, some just know, and a few receive data from all these arenas. We heavy-thinking, left-brained anal(yzers) may not register intake from any of those sources. If one, or more, sensory input makes a connection, wonderful—go with it. If, after several patient sessions, you still don't get any incoming impressions...not to worry. Simply *imagine* one of the suggested relaxation locations from the processing outline you just read. As you continue to practice, input sensations gradually grow in intensity. *You can not do it wrong!* Release those fear-based excuses. Breathe, relax, and go with the flow. You will definitely not be alone...especially during consciousness expanding attunements. However, you are perfectly free to imagine yourself in isolation, if that be your desire. A mildly disassociated orientation will not—in and of it self—prevent your achieving useful states of relaxation or purposeful contemplations. It may even be preferred.

Supportive Paraphernalia

This simple abatement (soft regression technique) I have given you will bypass the majority of Beta-Mind input. When repeated on a regular basis, it provides great rewards in enlightenment, general health, and well being. As an additional aid to relaxation and insightful clarity, some have successfully used soft, soothing, rhythmic sounds, or safely cradled incense. You can also create a special cassette tape with a message program to guide you. Give yourself calming, healing, motivating suggestions. As an induction guide, you may use my various narrative outlines (here and elsewhere) for your own personal use. If you dictate your own tape, be direct, positive, and speak to yourself in the present tense. Repeat your name (at least once) and the pronoun "you" or "your" rather than "me" or "my." Do not record "you *will* be relaxing," but instruct instead; "You *are* relaxing." Don't make unrealistic suggestions to yourself—they'll not be as effective. If your leg is broken, do not state "you are healed." Record, instead, "Every day, in every way, your leg gets stronger and stronger." When giving yourself an instruction, words that evoke feeling and emotion are always more powerful. You can purchase excellent commercial tapes to use either from the beginning, or at the appropriate time during your session.

Check out the large selection at Borders® or any *new-age* bookstore. Repeatedly practicing this relaxation induction will serve you well during facilitation of the "Cosmic Contact Visualization Process" presented later. This technique may be basic stuff for some of you experts. If so, be reminded to actually take the time to do your meditations. Ten- to fifteen-minute daily consciousness-relaxation sessions provide wonderful benefits to mind, body, and spirit. A short, regular schedule not only yields a wonderful break from the complexity and stresses of the physical world, but also grants more balance, clarity, and confidence in one's ability to peacefully embrace everyday challenges.

The way has been provided to replace old, tired, painful, negative thoughts and feelings with total liberation of mind and spirit. But, just like the fear-dancing process described in the next chapter, human free will and true liberation both require Second Reality awareness. As one awakens to Second Reality and beyond, much of the First Reality knee-jerk world becomes personally moot. Possessors empowered to engage internal healing and replacement therapies, greatly reduce the need for mental/emotional down time.

When we eventually realize everything has been provided—right on schedule—for us to complete our individual lesson plan, we experience a quantum shift in perspective. With synchronous *inclusivity*, no separate person, thing, or circumstance upsets us any longer. With Life's advanced suffering ☹ class completed, we are free to move on to ☺ FUN 101, 201, 301, and PhD, without ever looking back.

So…are you ready to climb out of that knee-jerk pain pit of First Reality and start claiming a greater slice of the cheese? In the next chapter, you shall receive your infusion of self-actualized empowerment. Enjoy!

THE OBSERVER

Of primary importance in the study of any and all ideas, is the role of the observer—you and I doing the study. Unless and until we have determined the means by which we comprehend reality—of whatever sort—there is a risk that we inadvertently omit the most important element in any study of consciousness.

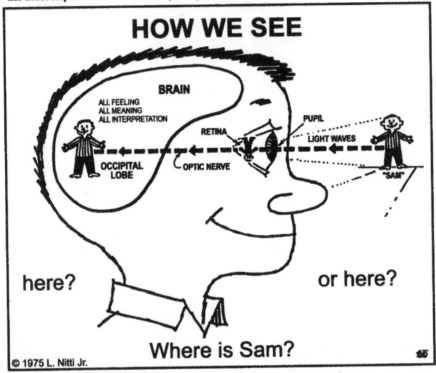

"THE LOCATION OF COMPREHENSION" cannot be overemphasized. Unless we realize the implications of this simple graphic, we insulate ourselves from the single most important factor in the understanding of consciousness. WHO IS IT THAT IS DOING THE OBSERVING? Understanding this chart allows countless problematic areas to be explained. We never do see the outside world other than in our own comprehension, fraught as it is with biases, prejudices and subjective opinion. These influences both color and determine "who" and "what" it is that we observe, evaluate and act upon.

Figure 2

CHAPTER THREE

Second Reality
Ego is <u>not</u> a Four-Letter Word

♥   ♥   ♥

Fast-Acting Holographic Fear-Dancing Technique...a Second Reality Empowerment Tool. I use this supercharged process to quickly clear myself of light, fear-based issues. With the exception of holistic energy-balancing healers, Neural Linguistic (NLP) practitioners, or angel author Barbara Mark—who all coach a process similar to this one, some therapy *experts* suggest the following technique too simple to be effective. I believe in the KISS system: "Keep it Simple Sweetheart."

Phase One

This releasing and healing process begins with a meditative attunement where you self-induce the basic relaxation I previously gave you. To do your *own* layered detective work, by mentally *"peeling the onion,"* helps you discover the core fear beneath any negatively expressing emotion. Although this task may seem Herculean, asking for clarity invites insights to start trickling in— eventually flooding in—as you continue your attunements. Release any desperate or forceful attempts to extract liberating information. Just deal with your most obvious challenge area. Trust me—you will not run out of curriculum.

Have a supportive friend with you for the holographic-image procedure. Use him or her to: ❶ prevent the inevitable interruptions from children, pets, and curious neighbors (turn off those phones and beepers); ❷ assist with the mechanics of Phase Two; ❸ be a friend you can feel comfortable with in the sharing, releasing, healing, and replacing that can result from accessing the inner recesses of your subconscious mind. Even if you feel complete after the first phase of purging, assuming you're capable, continue immediately with Phase Two. A quick transition reinforces any issue-dumping activities. Like going to your computer's rubbish bin to further purge a deleted file, following up immediately with Phase Two can help prevent further contamination or possible reintroduction of undesired issues.

Choosing Your Assistant

Ensure that your selected friend knows the importance of not engaging in a litany of helpful suggestions, or trying to correct or *fix* you, in any way—especially during your purging process. His, or her, job requires only support, empathy, and listening, while you share your feelings—rational or otherwise. If you prefer that your assistant chant a Hu, Om, or other tonal mantra, by all means go for it. This method enables *you* to take your power back, so *you* must completely run the show. Explain this ahead of time and get a commitment from your well-meaning friend to follow your supervisory instructions *to the letter.* Any non-compliance means: *try this procedure another day with a more agreeable assistant.* I emphasize the importance of *you* maintaining control of this entire process. An unwitting discharge of personal power during interpersonal exchanges may contribute to which issue you select. You'll be well served by healing and replacing particularly debilitating areas. Significant, emotionally involved, sometimes-controlling friends and relatives are generally not the best choice as partners. They might be the most threatened by your attempts at liberation; possibly even part of the energy vampire team working to keep your power sequestered. Carefully select your assistant(s) to prevent any psychological fear-based agenda(s) from competing with your fear-dumping process.

All preparations accounted for, begin the process of releasing any adjunctive or separate Earthly concerns—just as you've practiced. As you enter a state of peaceful relaxation, focus on a past experience that lovingly touched your heart. Take whatever time you need to sensitize yourself. The depth of emotional feeling you achieve during the preparatory attunement enhances your potential for releasing, healing, and replacing. While emotionally open, visualize, sense, or imagine the challenge area blocking you from fully getting on with your life. Focus all your attention on just this *one* debilitating issue.

Phase Two

Your partner needs advanced understanding of Phase Two, most of all. Stand up and face your assistant, with approximately three feet of separation. Practice interlocking your fingers and holding your arms semi-rigid, so that your partner can follow your lead. The practice completed, your partner sits down and waits for your signal to reconnect.

Directly in front of you, picture (eyes open or closed), sense, or imagine, a tall, semi-transparent holographic image of a cylinder or hexagon. The cylindrical chamber is just big enough for one person to enter by taking one medium step forward. For the moment, believe this *magical* holographic projection houses all your fear, issue, or condition that has you feeling stuck and victim-like. See this, feel this, know this to be temporarily true.

When ready, step directly in to your specially prepared cylinder. *It automatically opens for anything that approaches it, but once aboard, only you will be able to leave its containment.* Without resistance, fully welcome all the thoughts, feelings, and emotions contained in that self-limiting fear, or issue, you've courageously chosen to face, embrace, and erase. This confining cylinder represents the hold this issue has over you during your everyday life. Stuck here for a very long time, you're weary of it. You refuse to allow this symbolic *cocoon* to control you any longer. Brimming with renewed confidence, you suddenly realize you are stronger than the hologram's contents— contents that are and have always been: False Energy Appearing Real (F E A R). Seeing, feeling, sensing, and imagining your sequestered fear, or issue, a fragile illusion of psychological smoke and mirrors, you now know it as an intangible figment of your mind—just like the belief this fear-based issue ever had any real hold over you.

Spurred by the *appearance* of an affliction, to take this giant step, your dread actually took part in a supporting cast that guided you toward this defining moment. Time to say an appreciative good-bye to that old diagnostic *friend* (fear), its purpose has run its course and will not be coming with you.

The soon-to-be purged psychological noose hanging around your neck is remindful that you will no longer have it to use as a scapegoat. Assured that you no longer need this crutch or any other crutch, from this point forward, you feel a rush of power surging within you. A brilliant, supercharged, light-energy rainbow now joins you in the holographic cylinder. Feel, sense, or imagine this additional infusion of universal power as it courses through every atom of your body. While absolutely bursting with confidence, unwilling to put up with the repressive confinement any longer, raise your arms, again, to the horizontal position. Your partner reaches out to you from the other side of your mentally constructed chamber, and interlocks your fingers with theirs.

At the clear, prearranged signal (head nod, or the word "**now,**" as an example), you confidently leap forward, out of the hologram, while your partner simultaneously and quickly moves back in tandem. You can feel, visualize, sense, and—if necessary—just imagine the sensation of exploding out of that crusty old cocoon. Now your partner asks the prearranged question: "Where is your fear/issue/condition now?" That's right, sweetheart, you actually feel it *behind* you, left in the proverbial dust bin. Blessedly you finally begin moving forward, no longer encumbered.

Share this transformational realization with your partner in any way you wish—I promise not to watch. This is the time to *let it all go.* Congratulations and a *huge* thumbs up ✆ for your courage and success! You just took one giant leap for yourself and for all human kind.

To clarify: although not preferred, it's OK for your partner to help pull you out of the hologram as long as s/he waits for your signal and *you* initiate the blasting- ✆ free motion. Work this out ahead of time so your partner feels no confusion about when and how to assist.

It is particularly important for you to fully embrace the emotionally confining and torturous feelings that have been present, prior to pulling the releasing trigger. By no longer resisting that particular non-serving thought, feeling, or issue, your psychological sense of liberation heightens—as you depart. Be sure to use the additional love-bond energy provided through the finger-lock connection. If both of you keep your forearms moderately extended and stiff during this exercise (like ballroom dancing), no one should get trampled.

This process does not provide casual strolls in or out of the hologram. A *definitive power walk*, you must enter and eject with passion, faith, and determination. Remember, maximum flushing occurs when focusing on just one main topic or issue at a time. Also important: To stay in your heart-feeling mode, transition from Phase One to Phase Two without a break. With sufficient preparatory relaxation, you will normally reach an Alpha or Theta state of consciousness. Done as directed, this process can access the subconscious mind where belief-systems are housed and where many mental and emotional fears can be effectively expunged. Successful access requires preparing yourself with the relaxation process, so you can fully enter the psychological state the underlying issue produces. At least partially feeling the issue's hold over you signals your readiness for entering the holographic cylinder (Phase Two). Once in the chamber, torturously confining thoughts and feelings will amplify, as intended.

Now, here's the really neat part, and why this powerful process saves us weeks, months, even years of conventional therapy. Without wasting time wallowing in pathology, or trying to discover the origin of fear (or self-diminishing thought, or behaviors), we simply dump it, right now, and move on. Yes, we can search our childhood for debilitating events (I did that), and we can search through fear-based issues in a past life (did that, too). After finally believing we found the *originating* source(s), we then go through the whole agonizing ordeal again (yep, did that also). Afterwards, we try to pick up the pieces by *boo-hooing* our way through the old, standard grief process: denial, anger, bargaining, blaming, eventual acceptance, etc. The slow boat to China can eventually, *agonizingly,* lead us to healing. But, if this holographic shortcut process works, I'll let you do the math.

Whatever bonus years I have left in this lifetime I choose to spend joyously living, loving, and sharing. FUN, for me, does not include spending unending hours in psychoanalysis, when more direct, holistic alternatives abound. I've got people and animals to love...places to go-see-do. Anyone care to join me? One more prerequisite: MY FUN team members must embrace an unpredictable amount of dog slobber (Golden Nectar from God).

As I seek to not oversimplify the mental-emotional therapeutic process — nor overcomplicate it — consider that one's degree of success with this technique depends on a number of mostly psychological factors. Perhaps the most important: your ability to access a fairly deep, altered-state consciousness. You'll want to visualize all the steps and accept the subconscious suggestion that your actions lead to the desired self-purging result.

In spite of my previous humor about alienating professional therapists, and my spoof at other Second Reality tools for healing, I do not suggest you curtail the use of professionals when you feel the need for trained assistance. For years we bought into victimization of one kind or another. Most of us habitually get down on ourselves with strong feelings of anger, resentment, and worthlessness. Professional assistance may be indicated to help root out very deep-seated emotional fears and mental issues. The Holographic Fear-Dancing process can certainly assist and amplify other counseling or self-development sessions, while establishing for your psyche that essential feeling of self-directed empowerment and control over your life.

I have effectively used this holographic vehicle for my less-complex, but still-diminishing thoughts, feelings, and issues. Every time you repeat positive, self-selected results, and thereby create a habit of acceptance, the deeper the replacement resonates in your subconscious mind. The more you imagine *downloading* new, empowering software from the limitless and virus-free resources of the inner (Soul) mind, the better your hardware (brain-mind) performs.

With practice, you'll learn to do this holographic process on your own. *By relaxing and mentally going through the fear-dancing steps, you can achieve fast, on-the-spot grounding and balancing anytime and anyplace you desire.*

Gone in Sixty Seconds

Holographic visualization helps me center myself prior to important meetings or public speaking engagements. It's a great aid in settling stomach-churning butterflies, or to shake off light, non-serving emotions – all in a minute or less. When you don't have time for a full attunement, give **Holographic Fear-Dancing** a spin.

When I visited Dr. Pottenger to discuss, among other things, this model as a representative of a holographic-facilitated healing, his enthusiastic endorsement included the following: *"This is an awesome healing model!...a perfect example of the power inherent in one's awakening to reflection. When we understand how we react according to our own, inner psychological perceptions* [habits, beliefs, and self-image], *rather than any external causal action, person, or circumstance, we are instantly liberated. For those who can effectively incorporate this process, its use will provide an invaluable tool for their continued transition from victimization."*

Second Reality, or Humanism, was integrated into Science of Mind and other New Thought orientations in the early 1960s. The scientific community – spearheaded by psychologist Abraham Maslow – developed "Humanistic Psychology." Dr. Maslow's astute science and human-capabilities research involved knowing, understanding, and fulfilling the needs of the individual through self-actualization – identified by Holographic Psychology as the potential inherent within every Human Being.

Second Reality represents the birth of the awakening self. Its realization summons a quantum shift in understanding; an empowered recipient moves from a purely outer to an inner orientation. Awareness of this shift initiated in modern times with transcendentalist Ralph Waldo Emerson (1803-1882) and Theosophy Founder Madam Helena P. Blavatski. These two pioneers (and others) recognized the *infinite inner,* and taught that all forms of life are ONE with the Eternal forces.

Those awakening to Second Reality can, in degrees, realize their inner strength and power over environmental effects. The second level reflects the shift of perception to an "I AM" reality, thus replacing first-level defensive, confrontational, and one-dimensional motivations. Those in "I AM" reality believe the most powerful ten-word/two-letter sentence in the world: *If it is to be, it is up to me.*

Fully comprehending Second Reality automatically eliminates stress by shifting focus from outer confrontation and victimization, to internal actualization. To repeat: recipients of this potent replacement are fully empowered and gifted with a whole new set of choices and opportunities. Those operating in Second Reality realize (in stages) all beliefs and associated emotions, both positive and negative, activate solely within themselves, and not, as formerly believed in First Reality, *caused* by other persons, events or things. Others do not make us mad, glad, happy, or sad. To believe otherwise abdicates one's personal power, often surrendered to those closest to us. First Reality consciousness, preoccupied with *fighting the good fight,* does not comprehend this dynamic. With SR awareness, we can finally *choose* to be happy or sad.

The belief and accrediting statement, "You *make* me _____ (fill in the blank)," surrenders power, and as a reactive First Reality mindset, sacrifices self-sufficiency. Corresponding energy drains and imbalances, when used (exclusively) to manipulate interpersonal relationships, or sort out personal challenges, invariably result in psychological torture, emotional suffering, and physical dis-ease. Again, this does not label First Reality bad or wrong — just...*limited* in matters of the heart.

A Second Reality-aware person, feeling a negative emotion, takes a private moment for some spontaneous inward processing. Honest reflection normally reveals one's core source (fear) of discomfort. A self-empowered (non-victim) individual, expressing from early Second Reality, then decides what subconscious-mind process to use for healing, releasing, and replacing unwanted issues. *Advanced* Second Reality individuals more easily recognize replacement opportunities. As enlightened, direct channels to Source, they quickly resume their FUN — greatly minimizing personal down time and the need for any adjunctive therapy or facilitations. With the first inkling of Second Reality, we begin our self-empowering paradigm shift (replacement) and life-avowing liberation. In advanced stages of Second Reality, futile attempts at psychological cloning (manipulating for love) recede and fade away.

Meanwhile, First Reality still fights to control others in its desperate attempt to achieve some false semblance of security and comfort. Not yet awakened to other ways of thinking or feeling, suffering ones continue their feedback loop of misery. A wonderful, new world awaits those who achieve their intended quantum shifts of realization.

Agnostic Friendly

Of special interest to Secular Humanists and ones with agnostic or atheistic beliefs: access to early Second Reality consciousness involves a psychological dynamic. In and of itself, this shift in awareness does not require a belief in God, Collective Consciousness, or any *Higher Power*. Awakening to Second Reality simply requires self-actualization.

Location of Comprehension's reflective (observational) capabilities provide a structure for our understanding the psychological origins of our quality of life. Mirrored by internalized belief, our habit patterns determine our current self-image. *"Your* world is *your* reflection of *your* current level of understanding," is my research organization's mantra.   Positive achievements result from eliminating external blaming, and turning within for healing emotional fears and issues. This shift invites the *authentic* empowerment to which "Seat of the Soul" author, Dr. Gary Zukav, often refers.

By being the example through genuine sharing of our new empowerment, we gain even more options to help successfully deal with both the self-created and inherent challenges of our individually expressing lives. Our psychological response to hardship determines our state of Beingness. Not just some robotic DNA activation, the evolution of advancing levels of conscious awareness represents a congruent choice (co-creation) by a fully participating human personality. Others may disagree, of course. That's how it should be when we are free to choose. Humans expressing from First Reality awareness often say, "I have no choice." What they really mean: ❶ Based on the *facts*, [current level of understanding], as interpreted, all decisions have been predetermined (life spectator); or ❷ the fear of making a mistake (victimhood) is temporarily paralyzing. In either case, inadvertently accurate, First Reality represents a reactive behavior — not a true, choice-making capability.

In my own pathway, feeling the intimate presence of Eternal forces replaced the old feelings of loneliness and separation. Any separateness I occasionally feel originates within me and is mine to transform.

For my beautiful left-brained brethren/sistern: when we see our human and Spiritual selves irrevocably woven from the same bolt of luxurious cloth, we no longer need to separate any part of ourselves for intellectual or other reasons. As you partake of contemplative moments, feel yourself subtly prodded to seek balance. Rejoice in the synergistic power that results from harmoniously accepting *all* parts of yourself — including your role as co-creator.

Negative, fear-based choices are never Soul intended. Emotional fear, except when confronted by direct physical threat, is temporary, human-created distortion — not truth. Murder and mayhem, obviously not products of peace, harmony, and love, come from self-absorbed fear and greed. The reactive, non-reflective mind often manifests destructive expressions. Our true Self/self has been created in love. And when expressing disharmony, our inner voice (conscience) continually nudges from the background to cease, desist, heal, reframe, and replace. Statements like "the devil made me do it," provide humans with excuses for failing to take personal responsibility. Not proof of Satan's existence, or any other *cosmic shadow* minion, devils make convenient scapegoats for non-serving thinking and behavior.

The forces of creation do not step forward to stop or *fix* us when in the middle of our intended life curriculum. Even (or especially) when we've made a selection surely leading to suffering, we are gifted to discover, through the wonder of experiential life, all the Spiritual-DNA-provided gifts, talents, and abilities required for *self*-repair.

Bottom line. Souls want us to know that we — as humans — are not puppets on a Celestial string. We act and create in concert with the Eternal forces. The vast seas and even the ship, itself, may be gifts from the Creator, but with Second Reality we can decide — in concert with our Spiritual partner(s) — whether to go North, South, East or West.

Muti-directional or omni-sensory balance continually shifts and expands our awareness — moving from a *doing* (ego I) focus on life to *Being*. We then experience a gradual merging with Source and feel our congruency with the Divine. Upon realization, the ego "I" (little self) voluntarily moves into the background to embrace the forthcoming cosmic love from the expanded realms. In this broadened state of synergistic congruency, or ascension, an *individual* reawakens to his or her natural state (Big Self) of universal connection. Unlike many Eastern disciplines, this shifting process does not eliminate ego. I will *continue* to emphasize how we need a healthy Ego as our steering wheel and psychic junk filter, while on Earth.

Mood Swings Both Ways

If you sensitive right-brainers want to know why you have such huge mood swings, consider the omni-sensory, psi junk you are subjected to when left-hemisphere *anti-virus* programs are inactive or non-existent. Filters are *especially* needed when watching most news programs. *Note: "psi" is a letter from the Greek alphabet indicating "something associated with the psyche.")*

We require selective filtering and the harmonious balance of *both* brain-mind hemispheres to fully master the EARTH pathway and achieve maximum peace, harmony, joy, goodness, creativity, and everlasting love. My highly gifted and empathic sister—a natural intuitive—used to be absolutely tortured by psychic, *other world* input, until she developed left-hemisphere filters. Think about this the next time some *bliss* guru suggests your ego-mind is an enemy. *Balance* is the key. A healthy, reflective mind serves us, both here and beyond space and time. More on this in the next chapter.

Human "Choice" from a First & Second Reality Perspective

Let's review this human-choice category from the perspective of the first two of the three realities provided by Holographic Psychology. *Choice* has different interpretations depending on our level of comprehension. In First Reality consciousness, ones participate in physical-world selections such as picking out neckties or purchasing options on a new car. Dr. Pottenger's research would point out that even these simple selections are being motivated by a subconscious bias, which we can not know about without a reflective capability (Location). Why do some automatically gravitate toward red ties and brown suits, and others, blue ties with gray suits? And how about those folks that happily carry purple purses while wearing crimson shoes? Are *they* choosing? I gave up that combo several years back.

Seriously...real communication and successful dealings with life's multifarious relationships—whether interpersonal, philosophical, or analytical—require Second Reality. Going back to our definitions:

How is it possible for us to make substantive choices without realizing we have options in how we perceive and respond to both challenge and opportunity? Until making that inner discovery that all our behavior is of our own psychological making, rather than something *caused* by the environment, we're stuck. In the programmed *knee-jerk* world, we blame, judge, or credit the exterior world (luck, fate, etc.) for our condition in life.

The paradigm shift of human awakening has—in recent years—spawned the growth of the self-development industry. New Thought participants exist within the same material world, with the same events and circumstance, but with a more expansive and inclusive perspective. You, too, can reap the rewards that meaning-makers enjoy. FUN is the prize for completion of those First Reality relationship lessons.

With full mastery of this more empowering awareness, we cease stepping into other people's issues or drama. The fear-based compulsion to control and manipulate for validation and affection is replaced by a core understanding that peace, harmony, joy, goodness, and love must be achieved from within before it can be truly realized or shared with others. Blessed with a Second Reality perspective, we increasingly allow others to process their own Earth curriculum while we simultaneously engage in ours...eventually free from all codependency.

Awakening is Not Linear

Because the commencement process is not perfectly linear, experiences may reflect different realities at different times, generally proportional to the amount of practice one gives to any emerging consciousness level *and* to a particular activity. Inappropriate thoughts and feelings belonging to an earlier level of reality should be expected, on occasion. No reason for concern. Just because you awaken to the power of being your own CEO does not authenticate *total* replacement of your underlying mental, emotional, and Spiritual issues. Initially you may continue to encounter some interactions that push your emotional *buttons*. With the new reality comes the authority and responsibility to create new habit patterns. *Mastery is not about numbing input, OR any arrival point, but transforming current-moment perceptions.*

If we universally understood Second Reality, we would not suffer the indignant partisanship stress so evident during the concluding weeks of the US Presidential race of 2000. With the Bush/Gore contest we discovered how subjective a vote is—even when using neutral counting machines. Or, how about the worldwide blaming and righteous finger pointing that repeats itself with monotonous regularity? Can you see how wide-scale psychological intimidation— not military victories—is the real goal of fear merchants? With full appreciation for your paralysis, if suddenly afraid to get on a domestic airliner because of the very remote possibility there might be a hostile takeover; might you be temporarily buying into the coercion?

Let me be clear. I'm not talking about direct, physical, life-or-death threats with defensive reflex action not only appropriate, but essential for survival. Not wishing to be insensitive to those who lost loved ones September 11, 2001, or diminish the horrific attack on the Twin Towers, perhaps the following grim statistic will help put our fears in perspective. On average, we kill more people on our nation's highways, *each month*, than we lost at the World Trade Center. And you would rather drive?

Remember what I said in Chapter One: *Before there can be terrorists, there must be subjects agreeing to be terrorized.*

The next benefit to Second Reality awakening: Spiritually provided talents and abilities—especially our new, creative insights that suddenly become consciously vested. The grand prize: a huge reduction in emotional down time and a higher-quality, independently determined life. Practicing Second Reality enables our positive responses to challenge, and progressive self-empowerment. Initially, you use various self-development tools—such as this manual—to assist in healing, releasing and replacing of old, disturbing issues. After continually responding positively to what used to be *only* hardship, combined with a determined process of self-healing and forgiveness, you journey to advanced levels of Second Reality (ASR). Upon arrival...voilà! Almost magically we no longer identify *any separate* things, circumstances, or persons, and therefore require much less forgiveness and grief processing. Cause-and-effect, powerfully vital in lower vibrations, loses import and momentum...eventually dissolving as a limitation. Your expanded world still includes an awareness of cause-and-effect, but dualistic equations are no longer a limiting "law." If the rare disturbing situation occurs, ASR recipients quickly vent, release, replace, and reframe—returning to more beneficial and joyous states of Being.

ASR does not depend on desensitization, or the blissful *rising above* Earth and its suffering inhabitants, in order to transform one's awareness. While still grounded in physical reality, persons reaching this advanced level express a deep love, sensitivity, and understanding of life's challenges—including awareness of the mental, emotional, and Spiritual state of others. However, they no longer take situations or events personally. This state also corresponds to the Second of *The Four Agreements*: "Don't take anything personally," brought forth by the insightful don Miguel Ruiz and his Toltec teachings.

As an enlightened facilitator, you effectively *reflect* to others as a resource for the actualization of their preexisting potential. Those nearing mastery of at least a portion of their Earth lesson plan, transmit love, compassion, and reassurance. Also recognizing other humans have their own curriculum in progress, possessors no longer need or desire to fix, enable, or clone another. For those at the ASR level who choose to ask a mentoring one a question—indicating a motivation to further learn, heal, and grow—*internal* answers are more quickly awakened to, which greatly assists their further ascension.

Temporarily ruled by fear, and therefore squeezing out motivation to emotionally and Spiritually awaken, First Reality persons continue their repetitive, feedback-loop engagements. This is neither bad nor good—it just is.

Regardless of what's currently happening in your life, consciously taking more and more responsibility for your thoughts, feelings and actions, definitely places you on the fast track to empowerment and unique discernment. Before you bum yourself out by comparing your current state to the *ultimate;* rejoice that you've already achieved a monumental and unprecedented shift—in awakening to *any* level of Second Reality. Now empowered to chart your own course in life, partaking in old-paradigm patterns of human-indentured servility is no longer a requirement—*unless* you insist.

In Conclusion. Containing the highest level of choice-making options, or life blueprint, for your Earth adventure, Second Reality provides the opportunity to learn mastery over all aspects of your physicality. Consider how the second level is being missed by those Eastern disciplines that attempt to shift from First Reality consciousness—with ego-based desire allegedly the enemy—directly to bliss. Not criticism of any belief or discipline, but a subjective, observational difference.

Second Reality represents the beginning of the end to *win-lose* competition…replacing it with inaugurating *win-win* cooperation. The end of limited tolerance begins the larger expressions of allowance and acceptance. What a glorious, new Phoenix it is!

Now, let's see if you have the free will to exercise your freewill choices.

CHAPTER FOUR

Divine Guidance vs. Human Choice
Real or Imagined?

♥　　　♥　　　♥

Deep thinkers often ask, "Do we really have free will, or is human choice just an illusion?" Although I am attempting to answer that question with *Level* (three realities of consciousness) and Location of Comprehension, this question continues to be fundamentally important—one I often pondered, in years past. In fact, a frank discussion on this topic led to my first intensive, three-week, free-flow period—the precursor for this entire book. Deep reflection on this symbiotic relationship—an obvious Spiritual DNA trigger point—lifted my spirits and provided insights that virtually swept me away in a sea of inspirationally orgasmic thought.

As we open to trusting our intuition, or gut instinct, we feel the presence of subtle influences beyond our conscious awareness. I used to place any feeling or event that defied random chance in the "just-a-coincidence" category. Even one as stubbornly resistant as I, eventually awoke to how a critically timed fluke occurrence, or meeting, is more than a random event. When Guidance taps on my shoulder, I now shut up and listen. Coincidences, like all beliefs, continue to have the meanings we assign them.

Referring to subjective, multi-sensory areas not provable by five-sensory, empirical study, science cannot prove the existence of LOVE, either. Yet, most of us know love does, in fact, exist. Since evolving archetypes of expanded awareness cannot be processed solely through intellectual analysis, when our Spiritual DNA actualizes we feel and experience paradigm shifts in our core mindfulness. Certain triggering experiences and encounters, such as what we do here with this guidebook, facilitate our shifts. Consider the view that there are *no* coincidences. If still with me at this point, it's intended that this information be shared *with* you, and then, *by* you. When you've completely read my guidebook, and diligently practiced the suggested access exercises and processes, you'll be better able to evaluate the importance of it all—both now and later.

Using my intuitive gifts, now, I venture a *knowingness* that you want more than just left-brain, analytical information. How about a demonstration of the latent extrasensory perception innate to *all* of us...not just the so-called psychic person? I offer the following narrative to share a process that benefits me for the moment, but may or may not be a source of inspiration for everyone. Personal core issues should be pondered and formatted by each of us individually. Power-of-prayer demonstrations serve as conceptual premises for "Divine Intervention" considerations. Extrasensory perception results from one's determined search for larger truths. With the following extraordinary, but true, story as our guiding facilitation, decide who, or what, was working behind the scenes. *Boys and Girls...please do try this at home.*

Gravesite Search

My stepmother, Ruth Scholle-Stevens, grew up in St. Charles, Missouri—graduating from St. Charles High School in 1940. Still grieving over my dad's passing, Ruthie missed her 50-year reunion (Sept 1989). She was determined to return home the summer of 1997, and visit friends and relatives with her mind still reasonably clear. I made the arrangements and looked forward to seeing this special community that held so much history for her.

In the mid-eighteen hundreds, a strong contingent of Europeans— including Immanuel Lutherans—emigrated from Hanover, Germany, and settled the community of St. Charles. Ruth directly descends from these first settlers. Other than a few modifications to the high school, St. Charles, proper, appeared virtually unchanged from her childhood. Blood and Crypts gangs, alive and well across the river in St. Louis, and in most, if not all, medium-to-large cities, are nowhere to be seen in this community. St. Charles retains the majority of its native inhabitants. "Neighborhood Watch" is not an afterthought program in this Township.

In 1997 most station owners in St. Charles still trusted customers to pump their own gasoline, prior to paying for it. Through Ruth, I received a great education on the trust, community pride, and connection common throughout the heartland—until recent years. Could unifying traditions such as these still be the norm today, if we—as a species—truly committed to them? We would have to overcome our fears and refuse to let outside influences, and the negative acts of a few, dictate the lives of the many. Could it be that many of us created our own isolation and loneliness by surrendering to fear?

One of Ruth's main objectives for this trip was to visit the side-by-side gravesites of her mother (Elsie) and favorite aunt (Irene) buried in the Lutheran cemetery. She hoped—even at this late date—to find a nearby plot for herself. [*My father knew of Ruth's wish to be put to rest in St. Charles, next to her beloved mother and aunt, and did not want Ruth to deny herself this most heartfelt desire out of spousal loyalty. Out of Dad's sensitivity and love for Ruth, his Last Will & Testament provided for his cremation, rather than a burial.*]

We arrived at the spacious, peaceful, and very well-maintained cemetery purchased by the local congregation in 1850—the date of their first Lutheran burial. At Ruth's direction, we quickly found the headstones of her two relatives. No available plots existed near Ruth's mother's gravesite. But, as Guidance would have it, the senior cemetery manager who had worked there for over forty years—a former high-school friend of Ruth's—happened by. Upon learning of Ruth's plight, he went to work to actually *create* a plot-site bordering the access road, an area previously designated "not-to-be-deeded." The newly created site diagonally adjoins Elsie's grave. We met our Angel the next day, and with tears welling up in all our eyes, he presented Ruth the deed to her final, prayed-for resting place. He *felt* the extreme gratitude Ruth's slightly aphasic words could not fully express. We continued to hug one another for several moments joyously realizing that we all actively participated in creating this special gift. One more critical fact: the 70+ year-old sexton planned to retire in a few months, after which this unheard-of plot creation would most likely not have been possible. This miracle was not finished, however; the most dramatic happenings were yet to come.

After Ruth's benevolent emissary departed, we spent some additional moments at the newly created gravesite. Ruth shared the good news by speaking out loud to Elsie and Aunt Irene. I said a quiet thank you to those Guiding Souls I believed had actively created the good news. When getting ready to leave, a still-emotional Ruth stammered out a confession. She told me she had been prevented from attending the funerals of her two grandparents. Elsie, wishing to spare her only child any pain from the passing of the beloved couple, had not let Ruth attend either of the farewell ceremonies. Ruth had enjoyed a very intimate and loving relationship with her mother's parents; they had all lived together in their 6th Street Victorian residence. Even with her advancing age, distorted inner fear suggested to Ruth she was somehow responsible for the sudden departure of her grandparents. If not her fault (childhood reasoning), why was she prevented from attending their funerals?

As the confession continued, Ruthie admitted she always felt unworthy of visiting their gravesites. I later learned, from one of her closest cousins, that several years prior, Ruth *had* visited her grandparent's site. Regardless, with her ingrained burden, Ruth still suffered from intense anxiety. She remembered only that her grandparents were laid to rest somewhere in the same cemetery, not close to her mother and aunt. I silently prayed for the caretaker's return; he might know the burial locations off the top of his head. But he was long gone. After searching on our own, without success, Ruth and I got back into the rental car and started to leave the cemetery.

Unhappily, I drove with mind and heart working overtime on how I could—in a timely manner—offer a healing replacement. I sensed Ruth's almost desperate need for closure. Knowing her history of holding issues and hurts inside, I was mindful of just how rare it was for Ruthie to make this kind of opening. Once we left the cemetery grounds, I instinctively knew we would not have another healing opportunity. Temporarily suspended in time, with a remorseful stepmother fully absorbed in wonderfully mixed remembrances, this special moment could never be duplicated.

With my heart aching for her, and praying I could somehow help, I suddenly felt a strong pulling sensation from the left. This intuitive tug was so powerful I immediately stopped the car.

We were a little more than halfway to the exit, approximately one hundred yards and one street over from her mother's site, in an unrelated area. As Ruth questioned my stopping, I looked down a long row of plots—I was on total autopilot at this point. Approximately ten tombstones out from our roadway, I sensed the two names Ruth desperately sought. Without thinking or saying anything to my confused stepmother, I bolted from the car and raced down the long row of plots. Not entirely surprised by what I found, my delayed excitement finally kicked in and I raced back to the car to get Ruth. Now regressed to a young girl's state of confused loss and tortuous woundedness, she emotionally confirmed the side-by-side gravestones of her beloved grandparents. Dropping to her knees on the moist lawn, trembling hands reached out to lovingly caress the engraved remembrances. With an intensity and unguarded abandonment unlike any I had ever witnessed from her before, Ruth wept. Initially, her mood was pained and conciliatory. But as she revisited those childlike feelings with mumbled conversation, tears of wondrous joy and laughter gushed forth. While bathed in the warm glow of love from the *Souls-that-guide-us,* as well as the loving light-energy of the previously manifested Grandparents, I could see Ruthie, at long last, forgiving herself for those old, distorted feelings of unworthiness.

While Ruth experienced her long-overdue healing and closure, I, too, felt blessed to feel the warm, loving energy inherent in the amplified connection. Years of bottled-up, false, real-feeling guilt, finally purged, she stood to give me the most appreciative hug any son could imagine. My heart soared as the goose-bump producing *joy-juice* poured through me in celebration of a job well done. Our arms tightly wrapped around one another, we returned to the roadway.

Appreciating the Extraordinary

After seating the emotionally spent, but peaceful, Ruth, I opened my door and turned around to appreciatively look down that long, quiet row of resting knolls. With progressive-vision glasses and the tightest focus possible, I could decipher names only down to the second or third gravestone. Like a warm winter's blanket, the cover of recognition swept over me. Here was another Divinely guided event that heart—not head—had facilitated. This evidence, for me, extended well beyond mere circumstantial. Even *my* analytically skeptical mind accepted this astonishing visual comparative as the *real deal.* Smiling broadly, I affirmed the extraordinary becoming quite ordinary in my life.

Was this one of the great benefits of the simultaneous L-R brain hemisphere integration I had been practicing? Or, a simpler answer— my new acceptance of Universal connection and love? After this experience, I found continuing my Spiritual training an easy decision. Peace, joy, love, and happiness might just become the predominant habit! Bereft of further uncertainty, I felt worthy of the ministerial credential I'd been pointing toward.

Prayer, Power, and Results

As we begin this important topic, consider how everything you manifest through purposeful, focused thought—positive or negative—represents a prayer result. Presenting your thoughts as firm beliefs to the formless substance (Universe, Spirit, Higher-Self, et al.) guarantees a response, in kind. Remember that axiom from Jesus: "It shall be done unto you as you believe." Jesus' followers rarely understood when he said: "Your faith (belief) has healed you, not I." I refer to our previous example of this axiom: "I believe in _____." The power is in the subject "I," not in the predicate or noun.

Anything intended after the confirming "I believe," the Universe says *yes* to. The world always validates our current beliefs, until we are prodded to question. Examples of reflective questions: "Is it true I am clumsy (looking at the historical evidence), or is this *fact* just a distorted belief I've bought into, based on someone's opinion? Could I change my mind (belief) about this alleged condition and thereby transform my current experience?"

Spiritually and emotionally understanding prayer serves us in many ways, such as communicating with our Higher Power. Regardless how we name or label that inherent force, heart-based prayer ensures our *voice* is heard throughout the Cosmos—beyond any limitation of time and space.

People occasionally ask me, "What is the most beneficial *technique* for prayer?" Remember earlier when I shared with you how the Universe provides us what we require, not necessarily what our human selves want? Often that new challenge presented in your life *is* the response to your prayers—you just don't recognize it as such. Many folks continue to have difficulty finding the forest because of all those trees. Here's an example.

God Saves...a Classic

A God-fearing man, with an unwavering blind faith in the Almighty, suddenly found himself downstream from a busted river dike. With flash flooding imminent, the alarm sounded and officials ordered everyone to immediately leave their homesteads. Bob, a prayerful planter, asked the Lord to save him. He then prepared himself for Divine Ascension. Shortly after making his devout request, a Forest Ranger showed up in an all-terrain vehicle (ATV), with one seat available. Bob refused assistance, exclaiming, "You go on ahead, God will save me!" To escape the rising floodwaters, the faithful farmer—accompanied by his beloved cat, Samantha—*ascended* to the second-floor balcony. Just then, a volunteer fireman happened by in a Zodiac inflatable boat, carrying rescued animals. With room for a human passenger, Bob refused to climb aboard. Surrendering only his terrified cat, Bob insisted the fireman leave without him. "I'll be OK," he said, "*God* will save me."

The relentless floodwaters continued to rise until only the peak of Bob's gable roof remained above water. Miraculously, a helicopter crew spotted the solo summit occupant and immediately dropped a body basket. For the *third* time, Bob waived off the rescue effort by screaming above the prop wash; "You're not needed here, *God* will save me!" Shortly after the helicopter's departure, the floodwaters swept the farmer from his roof and he quickly drowned.

Upon arrival in Heaven, the human personality that had been Bob, chastised God: "As your most loyal subject, I sang your praises and never doubted you! Why did you forsake me in my time of need?" God answered: "Well, let's take a look, Bob. According to my angel network, we sent you a park ranger driving an ATV, a fireman in a Zodiac boat, and finally, a rescue helicopter. My beloved son, what exactly did you have in mind when you asked to be saved?"

Just like this anecdotal yarn, recurring challenges often show up in direct response to our repetitive requests to be rescued from adversity. A perfect system, is it not? *The more fearful we are that we can't fend for ourselves, the more obstacles appear in our path.* Might this "practice" be something created by you—as a Soul—for the *exhilarating* experience of realizing your preexisting empowerment? This feedback-loop continues until we experience, learn, grow, and eventually awaken to the salvation already within our grasp, waiting to be acknowledged. In our new HP paradigm, *cause and effect is acceptance by degree.* While not perfectly linear, *missing-the-boat* scenarios are a common happenstance. With prayer, even more so than with meditation, many of us place the emphasis on some prescribed—hopefully ordained—*method* of procurement. Otherwise, we fear our solicitations go unheeded. Like the farmer and his encroaching floodwaters, while absorbed with looking for outer solutions to inner conflict (form over substance) we often miss the practical current-moment solution that *hovers* right in front of our collective noses.

Outer-oriented fixation remains a partial reason why religious sacrifice and ritual so prevailed over the ages. Delving a little deeper into the human psyche, we find many that question why an all-powerful, all-perfect, all-benevolent force (when perceived to be separate) might care to respond or even listen to a Human Being's *pitiful bewailing.* Fearful desperation, if allowed to escalate, can inadvertently lead to subconscious or even purposeful alliance with negative energy. Intense fear may distortedly conjure an alleged Satan, or one of its advertised minions. If you'll recall, the movie script for "Forbidden Planet" based its plot on this *monster-from-the-id* concept.

Love-based prayer can be a very therapeutic and connecting process, providing we take the needing-to-be-perfect pressure off ourselves. From my trial/retrial experience and testing, the most favorable results emphasize purity of *intent* over specific mantras or techniques. When differentiating prayer from fear-motivated expressions — like begging and bargaining — more specificity may help you understand supplication from an expanded perspective.

Like many, I used to pray for material improvements, or the eradication of pain and/or my inner fears. Eventually, I learned that effective prayer is not normally evidenced by projecting a *Santa's wish list. Embodying a heart-communication vehicle, creates miracles.* For *Big Kahuna* prayer requests, feeling worthy of being an instrument of Divine intervention definitely helps — whether the intended beneficiary is you or another loved one. Ruth's Lutheran-cemetery experience embraced this dynamic. I did not have to say, "Attention God, I am praying now; please be mindful of my well-rehearsed ritualistic technique." Instead, I intuitively *plugged-in* through my intense desire to assist Ruthie in her earnest request to connect with the beloved grandparents. Although those damp plots represented only one, dualistic *location* of her family members, they psychologically symbolized a peaceful place of rest and the final closure to which Ruth had been lovingly guided. This wonderful result had as much to do with *her* heartfelt longing as it did mine. My prayer request was born from compassion, sensitivity and love, rather than a fear of failure. When we align in this manner, we act as an interpersonal conduit between Source and our loved ones — provided, of course, the beloved recipients open to (feel worthy of) healing and enlightenment. Consider for a moment that most examples of spontaneous love-energy healing you've heard about, or possibly witnessed, were created just this way. Through amplification of the cosmic-energy connection, a miracle is born.

Try to feel, or at least conceptualize, the difference between the facilitation rendered at the Immanuel Lutheran cemetery, versus some artificial fix. Take a moment to recall some episodes where you tried to manipulate, from a place of (your) fear, the choices of a loved one. Although labeled love, in my personal case, I perpetrated rescuing efforts on individuals not yet ready to begin the full, taking-of-personal-responsibility process. Conditioned to accept only a sympathetically applied external Band-Aid, my revolving partners were subconsciously attracted to anyone that would provide it. My portion of the concurrent interplay exhibited a subconscious effort to use the challenges of others to heal my own deep-seated feelings of unworthiness.

I've just described the poster child for codependency. In those painful, suffering, past periods, my desire to help others offered not just idealistic compassion, sensitivity, and reverence. The fear of being unworthy of love was an additional motivator.

The Universe answered my *prayers* with a hapless parade of challenging individuals entering my life with similar sets of circumstances. Boomeranging relationships reflected my own insecurities and were an essential part of my Spiritual DNA blueprint, or life-lesson plan. By experiencing the consequences of our behavior, again and again, my partners and I finally accepted (in differing degrees) that no amount of manipulating the *outer* would heal the *inner*.

Groundhog Day

The movie *Groundhog Day*, starring Bill Murray and Andie MacDowell, perfectly illustrates this law-of-attraction dynamic. I highly recommend you rent this movie to review a brilliantly presented example of the feedback-loop principle.

The Murray character (Phil Connors), mentally and emotionally stuck in a perpetual, negative, unhappy, self-absorbed existence, suddenly manifested a time warp—thus living the same calendar day, again and again. Then the real lessons began. With each second-chance replay, Phil had the potential to make new and different choices. After deducing what he perceived a dimensional trap, he cleverly tried to use his great intellect to control and manipulate his environment—to no avail. He attempted every outer-oriented solution to escape his predicament, or to numb his experience. Even suicide failed to release him from his horrific dilemma. *Prayers* produced more challenges and more Spiritual DNA-provided, First Reality curriculum.

All those outer-oriented fixes failed to yield what Phil Connors truly longed for—peace, harmony, joy, goodness, creativity, and love—the ingredients for true happiness. With all external options depleted, he courageously and authentically turned within for purging, healing, and replacing his unworthiness issues. Phil became the person his heart-self longed to attract. Then, after further enlightenment revealed the so-called *trap* an actual life-transforming opportunity, he finally achieved freedom from his phony-facade existence. With his shift in consciousness, Phil began experiencing the joy of helping others, and the mutual happiness that results. Upon his transformation, Phil emotionally connected with his healthy, loving, and non-dysfunctional costar, whose character (he learned) would never surrender her heart to any fear-based, con-artist pretender.

What a monumental gift to our species! *Groundhog Day,* as life metaphor, perfectly illustrates the futility of looking for outer solutions to inner challenges. Phil Connors needed to repeat the same place in time until cognition actualized. Most of us currently engage in a life replica of that movie plot, but not as obviously because our five-sensory, environmental scenery *appears* to vary. Because we create our own suffering scenarios, release requires inner-awareness shifts and life experiences combined with positive, non victim-like *action.*

Lottery Curricula

Money alert! Embrace this next principle and you instantly pad your purse or wallet. *When you pray for material gain (lottery hit) as a way to change your life, you unwittingly ask for more financial challenges as opportunities to transform your current belief in lack.* When we transmit the conviction that we don't already have that which we seek, the Universe says *yes* to our distorted belief in absence-of-abundance. When we give sincere thanks for having already received the totality of our gifts, the Universe says *yes* to that, as well.

Reflection on this dynamic, prior to your next lottery ticket purchase, will likely serve you. Are you just having FUN, or buying into the distorted belief you don't already possess all the riches of Babylon? One more thing: if you are supposed to win (Spiritual DNA) the mega-lottery, you need only *one* ticket. Conversely…I believe you catch my drift.

This overview will likely mean nothing to those who believe life a continual series of random events. Even if true, *how you interpret and respond to those events determines your quality of life, not the events themselves.*

How Prayer Works

To summarize, here's how the prayer principle works. When you say (pray) to the Universe (God), "I want (don't believe in) _____," the Universe says, *"YES; and you, dear one, shall continue to want _____until you accept the reality that what you seek is already yours."* Then IT (your God of choice) provides some tough curriculum so you can persevere—eventually realizing the potential within you, all along, to accept life's treasures. Is this not the *perfect* system to heal distortions of fear, lack, and limitation—opening us then to unlimited love and abundance?

If you awaken to a core understanding of this universal axiom, you instantly transform your life by replacing security and other fears with the self-realization that *you* reflect *your* current understanding. Now you have another valuable implement for your personal tool kit; the penetrating jackhammer of a reflective (non-reactive) mind, called *Location of Comprehension*.

Healing Compulsive-Addictive Behavior

In a meditative attunement, I asked Guidance for clarity regarding my personal use of food. Craving food as a substitute for love (most recently as an ongoing habitual form of unbalanced celebration), I desired a new way to harmoniously heal my issues with food. Accepting a new relationship with food, I made a clear-intent choice to balance my body weight out of love and appreciation for a healthy vessel. My old way used negative motivations such as potential disease, incapacitation, or the threat of being thought unattractive. I knew the key was to substitute better-serving, lifestyle habit-patterns. I need not become skinny, but I certainly could enjoy the benefits of physical conditioning and excellent health. I approached the challenges of body balancing just as I did mental, emotional, and Spiritual arenas. Although still a *play* in progress, I continue to project a laser-clear aim on my grandest vision. I make exercise and food selections a daily practice of FUN! Not always easy...change *can* be made more enjoyable.

The result? The search for inner, more expansive truth, as well as my resolute intention, *released*—without surgery—100 pounds of unneeded and undesired body fat between July 10th and November 26th, 2003. I've had some fluctuations since, but I strive toward excellence, rather than perfection. This perceptual shift presents the option for a healthy lifestyle, *without* beating ourselves up for lack of rigidity. I share this for the mutual benefit of others who struggle with some form of compulsive-addictive behavior. Be gentle with yourself as you seek out a mutual, like-minded support system committed to excellence and change.

In my personal attunement, I confirmed compulsive-addictive behavior a symptom of habitually accepted unworthiness. When we work, eat, exercise, drink alcohol, take drugs, go shopping, gamble, engage sexually, or practice any other behavior to excess, we normally use that conduct to numb or stimulate ourselves—an effort to override an underlying belief that we are not enough (lacking). Troubling feelings manifest as fear-based anger, anxiety, withdrawal, depression, frustration, or numbed boredom. Sufferers try to quiet the subconscious background chatter by obsessing over anything that temporarily silences the critical mind. When we finally come out of that self-created *ether*, we feel less respect for ourselves than before. Even after healing a self-limiting issue, old habit patterns can stick around until we replace them with a new, beneficial routine.

If you *want* love, joy and happiness, you must *practice* love, joy and happiness. When it comes to feeling victimized and powerless, few yearnings rival compulsive urges and their associated behaviors.

The key to healing these compulsions, say the Guiding ones: *"Realize that you—as a Soul—chose both your challenge areas and your creative opportunities for this lifetime. Consider your circumstances not the result of random bad luck, nor are they punishment from a vindictive God or fallen angel. You selected certain areas for mastering, and then came aboard with extra talent and ability to thrive within your chosen task areas. Make a gentle releasing...and rejoice in the awareness of who and what you truly are."*

Note how Guiding Souls speak of *thriving,* not just surviving. Knowing this helped me internalize my courage and determination to successfully deal with hardship. There's always a learning curve, for ourselves and those who interact with us, for as long as we have a pulse. Through an awakening perspective, we realize what our Higher Self wishes us to experience and master. Additionally, we gain the renewed confidence to make change happen. A far cry from being cast adrift and pounded on by relentless waves of repetitive victimization, is it not?

Expanded perception, often in the guise of confusion, evidences a rising consciousness. Even as we temporarily fall short of manifested perfection, we continue to possess all the necessary gifts, talents, and abilities to heal ourselves and create anew. If you accept the belief that we—as Spiritual Beings—can never be damaged by any human act, then you have what poker players call a can't-lose "free roll." The *smallest* possible outcome that could result from your choice to take the road-less-traveled: no *perceived* improvement.

Some of what I've just shared proves contrary to both secular philosophies *and* sacred (religious) orthodoxy. A multitude of teachings detail how *separate* Souls can be captured by evil influences. Although "devil" can be an effective synonym for fear, consider an alternative suggestion: simply quiet yourself through contemplative sessions. Invite your mental background chatter to first express itself, then lovingly take a back seat. Given time to bring your fears forward to share, vent, release, reframe and replace, you awaken to a more empowering reality that both emotional fear and self-diminishing mind chatter are your allies. You discover previously frightening thoughts and feelings represent a psychological *self-diagnostic*, rather than a demon's effort to possess.

Beware the Paradox

A fine line exists between believing a purposeful entity wishes to rain on our parade, and the psi (the Collective psyche) junk I address next in *Hardware Harbingers.* Every thought, feeling, action, or evidence of Intelligent Design—ever expressed or manifested—resides in the Collective Unconscious. Nothing within Creation can ever be lost. Just as we protect our important computer files and documents from corruption, so should we guard against non-serving energies that can inadvertently invade our awareness. A healthy, functional, left-hemisphere provides an unlimited level of virus protection. Be assured that the omnipotent, omniscient Soul-Mind is never at risk for schizophrenia or *any* form of damage; it's the human personality matrix I'm addressing here.

Although controversial and in contrast to many well-established Eastern disciplines, this author's *current* opinion: any system or modality that convincingly strives to eliminate (not balance) our rational-mind *steering wheel,* puts the human personality at risk for depressive and debilitating assault. This is why you see me continually stress hemisphere (intuitive-visceral *and* rational-cognitive) **balance**. Does it make sense to disavow your physicality in order to master it, or expand beyond it? What would be the FUN in that?

Consider that you — as a Soul — created Earth and the heavens with experiential intent and loving embrace.

The new-paradigm quantum shift I'm presenting, represents not only the simultaneous integration of both hemispheres, but the unprecedented potential to walk Earth as the multifarious master you've always been—and who doesn't want more of that?

Loss of Love

Internal Guidance delicately but continually encourages us to release our servitude to mental/emotional fear. Love, for which we sometimes grasp, has never left...awaiting the end of our fearful preoccupation with lack of love. "Loss of love" is a non-sequitur. Although you may be served by a change in the type of relationship you have with another, you can never *fall* out of love. Fundamental to your very nature, **you _are_ love.** By letting fear and non-serving emotions dominate, we momentarily numb ourselves to connection and affection.

Hardware Harbingers

With my flippant witticisms, narrations, and practical summations, I've addressed only the mental psyches not overly corrupted. Schizophrenia and other serious personality disorders can't be so easily addressed. When distorted thoughts and feelings run amuck, to the point of desperation or abject terror, ones may escape into the *elsewhere* areas. Untreated, this can—as I've articulated—lead to mental oblivion. Therefore, while we can, let's forgive ourselves for believing in boogie monsters and for being our own worst enemy. By not letting phobic apprehension and worry dominate our psyche, through either compulsive resistance or overindulgence, distorted fears eventually evaporate along with the mental background critic. Protective-filter placement for the subconscious-mind proves a simpler task for grounded left-brainers. Strongly intuitive empaths can be an open channel for psi garbage, until they too develop a left-hemisphere filtering system. When ignorant of the collective space junk, gifted psychics can find depression and immune-system disorders their crosses to bear. Disavowing the ego mind, rather than bringing it into harmonious balance, may render the gift of second-sight a curse. *"ALL THAT IS" does not mean all that's beneficial.*

Subconscious Self-Sabotage

Have you ever felt you were selecting options clearly not serving you—most certainly leading to pain and suffering—but you went ahead and chose them anyway? Or, perhaps not entering your conscious mind at the time, but in retrospect, you hardly believe you chose a path so obviously detrimental? Subconscious sabotage could very well be the culprit. You're certainly not the only one that struggles with invisible ghosts from the purported past.

The Patey Conglomerate

In the middle-to-late 80s, I attended a revolutionary workshop by leading-edge mind-development researchers from Orem, Utah: the "Patey Human Resource Group." Oriented toward behavioristic cause and effect with a humanistic cure potential, I now appreciate their research as an evolving precursor to Dr. Pottenger's LOC discovery—what eventually evolved into Holographic Psychology™. The researchers, then headed by Kenneth H. Patey, postulated all human behavior belief linked. Referenced behavior, not limited to *conscious* thought beliefs, also included subconscious influences (motivations). As they presented their persuasive evidence, including examples of irrational actions by persons lacking coherent explanation for their destructive behaviors, the facilitators introduced their special guest, Bruce. This man, out of extreme desperation, had attended this same lecture two years prior. I sat transfixed, as Bruce shared his incredible story.

Bruce had been to the mountaintop, not as the culmination of some great vision, but to take his own life with a .38 revolver. He went up that mountain with a chronic case of self-loathing—one with which he could no longer live. Bruce had experienced a consecutive string of business failures, with a similar track record in personal relationships. On the positive side, he was a strong demographics researcher and a detailed goal setter. Bruce was also a meticulous planner, with a charismatic personality and a powerful motivation to succeed.

In spite of Bruce's obvious talents and abilities, each time, at the very cusp of success, he made a detrimental decision that snatched *failure* from the jaws of victory. With the demise of several good relationships and more than one bankruptcy for him and his trusting investors (including friends and family), he could never explain why he followed a string of perfectly astute, beneficial choices with one fatal dagger to the jugular. On each occasion, just prior to a critical self-sabotage action, the last thought that entered his conscious awareness was an assured, "I have finally succeeded!" This extremely positive and confident person (on the surface) consistently brought forth brilliant ideas and sound business proposals. So, even with an *abominable* track record, Bruce repeatedly attracted new-venture capitalists, which fed the revolving cycle.

Finally, Bruce could no longer stand the humiliation and emotional pain of his repetitive pattern. He dejectedly climbed the closest hill to end the nightmare. An associate had told Bruce about the Orem, Utah, humanistic psychology facilitators coming to town. Having tried so many past (unsuccessful) therapies, and self-help programs, hope was all but destroyed. Something [we know what] influenced Bruce to not take his life, even though the cold, hard, deadly steel was pressed firmly against his throbbing temple. A moment before pulling the trigger, his tortured mind produced the thought to give success one final opportunity.

During Bruce's seminar, two years prior, wave after wave of realization poured over him like cool, clear, life-sustaining water down a parched throat. Bruce shared how he suddenly knew—in core mindfulness—this team of facilitators held the key (his key) to his own salvation. The workshop trained him in the process of uncovering buried memories. That his inner-core access involved altered-state visualizations should not surprise you. The facilitators helped the participants become their own *exorcist*. Subjects were mentally prepared (relaxed) and then given the suggestion to emblematically *peel an onion*. They mentally retraced the emotional pain, further and further, until arriving at its origination.

Bruce had eagerly volunteered as a demonstrational guinea pig during his seminar. A good subject, he entered a deep Alpha (possibly Theta) state of consciousness, eventually arriving at the long, sought-after scene from his forgotten childhood.

Environmental Conditioning

A five-year-old Bruce and his seven-year-old brother, Charlie, had a beloved uncle with permanent brain damage; the result of a recent car accident. A short time after visiting their comatose uncle in the hospital, Bruce and Charlie were playing hide-and-seek in a large, grassy field near their Boulder, Colorado, home. Bruce's turn to hide, he ran with reckless urgency to gain as much separation as possible during the count. Rounding an outcropping of rock, Bruce tumbled headlong into a large, granite boulder, knocking himself unconscious. After several minutes of searching, Charlie spotted Bruce slowly rising from a distant section of tall grass. Bruce had just awakened from what was later diagnosed as a mild concussion. Our shaky, dazed, and adoring five-year-old staggered to his feet. Charlie, stunned by the blood oozing down both his brother's forehead and the adjacent boulder, frightfully exclaimed; "Oh my God, Bruce, you will never amount to anything your entire life. You just lost all your brains on that rock!"

Just like any child, Bruce lacked sufficient rational-mind filters to block the emotionally delivered message from his admired role model. Right on the heels of their uncle's head injury, Charlie's statement immediately encoded as truth in his little brother's subconscious mind.

Bruce quickly recovered from his physical wound. But as he grew into adulthood, he only *apparently* forgot his belief-linked ordeal.

By replaying the childhood experience — this time as an intimate observer — Bruce's adult self perceived what the facilitating therapist was then suggesting. The previously hidden belief set the stage for an adult Bruce operating as if *incapable* of success. Now he realized he had lost nothing on that inanimate piece of granite. The adult self-sabotage, from a child's inability to discriminate incoming information, now acquired a *rubbish bin* as its new domicile.

When Bruce first accepted the reality of his self-empowered *re-born* awareness, he broke into deep, purging sobs. Finally… mercifully… it all made sense. He bid goodbye to his negative self-image. He replaced self-diminishing thoughts, feelings, and beliefs with a warm vibrant glow of love, joy, and knowing his suffering days and nights were over. The ancient and previously hidden fear of lack and unworthiness would never again sabotage his choices.

I found myself both envious of and intrigued by Bruce's breakthrough. I sensed that I, too, had a buried antagonist needing a voice in order to move on. I did not immediately follow up on what I now see as another Spiritual-DNA-provided opportunity to discover and heal my remaining issues of unworthiness. I apparently required a few more years in the stewpot, before taking action. Hearing Bruce's experience planted the seed for future actualization, however.

If you can slow yourself down a little, and step back from the material-world rat race, you just might discover some guiding bread crumbs along *your* path. A light-bulb moment awaits your decision to follow the clues.

Bruce's Full-Circle Transformation

Bruce beamed as he proudly introduced his beautiful new bride, along with the results of a stock deal he just negotiated with an IPO underwriter. That public offering made him and his new wife financially independent for life, while providing quite well for the many children they planned. Bruce was intimately sensitive and committed to never allowing emotional upsets or inadvertent negative outbursts to be directed toward open, unfiltered, and potentially fragile young minds.

I recalled how my own experiences at age 12 years (Chapter Eight) traumatically affected my self-esteem. After hearing Bruce's story, I felt some easing of the great burden I carried around, and began to glimpse the meanings to which I gave psychological shelf space. As a child, with no Second Reality mind-filters, negative validations were hurtful to my self-image. In early adulthood I distortedly believed unpleasant memories needed overriding, or at least numbing, as they seemed impossible to heal. After the Patey workshop I questioned myself: "Could it be true that an inner-accepted belief, rather than environmental circumstances, directly determined individual behavior and the resulting quality of life?" If I changed my perception of past events, as Bruce had done, could I set myself free of negative thoughts, feelings, and self-image?

The Patey Group provided strong foundational mortar for my sprouting emotional wellness and further awakening to Second Reality. I held myself back from any immediate leaps because (procrastinating fear) I thought the impressive teaching too simplistic and *too good to be true*. What if I trusted this story and opened my wounds for cleansing and healing—just to be left bleeding on the workshop floor? Could this be another fake Eden, like *"Forbidden Planet"*? I had invested a lot of time and energy keeping the beast sequestered. I didn't yet feel confident to open Pandora's Box. Still...something kept urging me to do so.

Much later, after my 1996 Spiritual odyssey, I could no longer justify holding on to those ghosts from the past. Finally identifying a likely source of my own enslavement (not a requirement) gave me the confidence to first acknowledge, then release and replace most of my self-defeating habits. I saw the evolving progression of assistance to which I had so obviously been directed, both before and after that fateful meeting with the Utah contingent. Remember our farmer who prayed to be rescued from rising floodwaters? Bruce received a continual string of answers to his prayers, but just like me, and perhaps you, he disavowed the gifts. When his will to live became stronger than his fear-based denial, he turned within and found the source of his salvation. First, however, his Spiritual-DNA-provided lesson plan (the red-rock encounter) engaged to prepare him for an emotional understanding of the facilitative importance of supportive, acknowledging, *love-based* models for children.

Positive psychological support for the young mind was to be the main theme in his future business and relationship undertakings. This Soul-desired selection made his heart sing—contrary to his previous squeezing and forcing exercises—all from a distorted, albeit temporary, perception. With some very challenging years in route, Bruce now believed his previous difficulties purposeful—perhaps vital. With his current awareness and feelings of synergistically connected purpose, he felt empowered as never before. Most importantly, Bruce no longer felt alone in a crowded room. His enthusiasm and passion for life were infectious, in spite of all previous *appearances* of failure.

Think Replacement...Not Cause

Not suggesting all reasons for self-sabotage are simply and categorically determined. I think it important to point out for pathology detectives that unresolved patterns may originate from unlimited sources. Fortunately, *we don't have to know the cause of a distorted, non-serving habit in order to achieve a life-changing replacement.* Expanding our philosophical and psychological awareness beyond behavioristic exclusivity eliminates the necessity to discover the originating source of a current, problematic function. For *mildly* disconcerting beliefs only slightly undermining your positive attempts at a quality life, first try to dump the unwanted pattern and associated behavior with a simple, fast-acting process like the Holographic Fear-Dancing Technique, provided in the last chapter. If you require more support, and gain insufficient improvement from using the other facilitations in this manual, consider a therapeutically structured group environment, or one-on-one assistance.

Remember the gift of Location: past *or* present events and circumstances do not ultimately establish human behavior. *Psychological and philosophical interpretations of any person, event, memory, thought, or feeling, determine one's well being or lack thereof—thus affecting one's direct experience.*

Bruce's belief—subconscious or otherwise—that he'd lost all his brains on a rock, determined his short-term behavior. My recommendation for bypassing the often frustrating search for definitive, past-memory recollection: in your *core of Being,* see all self-diminishing thoughts and feelings as temporary, distorted thoughts and feelings—*not truths.* Emotionally accepting your love-based reality empowers you to free yourself of any remaining mental or emotional burdens. Then, with self-sabotage forever moot, co-creation and creative free-flow become the norm. Even with co-creation and creativity always available to us, crafting our forms of destruction can provisionally prevent awareness of our more pivotal roles...until *shift happens.*

Regrets. Many persons at the end of their physical lives regret not having taken advantage of opportunities, dreams, and passions that resided in their hearts and minds. Almost universally, these same ones express little or no remorse over anything they actually tried and, perhaps, failed at. Since Spirit created us with the full potential for freedom of choice and expression, and since our species pretty well mastered suffering (in past times of Earth), might it be time to create new, more joyous chapters in your life? Unless it clearly serves you, do not be concerned **here** with reality levels or intellectual structures. When opening yourself to the power of prayer, simply follow your intuitive heart connection and take charge of your life. Most of all—take FUN with you on your journey. The final destination takes care of itself.

Bottom Line on Prayer

Much like dreaming, prayer remains a private and individually interpreted process. I hesitate to make any suggestions about how to pray; even the thought of that feels akin to trying to interpret someone else's dream state.

In previous passages you learned the different effects created by past-tense, or future-state, bargaining, begging, and fear-based pleadings, versus positively expressed, present-tense, subconscious-mind affirmations. Spontaneous requests to amplify an expressing belief—whether positive *or* negative—definitely influence the Universe. Even during in-progress, Soul-chosen transitions, or withdrawal of energies, human love-based prayer occasionally stems the tide of direct ascension. Although this result may not always be of benefit, the creative potential exists.

I wish to strike an appropriate balance (of discussion) between Spiritual DNA, chosen prior to this lifetime, and the influence of individual, or group-expressed, human will. If overriding the Soul transition blueprint should *not* happen, the person or persons praying for Celestial Intervention need not feel undeserving or inefficient in their prayer technique. Knowing in your heart that an Eternal plan— chosen by *you* as a Soul—follows its intended course, can release much suffering and hardship engendered by the passing of significant others. As we proceed, I share how the very aware *essence* of any transitioned loved one (human or animal) stays very much alive and present. This concurrency exists whether you feel the ascended Spiritual energy, or not. If you believe yourself separate and divided from the forces that animate all life, the preceding perspective may be difficult to incorporate.

When defining your own prayer philosophy, examining how *not* to pray may be useful, assuming you desire positive results. One most-common form of prayer, extremely effective conjuring up feedback loops of challenge, is *worry*. When we sit and emotionally focus — to the extreme — on worst-case scenarios, we often successfully create more of what we fear. I do not refer, here, to my previous recommendation of taking a few moments, each day, to acknowledge, vent, release, reframe (perceptual change), and replace distorted thoughts and feelings. I caution you against the gloom-and-doom mentality that perpetuates terror and powerlessness. Negative preoccupation is such a very powerful petition, it generally leaves you uninspired and wanting.

The reason I've spent so much time discussing the determining factors of human behavior: maintaining positive energy and getting the desired prayer results prove difficult when we believe in our hearts that we're undeserving. Waiting for and expecting God's punishing *bullwhip* often results in a self-fulfilling prophecy. You are, of course, free to believe negative results are the work of a supernatural entity and therefore beyond your direction, if that serves you.

My Prayer

Considering the dynamics of prayer and the correlation between desire and human challenge, I modified my prayer approach to one of expectant positivity, rather than powerless supplication. Instead of blaming, bargaining, and begging (the killer Bs) for what I prefer, I give regular thanks and appreciation for what IS. When I don't understand something, I ask for clarity so I might better serve others and myself. When any new challenge crosses my path, I vent any temporary feelings of anguish. Then, I go to work on my next grandest vision, with passion and continued effort toward achieving a graduate degree in human life. Even during the increasingly rare downtimes, I stubbornly refuse to see myself as a victim. I successfully do this because *I believe everything I share with you.* I don't always execute the most desired response to hardship. Sometimes I choose to wallow in the old, familiar, self-pity pain pit, for a while, or use my more-common practice of procrastination. But when I've had enough pouting, I climb back on the horse.

Through practice, actualizing the preferred response becomes more automatic. Seeing adversity in a more positive light makes me a stronger and more appreciative person. Reflecting on *your* past progress, has this been true in your life as well?

Most of my prayers convey heartfelt thanks for everything in my life—even tough challenges. I try to balance my energy between what I would prefer for myself (a degree of self-absorbency), and teaching, uplifting, and helping others. I discovered the more attention I give to the latter, the more joy, peace, and love flow into me. Regardless of Spiritual beliefs, we all benefit from turning our focus away from non-serving preoccupation. When I notice any temporary thoughts or feelings about what I'm not *getting from life*, I simply begin *giving back to life;* a quick cure without any side effects.

Buddha said: *"All you are is the result of all you have thought."* Jesus told the Centurion: *"Be it done unto you as you believe."* Jesus also gave us, *"When you pray, believe you have already received and it shall be done."*

Technique

Since some of you will hound me until my final days if I don't summarize my prayer technique, try doing this. First, keep your mind and your request positive and love-based. Avoid fear-based whining, begging, and bargaining. Enthusiastically speak in the *present* tense, expressing as if you already received that which you seek.

If you insist on asking for (rather than accepting) something you personally *want* for yourself, thank the Universe, in advance, for all the appropriate courses in life management you will soon receive. *Challenging curriculum continues until you awaken to the truth that you are never separate from **anything**, and therefore can never be without everything.*

If not able to see and experience God EVERYWHERE, you're not truly seeing and experiencing God anywhere.

Freedom in a Non-Free World? Let us Count the Ways...

Truisms from my great colleague-friend, Dr. Margrit Spear (simplyjoy.com):

Not knowing is innocence...not questioning is ignorance.

Beneath the veil of ignorance resides humanity's greatest potential.

When we leave mass hypnotism, we begin to discover our own power.

My shadow, whether large or small, is part of my physical nature…never obstructing who I am.

Pondering the yesteryears keeps me from celebrating this very moment.

Behind the darkest clouds shine rays of eternal hope.

What we cultivate…grows. Between excitement and disappointment there is a self capable of being consciously aware of the difference.

Toiling in a slumber impresses mass consciousness. Investing in potential uplifts and changes the world.

Between not knowing and wondering lies a great opportunity.

Love is an international language.

If humans could learn to purr, we would have a gentler world.

Imagine if at every stoplight we would take a conscious breath of joy.

When we breathe through our heart, we purify the air.

We can only listen with the awareness we've accepted.

Responsibility is a preference delivering great benefits.

Good and evil are chameleons changing with our level of understanding.

If you want to create a lasting masterpiece, you must use quality materials.

You can never find your self by looking outside yourself.

Do not compare, as new possibilities are unlimited.

Any canvas or paper is only as interesting as the individual's imagination.

Soul provides a link between the known and the unknown.

Real satisfaction entails a form of gratitude.

Have you phoned your cells today? They respond in kind.

You can cultivate sunshine in your heart, even if it rains.

No thing will be more miraculous than uncovering the inner gifts that advance our own evolution.

The greatest freedom will emerge from recognizing the benefits that come with self-reflection.

In the NOW lie the seeds of tomorrow.

It is estimated that humans originate from stardust.
How much star and how much dust do you cultivate?

If happiness is a state of mind, why is it not part of our teaching curriculum?

Between the four letters spelling LOVE, we can find world solutions.

Classics by the "Great One," *Ralph Waldo Emerson:*

Do not follow where the path may lead. Go, instead, where there is no path and leave a trail."

One of the most beautiful compensations of life…that no man [person] can sincerely try to help another without helping himself.

People only see what they are prepared to see.

The only way to have a friend is to be one.

What you do speaks so loudly that I cannot hear what you say.

You cannot do a kindness too soon, for you never know how soon it will become too late.

Spirituality according to George Carlin:

If you can't beat them . . . arrange to have them beaten.

Don't sweat the petty things and don't pet the sweaty things.

If God dropped acid, would he see people?

If you try to fail, and succeed, which have you done?

I'm not concerned about *all* hell breaking loose, but that a *part* of hell will break loose... it'll be much harder to detect.

The very existence of flame-throwers proves that some time, somewhere, someone said to themselves; *"You know, I really want to set those other people on fire, but I'm just not close enough to get the job done."*

More Power Quotations:

"The path to our own destruction may lie less in the weapons we conceive, than the violence within our hearts." ~ Quote from an *Outer Limits* episode.

"While we may not be able to control all that happens to us, we can control what happens inside us." ~ *Benjamin Franklin*

"The well of Providence is deep. It's the buckets we bring to it that are small." ~ *Mary Webb*

"Nothing on Earth is so powerful as an idea whose time has come." ~ *Victor Hugo.*

"Look well to this one day; for it and it alone is life!" ~ Found on a cave wall, dating back 2500 years.

"We don't see things as they are. We see things as WE are." ~ *Anais Nin* ♥

"There is nothing inherently evil, lest thinking [judgment] makes it so." ~ *William Shakespeare*

"It is our duty — as men and women — to behave as though limits to our ability do *not* exist. We are co-creators of the Universe." ~ *Pierre Teilhard de Chardin*

"All things in the world come from being. And being comes from non-being." ~ *Lao-Tzu - 600 B.C.*

"All Judgments are the tragic expression of pain and unmet needs." ~ *Dr. Marshall Rosenberg.*

"Happiness is a continuation of happenings which are not resisted." ~ *Deepak Chopra*

"The physical world, including our bodies, is a response of the observer. We create our bodies as we create the experience of our world." ~ *Deepak Chopra*

"The price of anything is the amount of *life* you exchange for it." ~ *Henry David Thoreau*

"One does- not fall 'in' or 'out' of love...one grows *in* love." ~ *Leo Buscaglia*

"Courage is resistance to fear...the mastery of fear...not absence of fear." ~ *Mark Twain*

"Don't let school interfere with your education." ~ *Mark Twain*

When asked, "What do you think of Western Civilization?" *Mahatma Gandhi* replied, "That would be an *excellent* idea!"

"A genuine leader is not a *searcher* for consensus, but a *molder* of consensus." ~ *Martin Luther King, Jr.*

Considering my previous descriptions about how we're never alone, we explore this intimate symbiosis, live and direct, in the following chapters.

CHAPTER FIVE

The Transcendent Reality

♥ ♥ ♥

Naval **Aviator is Born.** My father's enthusiasm was always infectious, but this particular Sunday he was definitely over the top. Anticipating a visit by two of Dad's most special associates, I knew our clandestine guests worked for Kelly Johnson at Lockheed Aircraft's ultra-secret, experimental aircraft-design and test facility — the "Skunk Works." Based in Burbank, California, the Skunk Works — formed in the early 1940s — got its name from the odorous fumes that drifted over from an adjacent factory.

Our special summer day in 1952 finally arrived. Who were these two men that held so much respect for my father, and he for them? My first look told me why Dad was so enamored. Two muscular men dressed in freshly creased slacks, brown bombardier jackets, and black shoes so shiny you could see your face in them, stepped out of a stretch limousine. They each wore gold-rimmed sunglasses and silk scarves around their bulbous necks. Climbing the steps of our spiral entryway in militaristic tandem, their swaggered confidence implied the world was their oyster. As Dad stepped forward to greet these two aviation giants, their tan, weathered, smiling faces radiated genuine affection. Nearly paralyzed with fascination, I managed a faint "hello" during my brief introduction. My eyes were riveted on the pilot wings, insignias, and aircraft-identification patches sewn into their flight jackets. In rapturous awe, I sat quietly as Mom brought out the lemonade, cold beer, and a bountiful array of finger food. Although a typical, always-hungry, nine-year-old, even the most tantalizing snack suddenly held no interest. I was not about to miss one gesture or utterance from either of our two impressive guests.

Lockheed's Finest

Our distinguished visitors turned out to be Tony LeVier and Herman "Fish" Salmon. Next to Chuck Yeager, whom my father knew more vaguely, these two characters are arguably the most successful test pilots in aviation history. Few would disagree they were *Lockheed's* most revered. Essential members of Kelly Johnson's flight-test team, as was my father, they each enjoyed long and illustrious careers. [*Tony LeVier eventually became the supervising test pilot on the U-2 reconnaissance (spy) plane, with its maiden flight in 1955.*]

Noting a young boy's almost rabid fascination, they delighted in sharing one hair-raising flight story after another. Several of these high-altitude, pulse-pounding, flight-test narratives included my father's trouble-shooting participation. Fearfully spellbound, Mom nervously gnawed her fingernails as Lockheed's most-famous took turns intently describing engine and electrical fires, oil and hydraulic failures, airframe stress fractures, and low-altitude bailouts!

Surviving a continual string of real-life emergencies seemed to suggest some form of supernatural ability or protection—like the heroes and heroines described in fantasy comic books. Was it possible for flesh-and-blood humans to be impervious to the perils affecting mere mortals? How could these three supermen successfully extricate themselves from a multitude of complex, often unrehearsed emergencies? In an unsophisticated but excited appeal, I repeatedly tried to get some understandable answers. Although they offered nothing more than their belief in continued good fortune and the grace of God, my young mind formed a tentative, almost subliminal answer. All three men seemed to have an unconscious ability to anticipate a previously undemonstrated problem *before* it actually occurred. This allowed them to be ready—with split-second timing—in advance of any and all emergencies. Was it really possible to predict future events? If so, where did this intuitive sensing come from?

Regrettably, I did not enjoy the pleasure of meeting either of these majestically courageous men again. One motivational imperative firmly planted itself in my subconscious mind, however. *I would either climb my way to Heaven, or—if need be—face the devil, itself, to get a definitive response to my unanswered questions.* After this fortuitous meeting, my child-self began to wonder whether a transcendent Spirit (Angel) might be influencing my daily life. Many years later—after several of my *own* extraordinary flying experiences in Vietnam—empowering and transformative answers would be revealed.

Born out of transpersonal psychology, the transcendent or "Third Reality" level of conscious awareness transcends—but continues to include—the individual. This science of Spirit correlates to individual mind, body, and universal consciousness. Third Reality perspectives expand the relationship between religions, philosophies, linguistics, and psychology. Beneficiaries of this level intimately embrace the synchronistic interweaving between the Earth environment and one's currently expressing human personality—all joined to what revered psychologist and philosopher Carl Gustav Jung coined the "Collective Unconscious." Current-day theorist Steven Kaufman calls it a state of "Unified Reality." Others call it the "Collective Consciousness" or "Universal Mind." Holographic Psychology labels this state of all-inclusive realization "Third Reality" reasoning or awareness. Regardless of moniker, recipients of this actuality fully unify with their universal connection. Separate human "choosing," a dramatically liberating component of Second Reality, becomes moot. A Third Reality human personality feels no limitations and no sense of separateness, or exclusivity, in relation to the Collective. This level of awakening equates to a full state of grace and Oneness with the cosmos. *With no **separate** person, event, or circumstance to grieve for, or to forgive, forgiveness and grief become moot.* With this expanded vision, beneficiaries possess a cohesive sense of inclusion, and not—as suggested by many Eastern disciplines—a dismissive *rising above* one's physicality.

The rare human reaching *full* third-level unification has totally mastered all Earth curricula. Walking the physical realm, while invested in pure bliss, s/he demonstrates unconditional love and total acceptance while Spiritually mentoring those still in the exciting role of actualizing. Very few humans have achieved a *conscious* state of congruent divinity, although available to all—in potential. In every corner of the globe, dedicated empowerment messengers have periodically appeared. They showed us how to experience *all* ongoing patterns—even the temporarily painful ones—as part of the continued evolution of every ray (Soul) of the Collective. They remind us that human challenge is temporary, and that *nothing we do can ever damage our true Being.* Ascended masters, intimately aware that all roads lead home, *live* in perpetual peace, harmony, joy, goodness, creativity, and love.

Overlapping Realities

Individuals realizing Third Reality comprehension also use—when appropriate—first- and second-level reasoning. A Second Reality consciousness knows the first level but not the third. The First Reality reactive mind holds little or no clue to the existence of second or third levels—until an internal shift occurs. Again, full Third-Reality-consciousness individuals, living in a monistic state of cosmic unification, not only think but *experience mind, body, and Spirit as One.* Expanded realities, always the higher truth, still remain unknown until Spiritual-DNA-provided (paradigm) shifts occur.

The bottom line in the exciting, new, all-inclusive field of Holographic Psychology: *by healing and replacing underlying emotional and psychologically based fear, we directly access all levels of consciousness.* Clearing out old-paradigm blockages opens love-based, expanded realms of awareness and associated existence. When unfettered, *you* are an extraordinary *(psychic)* channeler.

What modern humanity calls "mystical," or "clairvoyant," is just a deeper connection with the Infinite. Mystics, yogi masters, mediums, clairvoyants, etc., access the same Unified Field that connects us all. Clairvoyants and clairsentients exhibit more highly attuned awareness because they *practice* directing their focus toward expanded, multi-sensory realms. These achievements typify dramatic and real examples of the aforementioned Spiritual DNA (potential).

Realities Clarification

From a Second or Third Reality perspective, there is no *better,* or *worse,* level of consciousness. First Reality is not inferior to Second or Third; and Second Reality is neither inferior nor superior to Third or First, respectively. Different realities *do* produce different world views, however. As demonstrated in the comparative examples given thus far, level variance generates a huge differential in a recipient's empowerment and quality of life. Those expressing from Second and Third Reality claim their current operating level infinitely more expansive than First Reality—but not *superior.* First Reality, on the other hand, intellectually judges the various levels as better or worse. Can you feel the difference? Remember, all language is metaphor. The meaning you ascribe to these definitions is subjectively interpreted based on your current precepts, biases, and self-image (belief).

Not the intention of Holographic Psychology developers to create a new class system; we don't need another dualistic "ism" to separate ourselves. The process of comprehending the significance of paradigm awareness shifts is not intended as an ego exercise. As we open ourselves to more expansive levels, we automatically understand what these passages continue to clarify. By replacing any self-absorbed ego orientation, or feeling of superiority, with all-inclusive synchronicity (at the expanded levels), we regularly experience the continuity and inclusivity of all life. We *know in our core* that we are all of the same cosmic quanta and that every neutrino of belief, experience, *and* physicality is inclusive. One develops great peace and allowance for the universal plan when knowing with certainty that Human Beings are co-designers, rather than some crapshoot, eat-or-be-eaten artifact.

Intuitive Guidance suggests no relationship to current operating levels of consciousness and (for example) the age of our individual Souls (the same); our wisdom or prominence in a past life; or which church, religion, or god definition we affiliate with in *this* life. If you will, let's consider the world a grand playhouse. We—as Souls—have chosen improvisational roles with general themes (curriculum) to play. I suspect some of you are thinking, "There's no way I would have voluntarily chosen *my* current role!" Could this be your fear-based, ego-mind talking? Your Soul looks at your human self and your chosen path as magnificent and perfect. How could It not? It created you. If your life is not everything you want it to be, you have within your personality matrix all the preexisting gifts, talents, and abilities to create your life anew, from the inside out—where authentic change takes place.

Helping you first understand and then activate that Soul part of your DNA, what medical-intuitive Caroline Myss calls our "Sacred Contract," is our purpose here. If it is within your current belief-system to accept a shift in conscious awareness, it shall be done. This book was created to assist those truly ready to take responsibility for their quality of life, while simultaneously achieving the ultimate in personal liberation. That you are now reading this strongly indicates the arrival of your consciousness-makeover time. Do you still think the timing of this communication coincidental? Really? News flash— *there are NO, repeat, NO coincidences!* You can choose to **believe this**, or not.

Spirituality for Agnostics

I extend a special invitation to my beloved agnostic left-brainers. Many of you may be grasping for structure and tangible examples of the material presented so far. I certainly understand the fear of transitional jumps—especially those scary leaps into what many envision an esoteric void. The next several chapters provide you a golden goose from which you can pluck the rest of your preexisting potential. As I suggest in my opening, I feel a questioning agnostic perspective a beneficial prerequisite to Spiritual enlightenment. Without a positive, but inquiring, motivation, how can we grow and awaken to our evolving nature? That said...I find some forewarning appropriate.

In support of the analytically oriented person wishing to make a true cosmic connection, a preemptive caution. Because I know and respect your perspectives—like my own—I strongly suggest you not let your great intellect become an obstacle. If you *think,* that while limiting yourself to just five-sensory, scientifically based logic, you might both open to and prove the existence of the Eternal Forces, I absolutely assure you that you will *not* be successful. I'm sorry to burst your systematic bubble, but you need someone to give it to you straight. Intellect can be very useful in finding the door to the Collective. It takes intuitive heart (emotional feeling) to *open* the door to discerning connection.

I understand and emphasize with your frustration. While unwaveringly determined to get there without taking any emotional risks, I was terrified of making giant, heart-vulnerable leaps across unseen and psychologically unknown chasms. I once thought it foolhardy to consider *any* useful enlightenment, believable connections, or healing transformations from an intangible, visceral-based realm. When I intellectually reasoned the loftiest and final piece of the *Pyramid of Cosmic Understanding,* I was so proud of myself. "Finally Nirvana is mine," I exclaimed! Euphoric enthusiasm was short lived, as the previously exalted realization crashed an instant later. In my mind, a new pyramid suddenly appeared and positioned itself on top of the other with its point on the bottom — sides rising up to infinity. I then received a solemn summation from a loving but firm, purposeful voice that seemed to come from everywhere simultaneously: *"Congratulations Larry, you just completed Phase ONE of your purely-intellectual pursuit of the higher meaning and purpose of life. From this point forward, for every question mentally answered, two more will appear, exponentially, continuing to infinity. Create a wonderful day!"*

This dramatically delivered message produced its desired effect, leading to a final catharsis and the breakthrough Epiphany I so earnestly sought. So, if you intellectual wizards wish to continue beating your large, beautiful heads against an impenetrable wall, be my guest. I have shared the consequences. We are in the *feeling* business here, not just the thinking business.

Mediums, Channelers, and Clairvoyants

The famous trance medium Edgar Cayce (1877–1945) discussed at length the concept of a universal mind, or collective consciousness. Still studied by human potential researchers, energy healers, and leading-edge psychologists from around the world, at the Cayce Research Center in Virginia Beach, Virginia, this same genre of self-empowering wisdom flows to us today. Current messengers include Ron Scolastico, Lee Carroll, Gary Zukav, and Neale Donald Walsch — to name a few.

Edgar Cayce's heartfelt purpose was to help his current client in any way possible. He intended his communications as a specific aid, not a general truth applicable to the entire world population. Many studious readers find an astonishingly high percentage of diagnostic accuracy in Mr. Cayce's more than ten thousand medically oriented readings. His holistic cures continue to be studied and evaluated for their potential use to others. Personally speaking, if an external Castor Oil Pack will detoxify my body, or remove a boil, I'll take that over pharmaceutical drugs, or invasive surgery, any day of the week.

Slightly tempering our blind enthusiasm serves us by understanding that mediums like Mr. Cayce normally focus on one individual or group at a time. That person's blood type, pH, and general chemistry can be quite different from yours or mine. Let us take care in our generalizing, lest we distort ourselves — especially true when we ask mediums or clairvoyants to predict the future. The best way to reduce the risk of distorted or misleading information: *establish your **own** intimate and direct channel to Source*. This congruent purpose behind all New Thought and Unified Reality Theory, ideally models the facilitating aim of Holographic Psychology.

Humanity, metaphorically kissing the feet of symbolic gurus for centuries, believed it lacked sufficient *wind beneath its wings*. As unique and varied expressions of infinite Spirit, we are each prodded to leap from *nesting-security* illusions to soar with the eagles. So, I ask you: Is it *your* time to expand beyond worshipping the outer and attune, instead, to the unlimited power and potency of the inner? For most, co-creation feels a lot more empowering and connecting than servile supplication. For large segments of the world's population, prostrating surrender *is* the way to God. As one of the many options, there's nothing wrong or bad with being a blind follower. I surmise, however, that those who've read this far are looking for a more cathartic way to renew their power and potency. If you prefer *self-realized* actualization, I shall continue to assist.

Integrating the Reality Levels

Known levels of awareness, simultaneously used, provide quality-of-life choice making. A Third Reality-aware person operates in First Reality at various times—usually appropriately, occasionally not. The advantage here: *at any given moment, higher-frequency intuitives instinctively know which level they express.* Empowered to make quick changes in their thinking, feeling, and action, they understand mental and emotional responses lie fully within their domain, for any challenge. Enlightened ones recognize when they inadvertently slip into non-serving, reactionary behavior. This awareness stage, from its awakened level on down, usually makes the desired correction. As a conditioned-response manifestation, First Reality awareness has very limited options. Many times, however, a command of First Reality (reactive) perceptions greatly benefits us. Obvious examples include driving on the freeway, operating heavy machinery, or fending off carnivorous beasts.

To manifest an expanded realization, individuals benefit from additional life-changing, heart-opening opportunities. And with plenty of life-curriculum to go around, ones can expect their next lesson very shortly.

Work the Plan

In much of the world, at this moment in linear time, the pace of actualizing potential gathers steam. The many millennia of struggle have not been in vain. As we emotionally heal ourselves and create more heart-based openings, we invest a higher percentage of our precious Earth time in the more-elevated realities. This, in turn, unleashes more and more *joyousness* capability. Life experience generally matures us, as you've observed. But the general world population still lives in the dark about their creative opportunities to trigger underlying Spiritual DNA.

Now that your brain is up to speed, rest assured we are basically done with technical details. Foundational framing proves important to inquiring minds motivated to know more about Unified Reality Consciousness, Spiritual DNA, and Holographic Psychology. Left-hemisphere, *food-for-thought* orientations offer more options in our quest to understand how and why things work. Consider, however, that *Soul never intends that we — while expressing on Earth — ever comprehend the all of reality*. What would be the FUN in that? The entirety of the human race operates on a "need-to-know" basis. ☺

Now, for the many that don't care *why* or *how*, only *what* works…I invite you to sit back and let the process flow naturally. We've sufficiently fertilized our logic-locked left brains for the time being.

Universal Spiritual Overview

The following passage quotes Tenzin Gyatso, His Holiness the Fourteenth Dalai Lama — Spiritual and temporal leader of Tibet. "I believe the very purpose of our life is to seek happiness. The highest happiness is when one reaches the stage of *liberation*, at which there is no more suffering. That's genuine, lasting happiness. True happiness relates more to mind and heart. Happiness that depends mainly on physical pleasure is unstable — one day it's here, the next day it may not be."

The Dalai Lama also says that in order to obtain the ultimate in happiness, we must train ourselves. Or, as Holographic Psychology suggests: *practice* love, joy, and happiness until they become habits that replace undesirable worry, anxiety, and other underlings of fear and uncertainty. Fortunately, we are never alone as we practice change. The full power and potential of the Universal or Collective Mind makes itself available to us.

Universal Power Grid

To help us hold a picture, or concept, of the Eternals' awesome nature, let me suggest a symbolic organizational chart. This keeps coming to me both through dreams and more lucid attunements. Please set aside your preconceived notions for a few moments, as I share a simplistic, comparative structure for the intricate interweaving of Eternal Forces.

Attempting to describe *Celestial Fire*, I use a parallel to what humanity created to harness just a portion of the unlimited energy available from Source. Think of God, Supreme Creator, Big Kahuna (whatever), as the Boulder Dam, located outside Las Vegas, Nevada. Or imagine any other giant earthly source of human-harnessed energy.

Consider this crudely described hydroelectric process. Stored water from Lake Mead, released down long tunneled chutes, passes through an elaborate mechanical process. The power of the dropping water converts to the rotation of seventeen huge, turbine generators. Each main generator (15 of the 17) is 70 feet tall, 34 feet in diameter, and produces in excess of one billion kilowatts annually—enough *combined* energy to meet the needs of several hundred thousand households. Mega-giant, high-voltage transmission lines carry the power from these turbines to fifteen regional destinations throughout three southwestern states. Nevada retains approximately 25 percent of the total output. As the energy departs Boulder Dam, moving toward its intended destination, it passes through several step-up and step-down transformer sites that mold and convert the electricity. After traveling by over-ground poles, or underground cables, to individual tap sights, the electrical juice steps down again and reaches its destination junction box as manageable 220/110 volt, 60-cycle, 50-amp power. The final destination energy sufficiently supplies all houses and businesses within its service region.

Now, for our cosmic-character counterparts, let's divvy up the power grid. Of the seventeen symbolic pulsating turbines, each one a zillion times more powerful than the human-created Boulder Dam offerings, some maintain the energies that sustain the physical universe—including Earth. Others create and sustain the non-physical realms of existence. Still others are held in reserve to either, ❶ replicate more *turbines* as needed, or ❷ provide for any extraordinary power surges. The most common drain on the Earth power grid occurs during periods of extreme negativity—conflict between factions of a fearful humanity.

The Source current/power then radiates from the *Celestial Station* to certain Earth and human-oriented conduit forces of the Christ, the Buddha, the Krishna, the Eck, the Vairagi, and all masters whose energy, consciousness, and essence particularly focus on and love Earth and its inhabitants. These Earth-specific entities mold and transform the raw, creative energy to meet the vast requirements of the physical universe.

Upon arrival at the Earth magnetic grid, the next handoff—to Angelic Forces—again downsizes (to lower frequencies) the cosmic power energies. Angels and other cosmic assistants like the Kryon Magnetic Grid Being (read the books on Kryon) never incarnate, but lovingly maintain an Earth-life attention. Angelic divas pick up the energy at the second step-down transformer site (symbolized by Earth's mega-giant voltage transmission lines) and monitor its usage as it reduces and transfers to individual Souls. Souls, in turn, transport the manageable, but still somewhat raw, broad-based energy to its Earthly destination—where it forms and maintains all physical life. This gargantuan raw energy, selected and coordinated by the *Celestial Planning & Origination Center*, reaches finite destinations on Earth. Individually expressing Souls carefully wield Creation's energy, carrying it through Earth's power poles and underground lines.

Creation of the personality matrix—including the Spiritual DNA component—completes near the time of its respective human birth. Moving to and fro, individually expressing Souls coordinate the interlaced, intricately staged conception of fetuses.

In addition to various artistic areas Souls wish to express, each Soul commits to assist its human personality to experience, heal, and replace all negative mental and emotional patterns. Speaking linearly, this includes configurations that manifest as conditioned byproducts of current-life environmental factors, as well as archetypal patterns created during past times of Earth. Synchronized group plans can be considered Second Reality byproducts of intense, unresolved fear-based negativity—occurring at physical death by one or more of the Soul's previously manifested human personalities...or as a Third Reality *now*, experiencing *all* facets of experiential life. Note that differentiated patterns hold sway *only* in the physical realm—*within* space and time. Once a human personality comes full circle (during an incarnation) and realigns with the transcendent (Third Reality), consider its individual curriculum complete and the corresponding portion of any archetypical pattern restored.

What the heck did Stevens say? The bottom line: *Souls stage their scenarios from a desire to experience and eventually master all aspects of human life – not from karmic debt or Divine obligations.* The human personality, manifesting free will, may ignore subtle Soul influences. And an overly frightened or determined Human Being can either slow or accelerate actualizing his or her Spiritual DNA blueprint. No *slow* or *fast* from the Soul perspective – there's just *now*.

For those not resonating with dualistic, Soul-lineage concepts (I'm not suggesting you should), simply look at this energy-distribution scenario as a solo creation. Awakening to Third Reality consciousness actually makes reincarnation principles (and *all* dualism) moot. Collective Consciousness houses *all* memory and event records, all potentially available to us through the subconscious mind. Although it can be greatly therapeutic (Second Reality), a past-life recall is not always productive – especially when it distracts us from a clear focus on the *current* moment.

Even though you – as an Eternal Soul – are not new (in a linear sense), all human lives stand both alone *and* together. In contrast to the archetypal beliefs suggested to Eastern masses by their respective *elite* class, consider living your life without the burden of any past-due accounts to settle. Souls manifest lives to experience, reconcile, and eventually master their potential. Consider that *previous* lives do not, in and of themselves, determine current-lifetime circumstances. Since you *are* Soul, *you* decide whether you benefit from emulating the more empowering and less-limited, monistic, *all-is-now* perspective.

Without making any *right-and-wrong* judgments, can you see any obvious benefit to a comfortable, wealthy, elite class of folks when underprivileged masses continue to accept their assigned lot as "have-nots," so as to dispatch some dubious debt from a depraved past lifetime?

To completely balance the planetary energy grid and master Earth life, the majority of emotional fear and negativity must be released and replaced (healed). As you're perhaps sensing, the Soul's original intention was not for humans to turn toward selfishness and fear. Our ancient selves bought into the appearance of scarcity and separation. Rediscovering the truth ever since, we find no *real* poverty, only abundance; no emotional fear, only emotional love. This lofty observation shows little practical meaning to sufferers boiling in their soup pot. But you can say *no* to competition, and *yes* to cooperation. With more than just tolerance to consider, we experience the joyous communion of acceptance and allowance. Any concept of scarcity, lack, or unworthiness only *appears* real.

Human free will created much eloquence and creative beauty on Earth, but the reactive mindset also chose legions of expressions based in fear and greed. *Earth negativity, human-created, will be human-mastered*—as is being done.

As we live our life, especially the challenge areas, various shifts in consciousness occur. Depending on Spiritual DNA activation and our respective human choices, the results often manifest as sudden *ah-HA* light-bulb moments of awakening. Enlightenment arises after a monumental healing and releasing experience—often heralded by a period of confusion. If you find yourself bewildered a lot—like me—rejoice! Those rarely confused are generally stuck in a feedback loop of repetitive action. Any boat owner knows a propeller caught in cavitation, lacking a thrust quotient, creates only a non-productive vacuum.

Special completion events trigger preexisting components awaiting a healing precursor. Again, this domino effect normally follows a breakthrough in Second-Reality forgiveness and the release of the underlying issue or judgment.

As I continue with how things work, see if *you* can sense—not just intellectualize—a particular level of conscious awareness. Forgiveness—as a pertinent example—would be irrelevant at what level? And why is this so? If uncertain, you'll likely benefit from rereading the last several pages.

Guidance Within

To assist the amplification of its voice, Soul recruited certain guiding entities to travel along on your life's pathway. You may, if it serves, look at these benevolent masters as entities complete with their own incarnations. Guiding Souls share an intimate and clustered history. They—over many lifetimes (in a linear sense)—walked the Earth with your parenting Soul. This love-based synergy serves both the Soul and you. Guiding Souls can be felt, to varying degrees, depending on the healing and intuitive openings you individually and collectively make. Many metaphysicians consider this the true, Soul mate relationship. To me, we are *all* Soul mates.

Souls forcefully penetrate the human psyche if they choose to, but prior agreement generally keeps them in the background until invited forward. At times of strong, heart-felt emotional openings, intuitively creative moments, miraculous life-saving interventions, sleep (dream state), or other altered-state muting of the ego-mind, we more easily sense the presence of guiding Souls. A *conscious*-mind link is rarer, but possible with clear-channel focusing. Those reporting successful mind links prepared themselves through a repetitive sequence of meditative attunement and vivid contemplation. Efforts to force the connection normally fail. This author can personally attest that conscious-mind connections are best achieved during emotionally sensitive, love-based moments. Conversely, they almost always elude us when we engage in emotional fear or intense "in-your-face" confrontations.

The key to successful connections: *heal your feelings of unworthiness,* which frees your previously self-absorbed consciousness. This preliminary step proves unacceptable to instant-gratification-ers who say; *"Stove give me heat, then I will give you wood."* If so inclined, think of intuition as a subtle form of communication with Spiritual Guidance.

Once birth takes place, host Souls—intimately interwoven as are all Celestial Beings—never separate from the body, even during unconsciousness (sleep, coma, meditation, etc.). Normally only the parent Soul fully penetrates the human personality. It is not unusual for the personality-based "Spirit"—an extrasensory conduit or bridge between the human personality and the Soul—to leave a body still animated by the Eternal forces. This *leaving* or *traveling* sensation applies to human orientations only, as a creation made within space and time. Individually expressing Spirits sometimes pierce part of the amnesiac veil. Examples include Near-Death Experiences (NDEs), out-of-body visualizations, Soul travel, and other phenomena. Spirit energy can then make available, to the respective human consciousness, the information gathered by this means.

Souls, on the other hand, as omnipotent and omniscient, do not *go* anywhere, or *discover* anything. Like the Eternal forces, Souls exist omni-laterally—horizontally (*within* space and time) *and* vertically (*beyond* space and time). Therefore, Souls simultaneously express and create both within and without the physical universe. Manifesting themselves through the creation of a human personality matrix is viewed as their greatest (most expansive) undertaking. Yes, we **humans are a *very big deal* in the Soul realm of existence.**

Congratulations...it's a Human!

Assuming no last-minute, human-choice interventions, the Soul manifests the appropriate birthing energy to the specific site *junction box*. Then, in concert with the Eternal forces, a majestic, new Human Being enters the World. The creative magnificence inherent in the birth process—both human *and* animal—absolutely awesome, is it not?

NOTE: After reading what I've written in the past several pages, I apparently lied when earlier announcing we were done with technical aspects of our Earth adventure. One part of me accepts the futility of trying to explain infinite, non-linear realities with linear language. But the driven, questioning, part of my personality wants to keep trying. As reported, I'm sensitive to the inquiring mind that's often frustrated with the not knowing. For the few that may appreciate the additional but *non-essential* complexity within the Soul-human relationship (optional view), I'll leave some of the extraneous detail in. I caution you not to get lost in abstract particulars, as we are making it all up (the meaning) anyway. Regardless of how deep we go with *head*, we—as humans—will never grasp the full meaning of our existence by intellect alone. It always has, and always will, take **heart** to master the Earth pathway.

After absorbing your new, foundational left-hemisphere framing *and* your right-hemisphere (esoteric) layout, let's continue with the *practical-application* process. For those who have worked in the complex energy of a typical office setting, I see a "Hallmark" moment in your immediate future.

"**Before we allow ourselves to be consumed by our regrets, we should remember that the mistakes we make in life are not so important as the lessons we draw from them.**"

The Outer Limits® —1997.

CHAPTER SIX

Belief-System Makeovers

♥   ♥   ♥

Awareness Levels in the Work Place. To better understand how consciousness level determines behavior and associated quality-of-life results, consider this realistic narrative set in the typical workplace.

It's 9:03 a.m. and you've just settled into your desk chair to begin the day. With a steaming cup of coffee supplied by your smiling, ever-helpful secretary, you notice the red-hot, mostly delinquent to-do list staring you in the face. Before taking the first sip of fragrant mocha, your intercom beeps. Horror of horrors, it's the boss! In a strained, barely controlled voice, the Director demands your immediate presence. You feel the adrenaline surge through your plaque-filled veins, as trips to the boss's office are normally—for you—synonymous with disciplinary visits to the woodshed. Nervously jumping out of your seat, you spill hot coffee on yourself and all over your disorganized desk. After urgently sopping up the excess liquid from the closest, most-important piles of paperwork, you rush off to your boss's office.

The moment your coffee-stained self hustles through the Director's threshold, s/he launches into a venomous tirade. Seems your boss is more than a little disappointed that the report you handed in yesterday was late…again.

First Reality

How do you respond? In typical First Reality fashion, your mouth—already full of cotton—goes completely dry. Regaining a small amount of survivalist composure, you quickly sputter out some lame excuse about how it's really your secretary's fault. "S/he's the slowest typist on planet Earth, perhaps the Universe," you exclaim. "It's a miracle that I ever manage to meet *any* deadlines with *that* person hanging around my neck like a dead-sea anchor!"

Impressed, not at all, with your feeble, unintelligible explanation, and even more fearful this tardiness will continue, the Director gives you an extra stern warning. Not only are your Christmas bonus and stock options at stake, but you also risk your job if you don't shape up immediately.

After mumbling a weak acknowledgment, you slither your miserable heart-pounding bod back to your enclave, stopping only to give an evil eye to your bewildered secretary. S/he looks up briefly as 100-words-a-minute greased-lightning fingers fly over the keyboard, typing yet another report you dawdled over well past anything that could be described as last minute.

You slam the door behind you, hang out the do-not-disturb sign, put away the to-do list, and switch on a computer game. Desperately distracting yourself from your gut-wrenching feelings, you snarl at every person you meet the rest of the day. Why should they be happy when you're miserable? You ensure your underlings that you consider their performance substandard in every way. Each one of them (also expressing First Reality) transfer the hostility to their co-workers and loved ones, who in turn, pass ill tidings to everyone *they* come across — including any children or pets unfortunate enough to cross their reactive paths. When you get home that night, having accomplished little or no work, you fight with your mate and wonder why that wretched tic in your eye has returned. The nightmares that disturb your fitful attempts at sleep eagerly try to reach your conscious mind, suggesting you seek loving, understanding assistance in healing, releasing, and replacing your underlying feelings of worthlessness. You continue to deny the guiding message, labeling it just another unfair attack on your persecuted ego.

Early Second Reality (ESR) at the Office

Now let's look at the same office scenario from the perspective of someone awakened to early-stage Second Reality (ESR). You respond to the summons without the total-panic, coffee-stained experience of the First-Reality example. Concerned but hopeful you can deal with any *boss issue,* your confidence level expresses in direct proportion to the responsibility you've assumed for both your thinking and actions. With increased control and less anxiety over your daily events, and after listening intently — without interruption — to your boss' complaint, you take a deep breath to center yourself. Then you promptly apologize for your tardiness in completing the important report. You relate your understanding of the necessity for these particular documents in packaging the upcoming IPO stock offering. You acknowledge how your report delay likely put the Director in a tight spot with upper management.

You then reassure her, or him, that you better understand just how long it takes to develop these new financial readiness reports, and all future documents will be delivered accurately and on time. Your boss, visibly relieved, senses correctly that s/he may now count on you and your expertise for the currently demanding crunch time, and that you are also aware and sensitive to pressures from senior management. The Director feels a little embarrassed by perhaps over-reacting so dramatically. Obviously a motivated and competent worker, you need only a little guidance, now and again, to accomplish top-flight work.

Walking back to your office, you stop to thank your secretary for his or her valiant efforts speed-typing that last company financial report you delivered past deadline. You promise not to create unnecessary stress again through poor time-management or procrastination. S/he smiles radiantly, assured that you value and understand his/her (First Reality) world, as a compassionate—albeit imperfect—boss. S/he proves especially friendly and helpful to your team members and business clients who happen to visit or call that day. Subsequently they are better disposed toward you and your projects—making negotiations proceed more constructively.

Back at your desk, you take a moment to collect your thoughts and feelings—including the somewhat awkward ones with your superior. Closing your eyes, you take some cleansing breaths and allow yourself to enter those feelings fully and completely. Practicing techniques learned during a recently attended personal-development, emotions-management program, you mentally unlayer your *feelings onion,* and especially note the underlying unworthiness issues that lead to bouts of procrastination. Having struggled with the effects of these unresolved issues for years, you now set a *clear intention* to heal, release, reframe, and replace them. You're finally ready to graduate from self-sabotage curriculum. This resolve allows simultaneous blossoming of your infinite talent and creativity. You quickly visualize a peaceful river, and the accompanying self-forgiveness ritual, to wash away lingering feelings of inadequacy. Your short but potent attunement completed, you organize your paperwork, placing the most-urgent documents on top. Pulling out your calendar to work out timelines for completing all future reports on time, you break various tasks into manageable, less-overwhelming steps. Now you're ready to tackle the to-do list.

With the benefit of ESR reflection, you have a heightened awareness of how painful it is for First Reality oriented persons to receive negative feedback. At home, after some processing time in your private contemplation cave, you gently, courageously, share your previously embarrassing thoughts and feelings about the late report and your history of procrastination. Your trusted friend, partner, and mate listens attentively while you expose your vulnerabilities and list your alleged weaknesses. S/he loves and respects your courage and strength, feeling especially valued that you trust and openly reveal your human shadow. Together, using all the new tools you received in your self-development workshops, you strategize ways to overcome the troubling pattern. After an exquisitely passionate lovemaking session, you fall asleep nestled into each other like cradled spoons.

Level Recap

You are perhaps realizing these two diverse reactions to the same circumstance as simply the result of one's inner perception, and *not,* as most believe, differing environmental factors. Please also note that awakening to Second Reality is not the same as developed excellence. Repetitive practice of desired replacements dissolves old, non-serving habits.

In the office scenario just presented, the initial, heat-of-the-moment reaction might be to defensively complain about lack of appreciation, or not being given the benefit of the doubt. As a practicing Second Reality individual, you would — after returning to your office to settle down — see the situation from a larger perspective, including the upper-management pressures affecting your boss. You would then be ready to take responsibility for your actions, as did our sample subject. For one who temporarily *loses it* in the Director's office, an appropriate follow-up move would be to return to the boss and express regret for the temporary defensiveness. After a sincere apology, state the cooperative understanding and insight then evident. At this point, your expression is as balanced and empowered as the sample person that retained his or her equilibrium *during* the first go-around. A competent manager will be impressed by your ability to shake off criticism, refocus, and climb back in the saddle responsibly.

As enlightened ones continue their replacement practice during heat-of-the-moment situations, they learn to progressively release old, defensive patterns in favor of the understanding and excellence shown in the Second Reality example. Releasing and replacing worthiness issues also improve one's ability to master non-defensive responses. Reduced self-absorption enables us to better empathize with and counsel others caught in that feedback loop of reactive, non-serving action.

As dramatically different as our early Second Reality example showed regarding quality of life and diminished suffering, let's look at how our world shifts when expanding our consciousness further. At advanced Second Reality (ASR), this office scenario would rarely present itself in the original form. I modify it slightly to more accurately reflect a possible ASR challenge situation.

Advanced Second Reality at the Office

The boss' call comes in the same way. Consistently (habit) expressing both FUN and joyous personal responsibility for some time, you rarely experience internal sirens or adrenaline flows during the course of your days—even during heat-of-the-moment situations. You…easily coexist with various energy manifestations, including hysterical types.

You calmly respond to your boss's frantic call, with concern only for the plight of the company's supervising Director. Fully aware of your boss' pressures from upper management, you continue to be a sympathetic EAR, while holding your self-empowerment knowledge in abeyance until your advice is requested. Upon arrival, you observe your friend and boss now at the very brink of emotional overload. The sense of desperation is so great that s/he launches into a sequenced denunciation, accusing you—among a list of other things—of sabotaging company negotiating efforts by submitting late financial reports. "Maybe you are a secret *spy* for the takeover vultures who would like to steal the company at a bargain-basement price," she cries! Your temporarily crazed Director infers your general calmness during the current crisis, further evidence of culpability.

You take a moment to reflect: unlike your past, suffering, victim-like self, you feel no need to prove the timeliness of your reports, overtime hours, or the list of other supportive assistance you generously render in an effort to forestall the threat of a corporate takeover.

In the past, you would have been deeply hurt by these accusations, and felt intense suffering from your boss' lack of appreciation. Previously you would emotionally shut down for days—sometimes weeks—as you commiserated with your like-minded associates. Those well-intentioned friends and family agreed with your assessment that you were getting the *royal shaft* and that you should sue, or quit, rather than take any more abuse. Prior to healing your internal issues and retraining your automatic responses to challenge, your self-image and general quality of daily life used to revolve around what you perceived your supervisors, friends, family, spouse, and various acquaintances thought and felt about you.

At *this* very moment, however, you lovingly direct your focus toward a friend in crisis. You sense correctly and identify (to yourself) all the quite illogical accusations as nothing more than symptoms of your boss' abject terror. You actually delivered the reports two days early, but the Director's stressed-out assistant accidentally misplaced them.

With the expenses of three children in college and a humongous mortgage on a new custom home in the Heights, your boss' reasoning ability has been temporarily suspended through fear of losing a job. This feigned attack on your performance reveals a desperate cry for help from your ego-shattered supervisor. Not the time for recriminations (your current ego no longer buys into them), you immediately process and release your very temporary feelings of not being appreciated. You step forward to console a fellow Human Being asking—through trembling body language—for *life-saving* intervention.

You reassuringly offer all your knowledgeable assistance, expertise, loyalty, and most importantly your compassionate sensitivity and love. "You are not alone in this challenge. We will get through this temporary storm together," you state. Your unwavering confidence identifies the current crisis as serious...but solvable. After scheduling quiet time to jointly brainstorm a workable response to the latest takeover bid, you share a confident handshake or a hugging embrace (depending on the relationship) with your greatly relieved supervisor and friend.

With gratitude evident in his or her demeanor, your Director can't find the words to thank you for seeing—without judgment—past the panic attack. Because of your presence of mind (awareness level plus practiced replacement), you do not counterattack or take the directed onslaught personally. You intuitively sense your boss' immense gratitude and a bit of embarrassment for showing weakness in the heat of the moment. Realizing this, you compassionately share how understandable the venting was under the circumstances. You respectfully accept the veiled apologies, not from a superior knowledge of manipulating psychology, but from genuine, heart-felt caring, combined with a very healthy and secure self-love. Your spirit soars as you feel an inner appreciation for your heightened ability to be there for a valued friend and fellow Human Being. What a change from the old you!

With your generationally developed ASR talents, enhanced through practiced replacement, you now quickly enter, release, and reframe all illusions of temporary negativity. Practiced responsibility and pattern replacements have largely transformed all previous feelings of unworthiness. Concepts of "healing" and "forgiveness" dissolve as you gratefully realize the significance of every, single experience in your life. Expunging those past concerns (distortions associated with fear of change in your environment) leaves no lingering apprehension about losing *anything*—especially your corporate position. In your mind's eye, the current crisis with your company may be an intended catalyst for change, not only for yourself but for others. You've given a lot of thought to beginning a new consulting business—one that could potentially include your current company, regardless of ownership, as your first client.

Your boss, disabled by fear, could not open to this more independent, self-empowering perspective. S/he places security in the job, rather than in something deep and permanent within oneself. You recall how scary and painful outer-oriented beliefs were for you. For this and other sympathetic reasons, you intend to offer further reassurances and assistance to the troubled corporate director when and if the time comes for a transition. The key will be to center your friend on all of the gifts, talents, and marketable abilities already present. With a greater chance of success if your supervisory friend can heal and replace his or her own security issues, you mentally reaffirm that his or her Spiritually-created blueprint is not up to you. Your job: be a supportive *mirror* and loving, non-judgmental example; not the manipulator of another person's life curriculum.

ASR Orientation

You feel blessed, beyond expression, to realize your current mastery dealing with issues and relationships is not directly due to self-help tools acquired along the way. No particular religion, philosophy, process, book, tape, seminar program, guru, or *separate* Supreme Being gets the credit. You achieved success by assigning beneficially synchronistic, philosophical, and psychological evaluations to those inventoried items. *Your interpretation manifests ALL things and ALL associated meanings.* Along with your newly expanded consciousness, understanding how your confidence and belief gave those tools their vibrancy installs into your awareness that *you truly are your own meaning maker.* This more-expansive level lifts your discernment to an unprecedented level of empowerment—one where personal salvation and the ability to direct your resultant experience reside fully within you. Observational witnessing (which begins in Second Reality) invites you to lend a helping hand without enabling others to avoid responsibility for their own path.

Accepting the Gift

I hope this role-playing demonstration helps you further appreciate how these principles—defined by Holographic Psychology—greatly empower our lives. Yes, releasing and replacing fear-based issues allow a return to love and glorious free-flow options. The next time you feel upset with an individual person, group, or situation, ask yourself: *"If the vast minions of love guided me now, how would I respond?"* Regardless of current circumstances, you can successfully learn to actualize a state of love and grace. This book is your roadmap.

You'll note I did not provide an office-place example of Third Reality consciousness. When ones realize transcendent perspectives and the absolute perfection within *every* experience, they no longer require any guidebooks or illustrative metaphors. Throughout these passages, many terms replicate the presence and meaning of Third Reality awareness: Over Soul, Universal Mind, Cosmic or Collective Consciousness, Collective Unconscious, or simply "the Collective." Religious or sacred terms could include the multitude of names for Lord, God, Source, Creation, Souls, and Guardian Angels.

Consider that our supreme nature, ever expanding and all inclusive, encompasses the complete package of interwoven patterns that lead us to participate in a particular dynamic, at a particular time, in a particular place. Third Reality consciousness harmonizes with the operating system provided by our Spiritual DNA. Third-level individuals no longer limit (to earthly human dynamics) their understanding of the complexity and synchronism of life. In full Third Reality, constant feelings of joyful love maintain our waking cosmic connection, with omniscient understandings of the *how and why* of the syncretistic practices with which mortal Beings continue to work and play. Third Reality lacks even the *appearance* of any differentiations. The transcendent level represents the maximum in congruent synchronicity, or **Oneness**.

In addition to those great prophets mentioned earlier, mystics like Socrates, Plato, Aristotle, Emerson, Jung, Gandhi, and others undoubtedly danced in the domain of Third Reality awareness. Mastering Third Reality leads to further rejoicing as the veil of partial amnesia *completely* falls away, and we (again) directly experience our oneness with the cosmos. The ultimate accomplishment, from this author's perspective, is to achieve this state of grace, divinity, and connection *during* an incarnation, rather than as a right of ascension granted only to transitioning ones. I have it on very expansive authority that establishing multi-realm congruency, does, in fact, represent humanity's completion and mastery of the Earth adventure. For here-and-now practicality, rest assured that achieving a continuous Third Reality state is not necessary to experience substantial cosmic connection, or to have a successful and joyous life. Second Reality awareness gives us all the openings we need to master our own psychological dynamics in the Here and Now. That said; I *still* intend to help facilitate your own cosmic interface in a later chapter. Why? Because you deserve it—of course!

Practical Application

If we can't use advanced concepts to improve our human condition, what use are they? After declaring that more expansive levels of consciousness offer a realistic potential for a more bountiful life, how do we generate these shifts? The doorway to the Infinite resides in our subconscious mind, where all beliefs are stored. And we need more than one magic pill or technique to open that door.

It is intended that our time together be spent applying layer upon layer of practical, productive use of this information. The several visualizations and other facilitative tools—when practiced—help you purge non-serving thoughts and feelings while simultaneously forming more beneficial habits. After taking out the garbage, let's fill the void with idealistic, love-based connections. *You*, not I, decide the nature of that new content. I support you in choosing wisely. Here's an interesting group that did not.

Hale-Bopp, Anyone?

Separatist disciplines commonly bypass most or all the *here-and-now* creations or remedies, while simultaneously bashing the ego mind. Taken to the extreme, this can have dire circumstances. The 39 Heavens-Gate suicide grouping distortedly believed there was nothing of value left on Earth. Doe, the group's embittered leader, erroneously concluded that victimization could be avoided only by reaching some "other-world" sanctuary.

Extreme hopelessness will normally squeeze out (prevent) Third Reality (transcendental) connections. Had the Heavens-Gate membership more patiently worked through their pain and fear, or desired an independent evaluation—by challenging (questioning) their so-called *authority*—they might have discovered the warm, fluffy blanket of inner-salvation and joyous celebration. Instead, they blindly rejected Earth in favor of an orbiting ice ball. If there *is* a purgatory, the "Hell" Bopp Comet appears as likely a candidate as any. Bring your overcoat!

Fortunately, other non-limiting alternatives exist. If you truly believe you need saving, why not save yourself? Choosing a courageous, non-escapist program definitely leads to positive change for you *and* for the entire human race. *We now have the potential to self-actualize our Heaven, just like we unknowingly created Hell for ourselves.* And we don't have to leave physical Earth, or disavow our materiality and ego-mind, to achieve grace and serenity. If our ego is *fear-based*, however, thereby limiting our capacity to love, this clearly needs attention.

Complacency Trap

As a related procrastination challenge, most of us feel even less motivation for change when moderately comfortable. From our human history, we know fear as an effective motivator. In First Reality, fear rates number 1 on the motivational hit parade, with physical pleasure a close second. Most individuals beginning various self-development programs, books, tapes, etc., are opening to expanded levels because they are: ❶ unsatisfied with their current state of affairs, and ❷ now realizing they can make a difference in their lives through their own, independent choices. Perhaps we embrace self-development initially because of our fear of abandonment, or losing love. Regardless, this priming activity, the first stage in taking the reins, often denotes the onset of a significant shift in perceptual awareness. Newly created action, designed to blast free of the comfort-zone nest, indicates your innate willingness to expand beyond the old-paradigm *slave* role. *Captaincy momentums* really start steamrolling from this point. Initially (ESR) you feel a particular *process* correcting your condition. Later (ASR) you discover how ones spell (place) the noun or predicate does not matter: "**I believe** in _____." Second-stage power is, and always has been, in the *subject*...YOU!

Although involutionary and evolutionary science can be quite captivating, I primarily focus on *what* works, not in how or why something works. If practical considerations don't reveal themselves, I'm quick to move on. In this chapter I attempted to demonstrate — through everyday scenarios — various applications of the previously described levels of reality.

In the following three chapters we use our knowledge — from our new-paradigm model — to examine grief, vengeance, forgiveness, and concepts of right and wrong. Lastly, using the three levels of human consciousness, we examine our propensity for separateness and judging...versus connection and unity.

"Love...much like
meditation...is not
something we give, receive,
earn, or do;
but rather, something we
allow to be visited upon
us."

—The SoulMan

CHAPTER SEVEN

Grief Healing
The Holographic Perspective

♥   ♥   ♥

The Gift of Caring. On my very first assignment as a hospice volunteer, I was introduced to a wonderful Latino lady—named Lupina—who was living in a hospice hospital. Our frail matron, slight of build and quite old, was completely blind and now bedridden, due to her weakened state. Rapidly approaching her time of transition, her weight had dropped below eighty pounds. She slept a lot, but when awake her mind was clear. Lupina spoke a little English and I can speak a little Spanish, so verbal communication presented no problems.

In the case briefing, my hospice supervisor mentioned that Lupina did not know of the death of her younger brother, Hector. Her adored sibling passed away several weeks earlier and the family issued explicit instructions not to tell Lupina of Hector's earthly departure. They collectively believed this negative information might lower Lupina's spirits. Lupina's children had not visited since their uncle's death, fearing their mother would ask uncomfortable questions. This sensitive, loving, but fearful woman was desperate for companionship. Lupina knew her time was short. She was both dispirited and depressed, not so much—surprisingly—by her current ordeal, but mostly because of her family's absence.

From my first meeting with Maria, Lupina's full-time ward nurse, I was accepted with encouraging arms. I instantly bonded with this impassioned caregiver. So much so that she admitted that Lupina did, in fact, know of Hector's death. Seems Lupina had continually pestered her only contact, Maria, "Donde está es (where is) Hector?" Although Hector had been very sick himself, he never failed to make a weekly visit to his beloved sister. While conversing with the immediate family by telephone—encouraging them to stop by—Maria was told of Hector's fate. Bombarded by Lupina's aching heart and mournful questioning, Maria gave in and revealed the awful truth.

Armed with this more current and intimate briefing, our compassionate charge nurse officially introduced me to my fearful client. Maria made a big deal about how I had volunteered to be Lupina's private companion. "Lorenzo is here just for you Lupina," she said. Even without those once expressive eyes, Lupina's face lit up like a glorious sunrise. I could see and feel how precious this visit was to her. However, my heart told me *I was the blessed one*.

Lupina was especially happy about being visited by a man. Perhaps my gender was suggestive of her special sibling relationship, although she had not yet mentioned Hector. In the course of describing her general fears, concerns, and loves, she abruptly tensed. In a clear, purposeful, solemn—almost disembodied—voice, she asked, "Why did Hector leave me?" Had Maria not made her reticent disclosure, I doubt I would have responded as I did.

Because Hector had been the younger sibling, Lupina expected to pass on before him. He had also made a promise to be at his sister's side for the entire duration of her transitional ordeal. Later it dawned on me that Lupina, fearfully dealing with feelings of abandonment and unworthiness, along with intense grief, could not understand why the *rest* of the family had forsaken her. Did they blame her for Hector's early passing? Were they too horrified by her impending death to come and say goodbye?

With tears in my eyes and compassion in my heart, I spontaneously answered her question before I had a chance to think: "Hector went first so that he could assist you in *your* crossing and arrival in Heaven. He is with you both *now* and always." At this point, an amazing thing happened. The bright ecstasy of realization dispelled Lupina's rigid and frightful scowl. As her previously tensed body returned to the soft comfort of her reclining hospital chair, her mouth opened in wondrous awe; "Sí...claro...es verdad! (Yes, it's clearly the truth!). Muchas gracias, Lorenzo," Lupina enthusiastically exclaimed as she tightly grasped my arm in loving gratitude. In her weakened state, I had not thought her capable of such strength.

After a few more moments of celebratory conversation, and with promises of a return visit one week hence, I got up to leave. Lupina would not let me go without my giving her a good-bye "beso" (kiss). On my way out I told Maria of our miraculous breakthrough and how important it had been for me to know about Hector's passing. Secretive about her selective communion, Maria now worried about repercussions from her superiors. In spite of managerial fears, she had felt a sudden compulsion to confess her involvement. With religious faith and a special love for her charge, our mutual breakthrough deeply touched Maria. We rejoiced in the realization that Lupina's family need not worry any further about the passing of Hector. I would send them a tactful "all clear" message.

Fear vs. Love

Hoping to end the family moratorium on visits, I reported my successful sojourn to the hospice director. The following section represents my best, paraphrased recollection.

"Your behavior with Lupina represents a huge risk to our agency. You were expressly told not to discuss the status of the deceased brother, yet you went ahead and did so anyway. I have just spent two hours on the phone trying to justify your actions to the family. This time we may have dodged the bullet. They are hopefully not taking legal action for having violated their contractual wishes."

"We are in a very volatile business," the director anxiously explained. "People come to us under tremendous stress and fear. Family members are terrified about the impending death of their loved one(s), and are often in denial. If we breach a confidence, even a distorted one, we can be and often *are* sued for punitive damages. As a result, we constantly cover our backsides. Perhaps you can understand why we can't have any independent mavericks—even if well-intentioned—running around ministering to our clients. We have ordained clergy on our staff to do that job. The law extends more interactive latitude to legally ordained ministers. You are *not* a minister—you *were* a volunteer." [*Note: This experience was a major impetus toward continuing my ministerial studies and obtaining credentials.*] "I take this extra time with you because you seem to be a sincere, giving person who just got caught in the switches. I felt you deserved an explanation for our expedited action on this matter. To further isolate ourselves from the potential of future liability, you have been replaced and your services are no longer required."

As the director concluded his somewhat prepared oratory, I was a little too stunned to reflect on how my spontaneous but certainly beneficial actions became a threat to the hospice staff. My main concern continued to be for Lupina, however. I had made a commitment to return. How would she feel if yet another person abandoned her?

Shell-shocked, I left the hospice building mumbling to myself. Should the family still want me, I was prepared to be Lupina's *independent*-caregiver companion—right through to the end. I called Lupina's children to offer my apologies for any misunderstandings, and to answer questions. They expressed displeasure at no longer having a valid reason to avoid visits to their transitioning loved one. They kept rambling about the depressive nature of the hospital. The family had only one question: "How can you stand to go in that place?" I told them of my experience with the passing of *my* father and how thankful I was to have been able to say goodbye to him personally. Feeling their dread, I reassuringly shared my willingness to be there for them—passing on messages and so forth—if that be their desire. They seemed unsure; the hospice director had sent word that I had been permanently dismissed for unspecified reasons. Expressing best wishes for their final outcome, I asked them to call if they needed me.

Later, after reflecting on this bizarre experience, I reassessed the degree to which fear pushes love out of our lives. Even in an organization created to tend to the terminally ill, administrators can be found stewing in the fear-pot of loss-of-license and livelihood. Dealing with a terrified public, might management (in general) be focusing more on self-protective shielding, than service? With defensive self-interest reigning supreme, how do we provide quality care to the Lupinas of the world?

The more I looked into it, the more aware I became of suffering victimization—a worldwide byproduct of this fear-based dynamic. With the director's plight not just an aberrant exception, no wonder we have so much stress, unhappiness, and dis-ease in our daily lives. By living outside of natural law, we subject ourselves to a continual, depressive energy drain.

Although I never saw Lupina again, she and her family left me a great gift. Now that gift is yours, as well. As you read the next segment, consider the consequences of pushing love and final-sharing opportunities away—as did Lupina's surviving family.

Grief Process via the Reality Levels

This chapter includes my own "up-close-and-personal" experience with the grief process. Revisiting these memories revealed love and joyous reunion, as my predominant feelings, rather than the fear and pain so predominant in the past. Even so, this was not an easy segment to record. The personal realization from this chapter's grief comparative embodies one of my most-transforming insights. With just this one topic, alone, I hope to alleviate a great deal of suffering — especially regarding the physical passing of our loved ones.

Letting Go...Power Intimacy

My stepmother, Ruthie, and I achieved intimate breakthroughs with my father during the post-stroke years of his life. Dad finally accepted love as his due — not because of his brilliant talents, or hard work, but for no other reason than he *was* love personified. In the final months, he developed (I now believe he subconsciously created) lung cancer. This most-dreaded disease seemed to come out of the blue — he gave up cigarettes almost 40 years ago and had no history of lung problems. At first I was unwilling to accept the diagnosis. After finally achieving a deep, shared, loving relationship with Dad, I was not about to say goodbye. I became self-absorbed with my own fears of potential loss of love, and for a time, avoided asking Dad questions about *his* thoughts, feelings, and preferences. "Surely he wants to fight this malignant invader with all the resources and energy at his disposal," I convincingly told my terrified self. After all, what was the alternative?

I quickly moved into *rescue mode* — a state I was well versed and secure in — before emotionally considering any unacceptable answers to my question. I possessed a fair degree of knowledge about various non-toxic, holistic-based remedies, and I immediately began researching alternative treatments. No organ-eating disease was going to get *my* father! I would not, could not, let that happen.

Still not asking Dad what he wished to do about the insidious cancer, I began dragging his less-than-enthusiastic bod around to see alternative-medicine specialists. Determined to find both an appropriate holistic treatment *and* a motivational partner, I hoped natural practitioners could also strengthen Dad's emotional resolve. My stepmother, Ruth, supported my actions out of her own fear. As I was to eventually realize, Dad went along only because he could not bring himself to tell the truth about his feelings — a declaration he believed would devastate our family.

To my credit, it didn't take me long to acknowledge Dad's continual *hangdog* body language. Due to the aphasic nature of his strokes, my father endured great difficulty phrasing even short sentences. Successful communication required much intuitive interpretation and a long, twenty-questions type of procedure. A perfect example of *"what you fear comes upon you,"* I gleaned from my sensitive, loving, outwardly expressive father (boy, how he had changed!) that not only did he not want to fight the cancer, he actually welcomed it. I put great effort into reconciling what I heard, while hiding the pain of having my worst fears realized. I failed miserably at both.

As we both wept, my father demonstrated the patience and strength of Job. He painstakingly described his boredom with limited, routine existence, and his tiring daily struggle. Dad acknowledged how wonderful he felt about the love-affirmation breakthroughs achieved with Ruth and me, but he felt it time to move on. Never an overtly religious man, after a brief-but-disappointing childhood experience with strict Catholic schooling, he became an Agnostic. During his last few years, Dad accepted—without protest—daily inspirational scripture readings from a loving and supportive Lutheran spouse concerned mostly about the condition of his Soul. He seemed to have a great peace about his decision to let go and surrender to the forces withdrawing energy from his mind and body. At first I worried he was despondent and therefore expressing some tired acceptance. But Dad's fearless reconcilement and lack of depression signs, reassured me. With no psychological pathology to sink my teeth into, I pushed myself to listen to what was initially a very painful message. With a shaky voice, I asked the final questions. "Are you sure this is what you want, Dad? Don't you wish to wait for the remaining test results, get more information—just think about it a while longer?" His answers were, "Yes, no, no, NO," respectively. I looked deep into this tormented man's eyes and confirmed his current anguish was caused, not by fear of impending death, but by his concern for how Ruth and I would respond to his declarations. Although Dad sensed he had only a few short weeks to live, this hero's focus was clearly on his family.

Then—for the first time—I saw the world from his perspective. I finally appreciated how Dad had already completed a great life full of wondrous achievement—up to and including this challenging moment with his son. My father patiently explained how his important goals and aspirations were accomplished; he declared it time for final goodbyes and intimate sharing, not more fighting of the cancer (out of *my* fear of loss). Choked up, I told Dad emphatically that I understood and would support his decision. We fell into each other's arms—sobbing deeply—as we released a torrent of emotional stress. Ruth, quietly observing the entire exchange, also accepted the inevitability of her husband's impending transition. Without censure or comment, she joined our collective embrace.

Dad's coming to us so directly with his wishes showed tremendous love and courage. In retrospect, I know he could have taken the easier route—avoiding all potential confrontations and quietly slipping away. In emotion-packed encounters, this had always been his *modus operandi*. Having healed and replaced most of that old insecurity, Dad wanted his beloved family—especially me—to face that he was dying. Seeking quality sharing time without any more tiptoeing around his terminal illness, Dad refused to squander his remaining energy on an exhaustive therapy program. This was to be the case, as we now took our lead from the person *clearly* in charge.

The Choice to Celebrate

At Dad's request, we rented a motor home and comfortably drove two hours north of Escondido to visit his remaining relatives in Canoga Park, California. Upon arrival, now able to openly discuss this sad topic without my previous gut-wrenching agony, I explained to them this was a goodbye trip. Knowing and believing a final earthly goodbye was his choice, rather than some fostered injustice, karmic punishment, or other victim-creating scenario, made a great difference in allowing this to be a pleasant visit—even a celebration. The childhood stories told by Dad's remaining and very lucid cousins were terrifically entertaining, and provided some additional history on my father that I cherish today. I had a choice of how I responded to this phase of the family crisis. I am grateful beyond expression for my choice to go with my inner, love-based feelings that suggested it be a festive occasion enjoyed by all—especially my surprisingly exuberant father. The visit concluded, we returned to Escondido where my greatest learning from Dad was yet to occur.

Within a couple of weeks, we obtained the compassionate services of the Elizabeth Hospice Care people. My father was shutting down rapidly. Dad wanted to die at home, so we arranged for full-support assistance for the home passing. The final, complex matter Dad needed to communicate, and his last really coherent communication, was to ensure we would not resuscitate him or prolong his vital functioning with artificial life support. We were advised by hospice to *not* call 911 when he expired, as paramedics, by law, administer emergency, life-*saving* care—which Dad did not want. We prepared a directed legal document for the family doctor, just in case it was needed.

My dear father spent his last few weeks mostly in a coma-like sleep, waking occasionally for liquids before returning to a quiet rest. I spent some quality time holding, stroking, and telling him how happy I was to have been his son; as I continued to feel at peace with his departing process. My Agnostic beliefs, at this juncture (fall of 1989), did not preclude a reassuring sense of father-son completion.

We of course did not want Dad to suffer unnecessary physical pain. Empowered with the doctor's order, the hospice nurse stood by to administer whatever amount of morphine he required. In spite of Dad's normally difficult and agonizing disease, he didn't need much pain relief. He (and we) allowed his sleep and dream states to be more natural. Later, I asked myself: "Could Dad's pain-free passing have been due to the peace and closure he felt about our celebratory goodbyes? Does a sense of completion with one's life dictate the quality of death?"

From the time of that Motor home trip, where my temporarily energized father acted like he might live another ten years, he was gone in about five weeks—September 19, 1989. We scattered Dad's ashes in the Pacific Ocean, which had been this *fisherman's* request.

Where's the Grief?

After accepting Dad's decision to not fight the cancer and to enjoy what he knew to be the last few weeks of his life, I felt at peace about everything. At the time, I could not fully understand the rationale behind my pain-free emotional state. Analytically I reasoned that perhaps I was in shock, or at the very minimum, experiencing some form of denial.

`My stepmother Ruth, who also accepted the finality of her husband's rapidly approaching death, did not fare so well. She rallied around the job at hand, coordinated support services, ran the household, made final arrangements, and the like. Even though— with my assistance—she performed these functions satisfactorily, she struggled emotionally, as expected. I could not understand why Dad's deteriorating condition did not leave me tortured and saddened, especially as the final days, hours, and minutes approached.

I reasoned that I was experiencing delayed-reaction grief—a theory supported by my professional counseling friends. They told me not to worry. "The *sledgehammer* of grief will come slamming down on you days, perhaps weeks afterwards," they assured. In spite of my consistently tranquil mood, their psychoanalysis seemed rational. Disturbing thoughts about not having loved my father enough...I pushed to the back of my mind. Culturally indoctrinated to believe we suffer proportionally to our love for another at their passing, I discovered later that both my concerned observation *and* the opinion of the experts was not the higher truth.

Show Me the Pain!

Several months after the funeral, the anticipated onset of the *normal* grief process was still absent. I remained comfortable, even happy about where Dad was—and very content with the memories of our father-son relationship. I did *then* and *still do* miss those great hugs and his special scent, however, which I partially experience during contemplative moments. Meanwhile, Ruth and other close family members displayed more traditional grief—the Elizabeth Kubler-Ross model we expect in a normally functioning, non-dysfunctional psyche. So, once again, I wondered why I was feeling great, experiencing only pain-free memories. Conventional wisdom suggested this abnormal.

Not content to leave well enough alone (I never said I was the *sharpest* knife in the set), I decided to check for buried denial issues. I headed in to see one of the friendly family counselors at the Las Vegas chapter of the non-denominational Jewish Family Service Agency. Pleased to be introduced to a wonderful, sensitive, intelligent lady, we did several sessions of, "let's turn Larry upside down and see what drops out." Cooperating fully with the process, I was very open—and withheld nothing. After about six emotionally intimate visits, we reluctantly brought our sessions to a close. I really liked and respected my counselor, but we detected nothing new or untoward. We could not find any hidden feelings, submerged childhood issues, or relevant pathology.

With the mutual analysis of *"if it's not broken, don't fix it,"* we bid adieu with hugs and shared best wishes. Although I still had the feeling that the real answer—and main message—awaited discovery, I decided to release my concerns.

Again, the Universe provides us what we require to complete our earthly curriculum—not necessarily what our human selves *consciously* desire. I was to get the answer I sought in the aftermath of encountering what the big-time *traditional* grief process feels like. To teach me to be careful about what I wish for, delivery of the coming realization package arrived via the *pain express!*

Traditional Grief

Two years after Dad's transition, I was in the throws of another half-hearted rescue job. This was my graduate course. It was finally sinking in that love and personal feelings of completeness are not to be found (*out there*) through another person. But, while assisting an abused woman and her three dysfunctional children, I was grossly neglecting a very special 14½-year union with my Spiritual mentor. My universal tutor had given me a greatly expanded view of life. Much of what I know about unconditional love, loyalty, camaraderie, responsibility, and how to establish an actual psychic connection with another Being, I credit to this special angel. These incomprehensible gifts—and more—came from a beautiful, sensitive, caring, engaging, passionate, and very *cool* Doberman Pinscher named BLITZ. I raised her from a six-week-old pup, obtained from a Dobe-loving, Phoenix Arizona couple.

Animal Kingdom—Masters of Love and Presence

Blitz was unlike any Doberman you've seen or read about. She was a Spiritual master that alighted on this planet to teach a few fortunate individuals, even me, the many wondrous things beyond the temporal world. She opened my mind and heart to the possibility that, if there could be a *Blitz* created, there must at least be a Canine God. She almost instantly transformed anyone that met her, even those who feared big dogs—especially Dobermans. I may slightly exaggerate her importance to others, but not her significance to me. All the dogs, cats, birds, and other pets I've known were unique and special—each with their own one-of-a-kind personality. But Blitz was...mysteriously different.

A River in Egypt

During the time I provided temporary sanctuary to my latest rescue ensemble, I ignored Blitz's emotional needs—as well as my own. I loved Blitz dearly, but now she was dying—just a few months short of her fifteenth birthday. Blitz had inoperable tumors in her mouth. Because they were beginning to bleed, I kept her in the garage that was open to the enclosed patio and the nice, mild weather we were enjoying in the late summer and fall of 1991. Blitz had always been a house dog, so this posed a difficult change for both of us. During the last few months of this delightful Dobe's life, while I was still smack dab in the middle of a challenging relationship with a cocktail waitress and her three kids, I gave Blitz very little extra attention. Not in any apparent physical pain, she ate well in spite of the spreading growths. Blitz got her vet visits with Joanne, a compassionate, holistic doctor who, as good as she was, could do nothing about the tumors' advance. She said only that I would know *"when it's time."* Even today those devastating words somewhat challenge me. At the time I did not realize I was avoiding the special walks and playtime we had always enjoyed—partly out of my unwillingness to accept that I was going to lose her. As my mainstay—the rock in my life—Blitz had been with me through thick and thin, including three, very different live-in relationships.

With a keen interest in everything, Blitz was curiously and patiently accepting of everyone—especially children and any species of animal. Very un-Doberman-like, she never growled or made any discouraging gestures. There came a time, during my ignorance of her full abilities, where I decided she should be more of a watch dog and protector for Marge—my partner at the time. I went through three different dog trainers trying to get her to alert on command. They all gave up, when regardless of how they pretended to be a threat, Blitz always knew it was a game. They said they would have to physically provoke Blitz to make her more suspicious of people. I discontinued the training at that point, because what we loved most about her was her loving and trusting demeanor. I had a heart-to-heart with Blitz and she obliged me by at least feigning a threat-bark, when I commanded, "watch-em!" This bluff was intimidating enough to meet our needs. I reasoned she would probably lick the hand of any *real* burglar.

One day, about to insert my key into the front door of our Phoenix townhouse, I heard Blitz ferociously barking at something inside. I nervously entered to see her silhouette positioned by the rear patio door. With teeth bared, Blitz was angrily riveted to movements outside. Quickly stepping forward, I saw two guys with duffel bags diving over the back wall. Just then, the sliding glass door exploded in shards of glass, which sounded like a torrential rain storm. Because of its protective film, the door glass gave way in large interconnected chunks. The would-be burglars had attempted to pry open the rear patio entryway, when an irate Doberman arrived on the scene. I had never seen Blitz in such a state of arousal. With her body rigid as a board, her hackles fully erect, it was quite clear she meant business. "Was this the same dog?" I asked myself. I suddenly understood why those professional trainers, although *acting* the part of threatening degenerates, could not deter Blitz's tendency to play. She knew the difference between make-believe posturing and the real deal. *I* was the one in need of training, not Blitz.

Honey...I'm Home

Anytime I returned home—often after a tough day—I could walk in and have my spirits instantly lifted by Blitz's enthusiastic body wag. She had a good vocabulary of understood English words, but the *psychic* connection made our relationship unique. I have never experienced anything like it—with animal *or* human—before or since.

I admit that along with a healthy genuine affection, I also possessed a degree of codependency in my relationship with Blitz. I made myself emotionally vulnerable in ways I less often expressed during human interactions. As Blitz's terminal condition occurred while in the middle of a relationship distraction, I continued with only the basic *autopilot* type of pet care. After all, as special as she was, Blitz was just a dog for God's sake. I'm sure you thought it silly to sit down and have a heart-to-heart *settee* with a dog...right? Before you answer, ask yourself if it's just a coincidence that "Dog" spelled backwards is goD.

One day—with heavy heart—I finally took a serious look at my precious Blitz. I didn't stop crying for weeks. The mouth discharge had increased to a continual, slow, bloody drool. Even though she still ate slowly, but well, and wagged her butt with the customary—albeit slower—greeting, plainly her strength was fading. I knew I could not live with myself if I let her condition deteriorate to a hemorrhaging death on the garage floor, all alone. This was a possibility about which my humane vet, Joanne, warned me.

Finally, I peered deeply into those expressive eyes. Speaking with an aching heart, and a faltering voice: "Well, it looks like it's about time to go, old girl." I waited for that familiar psychic connection to tell me I was *wrong* and we still had more time. Painfully, my beloved mentor expressed no disagreement in her eyes. I reluctantly called the animal hospital and requested an examination room with some big pillows and a blanket. Out of curious interest, the two youngest children asked to accompany me. At the time, I entertained no thoughts about how this experience might or might not penetrate their previously wounded little hearts. Fighting back anguished tears, to maintain some semblance of control, I was too self-absorbed with my own misery to do more than agree to their request. We gently loaded Blitz into my Utility Vehicle and took our last, short, 15-minute drive together. Blitz always loved to travel. She quickly learned this was the way to the best smells and adventure opportunities.

And Then There Was Misery

After arriving and paying the pre-arranged fee, we were escorted into a specially prepared room furnished with soft floor coverings. Joanne said I could stay there as long as I wanted, and that the transition process would take about 10 minutes after the injection. [With today's meds it's almost instantaneous]. I looked again into those still-clear (thanks to wonderful homeopathic vet care) dark, liquid-brown eyes, to confirm this was the needed thing to do. This time I got an unmistakable answer—*yes!* Just like my father, some twenty-six months earlier, she was ready to go. The difference this time: *I was not ready to release her*. With my love and sensitivity for Blitz stronger than my intensely felt grief, I gave the OK for the injection and my sobbing kicked into overdrive.

Through copious tears I talked aloud of our great years together, especially the two visits we made to a campground in the Sierra Nevada Mountains called "Holly Meadow"—a sacred location where Blitz had frolicked to her heart's content. These were the only two times in all our years together that Blitz became so excited about the environmental playing field that she left my immediate vicinity to run with the speed she had been named for. When she was a pup, we used to play this game where I would try to hide from her so she would have to search for me. I successfully eluded her only once. From that *panic-point* on, she always kept one eye on me no matter where we were.

The Appeal of Nature

Uncharacteristically straining against the leash, I released her on our first visit to Holly Meadow. Blitz began running in huge figure-eight patterns. Her repetitive course extended throughout the entire breadth and width of this five-acre parcel of beautifully abundant flowers, plants, and streams. Each exercise period, I positioned myself in the middle of the field to joyously watch my energized Dobe speed to the far edge of the meadow. Then she would reverse direction and *blitz* past me again at full-impulse power. Blitz had an elegant prance, her gait similar to a gazelle or proud racehorse. She delighted in this looping game until totally exhausted. We enjoyed two to three glorious runs every day of our visit to this majestic venue. So many wonderful memories…where had all the time gone?

As I affectionately recalled those shared experiences, it suddenly hit me between the eyes—like that *promised* sledgehammer—how I wasted the last precious months of her life. I begged—yes, begged—for forgiveness for my grievous error, but she was too far gone for any psychic response. Either that, or I was too overcome with guilt, remorse, and shame, to hear her answer.

During the entire euthanasia ordeal, the two kids sat quietly—thinking and feeling who knows what—while I talked to a dying animal and unashamedly wept. These children had already known so much violence and fear in their short lives, they did exactly what I had done—as a child—to protect themselves from potential pain. Having been numbed by anger and fear, seeing a grown man cry and tenderly express love may have been a first for them.

The more I mentally chastised myself, the guiltier I felt for what I had done; or more accurately, what I had *not* done. When I first found out her illness was terminal, why did I not drop whatever insignificant thing I was doing and take Blitz for one last hurrah at her beloved Holly Meadow? Surely she deserved at least that much for all she had given me. How could I so selfishly ignore her in her time of need? The self-flagellation escalated in proportion to her fading pulse. With Blitz's heart still beating slightly, and believing I might pass *with* her, I shrieked, grabbed the kids, and quickly bolted from the building.

In those long, painful months that followed, I greatly regretted my premature departure—and beat myself up even more. "How could you abandon her at the time she needed you most, you spineless coward?" was one of the more printable things I said to myself after her passing. No scolding at the hands of another would have been more punishing than the dressing-down I continually gave myself. Ladies and gentleman—*boys and girls*—I had officially entered the wonderful world of the *normal* grief process. Believe you me...it burned like HELL!

The virtual discomfort that differentiated my experience with Dad's transition, relative to Blitz's passing, was not to be lost on me. During my intense grief I could not come to the true significance of this disparity, however.

Before reading further, take a moment to search your feelings and reasoning abilities. Prod beneath the surface and discover the empowering truth within these comparative (Dad and Blitz) bereavements. This is the realization I have pointed toward for the past many pages. The buildup was intended to be gradual so that, during the narrative, you could fully enter your innermost feelings. All transformational processing and change to your underlying belief-system takes place in your deep *core* emotional center. We are now at the center of this issue, one of the most important insights I hope to communicate during this entire writing. If you core integrate this one—not just intellectualize it—you take a giant leap into practical awareness, and you purge any need for similarly painful learning situations. Why was my suffering more excruciating with Blitz's passing than it was with my father's transition? Consider these two diametrically opposed responses to the loss of a loved one, before reading on. What's *your* conclusion?

Grief Process Conclusion

Hoping you were well rewarded for your contemplation, let's see if your subjective deduction is similar to mine. It took me until after the intervention experience in Escondido and the spectacular 30-day Spiritual odyssey that followed—five years after Blitz's passing—to fully get it.

Those compressed but very transformational 30 days included some wonderfully facilitated assistance from a kind, compassionate, very gifted pet communicator and animal psychic—Vicki Allinson, of Lake Forest, California. After a short but dramatic healing process with Miss Vicki, I finally released the last of my suppressed remorse. Not particularly surprising, my *unresolved* grief came from not forgiving my *self* for perceived shortcomings dishonorably demonstrated during the final months of Blitz's life. Prior release of those distorted thoughts and feelings might have allowed me to *earlier* embrace Vicki's present insight—Blitz had *not* remained at the Vet's office. The true essence (Soul) of my beloved Doberman *walked out the door with me;* leaving *her* body, and potentially *my* suffering, behind. As usual, I sat on the backside of the learning curve and played catch up.

My self-created guilt paralyzed me so much that I waited—even with my great love of dogs—over four years before adopting another one. I continued to get very emotional whenever any Dobermans crossed my path. How's that for subjective differences? Most people shun Dobermans out of gripping fear. I avoided them lest I break down in uncontrollable sobbing.

Dad & Blitz – Summer 1979

I know now that the distorted (subconscious) belief I was not worthy of owning another companion animal, delayed my obtaining a new dog. That incessant, negative, background mind chatter kept reminding me how I let Blitz down in her time of need. It strongly suggested I do the dog world a favor and not compound my *sin* by creating disappointment and pain for any more members of the canine species. By not accepting a slothful, guilt-ridden attitude as the final tombstone inscription, I listened to my more supportive internal Guidance. I got the *recommended* therapeutic assistance that allowed me to finally forgive myself for having not performed perfectly. Releasing the immobilizing afflictions of guilt and remorse gave me new life! Difficult to describe the unburdening feeling associated with self-forgiveness...it's something you must experience to truly understand. What finally came to me: *I already possessed the power and wherewithal to heal myself any time I chose.* Not aware how heavily burdened and emotionally shut down I was after Blitz's transition, and oblivious to the self-healing power awaiting my acceptance, I suffered. Upon awakening to ASR, the actuality of my powerful and preexisting healing abilities came into clear focus.

Within moments of the Vicki-facilitated healing experience, my mental and emotional vision switched to full, wide screen. Suddenly, I got it! When my father passed, the no-show *normal*-grief-process was not due to loving him any less; I was *free* of unresolved issues—denial, anger, guilt, remorse, bargaining, etc.—with my father's passing. Feeling good about what I accomplished with our healthy, non-codependent relationship, and accepting my father's transition decision, allowed the peace and closure I experienced during his passing. I actually *stepped through* the grief process—almost immediately—when I chose to celebrate, rather than just mourn the loss of him. Psychologists call this "anticipatory grief processing."

Although I still miss my father's physical presence, I never experienced the intense pain I later endured with Blitz's passing.

If you can open fully to the following, you won't need any of the previous steps or processes. The next step (shift) beyond the previously explained level of empowerment can be difficult for most to even comprehend, let alone actualize. Our intense participation in the five-sensory world usually squeezes out our *beyond-space-and-time* connection. If you've followed the progression of realities, or Level Consciousness, you at least theoretically understand how Third Reality awareness makes grief, healing, forgiveness, and emotional pain, of any sort, *moot*. I am not talking about anticipatory (advanced) grief processing now. Consider that *all* grief, loss, etc., ceases to exist at a *certain* level of consciousness. Without a belief in, or sense of, separation, how can grief, or loss, be relevant? *How can cause and effect be germane at a level where effect co-exists with cause?* Third Reality embodies this elusive out-of-the-box realm; a level not limited by Space and Time (linear) equations—including all forms of duality.

In Third Reality, or the transcendent connection, *Oneness* stops being an abstract theory and becomes a core actuality. Self-forgiveness, a very powerful and important facilitation for Second Reality emancipation, represents only one important step in our evolutionary, *power and potency* process. Third Reality, an expanded state capable of *full* right-hemisphere, or heart, requires no separate DO-ing. Prayer, attunements, out-of-body, NDE, subconscious-mind accessing, and other altered-state orientations help gain access to Third Reality—where they are then...*no longer required*. Again I emphasize that each expanded stage continues to include the lower vibratory levels—but is not limited to them. Nothing is ever lost, or made wrong through enlightenment. In the exciting business of actualizing, *all* is appreciated.

For me, and I hope for you, as well, the lesson glistens crystal clear. Love everyone and everything *now!* Don't hold back. Ask yourself this: "If, at this very moment, I permanently *lost* the physical presence or well being of my significant other(s), how would I feel?" Are there any unresolved issues, unfinished business, or things to be spoken/shared/experienced left in your closet of fear, anger, righteous indignation or self-absorbed complacency? We humans seem to take our lives and those around us for granted. Later we beat ourselves up while accepting membership in the *"Shoulda-Coulda-Woulda"* club. I used to be a dues-paying member, so I know what that affiliation feels like. IT...say it with me now...SUCKS! As of late, I let my membership lapse in that old-paradigm club.

I sense some of you—especially counseling professionals—thinking that I oversimplify the grief process, and that each case is different. Since I am not an expert in the *limitations* of Human Beings, let me reinforce two points:

❶ Regardless of the circumstances, or an individual's ego-based need to be right, doesn't it make sense to clear all or most unresolved issues *prior* to an injury, or transition, of a loved one? Consider the benefit of minimizing guilt and regret sure to be experienced *after* their passing.

❷ Much more importantly, how about the opportunity for additional quality time whilst they're still here?

No Mistakes

The Soul recognizes no dilemma with humanity's right or wrong choices. *The Soul sees all experiential life as purposeful and valued.* Note the painful consequences regarding my choices about Blitz. Not experiencing that lesson, thus still ignorant of current realizations, might (likely) have precluded the appreciation for life I now enjoy. Today, I can reflect on and compare what had originally been *only* a painful human experience, with the Soul's more expansive perspective...thank you, Spirit! Yes, we all appreciate our health more after recovering from a bout with the flu. But advanced mindfulness practice magnifies levels of joyous communion *without* tortuous precursors; not that I wish to *choose* for you...wink, wink.

We quite commonly focus on certain aspects of life (the *doing* portion) with self-absorbed, tunnel vision. We can choose to take the blinders off and smell the roses (just BE), rather than stomp all over the foliage on the way to the next goal line. Reflective pausing is the preferred method for actualizing your potential (Spiritual DNA), unless you wish to explore additional *pain* options. Making what almost everyone calls an *error* potentially manifests great transformational awakening. Guiding Souls wish to reassure you: *there are no mistakes.* So-called mistakes provide learning, growing, awakening opportunities. More accurately, Soul realizes no concept of "learning" or "growing"—only the gift of intense human experience and the involutionary and evolutionary development of expanded awareness that accompanies it.

The bottom line, here: ***Souls desire a full spectrum of human experience.*** We, standing beyond Earth, *are* the Souls that pre-chose that variety. Souls have loving, supportive intentions and preferences for us, and gently guide our human selves from the background. As human personalities, we own the potential for free choice and can deviate from the intended Soul purpose—creating negatively versus positively—if determined to do so. Consider murder, mayhem, and all other demonstrations of destructive behavior the sole byproducts of human fear and greed. These negatives create the beliefs and repetitive habit patterns associated with a poor self-image. Distorted thoughts and feelings often dominate human conscious awareness, thus temporarily squeezing out the universal healing and communion energy. Souls see our human choices as *Large or Small*, rather than good or bad. Obviously a main theme, I know I've repeated this to the point of redundancy, perhaps beyond. However, its significance may inspire sufferers—allowing them to retire from the right-and-wrong, *judging-of-others* business. Prior victims may then open their hearts to all the love in the Cosmos.

How empowering is it for us to believe supernatural devils exist just to jerk our chain? As an alternative, consider that we, as Souls, wield the forces of God and call the shots—deciding to incarnate to this so-called physical reality, *and* structuring our Earth-specific lesson plans. If we—as humans—had full knowledge of our unfettered magnificence, we would find it extremely difficult to keep an intense focus on Earth life. You don't have to take my word for it, ask any *bliss-aholic*. Other controlling elements dwell in our lives, however. The following narrative will explain.

Who's in charge?

Adam and Eve said, "Lord, when we were in the garden you walked with us every day. Now we do not see you any more. We are lonesome here and it is difficult for us to remember how much you love us."

And God said, "No problem! I will create a companion for you that will be with you forever and who will be a reflection of my love for you. This way you can feel my presence even when you cannot see me. Regardless of how selfish, or childish, or unlovable you may become, this new companion will accept you as you are and will love you as I do — in spite of yourselves."

And God created a new animal to be a companion for Adam and Eve. And it was a good animal. And God was pleased. And the new animal was pleased to be with Adam and Eve, and wagged its tail.

Adam and Eve said, "Lord, we have already named all the animals in the Kingdom and we cannot think of a name for this new animal."

And God said, "No problem! Because I have created this new animal to be a reflection of my love for you, its name will be a reflection of my own name; you will call it DOG."

And Dog lived with Adam and Eve and was a companion to them and loved them. And they were comforted. And God was pleased. And Dog was content, and wagged its tail.

After a while, it came to pass that an observing angel came to the Lord and said, "Lord, Adam and Eve have become filled with pride. They strut and preen like peacocks and they believe they are worthy of adoration. Dog has, indeed, taught them that they are loved, but perhaps too well?"

And God said, "No problem! I will create for them a companion who will be with them forever and who will see them as they truly are. The companion will remind them of their human limitations. Adam and Eve will learn that they are not all that."

And God created CAT to be a companion to Adam and Eve.

And Cat would not obey them. And when Adam and Eve gazed into Cat's eyes, they were reminded that they were NOT the most superior beings on Earth.

And Adam and Eve learned humility. And they were greatly improved. And God was pleased.

And Dog was still happy, and wagged its tail.

And Cat didn't give a s - - t, one way or the other!

Remember, boys and girls...all work and no play makes us dull and uninspired.

Soul Touch

Have you ever wondered about how much guidance you may be receiving from beyond your conscious awareness? For a moment, assume cosmic persuasion real and ongoing; does its presence suggest we are puppets dancing on some celestial string? As we become more sensitive and open to the presence of Spiritual influences, we inevitably step up to question this *human-choice-versus-cosmic-guidance* area of our lives.

Our next chapter delves deeper into the *core* power of forgiveness. I share a story from my early childhood—a story told, for years, as judge and victim. Looking through the lens of Second and Third Reality, rather than the joyless and limiting blame-game of First stage, I finally liberated myself from endless suffering. An all-inclusive world comprises no right or wrong answers...just choices and consequences within the dualistic realm. Concluding analysis presumes you free to choose. Shall we find out?

Larry and ♥ Tanner — March 2005

"Life is not measured by the number of breaths we take...but by those special moments that take our breath away."

—Unknown

CHAPTER EIGHT

♥　　♥　　♥

When In the Pot...
You Can't Taste the Stew

First Love. In the spring of 1955, at the ripe, old age of 12½, the world I knew ceased to exist. The little girl I fell deeply in love with (Celeste), also lived in Studio City. "Me amour" was the daughter of two celebrated entertainment moguls. All the star power meant little to me, although I was slightly impressed to have Captain Zoom — and his warehouse of gifts — in our neighborhood.

The day, for which I had been building my courage, finally arrived. After many weeks of intense *show-but-don't-tell* and other intimacies, I stepped forward to declare my love and lifetime commitment to the object of my blossoming affections. By all visible accounts, I felt confident Celeste held the same interest. Shock is not the word to describe my emotions when Celeste rewarded my trust and courage by declaring that, although she was flattered and pleased with her successful manipulation of my feelings, she did not love me. My story gets a little weird, here, considering this behavior came from one approaching only her thirteenth birthday.

Celeste informed me she was *in love* with a young man of celebrity parents. The other boy attended her same private school, and it seems he was not returning her interest. So, my heartthrob concocted an elaborate plan of deception. The lad in question would attend Celeste's birthday party, scheduled a couple weeks hence. The reason we had been kissing so ardently, she explained, was to *practice* for the upcoming celebration. I was to be fodder for her attempt to get the attention of the desired boy, through manipulative jealousy. As the only public school kid in attendance, no one else would know me. Celeste imagined that ardently kissing this unknown boy (me), in front of her intended, would finally elicit the desired, attention-getting result.

Still reeling from her first salvo of emotional jolts, trying to grasp the intricate deception plan without any clarifying charts or graphs, the conniving vixen dropped her final bombshell. After taking me into her special hiding trough, Celeste offered additional enticements. For my compliance with the birthday plan, she would *make a man* out of me in the same manner others had *made her a woman*. I lost count of the many times throughout adolescence that I was chastised for turning down this Celeste-*ial* offer. Years later, my converted hedonistic self thought that perhaps I should have stuffed my pride and enjoyed the fruits of her third-party maneuvering.

When I went home to my sensitive, loving, supportive, but occasionally explosive mother, hoping to get some much-needed consolation and relief from the excruciating pain in my heart, I received my second back-to-back hit. Mom was in tears, packing several suitcases. My preoccupied and generally aloof father sat on the roof, hammering nails, as *always* after a confrontational upset. Without fanfare or drum roll, Mother informed my sister and me: "We are going to be living with Nanny and Banco (our grandparents) from now on. Mommy and daddy are getting a divorce."

I was to be instantly severed from my wonderful, oak-forested adventure land...complete with pet gophers, squirrels, ducks, and:

- **My playmates and friends from our "Poco-Mas-Arriba" hill...**
- **My best friend Clark, with whom I shared my childhood adventures and trusted enough to fully confide in...**
- **The view from which I could see one-fourth of the entire world...**
- **My classmates at Dixie Canyon Elementary...**
- **And Ms. Keller, the teacher I loved enough to torment unrelentingly... <u>all</u> suddenly lost to me.**

From an adolescent perspective, my greatest indignity: trading in a Garden-of-Eden paradise for a small tract home in the suburbs of North Hollywood, complete with three chain-smoking adults. I could feel the just-barely-outgrown asthma renewing itself deeply in my chest; but I was too numb to care.

Later in life, I summarized my 12-year-old sensitivities and open innocence as culturally atypical of most curious, male children of that time. When finally able to reveal the emotionally devastating secret, none of my hedonistic, peer-group associates seemed capable of relating. They suspiciously rebuked the idea that a curious, hormonally active boy would pass up *any* carnal opportunities, or that I had—in fact—been disabled by a broken heart. Any emotional maturity I had at 12½ was *deleted* and sent to the rubbish bin. After the described combination of traumatically charged events, plus some other minor episodes during the same adolescent period, I joined the ranks of the emotionally dysfunctional. This impaired state rigidly served me for the next 14 years. The defrost cycle beginning at age 27 took many more years to complete. I continued to be terrified of potential rejections or alienation of affection. Go figure!

Ask yourself if I was capable of making freewill choices during those fearful years. Or had I been effectively conditioned to predictably respond to environmental situations based solely on fear and threat of emotional pain? The journey to heal those feelings of unworthiness, thus opening to our true magnificence, is the main theme of this writing. It is hoped that the sharing of my personal journey will serve others trying to reconcile their past, empower their present, or both.

Misery in Perspective

Today, as an advancing, middle-aged adult, I realize my traumatic adolescent experience pales in comparison to the daily toil of a starving child in fly-ridden Somalia. Still, perhaps you appreciate how the unresolved trauma of this western-based cultural experience tempered a child's zest for life. I continued to question as a way to learn daily *survival* practices, but it would be many long years before I even approximated the enthusiasm and fullness I enjoyed as an innocent, 12-year-old boy. Determined to never entrust my heart to another Human Being, I relied strictly on myself, just like *good old Dad* had done. I kept all my turmoil bottled up inside, with *"Never let them see you sweat,"* as my mantra. I denied my emotions, and focused on the *happiness-and-success* model gleaned from billboards and advertising agencies.

Defining Life Success

One day, 14 years later—while focusing on some recurring gray whisker stubble—I peered deeply into the mirror to study my entertaining but basically unhappy self. In a rare, reflective moment, I mentally reviewed *society's* success checklist.

❶ ✎ The perfect glamour job and a high-paying future as an airline pilot for a major Los Angeles-based airline ✈.

❷ ✎ A deluxe, bachelor beach-pad complete with private sundeck and unrestricted ocean view, in *happening* Marina Del Rey, California.

❸ ✎ A brand new, paid-for, Jaguar XKE, with a custom, *head-turning* paint job.

❹ ✎ A healthy, muscular body, with handsome features and a charming, albeit *spurious*, personality.

❺ ✎ A bevy of beautiful, professional, bikini-clad, sun-and-pleasure-seeking ladies eager to be with me.

Yep...pseudo appearance checklist complete! I created the perfect hedonistic lifestyle and the envy of all my superficially oriented male friends. This jealousy was also begrudgingly apparent from my supervisory peer group of airline captains, many on their 4th or 5th marriage, the current offering a twenty-year-old stewardess or other glamour groupie. I know some of you (mostly men) must think: "What the heck is this guy's problem? Stevens had it made in the shade! All he needed was a minor attitude adjustment to continue the one-hundred-percent, full-time pursuit of pleasure, block the potential for any kind of pain, and just sit back and enjoy the ride. I have no sympathy for a guy who screwed up such a sweet deal, just because he had a little guilt about being a taker. To the victor go the spoils!"

The above male perspective is a familiar one on the road commonly traveled. The very human desire to seek exclusive pleasure, while avoiding (like the plague) any type of potentially deep and expressive feelings, often results in a full range of emotional suffering—including the debilitating effects of depression. I maximized the self-indulgent lifestyle, and like others who traversed the same path, *emptiness grew inside me like a malignant tumor.* Using my manipulative charm to control others gave me a false sense of power over my environment. The self-imposed facade momentarily masked my inner feelings of unworthiness, until the time of reckoning was at hand. I was quickly opening to the idea of a *road less traveled* where a natural, internalized type of FUN was again possible...rather than the artificial, outer-fixated variety I'd been living. Before I fully embraced this new path, I had much work to do learning to forgive, heal, and eventually trust in life. I desperately wanted to move past the old, non-serving agenda. Making an inner and resolute commitment to change, I felt calming reassurance and an inner enthusiasm, both of which were off my radar screen for the previous fourteen years. Beyond any general sensing, I *knew* this new direction would create a love-based resurgence of FUN—once I got unstuck.

Who's the Man?

Regarding my emotionally evasive, self-gratifying relationship entanglements, the old me prided itself in some semblance of distorted integrity. Although I recall instances of expressed exaggerated interest, the reason I would not tell a woman I loved her to manipulate sexual favors was less than the idealistic one I professed.

The truth I awakened to was the near-catatonic terror I felt when confronted with vulnerability. Beneath the semi-conscious fear lay a deep, negative feeling not totally unearthed for many *more* years. Didn't a 13-year-old girl clearly infer I deserved only being used? After Celeste's convincing, effective, and purposeful manipulations, rational-mind affirmations were not overcoming my subconscious unworthiness. Having additionally witnessed my own mother suddenly bail out of a committed marriage, how could I trust *anyone's* love? In *my* mind, those eager, often aggressive women in my young Navy and airline-pilot's life were just looking for a good meal-ticket. Maybe a valid assessment of some, it certainly was not true for the full assortment of bountiful opportunities that passed my way. In my ignorance of true empowerment, I used female conquests as a way to validate my desirability.

As my childhood friend, Clark (with whom I've continued to enjoy great sharing), pointed out to me a few years back, I used to present a lot of personality bluster to cover my deep-seated insecurity. Yes, I had done a perfect job of not being used again. So, there I was, staring at my mournfully reflective self, lonely and miserable even though quite proficiently pursuing the *advertised* American Dream.

Soul-Searching Begins

I saw that any blissful prospects for the future, as a controlled-emotions airline captain, were no better than my current woeful state of affairs. This honest, though incomplete evaluation effort, combined

with the arrival of an incredible support partner, began my journey to unearth the authentic source of peace, harmony, joy, love, and guilt-free happiness.

Touched by an Angel

In the spring of 1969, a beautiful, sensitive, giving, kind, functional, *real* woman entered my life. Suzanne, out of unselfish love and compassion, saw past my carefree facade to the wounded little boy that just wanted to love and be loved. With Suzanne's extremely patient, but often unrewarded facilitation, I began cracking open the hard shell around my frozen heart. Terrified, but reassured by my future wife's rock-solid sincerity and heart, I tentatively sampled the potential rewards of a fully engaged life—one that my child-self had joyously frolicked in *before* my head-on crash with the *Celestial body*.

Suzanne and I had five wonderful years together. When it became painfully clear that my goals and objectives were preventing my gracious wife from accomplishing *her* particular plans and desires, I sadly let her go. Not a day goes by without me giving thanks both *to* her and *for* her. With quiet gratitude, and often a tear, I celebrate Suzanne's birthday (August 22nd) every year. She will always hold a special place in my heart.

The great thing I've discovered: *when we release our fears and regain our core balance, we can never be separated from those we love.* In my original decision to take advantage of the Soul-guided opportunity with Suzanne, I sensed the forthcoming rewards should I face and slay my inner demons. My continuing goal—then and today: to achieve the true grace and serenity so natural for my ex-wife's entire family. Not always easy, awakening to what comes naturally for our Soul selves, but more than worth the price. *We did not come to Earth to scrimp and survive, but to blossom and thrive.*

I resurrected this little trip down memory lane not to obtain sympathy for the plight of little boys, little girls, or myself—although sensitivity to a child's psychological world serves us well. The important issue, and now hopefully your seat of attention, is how *interpretation* of certain experiences—not only in childhood, but throughout our lives—can provide fuel for our internal motivations and subsequent life choices. Since unworthiness is such a common theme, I feel the import of publicly sharing my transformative process. I conclusively proved to myself there is no such thing as "ordained victimization." The emotionally delivered rejection and manipulation scenario, experienced as a 12-year-old, began my life's grand melody. It helped me maintain a search for how every person on Earth can heal and replace temporarily accepted feelings of lack and negative self-image.

A Challenge of Perception

Can you now open to at least the *possibility* of there having been perfection (higher purpose) within your adolescent happenings? Regardless of how psychologically and physically complex your life, can you consider yourself the co-designer of a carefully created Earth lesson plan? We're talking Mastery Level now, so observe with me for a few moments. You can always return to the…*"but-they-did-me-wrong"* song…if that truly serves you.

Like the ripples created by a stone tossed into a smooth lake, all persons that Celeste and I later encountered received their portion of Earth-school curriculum. An emotionally starved 13-year-old girl tried to deal with self-esteem issues by imitating behavior she witnessed from those in *her* world. That intricately interwoven manipulation was all new territory for me, however. All pain and regrets are gone now, along with the glamorous airline life that ceased to serve me after I began my awakening to Second Reality. Today, I could shift my focus between the controlled emotions a professional pilot must have *on* the job, and the free-flowing emotional depth desired in any healthy relationship. I know now it was never the job that limited me. Conflict, stress, and lack of fulfillment were fashioned from ignorance of my inner psychological dynamics. Eventually I learned the greater truth that real, permanent healing and change do not come from another person, vocation, or *anything* in the external environment. Special facilitators *do* help trigger significant *wake-up* calls, however.

Today I stand on that symbolic mountaintop largely free of negative judgments, debilitating thoughts, or depressive feelings. I can truly say I accept, love, and respect the person I've become — even when not manifesting my full potential.

You are free to reject that we — as Souls, standing beyond Earth — choose our planetary environments and pre-select certain areas for creative emphasis. What you are then left with is classic victimization; including random fate, God, and/or the devil's will, as the continuing explanation for both the creativity and tragedy of Earth life. I know this is controversial, but ask yourself which perspective serves you at this time in your life: God/devil dictates, or human/Soul choices? What I encapsulate, here, is a condensed appreciation for the empowering difference between dictatorial *commandments from* God, and the preexisting potential so generously *gifted by* God — whether we be a Soul-Being, a Human-Being, or all of the above.

As my childhood story illustrated, we find it difficult to embrace idealized, all-inclusive empowerment principles in our reward-and-punishment-conditioned culture. Consider how our early, behavioristic-based educational system intensifies relationship difficulties. Imagine what joy early schooling would bring for a curious, eager student who receives only *encouragement* for what is correct, and therefore *never criticized* (RED X) for those portions still awaiting mastery. This more supportive system is currently being field-tested in a small sampling of public schools. It's called "Inspired Learning (inspiredlearning.org)," and it's getting fantastic results. In the traditional model, young children are taught that *right and wrong* judgment is the most important foundation for successfully functioning in society. Most courts of law establish whether an accused person understands these dualistic opposites before they can be found *sane* and qualified to stand trial. So, we as a society take a census of the majority opinion, while those in authority — at any given moment — decide what rules and laws to establish for governing our citizens.

Our *anointed ones* also determine appropriate punishments of those in violation of rules and laws. All quite arbitrary…a minority of leaders decide what is moral and decent for the majority. Fortunately, a democratic society comprises a degree of checks and balances. But we continually wrestle with what some desire as universal moral codes, and what others want as independent rights to free choice. One person's *sinful* activity is often another's *private act between consenting adults.* Shifts in the designated moral center of human behavior are more noticeable in free societies. In the West, we arbitrate only the most inflexible issues of right and wrong—good and bad. With this dualistic focus, competition and belief in lack and limitation generally overshadow acceptance of multiple, all-inclusive realities and the liberating benefits of mutual cooperation and shared abundance.

Right and Wrong vs. Varietal Experience

Imagine that you have always owned the same kind of nice, comfortable, multi-purpose shoes…for walking, working, and everyday activities. You appreciate their practicality and the way they look and feel. In the past, every time your shoes became worn, you replaced them with an identical type. All your acquaintances agree on your footwear's acceptable appearance and functional norm. You comfortably walk and run in the standard issue, and all your friends use the same type of shoe—with very little variance.

One day, you awake to inexplicable boredom with your societal *clogs.* While looking through a French magazine, you notice a completely new shoe design. Intrigued, and since you now grow weary of your regular shoes, you order two pair of these bright, shiny, pumps, with 3½-inch heels and pointed toes.

When you receive and try on the stylish footwear for the first time, you're unable to maintain stability. After sufficient practice, you adjust to the required balancing act that's part-and-parcel of their use. Although they tend to pinch your toes, you love their radical design— so different from the common, everyday shoe. When you wear your *sparklers* in public the first time, everyone is shocked. "How horrible!" they say, aghast at your brazen effort to be different. They repeatedly ridicule your choice: "You can't run in them, or even walk in them very well," they adamantly declare. "Your legs look funny and misshapen. Those shoes are ugly and inferior—only a sadist would make such grotesque and torturous footwear," friends say. Steadfast and practical, your feminist acquaintances play the same tune with, "Those shoes certainly were not designed by a woman!" They tell you it's *bad* and *wrong* for you to wear those shoes, instead of the nice, practical, comfortable, *normal and acceptable*, standard shoes.

Your well-meaning friends, with rare exception, demand to know your logical reasons for wearing such ugly, uncomfortable, fundamentally different footwear. You silently wonder if this intense resistance is due to jealousy of your courage to express yourself differently — daring to stand out from the crowd.

Consider how the fancy French shoes are neither *bad* nor *wrong* — even *if* uncomfortable — just different. You choose the road-less-traveled even after your selection proves publicly unpopular, labeling you a subject of ridicule. You urgently want more variety in your everyday experience, even if resulting in anguish and rejection. After all, you do not demand anyone else wear high-heeled shoes.

As it would happen, one person quietly comes over and invites you to a mysterious, *secret-society* gathering. This underground assembly comprises others who, like yourself, wish to express themselves differently. You happily accept both the invitation and the implied support. Upon joining the festivities, you delight in seeing virtually all the women and even some of the men in similarly elevated footwear. Various kinds of exotic clothing and adornments, most of which you've never seen before, are also on display. Practically all the specially invited guests report painful rejection experiences associated with public use of their expressive ornaments, but enjoy them anyway because of the intensity of varied experience. This courageous grouping rejoices in their shared association, even though they risk discovery by the main majority, certain ostracism, and possible morality charges.

The details of this little parable represent — I'm intuitively told — a simplistic version of the Soul's perspective on experiential Earth life. Souls enjoy *every* human experience — not just the *comfortable* ones. The animalistic human perspective sees all pain as bad...all pleasure...good. The first thing most of us do when we have a headache is take an aspirin, even though irrefutable, empirically-based evidence proves that *headaches are not caused by a lack of aspirin*. We generally just treat the symptom(s), returning as soon as possible to pain-free pleasure, instead of taking time to discover the true cause of our discomfort. Later we think ourselves *unlucky* when our symptom-treating, instant-gratification lifestyle results in serious, even irrevocable dis-ease. Taking imbalance to the extreme ensures human suffering.

Revenge and Justice

Consider that choosing a life obsessed with revenge, to reach any type of personal or societal comfort zone, prolongs our life as a victim to the offending perpetrator. Although there may be a temporary feeling of satisfaction from gratuitous revenge, it rarely, by itself, results in the closure and return to a joyful life we ultimately desire. The following narrative represents an all-too-common scenario.

The Gibson Family

Various studies conducted by psychologists and other behaviorists have followed the experiences of intimate family members who lost loved ones through the heinous crimes of another. Take the example of Mrs. Gibson, suffering the loss of a daughter that was tortured prior to being murdered. I think we would be hard pressed to imagine a scenario more horrific.

Mrs. Gibson's grieving process is stuck on hold since the perpetrator has not yet been identified. Told by well-meaning friends and professional caregivers that being frozen in the grief process is to be expected, she waits until there is *satisfaction* in the case before resuming any healing regimen. The parent, predisposed toward justice, accepts this edict. With a wretchedly aching heart, she awaits action by the police.

Finally, a prime suspect is identified and a nationwide search begins. Mrs. Gibson continues the vigil while the newspapers and television stations report daily on this sensational case, even with nothing new to disclose. She remains fixed on the need for *revenge and justice* for her departed child. Because of this outer focus—which most of society agrees appropriate—feelings of revenge override and mask her underlying emotions of remorse, guilt, shame, and regret.

After a year of continual stress, and the resulting deterioration of her health, Mrs. Gibson learns the suspect has been captured. The surviving family rejoices! "This will be over soon and you'll be able to go on with the rest of your lives," they are all told. Mrs. Gibson continues as parent *"in waiting."*

The hearings to determine competency, depositions, and various legal motions take six more months. Due to the heavy publicity in this sensationalized case, the defense wins its argument for a venue change and the trial moves to an adjacent county. Having not worked for eighteen months, Mrs. Gibson's financial reserves are kaput. Two victim's rights groups step forward to provide a temporary family residence in the trial city, but to cover her travel and food expenses, she takes out a high-interest equity mortgage on the personal homestead. Other family members do the same. They accept the prosecutor's imperative that they must be prominently visible to favorably impress judge and jury. The grieving process for the parent and family sits on the *back burner*, pending the trial outcome. With continuous motion filings and delays for appellate decisions on judge's rulings, the trial lasts a grueling 10 months. Weeks were consumed with voluminous and labor-intensive presentations of expert witnesses, charts, graphs, and other evidence. Mrs. Gibson attends every session. The horrific details of the rape, torture, and murder are nearly overwhelming. Then…the concluding insult: To try and impugn the integrity of the young, teenage victim, the defense parades one deprecating character witness after another.

The emotional pain and torture of this final defensive ploy proves more than the parent can endure, and she collapses in court. Rushed to the hospital, Mrs. Gibson's doctor diagnoses her malnutrition, extreme fatigue, dehydration, and complications from high blood pressure. Against doctor's orders, she continues to watch the trial on Court TV. Mrs. Gibson lives *only* for the moment the judicial system *judges* the guilty party. The tremendous pressure of holding on to pent-up emotion continues to take its toll—regardless of medical intervention. "Surely the end is near," the family members advise. "*Then* you will have closure."

The defendant's family has substantial resources. Competent, high-profile attorneys present a strong defense and neutral observers are not surprised when the jury ends up hopelessly deadlocked. The judge, sympathetic to the victim's family, sadly declares a mistrial. More than devastated, the victim's family feels the justice system failed them.

After almost three years, Mrs. Gibson still receives no satisfaction from *justice*—alleged to be required for closure and the continuation of her life. During brief, reflective moments spent addressing her emotions, she feels even more bitterness toward the defendant, the justice system, and especially God—the One *most* responsible for this miscarriage. Mrs. Gibson goes home to await the new trial. As foreclosure is imminent, she returns to the workplace to forestall loss of the family residence. Unfortunately her work performance is substandard, and after several warnings, management terminates her employment with a small severance check as a parting gift. Sympathetic employees take up a collection to assist their fallen comrade with moving expenses to a room offered in the home of a friend. The former principal residence, and adored rallying point, is surrendered to the Mortgage Company.

Suffering Continues

After six additional months, the new trial begins *without* the victim's principal supporter. Mrs. Gibson can no longer afford the travel expense. The county of jurisdiction provides supportive funds only for actual witnesses. The second tribunal does not have the same level of sensationalism as did the first. Not surprisingly, the prosecuting AND victim's aid budgets conform to the reduced media interest. With great frustration, the family gets their new trial updates from the now less-than-committed media.

The codependent, albeit supportive, family members feel guilty about losing patience with their mother. Most of them wish to grieve, heal, and go on with their lives. But Mrs. Gibson reminds her clan of their earlier declaration that closure and *moving on* are not possible until justice is served. She admonishes them for not showing more loyalty to the memory of their deceased sister: "How can any of you lead productive, *happy,* fulfilling lives while this travesty awaits redemption?" Martyred and estranged, loneliness and deep depression are her only companions.

The new trial starts and ends with less public prostrating and more expediency than the first. Mrs. Gibson and a few supportive — less estranged — family members travel upstate for the final arguments. Because of continued public sentiment over the victimized family, they are granted two state-provided hotel rooms.

The jury deliberates for seven, long days. Anguished families wait, on both sides of the aisle. Finally, the jury completes its exhaustive examination and declares its verdict — GUILTY AS CHARGED! The victimized family members, relieved beyond expression, assert, "Finally justice, closure, and a return to normal life."

Mother reminds them this is just phase One in the justice process. They must be ever diligent to prevent the defense from beating the death penalty, surely deserved for the *monster* that sucked life out of a vibrant and beloved young girl. "*Then* we can say there has been justice," is the cry from the still intensely bitter and pained Mrs. Gibson. The surviving clan's earlier enthusiasm quickly evaporates. Some sense correctly that the nightmare is still in its early stages. After another excruciating three weeks, including instructional motions, character witnesses, influential posturing by both sides, and mutual hanging out of the obligatory dirty linen, the judge declares the **death penalty**. Family members, more relieved than satisfied, feel grave concern for their mother. Mrs. Gibson has no interest in life and appears emotionally dead. During the long, arduous process, her life *became* the facts and events preparatory to trial. Still no letup in sight, the family finds the appellate process takes years—something the prosecuting attorneys failed to brief them on earlier. So, for twelve more years, Mrs. Gibson lives for the day the guilty man is to be put to death.

The family is coached on how to play the important political game. They are instructed to keep the pressure on at home, so that elected officials do not forget the severity of the crime and the innocent victims left in its wake.

Mrs. Gibson attends all the hearings, continually prodding the sensationalistic media to retell the gruesome story. Politicians, with their feet kept to the fire, resist every attempt to reverse the order for the death penalty.

Out of the blue, the murderer asks for a consult with Mrs. Gibson. He wishes to answer questions, define circumstances, and ask for forgiveness. The state representative labels this a ploy to gain public sympathy and a reversal of the death order. Although Mrs. Gibson feels something deep within urging her to meet, the sit-down is never consummated. She goes to her death regretting that decision. While all attempts to help Mrs. Gibson release the consuming anguish go for naught, time ticks on.

Slowly…agonizingly…execution day arrives. Regardless of not staying the intensely negative course demanded by their mother, previously estranged family members make the pilgrimage to the state's lethal-termination facilities. They earnestly hope the execution brings relief and final closure to this sad, sad, chapter of life—in time for final good-byes. No surprise…Mrs. Gibson is terminally ill from a rapidly spreading cancer. *"So many victims—so little time."*

The execution chamber is made available to select media, family members, and certain state witnesses. As the curtain pulls back, the convicted, now middle-aged man visibly cries—but not out of fear. While fighting to control his emotions, he stammers an almost incoherent apology to the stoically frozen survivors: "I hope my death brings some measure of peace and solace to your family." To absolve them from any implied responsibility and to ask for forgiveness, he then turns to his own disheartened parents: "I am so sorry for letting you down and for not being the good, untroubled son you hoped for and deserved." With those final words, the IV drip began. After a few moments, and just one, large, convulsion, the repentant fiend was gone. With nothing more to see, the press and the state witnesses beat a hasty retreat—some urgently needing to visit the facilities. Final closure at hand, in a disembodied voice, Mrs. Gibson utters one statement: "It's over…I can leave now."

This once-vivacious, energetic, hopeful, loving parent, a shell of her former self, said not one more intelligible word. Emotionally and physically shattered, she slipped into a coma three days later, and passed within two weeks.

After Healing Comes Realization

The surviving offspring now had to fend for themselves. In time, they realized their ordeal as not *only* horrific, but also an extremely important lesson. In totality, values shifted as they opened to an emotional understanding of the futility of putting their lives on hold. They recognized the uselessness of looking to outside events, such as justice and revenge, for inner healing or personal salvation. They committed to never repeat their mother's ongoing victimization. After a healthy grief process for the passing of their beloved mother, the Gibson family began to see their tragedy from a more expansive perspective. They sensed a great empowerment welling up within them in direct proportion to their ability to value the experiential lesson. As the bonds between the remaining siblings strengthened, they shared the more positive purpose to their long, arduous journey.

The transformed family members stopped seeing themselves as victims of a horrific crime, or as *survivors*. Rather than interpret the lives of their departed sister and mother as wasted, they gradually experienced new appreciations for life. With a newly emerging transcendent perspective, they speculated whether their mother's Soul wished this experience for its intensity and opportunity it provided to the Gibson offspring to discover higher and larger realizations.

From the Soul perspective this supposition was true, but incomplete. The preferred scenario was for the mothering one to *also* awaken to these all-inclusive truths. Because of her exclusive focus on self-absorbed negativity, Mrs. Gibson did not act on the not-so-subtle background influences from Soul. She repeatedly ignored her deeper and insightful thoughts and feelings in deference to revenge and a distorted obligation to the memory of a departed child.

The surviving family members shared their discovery of a new, positive, empowering process with the family of the executed man. The deep, personal dialogue led to awakening and healing for the other family as well. They appreciatively expressed mutual forgiveness; not because it was politically correct, but because both families genuinely desired it. New friendships formed as the bonding circle expanded.

Several surviving siblings began writing and speaking of their experiences while recreating their lives anew. Invited to various talk shows, they inspired millions to see extreme challenge differently. Viewers and listeners began taking more personal responsibility in their own lives—*and the Souls rejoiced!*

After such devastating adversity, this embodied the highest possible outcome. Miraculous breakthroughs occurred because members of both families selected healthier choices. Of course they received supportive help (as we all do) from a team of loving entities, operating within and without the amnesiac veil. The family members were glorified in the Soul realm, which includes *all*. The cosmic adulation included those two individualistic rays of the Infinite that had expressed as mother and daughter.

Perhaps now you can at least *imagine* why a loving Soul would volunteer for *hazardous duty* here on Earth. Souls continue to support us in remembering that no power, entity, or manifested event—anywhere in the Universe—can damage our true Being. Being Eternal, the Universe provides us unlimited opportunities to awaken to the higher expressions of Earth life.

"The *fairytale* outcome of the Gibson family seems too good to be true. How do you justify this *SoulMan?*" you ask. Would you prefer it too *bad* to be true? All this is testable. You don't have to accept my words—or *blind faith*—to prove the validity of these principles. Test the various perspectives in your own life.

Which serves you better? ❶ The suffering, *poor-me* victim scenario with everyone expressing their subjective pity and agreeing how cruel and unlucky life is—especially for you? A life lived from this perspective often results in the powerless, suffering misery depicted by Mrs. Gibson. Or, ❷ allowing the possibility of that previously proffered perfection—a miracle found within *every* experience if you care to prod beneath its surface?

As ones who *chose* Earth, and carefully crafted a unique blueprint for life, each challenge area offers us a character-defining, strength-building moment. Yes, we do—from time to time—get our proverbial butts kicked. But what prevents us from standing up, dusting off, and beginning the trek up the mountain again? Do you wish to be defined by fear of failure, or the false belief in not being enough?

Try these opposing perspectives—actually live them in your everyday expression. See which viewpoint and its resulting quality of life suits your needs. Again, no right or wrong here—just a choice and the corresponding consequence.

Human Reality or Subjective Choice?

As much as I am tempted to leave this tough subject with the nice, pretty ribbon wrapped around the package of "and they all lived happily ever after"...I can't. I feel the need to be honest with all viewpoints and that means I must be a First Reality realist—if *only* for a moment.

In a perfectly enlightened reality, we would immediately move on from any personal crisis—no matter how grievous—with a great Soul-like appreciation for how nothing is ever lost to us. As a Soul, perhaps we can experience the physical torture and murder of an Earth-bound loved one and incorporate it as another valuable and meaningful (although not preferred) experience. In a dualistic world of cause and effect, this perspective is rarely if ever considered.

First Reality Response...a Human Certainty?

I intuitively hear some of you shout, "Get *real*, SoulMan," when I describe the recovery process of the surviving Gibson family members. I imagine those dissenting declarants following their expletives with the following diatribe.

> *"Let's see how you'd deal with it if it were **your** daughter raped and murdered. How high and mighty would you be if one of those precious dogs of yours was soaked in lighter fluid and set on fire (similar to an actual crime committed in Los Angeles in 1999)? Are you telling us you would not be consumed with thoughts of revenge? You're not so tough now, are you buddy? It's real easy to espouse beautiful philosophy from your ivory pedestal. In the real world, it's DOG-EAT-DOG!"*

Ok, **yes**, I might temporarily wallow in First Reality knee-jerk, including the full spectrum of negative human emotions. But *then*, I feel the depth of belief in everything I've shared with you, *to not let negative experiences ultimately define me*. Determination to heal, not the product a stubborn ego or cultural imperative, but from a genuine love of life and a knowing that the *Eternal connection* to a deceased loved one can never be damaged or lost. I cannot sit here in a negative hypothetical and tell you exactly how much time I would require, but I emphatically refuse to look at emotional pain as my enemy. Healing and replacement takes whatever time I choose to give it. Stuck in revenge mode, I would *never* heal. I might numb or bury the painful feelings, but never truly heal, release, reframe, and replace them. The ensuing powerlessness would characterize my human existence, and I would likely go to the end with bitterness still stuck in my craw.

Now let me ask *you* a question. How would righteous indignation and revenge-oriented retaliatory images and related actions serve me, you, our friends, or family? Self-sabotage is a significant consequence of negatively expressing ego, as well as a direct reflection of one's weakened self-image. Circumstances so perceived typify why many Eastern, meditative traditions consider the *ego* the enemy of a prospective enlightened one. When stuck in First Reality appearances, an "eye-for-an-eye" represents the only apparent semblance of illusionary power. This includes relentless attempts at psychological manipulation of those who push our internal buttons. Wise ones who walked this path before us have said: *"Lusting for revenge, or holding a grudge, is like swallowing poison and waiting for the other person to die."*

In opening to Second and some level of Third Reality awareness, I now connect to *all* life. This includes my deceased father's essence, and all I love and experience—whether physically on Earth or not. I feel their essential quality of Spirit, both in my heart and throughout my entire Being. No longer is anything lost to me.

Even with all the detractors, this is my current World perspective. Ours is a Universe full of love, joy, adventure, and creative opportunity. To not embrace life fully and completely is like being invited to a magnificent feast, containing a multitude of delectable delights, but having only lettuce. Whatever the scope of the feast you currently sample, I assure you many more selections reside on life's menu. If it serves you, I will continue as your *banquet maitre d'* as we unearth your bountiful array of preexisting potential and open to the awesome continuity and synchronism of life.

In addition to reflective reviewing of our behavior, the second key to Earth "Soup Pot" Mastery?—the releasing of judgment. In our next shared chapter we learn how to accomplish that liberating feat.

CHAPTER NINE

Releasing Judgment and Separation
Embracing Unity

♥   ♥   ♥

Unconditional Love — the Real Deal. Several years before the Escondido Intervention, I was given a very practical demonstration on how mental and emotional squeezing represses love connections. The full import of the following narrative took a while before sinking in. I told you I was slow…but also determined.

I had the good fortune to be accepted as a volunteer with the Opportunity Village, in Las Vegas, Nevada. This fine organization is mandated to train and support those persons with Down 's syndrome (DS). The first time they escorted me into the main workshop room and campaign button factory, I experienced what *real* unconditional and ego-free love was all about. Having never seen me before, and knowing only that I was there to help their organization, several of the *so-called* mentally handicapped residents walked right up and welcomed me with the most enthusiastic and heart-felt hugs I've ever been blessed to receive. As human *heartbeats,* they possessed not a hint of fear or standoffish behavior. Their love was freely given without self-serving expectation.

Give or Take? I had always prided myself on my ability to spot scoundrels during common human interaction. In Las Vegas casinos, and perhaps gambling halls throughout the world, they have a saying: "Are you *giving* action (the sucker) or *getting* action (the beneficiary)?" After my initial meeting with those DS folks, I began asking myself some pre-transformational questions.

- **Is loss of intimacy (heart) the price I pay for my determination to never (again) be conned or hustled by those pretending to love?**

- **While continually scanning for possible energy *muggers*, do I miss the color, beauty, and texture of everyday life?**

- **Is my "never-be-a-sucker" cleverness contributing to my intermittent bouts with loneliness and depression?**

When answering these questions, I realized the "Village" also extended an opportunity to me. My ah-*ha* enlightenment bulb focused its laser beam on the quality-of-life consequences of emotional aloofness, or ego-only intellect. Time to upgrade my emotional IQ!

The uncomplicated DS workers owned none of these limitations. As a result, their lives were pure, unadulterated, and much less stressful. In the throes of first contact, I could not fully grasp why I felt intimidated by their freely given intimacy. Later it occurred to me: *I was the handicapped one.* Could these special Down's syndrome *masters-of-love* persons be here on Earth for a special reason? Have they tasked themselves to teach an anxious and fearful humanity the wonderful benefits of eliminating psychological barriers to love?

As our individually expressed Spiritual DNA actualizes, we open to a much deeper understanding of the revered mystics. We feel freedom, liberation from victimization, and the lifting of burden. For me to join this progressive shift-track, I first had to heal my feelings of inadequacy. Escape options were dying, as I continued peeling back the layers of my worthiness issues.

Negative emotions of anger, jealousy, envy, and possessiveness represent fear-based imbalances—not truths—although troubling thoughts and feelings may appear truthful. Our true Being embodies only love and the byproducts of love—joy, happiness, goodness, peace, and harmoniously creative free-flow. Once acknowledged and shared with others, distorted thoughts and feelings are potentially released, reframed, and replaced by a sea of gratitude; an appreciation that reveals one's true magnificence. Although there are no "Star Wars," the Force, itself, lies truly within us.

Consider again my previously stated premise that we are not here on Earth as an assignment from God, or to *perform* for God. Nor is God, or any other Supreme Being, judging our actions. Instead, if you suggested the forces of the Eternal intimately observe, participate in, and even animate our life-force energy, I would unequivocally agree. Most cultures repeatedly pound on us to accept that judgment day is coming, and that God, or some other representative (St. Peter, etc.), determines our afterlife future based on whether we've been good or bad. The Santa Claus *"naughty or nice"* approval list patterns after this pronouncement. Conditional-love definitions are a major reason why so many choose agnosticism, atheism, or *God-fear-ism*. These three diverse groupings don't normally manifest because of their inability or unwillingness to believe in some form of love-based higher power, but because of the *definitions* for God they feel compelled to accept—or else. Many continue to search for an Eternal (NOT external) source of power in which they can believe—one that uplifts and inspires from within. And not as indentured servants or programmed puppets dancing on some celestial string, but as non-judged, independently expressing co-creators.

Throughout much of human history, excepting the mystical Pagan, Hermetic, and Gnostic periods, existing authorities extolled our unworthiness while commanding that we not expect to know any supreme deity directly. They either implied or downright stated the God Force had instituted some arbitrary *chain-of-command* to meter out its power and influence.

Might it now be time for us to awaken to our true power, potency, and synergistic connection to *ALL* life, including the holographic cosmos? Consider that we—as Spiritual Beings—designed our ingredients for Earth life. We are not accidental manifestations or sacrificial meals boiling in some cosmic soup pot. A fundamentalist persuasion may label a person giving credence to an unconditionally loving God as "a *sinner* looking for an easy form of salvation." Here we have the same world, but with different interpretations of the meaning and purpose to life. If believing your human or Soul existence to be dualistically separate from Universal Energy Forces (God), then you stressfully choose between two (dualism or monism) diametrically opposed foundations of belief.

Throughout the world, we generally follow the one-god principle (monotheism). Most persons of monotheistic belief, however, believe God this mysterious, *separate* Force that we are never intended to know. From history it seems polytheistic pagans enjoyed a much closer relationship with their deities. From an *all-inclusive*, monistic perspective, all pathways serve their intended purpose. Opening to this more inclusive potential propels you on your way without further need for arm twisting or other forms of suffering debate between *the good, the bad, and the ugly.*

God as Energy

Again, let us perceive God as this humongous power generator—supplying the foundational energy that animates all life. Just like the electricity many of us enjoy everyday, we have the choice of utilizing the energy flux *constructively* or *destructively*. We can use it to bring light and animation to the world, or to electrocute ourselves. After the vocalized expletives, when we accidentally put our hand on a hot stove, do we spend a lot of time deciding whether the stove is good or bad? We learn to pay more attention to the heating element so we don't burn ourselves again. If we fool around with a defective circuit and accidentally shock ourselves, do we say; "*Bad* electricity...leave the wall Satan?" In past times of Earth, before familiarizing ourselves with electrical properties, we would have likely interpreted being shocked as punishment from God or the work of the devil.

Personally, I do not perceive God a separate SHE, HE, or IT. Nor do I think of God as good or bad. In my world, God just *is*. And **"is"** means *all the above*. I respect God as a provided Force I can use to joyously turn on the lights (FUN life), or plunge myself into suffering darkness (SUCK life).

For this place and time, you need only decide which perspective works for you. Can you feel how much more love and creativity you can open to with your life force *not* being discharged through the moralistic judging of another person's belief? The following passages illustrate some of the ways we utilized our energy choices in the past. For some, this may be a difficult segment.

Slave Creation 101 - "Original Sin."

Lines continue to be drawn in the sand as many of us stay separated and Spiritually disenfranchised. For thousands of years, the reigning authority used fear and superstition to control the masses. If we accept this type of leadership now, we doom ourselves to continued victimization and more bowing and scraping as we try earning our way to salvation and/or Heaven by adherence to rules set by Earth authorities. Authorities who often — out of their *love* — use the fear of God like a bullwhip flogged across our backsides.

Even today, many well-received authority figures perpetuate fear-based myths of a vengeful, wrathful, judgmental god. Some cult leaders keep their followers ignorant of more empowering perspectives, as the uninformed are easier to manage. "Salvation later" proves an effective tool for *flock* control. Could some of this authority-insistent manipulation be motivated by the fear of what would happen to their sequestered congregation if previously submissive masses became enlightened? What if followers developed into strong, self-empowered, independently thinking leaders in their own right? Are segments of authority, as well as ourselves, culturally predisposed against opening to more expansive, inclusive, allowing, purely love-based theologies? Some leaders still use an exclusive combination of love/reward and fear/punishment as their motivational imperative. How do you respond to those that suggest you are a weak, puny, undeserving, half-person, needing their (or God's) pity, approval, and forgiveness?

Consider both *approval and guidance from the forces of the Eternal as constantly ongoing and never conditional.* If we are not separate from the Collective (or God), how can Spiritual Guidance and loving cosmic acceptance ever fail to be with us? How would you benefit if forgiveness and salvation were decreed internal matters fully within your realm of influence? "A bit more empowering," you say? Your use of caring facilitators—including clergy—as tools for your healing and transformation, keeps the ball firmly in your court.

Most orthodox religions still adhere to their principal that we were born in immortal ("Original") sin, and are therefore Spiritually impure. They tell us we should confess and beg forgiveness for humanity's or our own pre-birth wrongdoing, to achieve the salvation *they* consider a requirement to enter Heaven. These creeds require a lifetime of faithful tithing to support the respective church, synagogue, temple, mosque, etc., *and* to ensure good standing on *judgment* day. Consider the more-empowering perspective proffered by Toltec Facilitator and Life Coach, Allan Hardman: **"NON-judgment-day is at hand."**

Many religions, including some of the most popular theologies in the West, espouse how it is a sin to love life more than God. How can the passionate loving of life and its creations not be one of the greatest gifts we could bestow on the Divine forces? If never separate from the Eternal, by loving life fully and completely we celebrate those very forces *with us* and *as us*, do we not?

Perhaps some of my discordant challenge here lies in the definition, "loving life." If we go through our entire human existence expressing only selfishly greedy desires and materialistic, fear-based thoughts, feelings, and actions, we are not manifesting our highest potential. An unconditionally loving Soul-God perspective judges this neither bad nor wrong—just small. As suffering ones can certainly testify, the consequence of living a negatively oriented life is a self-created hell.

Differing beliefs and interpretations—all subjective—illustrate just a few of the ways we allow ourselves to be divided and made confrontational with one another. One of the more striking examples: "My god is bigger, better, tougher, and more righteous than your god." Apparently *size* does matter in much of the religious community.

When we take rigid, inflexible positions inherent in absolute-truth dogma — then defend them to the teeth to avoid being proven wrong — conflict, separateness, and suffering are common byproducts. All this is part of the dualistic First Reality world that humanity, in slave and victim roles, has been subject to for thousands of generations. Now time to rejoice…liberation day is upon us!

In case you wonder, I no longer take issue with *any* religion — whether I agree with a particular theology, or not. Today, I can and do enjoy attending all love-based religious services. I appreciate the positive energy that brings folks together for deeper connections and the amplified effort to make the world a better place. I admit I have not primarily focused on political correctness — especially the last few pages. If you recall, I promised a guide to facilitate the *releasing* of those shackles that bind us to emotional, psychological, and Spiritual victimization (slavedom). I point out some major examples, including the religious arena, where we humans bought into *unworthiness of love*. Even the God-fearing religious sects are in business, not because of God, but because of people that support them. They obviously serve many and I strongly support free choice and firmly believe in inclusivity. Consider how the multiplicity of faiths can benefit you even more, however, if you keep your mind open to an ongoing (reflective) examination. If you require an eminent expert to validate this previous point, take Socrates, the respected Greek philosopher. He said, *"An unexamined life is not worth living."*

My belief in inclusiveness releases me from emphasizing right and wrong — good and bad judgment. I've largely purged my previous issues with philosophies and perspectives that fail to serve me.

Defending ourselves and our way of life without going over the line, forcing other cultures how to think, feel, and act, invites an improbable balance for those expressing exclusively from First Reality. In the past, feigned respect exacted the price of fear-based coercion. Human suffering — whether global or in family relationships — ends when we awaken to the empowerment and liberation in freely and lovingly respecting each other's right to seek respective pathways. Releasing emotional fear makes way for additional inflow of blessed love-energy, and allows the mind, body, and spirit to flourish. The knowledge that true respect is not obtained from another, but something found only within one's self, lies undiscovered by fear-based gang youth, today's terrorists, and world leaders intent on bombing their way to security. Embracing harmony supplies the recipe for mastering relationships; and ultimately life itself. Fortunately we don't have to wait for the rest of the world's population to "get it" before enjoying our own liberation.

My continuing purpose: to assist those ready to get unstuck from the muck of self-diminishment. The transitional process we attempt is certainly not for everyone. I don't have to remind you that Earth is a tough school, with nothing inherently *wrong* or *bad* in being a psychological slave. In one form or another, we have been good slaves for tens of thousands of years. If, however, you've had enough of the standard grade-school, revolving-door types of classes and are ready to choose some elective courses for a change, then stay the course. You may be ready to add a *hacksaw* to your tool kit for cutting through the ball-and-chain limitation of dualistic perspective. This is the time and place to reveal how truly exalted you are in the Universe. No more fooling around…it's time someone told you the truth about *how great thou art* from the viewpoint of unconditionally loving Souls.

It feels appropriate to remind readers that my brief and (some would say) critical overview of religious philosophical dogma is most certainly subjective—just like all opinion. Many theologians strongly disagree—at least publicly—with my premise that being in God's grace and power is much less complicated and quantified than we've generally been told. Notwithstanding any revolutionary implications, I certainly do not suggest we throw the baby out with the bath water through wholesale nullification of one's existing faith. But we *can* be more open, allowable, and inclusive. Could this have been the original message delivered by Allah to the prophet Muhammad, which led to the Koran, Mecca, and the nation of Islam? Intuitively follow your inner guidance to the healing and salvation awaiting actualization. In other words, *keep* the baby, but *change* the stale water. As you consider your options, be assured, again, that no one exclusively owns Divinity. No person or group can block your access to the forces of Creation…without your acquiescence.

Congruency of Life's Purpose vs. Outside Motivations

Even before we kept any official body counts, it was generally known that throughout human history, we tortured and killed more humans pitting one god definition against another, than from any other motivation. In another more-modern example of First Reality cultural programming, some so-called New-Age relationship gurus suggest you must find your one special Soul mate to be truly happy and fulfilled in life. Some "ex-spurts" call it normal to be an incomplete, wandering, half person until one finds his or her "other half." Listen to just about any love song—especially the old style country music— and you'll hear our strong identification with codependency. The implication is we should not expect to feel complete and fulfilled while on our own personal pathway. Our cultural norm is to seek outside validation to feel worthy of peace, harmony, joy, goodness, happiness, and LOVE. This so-called *normal* way of thinking and feeling does not exactly rouse an endorsement for self-empowerment. If it serves you to believe in structured dogma, conflict, self-imposed separation and codependent relationships, then rejoice. No further enlightenment is necessary or perhaps even desired. There is nothing *bad* or *wrong* with your decision. Only you can decide if that choice is less than your full capability. If, on the other hand, you believe that living a life as fodder for others, while being controlled, manipulated, told not to question authority, etc., sucks *big time* (pardon the crass pun), then might "we" respectfully suggest you awaken and further actualize your preexisting potential? Human history demonstrates that any structure that attempts to keep humanity divided and feeling powerless and alone does not serve us—unless we desire murder, mayhem, or today's lonely antidepressant existence. A higher truth can be shared now. As descendants from Creation...**YE ARE GOD!**

Not saying we currently express the entirety of our God potential, but we are—in stages—actualizing it. Consider your rightful place, not as a complacent slave, but as co-creator. I believe it the height of *blasphemy* to teach that we were created only to be servants and followers rather than creators and leaders. We can choose to take our power back from the naysayers, just as we chose to give it away. That Human Beings can ultimately be denied their potential holds true only if one fails to claim his or her right to self-determination. In the face of all this earthly abundance, uninspired manifestations represent only the *appearance* of scarcity and lack—not the higher truth.

The new powering-up process requires healing those underlying unworthiness issues, which then allows actualization of preexisting potential. As a reminder, a process that can prove helpful is to mentally and emotionally acknowledge distorted thoughts and feelings. Courageously enter them—fully and completely—for a few moments, before venting, releasing, reframing, and beginning the habit of replacement. You can even exaggerate the fear by imagining the worst-case scenario, for a short while. Through this process, we build courage and learn that nothing ever damages our true Being—the opposite of ignoring and *stuffing* negative issues. If numbed denial had worked in the past, you would not have ongoing challenges and that disparaging, mental self-critic in your life today. Use the venting, healing, releasing, reframing, and replacement series whenever you feel the need. Combine it with the Holographic Fear-Dancing Technique. Share those temporarily debilitating feelings with a trusted friend who will just *listen*, rather than try to fix you. You can and will fix yourself—thank you very much! If you *need* salvation, and you'll be the only entity requiring it, you can learn to turn within and forgive yourself.

Awakening to *advanced* Second Reality awareness makes this and all other psychological processes moot. At this totally reflective level you simply thank the Universe for all your learning, growing, awakening opportunities. All challenge, no matter how difficult, facilitates opening an empowered recipient to more and more of his or her magnificence. Creation supports us in this discovery of our authentic inner power. Only *love* is real and permanent; it represents who we truly are.

I say again, awakening to your inner potential does not necessarily call for a belief in God or any *Supreme Being*. Your acceptance of the truth that authentic love-based personal power preexists within you *maximizes* your results, however. A faith in a collective Spiritual base does—for many—provide connection and sanctuary during times of extreme challenge; like the following.

Extreme Human Challenge

Philosophizing about all this is much easier than actualizing—especially when faced with a challenge like *Christopher Reeve's*. We can see extreme difficulties as part of our life lesson plan, or as a platform for surrendering victimhood. We can hold ourselves hostage by waiting for human *justice* or some outside force to correct the inadequacies of the world, or we can choose to open to the healing power from Creation already within us. We all note that Christopher Reeve—in spite of what had been an incapacitating injury—chose *not* to be a victim. By recreating himself, he not only healed many physical and emotional feelings of loss, but he *uplifted* himself with a new path in life. Christopher, named after the Saint that protects travelers, obviously discovered a great power within—perhaps one not fully recognized until after his injury. As an actor, he directed his major focus toward *outer* expressions. At this he was quite accomplished. While stimulating and elevating himself in what became his new life role, he continues to inspire many — even *after* his Earth "graduation" and glorious transition. I share the loving observation of millions when I say Christopher Reeve evolved into an even more renowned SUPERMAN on the movie screen of LIFE, than during the *make-believe* period.

Because Christopher's injury and great struggle to survive, stabilize, and even thrive, was so public, we've been spurred to experience our own emotions in this area. Our choices include the following range of options:

❶ **Cowering in fear as we mumble "there but for the grace of God go I."**

❷ **Refusing all acknowledgment of the former Super-man, who must have been exposed to kryptonite.**

❸ **Rejoicing in amazement over the power within a Human Being when tested or otherwise motivated to fully actualize preexisting potential.**

❹ **All or none of the above.**

Quite obviously, great daily struggles (how can there not have been) existed for both Christopher and his very loving and supportive wife, Dana, who continues to experience her *own* redefining process. Christopher could have surrendered to *permanent* feelings of mournfulness and depressive melancholy, as we all can when challenged. He might have turned to drugs and alcohol to numb himself, or if denied those selections, simply withdrawn into a deep permanent despair and early death. Few would have blamed him for that choice — perhaps even distortedly agreeing nothing was left for him in his post-injury state. Many of us thought and some publicly stated that the best choice, under these circumstances, would be to arrange a painless departure — perhaps a quick call to Dr. Kevorkian.

Unconditionally loving Souls, who animate all life, remind us that a fearful suicide selection would be *extremely small* compared to the mentoring choice that Christopher and Dana *did* make. Souls wish to reassure us that human pain is temporary. Even death does not have to be the horrible ending to life that most persons envision. This more expansive and inclusive concept might be difficult to imagine by the many convinced otherwise.

[NOTE: *The controversial perspectives expressed throughout this life-guide are not intended to imply suicide a no-consequences choice. I wish only to emphasize the benefit in releasing the fear and self-deprecation that habituate an ongoing belief in Celestial judgment.*]

Although theirs (Christopher and Dana) is not a path any mortal human would volunteer for, both they and we have been immeasurably enriched by bearing witness to their recreation. We have been privy—via personal media interviews—to share the knowledge, experience, choices, and consequences rendered by this pioneering couple. Their supportive cast of friends, relatives, and volunteers have opened their homes and their hearts so we could share their incredibly transformational reanimation of the human Spirit. For me, this perfectly illustrates how we are here on Earth to co-facilitate each other's process.

From isolated, angry, mad bombers, to the Mother Teresas and all expressions in between, we each have a special function in our experiential process that transcendent medium Dr. Ron Scolastico calls the "Earth Adventure." For many of us, nothing is more fearful than the thought of being trapped inside an immobile body with a fully active mind. When terrified of pain and incapacitation even more than death, that level of fear prods us toward a different, more expanded perspective to this type of crisis. We can choose to use our fears as facilitations for healing, as well as for creating a new, more appreciative life.

If you currently suffer with crippling physical or emotional challenges, Souls remind you that after using all your latent gifts, talents, and abilities to turn what may appear to be only tragedy, into triumph, the suffering you are left with is temporary. For those in continuous physical pain, this message might not feel as reassuring as a morphine drip. *All pain and suffering*—physical, mental, emotional, and Spiritual—not purged during an Earth incarnation, is *left behind at transition.* Joy, peace, goodness, and love prove central to our expanded realms of existence.

Time Relativity

I feel blessed that the Eternal gift of conscious awareness is not limited to worlds located within space and time. I can hardly believe I graduated from high school forty-five years ago. I would now be forcibly retired had I stayed with the airlines. As a young child, it seemed I continually waited for some arbitrary chronology in order to participate in something that held my interest. Did you have that same hurry-up-and-wait sensation? Ask any older person living in a more-or-less free society—with a currently stable and pain-free everyday existence—and most will tell you that time feels like it's speeding up.

Some of us have taken on extra-tough curriculum for this lifetime, and, for those, time may seem way too slow. The best we can do is dig deep within ourselves. Try to discover the higher purpose to extreme challenge, whether physical, mental, emotional, or Spiritual. Let's listen and learn what the Christopher Reeves of the world share about thriving in an environment of extreme adversity. Be determined you will not surrender to permanent victimization. Transform yourself into the magnificent hero or heroine that you—as a Soul—envision as your highest possible achievement. Then you can say you have truly mastered this time on Earth...*and the Angels rejoice!*

Living in the Moment

This presents an excellent time to give thanks for our blessings and to remind ourselves to not take any aspect of life for granted. Live in the moment. If you want to learn how to do this, just watch any young child or animal. My dogs never carry a grudge from the day (or even minute) before. Always ready to play or work with the same enthusiasm, they always have a positive attitude. At no time do they miss an opportunity to engage in FUN. When I've fully awakened, I know I will embrace life as do my dogs. What great mentors!

Speaking of Great Mentors; let me reintroduce you to one of my two most-revered human teachers.

CHAPTER TEN

The Many Faces of Mentorship

♥　　　♥　　　♥

My Greatest Mentor. I previously introduced you to my father, Thomas (Steve) Stevens. He lived for seven years after two debilitating strokes left him partially paralyzed on his left side and unable to speak coherently. For a man of great wit and conversation, as well as an engineer/inventor who always relied on himself for success in life, his illness was—at first—quite devastating. Eventually my stepmother (Ruth) and I came to see Dad's disability as a type of blessing. It led to a more deeply loving emotional closeness with him not possible before, largely due to his lifetime of fear-based choices.

After his strokes, Dad ultimately learned to heal his old child-abandonment issues and trust others. This, in turn, allowed his emotional walls to come down. Together, we learned to release our mutual preoccupation with the seriousness of his injury. We reached the point where we all joked—especially Dad—about the advantages of paralysis. He could no longer run away from us during our love affirmations. My father learned to give and receive love in a direct way, which he fearfully avoided *prior* to the strokes. We shared the greatest hugs, tears, and intimate connection during his "disability" years, even though we could not share many words together. Spoken language became unimportant. We learned to communicate in deeper, more-cherished ways.

How often does verbal interaction get in the way of real heart communication? In the past, I often used my gift for words to push people and love away. I would remain safely sequestered away in my head, through analytical contemplation. By creating this inward avoidance procedure, like my dear father did before me, I denied myself true intimacy. I witnessed Dad's great post-stroke example of turning inside to psychologically heal, release, and recreate his presence. As a result of my choice to follow in my father's liberating footsteps, I continue to break the *big boys don't cry* myth in my own life. This recovering left-brainer lives more and more in his heart. As a result, I appreciate life more and more.

Although my father made his glorious transition in 1989, I often feel his presence and know he is not lost to me (Chapter 15). I learned intuitively, via Dad's great emotional embraces, one of the main reasons why we as Souls participate in this reality. Something very special and unique exists within the intensity of shared physical love—whether expressed with a parent, child, mate, beloved pet, or any other segment of nature. What a loss it would have been to *call Dr. Kevorkian* and not experience those final and best gifts of affection shared by father to son, and stepson to stepmother. These were bestowments very unlikely to be exchanged with the unworthiness-of-love issue my father still struggled with prior to his vascular strokes.

Suicide Alternative

I use "Dr. Kevorkian" here as an illustrative metaphor. I do not pass judgment on the Doctor, or the assisted-suicide issue. For you wonderful caregivers entrusted with the responsibility of counseling those *considering* assisted-suicide, and you probe for a motivational theme, contemplate the following.

Is your patient considering the potential for life's final, interpersonal gifts, or is his, or her, intended choice solely a reaction to fear, disability, and/or pain? As a sensitive, caring person, is the hardship for others factored into their decision? If they internalized their critical situation as a mirror for significant others to reflect on, leading those loved ones to emotional purging and a newfound appreciation for love and relationships, how would that affect your patient's decision? Alternatively, could modern medical intervention bridge the physical pain with those final and most precious moments of unguarded love?

As unique human personalities, we are here only once. As ascended Spirits, we experience ultimate joy if we maximize our earthly opportunities. I hope the message is getting clearer that we have complete power over our perceptions. If open to the belief that standing beyond Earth, we, as Souls, actually wrote the curriculum for our lives, perhaps we can relax and let the process unfold naturally—even the challenging parts. Or we can choose to play suffering victim for the entire journey.

When it finally occurs to awakening individuals just how united we all are, it's a defining and uplifting moment. A huge burden lifts when liberated from our previous beliefs—regardless of how formed—that we are separate, lonely, isolated Beings. In the new paradigm explained so well by Holographic Psychology and other mediums, humans are like trees in a beautiful, expanding forest. Even as we learn to uniquely blossom, we are continually connected via our *root* system. Souls enjoy creating individualistic themes for the intensity of the physical experience then provided. To vividly *imagine* a clear, clean, cold running stream is one level of manifestation. But it's a very different experience to actually *feel* the cool water coursing over our physical bodies and down our throats, as we quench a great thirst.

Physical Death...or is it?

Only through facing and replacing our fear of death can we release its icy grip. Then we open ourselves to the full engagement of *life*. Sogyal Rinpoche explains this great Buddhist teaching so well in the *Tibetan Book of Living and Dying*. The eminent Elizabeth Kubler Ross, MD, former hospice and doctor consultant, wrote about Soul-connecting teachings as the *final gifts* available to us if we stop stuffing our feelings and walking on eggshells. She explains how to be much more than caretakers for the transitioning ones in our life. Those with a terminally ill loved one *must* read Dr. Ross' book, *On Death and Dying*. We can choose to maximize our potential for human expression, or live in tormenting regret for past opportunities.

One of the most comforting messages delivered to me during my Spiritual odyssey: my *Being* never dies. Even though my physical body eventually recycles itself, as in the common succession of all life, my *Being* and all memories of human experience always exist. Instead of death, my focus transitions from one realm of existence— experiential physical life—to another, more expansive awareness. This extended realm comprises exquisite joy, peace, harmony, goodness, creativity and love, as consistent themes. For those supposing the finality of human existence, and physical death the end of all awareness, these convictions are neither wrong nor bad. But it's doubtful those of this persuasion will trust in and thereby unblock much of the expanded realities while still here in the physical plane.

In order to prove the existence of these expanded realms to yourself, you must open your mind beyond five-sensory preoccupation. Relaxation and regular power attunement sessions greatly assist your expansion beyond the Beta mindset. ECKists (followers of Eckankar) refer to this process as *Soul Travel ™*. For orientation purposes, consider that we don't really have to *go* anywhere—we're already there. To feel a strong union with the Eternal forces, it's helpful, perhaps even essential, to dial in the right frequency of light and sound. Heart-opening, altered-state sessions provide cosmic connection. Attunements also present an excellent vehicle to help release devils, demons, fallen angels, Darth-Vader types, and other *illusionary* forms of cosmic riffraff.

Human Shadow

Accepting our magnificence often proves difficult for us because we judge ourselves imperfect. Many sense what they perceive a dark side within themselves, which *escapes* from time to time. This evil *allegedly* proves itself by our regularly — or occasionally — performing less-than-honorable deeds. A self-diminishing perception makes it seem more plausible that an all-knowing God will surely inflict punishment, just as our loving parents did when we were *bad*. I discuss our history with satanic forces and their relationship to God in a later segment. For now, know that fear of Celestial discipline continues to significantly affect and separate our respective cultures. And this divide shall continue until realization of how *we* create a very real (the only) hell right here on Earth—through destructive thinking, feeling, and action.

Here, perhaps, lies another very practical reason for atheistic convictions. I certainly understand why persons don't embrace a force that, once accepted, might punish them for having not perfectly expressed their potential. Obvious in our fear-based choices and negative self-image, *true* peace, harmony, goodness, balance, joy, happiness, and love continue to elude us. Again, I emphasize that we over-packed our suitcases for this lifetime on Earth—and we did not come alone. Loving Beings, manifesting both in and beyond space and time—as does our own Soul awareness—guide us on our selected journey. We all feel them to some degree. *Contact* is often described as *intuition* or *conscience*. We continue to blame outside circumstances for our lot in life, or...we choose to put our creative magnificence to work. *We are omniscient, omnipresent, omnipotent, Eternal, Universal, Spiritual Beings.* Choose to believe this and rejoice!

Tough Questions from Agnostics and Atheists

The following four questions encapsulate what many thinking, reasoning persons see as the most difficult mental and emotional obstacles to accepting and opening to the Divine realm.

❶ "If a benevolent, unconditionally loving, non-judgmental, all powerful-knowing-seeing God/Goddess (whatever one wishes to call it) really exists, and *it* is the force behind both creating and maintaining the energies sustaining the entire Universe, then why is there so much negativity in the world—including but not limited to the torture of little babies? And please spare me 'the devil made them do it' speech."

❷ "If all this *our choice* stuff is true, why in the world, or more specifically, why in God's name would we—as Souls—ever choose to incarnate into negative and distressful environments? Who among us would wish for a life of starvation in fly-ridden Somalia, or ask to be born to ignorant, immature, violent parents who don't want us and will mentally, emotionally, and sexually abuse us every day of our childhood days and nights?"

❸ "Do Souls and that supposedly omnipotent God Force lack compassion and sensitivity?"

❹ "Are the Eternal Forces oblivious to the murder, mayhem, and daily torture of Humans Beings? If I am ever to believe in any benevolent Higher Power or Supreme Being, answer *these* questions SoulMan. And lose that Blind-Faith, *God-Works-in-Mysterious-Ways* religious claptrap! I didn't accept that nonsense before, and I'm certainly not buying any of it now!"

Since I probably alienated the vast majority of belief systems on the planet with my previously encapsulated overview of orthodox agendas, what the heck, we might as well go for the *Full Monty*. I didn't start this to run for cover when the *flack* started flying—so, let's do it! To my beloved atheist and agnostic friends: did I hit the major questions that intelligent, rational humans grapple with when trying to open to the existence of a Divine force or presence?

These queries continue to haunt us as we persist in looking toward *outside* causal factors to explain our condition in life. In *not* accepting an inner-actualized determinate of Earth events, psychological dynamics (beliefs) essentially point to the *will* of God/Satan, or *blind faith,* as causal factors for the human condition. If you connect to the forces of the Eternal through a blind-faith love in your heart, rejoice! Much of what we say in response to those tough questions will hold little interest for you. With the committed courage to discover your highest inner truth, try prodding deeper for preprogrammed, subconscious-mind denunciations of thoughts and feelings that contradict established belief. Many of us resist serious questioning of outer-validating *authorities,* fearing ostracism and abandonment.

Many worshipers who believe themselves unconditionally God-loving are—to one degree or another—actually God-*fearing*. The "tell" is whether God's love comes with conditions. *God fearing* is a very strong, very old, societal belief within our species. Such an indigenous part of the human culture for so many millennia, we are often not consciously aware of this doctrine's influence on our thinking and feeling. In contrast, many wear "God Fearing" as a badge of honor.

Recalling that humanity has—for thousands of years—been very efficiently conditioned to feel unworthy of love from the Divine, cradle-to-grave shame and guilt lead a populace into abject slavery. The implication that the power—and therefore God—exists only in some *separate* realm, typifies just one example.

In the early days, fledgling religious leaders had their own survival interests at stake, so let's not be too hard on them. Well-meaning control and manipulation are certainly not the only expressions coming from Orthodoxy. There's also a strong effort to emphasize the goodness in everyday expressions (Golden Rule, etc.) and to forgive and love all others. Forgiveness and love prove quite difficult to have for others, however, when we do not—as yet—have loving thoughts and forgiving emotions for ourselves.

Absolute or rigid atheism illustrates *another* expression often born out of worthiness issues, although not acknowledged by those expressing only from First Reality perspectives. If we don't feel worthy of love, whether human or Divine, we usually experience an exaggerated fear of the potential loss of love. Faced with this dilemma, many choose the expedient prospect of disavowing love altogether with statements like, "Love is overrated—give me *lust!*" I played this game myself in years past; I'm quite familiar with intimacy avoidance.

The beliefs possessed in higher realities are not blind, but directly experienced by every fiber of one's essence. The proof is very much *in the pudding* with Second and Third Reality awareness. Through stubborn determination, I eventually discovered that fearing the Divine creates a temporary barrier to opening to the forces of the Eternal, just as loss-of-love fear roadblocks the deeper human emotions. In Second Reality, we choose to acknowledge, share, vent, release, and replace—just like we dump *any* human fear. Advanced Second Reality (and above) ceases any need to confront anything or forgive anyone. All pathology vanishes in the more expansive realities, as if never existing. With a core shift, we suddenly envision synchronistic order to the universal continuum; *no more feelings of victimization or needing to fight to be right.* This is an awareness whose day has come and come again. This time, we humans, in ever increasing numbers, hear/feel its calling from the joyous FUN zone. Expanded levels of consciousness provide the tools for immediate processing of temporary problem situations. Enlightenment brings understanding to our current dynamics and overall appreciation for life's lessons. No longer limited, recipients see manifested negativity as a subjective distortion and part of the world's ongoing curriculum. With life in these expanded realities an absolute joy, we even embrace the occasional hardship for its intrinsic *perfection.*

An analogy might be the mindset of successful body builders — just before a workout. They intellectually understand they must exert themselves to the fullest to get a good result. But instead of focusing on just the proposed work effort, or temporary strain, they choose to envision the look and feel they have when "pumped." They thereby minimize the degree of suffering necessary to overcome obstacles to success. Regardless of the type of challenge, one person's devastating crisis is another person's growing, learning, awakening opportunity.

In this manual we attempt to show the extra opportunities that await us when we embrace the current moment with sensitivity, passion, and tenacious confidence. Not to worry, this guide includes something for everyone regardless of current awareness. The valuable tools offered, along with the corresponding structured understanding, give you a sense of where you are now and the levels of expanded consciousness that await actualization. You connect to the parts of this intended for you now. You could pick up this book again — in a year or two — and discover a whole new world you hadn't noticed the first time. This is the evolutionary property of Spiritual DNA. It is suggested you not compare your progress to anyone else's. You are exactly where you're intended to be, but only for the moment. Upon awakening to Second Reality, and no longer frozen in any feedback loops, your future is yours to create.

You can tell what level you express from — at any given moment — with the following self-diagnostic. Faced with a challenging situation, determine whether you are making a coherent, inner, psychological evaluation as subjective interpretation, or a reflex response to an event pushing one of your faultfinding buttons. If you can make this distinction (at *any* point) after an emotionally upsetting incident, then you are definitely operating from a degree of Second Reality. If capable of realizing this differentiation *during* a rare confrontation or upset, you are an advanced student already demonstrating replacement. If you have no buttons left to push, and confrontations no longer exist in your world in *any* form, **and you still have a pulse**, you remain on Earth as an ongoing example (Master) of humanity's innate and Collective potential—a fully awakened Third Reality beneficiary.

Finally grabbing the reins to your own inner power is no small accomplishment. For others, your potential preexists as well. Awareness shifts are invited by the releasing of emotional/psychological fear and replacement practice.

Letting Go...and Letting Love

The following narrative wonderfully demonstrates synchronicity and co-facilitated transformation. Additionally, this account shows how one man healed his non-serving fears, experienced and accepted a whole new set of love-based options, and in so doing created a ripple effect that continues to change lives everywhere. An actual event, and not intended to criticize or judge any person, religion, or philosophy, our *collective* story exemplifies the many ways we push love out of our lives by letting fear rule us. Many persons, at this very moment, experience great challenges reconciling their respect and love for the *Almighty,* with their desire to open and commit to loving Earth-bound relationships. Often in tormenting dissidence, they struggle with what they believe to be *evil* influences, while fearing all along they will fail at either human or Divine love—or both.

In 1996 I attended a Christmas party in Las Vegas, Nevada. A very interesting group of metaphysical types—many in professional counseling and service—we had numerologists, astrologers, and assorted psychics in attendance. Even an ex-CIA parapsychology researcher showed up. No, Art Bell was not present. In spite of this famous radio personality's metaphysical interests, he enjoys his privacy.

We all sat around in a large circle while the designated gurus took turns fielding questions from the forty-five, or so, guests. One *civilian* invitee, a respectful man in his early 30s, had what I easily sensed as some intense issue to resolve. Overtly nervous, the gentleman tried several times to get his question answered. While our "ex-spurts" partook in some orgasmic, *cosmic-zone* rapture, they were temporarily unable to fully embrace anyone expressing from the more basic, human level. Sensing the problem he struggled with, I felt a knowing tug in my gut. Since I was physically close and fully empathized with the frustration of having a burning question ignored, I leaned over and introduced myself. I told him I basically understood his issue and would talk to him privately when the *show* was over. Within his deep blue eyes I saw a look of relief that someone finally heard his plea.

Afterwards, while everyone stood up to circulate and say his or her respective goodbyes, we stepped into a back corner of the large living room. Without any more words spoken, I felt an immediate heart connection with this sensitive, pained young man. I put my hand on his shoulder and said, "Obviously you are in the middle of some fearful hardship." When I asked, "Are you ready to let the burden go?"—the vestiges of resistance crumbled. While fighting back a floodgate of overdue tears, he related his story. He told me he was the father of five-year-old twin boys. He described how happy, outgoing, joyful, and loving his sons were. He felt their great pull to fully engage him emotionally. Although he kept putting them off with a self-imposed wall against too much intimacy, they kept coming at him relentlessly—pulling at his heartstrings. His center-core self desperately wanted to surrender to these two dynamos of pure love energy. But he carried a tremendous fear of doing so.

The young man had been raised by very loving parents, whom he continued to admire. At a very early age, his parents taught him that overtly embracing people, things, or life on Earth, with unfettered joy, was not respectful of God. His family believed it wrong to demonstrate too much exultation in life, as the sinful would be telling God that *Earth* was heaven. Forgetting *God's* Heaven, and not living the intended suffering life of a *chosen one* would provoke severe consequences—both here and in the afterlife.

When the young man went to his parents and courageously told them of his dissidence, they counseled him that this was his great test—sent by God. They immediately called their religious cleric to schedule a prayer vigil to deal with their son's crisis of faith. Our discordant sufferer held the prayer meeting at bay while deciding what to do—something that upset his parents even more. His family said they would pray for his Soul until he came to his senses and *saw the light*. Our troubled seeker explained the cultural conviction common to a localized minority in his country of origin—and their ultra-orthodox religion. He felt a great sense of betrayal in disavowing his foundational values. He knew his current actions would estrange his entire family and embarrass his parents. He had already made the courageous decision to forego his entry into Heaven, if necessary, to fully respond to his sons. I stood amazed as this brave but terrified man shared an even *larger* demon—one that hampered the dismantling of his remaining obstacle to love.

His learned fear of Divine Wrath was so great, he believed God would actually take his sons from him or leave them crippled as punishment for his non-repentant *sin*. By giving in to complete joy, peace, harmony, goodness, and love while still here on Earth, there would be hell to pay. In the presence of empathetic, non-judgmental company, long-overdue tears streamed down his tormented face.

Although happening in a very public place, amazingly no one interfered or even noticed our emotional exchange. Totally our moment, I embraced it fully. Listening intently, I sorely needed to release temporary flashes of judgment about *any* institution propagating this kind of torturing tenet. As we embraced in an almost crushing hug, I experienced the greatest intimacy imaginable with a person (officially) unknown to me. A later insight told me how truly connected we humans must be for any person to suddenly feel as if they've known and loved another all their lives—like a brother.

I felt purposefully guided with my next question: "Let's say that when you go home tonight you find your greatest fears realized. Through some horrific tragedy, your sons are no longer with you. Will you feel *fortunate* and *relieved* you hadn't let your barriers down to love them fully and completely while they were here?"

Our eyes locked as I asked this deeply probing, heart-wrenching question. Those baby blues went distant, as he painfully experienced this dreadful scenario. When my new friend came back to the room he stared at me tearfully, apparently shocked I would ask the core question. After being prodded to imagine such a devastating loss, his grief-stricken realization was clearly evident.

All bets were off. All emotional and psychological obstacles...gone. This Dad finally realized the enormity of his opportunity. With an instantaneous shift, he no longer conceived of a God that would not want him to embrace life fully and completely. As we both began sobbing again in earnest, I felt my friend's previously tensed muscles relax with eradication of that ancient pain. After several deeply connecting and healing moments, we broke our embrace in time to see his very puzzled wife standing near the exit. What else could we expect from a loving spouse just now noticing her husband hugging and crying with a strange man? We must have been quite a sight! My new young friend, embarrassed not in the least, continued to engage his enormous breakthrough.

He thanked me profusely for my caring and help. He'd been invited that night for some unspecified reason that he now understood. I answered that no thanks were necessary, as the gift was mine also. I, too, recognized my real purpose in attending. When I asked what he was going to do now, he emphatically exclaimed: *"I am going directly home to wake up my sons. I can't wait to tell them how dear they are to me; and how much I love and adore them. Holding nothing back, I will share how overjoyed I am at having been chosen to be their father. I will promise my boys that I will **never** push them away for the rest of our precious lives that I am blessed to spend with them. Then I'm going to give each of them the biggest hug of their still young and impressionable lives!"*

My emotions kicked into overdrive as I remembered the terrific hugs I experienced with my own father after he overcame his barriers to love. I now have even *more* appreciation for my recovery from traumatic childhood experiences. In *my* life, I have feared only Human Beings. Gifted with a measure of what it must be like to be afraid of an omnipotent God, I feel doubly grateful for my past healing opportunities. I shared in the glorious realization that my new friend and his sons would now enjoy for a lifetime.

We said our goodbyes, and in his rush to get home, I never got his name, address, phone, or the identity of those who invited that precious couple. I may never see that specially delivered Human Being again—in the physical—but I will never forget him or the deeply bonding moment we shared. I hit the Mega-Bucks jackpot with an encounter that irrevocably changed my life. I actually *feel* (now) what I used to mention in my past lectures: *"A stranger is just a friend we haven't met yet."* He and I are destined to share our special, synchronized moment for the rest of our lives—just as *we* do here. The people touched by that sharing then pass it on to *their* direct circle of influence, and on it goes.

*Can you see how we, as **individuals**, effect a great change in the world? One person at a time...one intimately shared experience at a time...multiplies like ever-increasing circles in a reflecting pond, to infinity.*

When I was with *The Man Who Learned to Love,* an instant love-bond arose through our intense emotional sharing and purging. By opening our hearts, we enter a new, expanded zone of intuitive communion. This saves our lives in more than one way...as we discover in our next chapter.

"There are only two ways to live your life. One...as though *nothing* is a miracle. The other...as though *everything* is a miracle."

—Albert Einstein

BOOK TWO

Pushing through the sensory overload, one thought dominated:

"Aviator skills, alone, are not going to save us"

—The SoulMan

CHAPTER ELEVEN

The Life-Enhancing Power of Intuition

♥　　♥　　♥

Traditional psychology, even today, does not consider intuition a reliable data source. Orthodox researchers attempting to rationally consider psychic abilities ask this question: "If intuition is a real and measurable ability, where in the brain is it located?" Could it be that Science—with its First Reality (reductionist) blind spot—needs to *feel* more and look less?

In addition to our expanded *look* at intuition, my Vietnam stories may help give noncombatants a sense of living and performing under the continual pressure of a physical, militaristic, life-or-death existence. The following account reflects both these themes.

Mid-1960s, Vietnam

The two most-secure airports in South Vietnam were Da Nang Air Base, just south of the DMZ, and Tan Son Nhut Airport in Saigon. Our squadron (VR-21) occasionally flew into less-protected bases such as Phu Bai, Chu Lai, and on this one occasion—Cam Ranh Bay (CRB). I was the left-seat qualified Second Pilot on the very first four-engine transport aircraft assigned a cargo delivery to Cam Ranh Bay. We planned to land on CRB's metal-mat runway, which had been recently constructed by a Naval Seal Team unit.

We found ourselves in the middle of a torrential monsoon rainstorm, as we began a Visual Omni Range (VOR) approach.

Pre-Approach Background

Pilots know this Omni Range navigational aid is adequate for high-altitude point-to-point navigation, but not what we prefer for an instrument approach in heavy rain or reduced visibility. An Instrument Landing System (ILS) with continuous cross-hair glide slope and radial direction readouts would have been perfect. ILS was available only in major, well-established airports in 1965–68. A Ground Controlled Approach (GCA) uses ground radar personnel to verbally report the same information as the ILS provides by avionics instrumentation, and would have been a good second choice.

With only radial direction and stopwatch timing, we crossed over the top of the VOR to begin a looping decent. With *accurately* provided surface winds, and *correct* seat-of-the-pants adjustment for crosswind drift, we would hopefully line up with the approach end of the runway when emerging from the cloudburst. This less-than-optimum approach procedure provided a minimum-allowable descent altitude of 500 feet above ground level (AGL).

The CRB field operations officer told us of the ground unit's desperate need for the ammunition, medical, and other logistical supplies we had on board. I convinced the Aircraft Commander (A/C) for this trip of my confidence in making a successful approach. The A/C, a full Navy Commander and jovial man with whom I'd flown many West-Pacs, wisely trusted my current abilities more than his own. With collateral duties keeping him from full-time flying assignments, the Commander barely maintained enough flight hours and recurrent training to stay qualified. It was standard procedure to match up lower-hour A/Cs with high-hour second pilots. It was decided I would make the instrument approach and landing, while the A/C flew right seat (copilot).

CRB operations personnel, safely sequestered in their makeshift control tower, withheld one vital piece of information. Foreknowledge of this little *tidbit* would have precluded any landing attempts. Later, the operations staff would sheepishly tell us (lie) they thought us a C-130 Hercules—a short takeoff and landing (STOL) turbo-prop aircraft. Thus they considered irrelevant the critical piece of landing-condition information. Although VR-21 did have three C-130s, the majority of our fleet consisted of approximately twenty, four-engine C-118b/DC-6b "Liftmaster" aircraft. At this particular moment, we were more in need of a "descent-master."

The metal-mat landing surface installed at Cam Ranh Bay comprised heavy-gauge steel, honeycombed with 2- to 3-inch diameter holes for water abatement. Even with the drainage assistance, traction would be poor-to-worse under these conditions. I was fully prepared to use asymmetrical reverse thrust on the rollout, as anti-skid brakes would be ineffective until we approached taxi speed. Reverse thrust utilizes the engine propellers—which pull an aircraft forward during normal flight—to help push the plane backward. With appropriate speed dissipated, safe brake application could then be applied.

The asymmetrical application would be the tricky, finesse part. In super-wet hydroplaning conditions, a landing and rollout proves similar to gliding on ice. Unlike the rudder—which loses effectiveness as the plane slows—asymmetrical reverse thrust both slows *and* correctly aligns the aircraft similar to the action used to rein in a horse. Landing as close as possible to the apron (first part of the landing surface), provides for the shortest stopping distance. Freestanding water is slippery all by itself. Add unpredictable gusts and a torrential rainstorm to the metal-mat factor, and you have one delicate touchdown and rollout. We wanted to have every inch of that 7000-foot landing surface available. Running off the runway into the thick, clay-based mud would detain us indefinitely. Quite selfish in retrospect, I had scheduled a hot date for our upcoming layover in Atsugi, Japan. Becoming a temporary ground-pounder for an extended stay at the newly secured and very vulnerable *Hotel Cam Ranh Bay* was definitely *not* in the game plan.

On Final. Since this was advertised as a "minimums" approach, we anticipated the heavy moisture right down to the lowest permitted altitude. At that point we either had the field in sight or we waved off the approach attempt. As we carefully approached five-hundred-feet AGL, the precipitation was relentless. During instrument approaches, the concentration required for continual rapid scanning of pertinent flight instruments really got my juices flowing. Nothing boring about an instrument approach during a blinding rainstorm!

The engineer monitored the engine instruments, and an operative radar altimeter acted as backup to the basic atmospheric altimeter. As a warning cushion, I set the radio altimeter at 550 AGL—50 feet above published minimums. When approaching an altitude threshold, standard procedure requires a copilot callout every fifty feet of descent.

As we hit minimums, I already had partial power back on to prevent further loss of life-sustaining elevation. After carefully maintaining that lowest-safe altitude a few seconds, the right-seat copilot—entrusted with getting a visual on the runway—reported, "NO FIELD...NO FIELD!" I immediately shoved the throttles to advanced stop position while commanding, "WAVE OFF...WAVE OFF!" Just as full power came back on, the rain mist cleared and the runway's approach end became barely discernible. The copilot's visual came too late—we were past the decision point. Any attempt to land now would likely result in overshooting the landing surface.

Try, Try Again. Since we belatedly saw the runway in the pulsating squall, we decided to try the approach again. With Monsoon weather conditions quite variable, rainfall density can change dramatically from moment to moment. Making a successful instrument landing—or not—is often just a matter of fortuitous timing. I took a moment to *wish* Lou, our best flight mechanic, into the engineer's seat. First-Class Petty Officer Lou and I had a running debate about which of us was the *real* rabbit's foot; regarding our mutual ability to extricate ourselves from hazardous circumstances. After dismissing that non-productive thought, I immediately psyched myself up for another go. Instrument approaches are both mentally and physically draining, and this would be our final attempt. We would not risk a third effort in a fatigued state.

The second approach proceeded just like the first, but just as we reached the minimum descent threshold, the field came into view. After the copilot reported "runway in sight," I coaxed our bird down to a perfect landing on the very tip of the hardpan. Because of the mist and pummeling rainfall, we could see only a short distance down the runway. I took no chances, as something told me to get this baby stopped—ASAP. I quickly reversed the engines [*actually the pitch or angle of the propellers reverse*], keeping my toes away from the top of the rudder controls where the wheel brakes are actuated. I cautiously began a combined directional rudder adjustment and asymmetrical reverse thrust. When comfortable with my rollout alignment, I called for maximum redline throttle. Preventing over-boost of the engines was the flight-mechanic's job. In perilous landing and rollout conditions, the pilot can ill afford to take his or her eyes off the runway—even for a fraction of a second—to look at cockpit instruments. Fortunately, there was no significant crosswind during our touchdown and rollout. Everything proceeded perfectly...until horror reared its ugly head.

Looming ahead—*like a ghost emerging from a gray fog*—was the little secret that ground operations had kept from us. Somehow I wasn't totally surprised to see the last forty percent of the runway totally under several feet of water. When the submerged section first came into view, we judged our reduced speed still too fast to stop in time. Just starting to ease on the anti-skid brakes, I now risked skidding and possibly spinning the aircraft as I gave those landing brakes more pressure. I could feel the perfectly performing pulse of the anti-skid function through the brake pedals. Prior to plowing into the human and nature-made duck pond, I instinctively put the four engines at idle. This action automatically brought the propellers out of reverse. Firmly grasping the hydraulically assisted nose-wheel steering, we slammed into the floating debris. Muddy water and foliage blasted up and over our cockpit windshield, temporarily blinding us. The windshield wipers, on high for the entire approach, took a beating but continued to function. After the jungle flotsam receded, we were astounded to discover our aircraft still on the narrow, metal-mat landing surface they called a runway.

Finally at rest, with legs and arms trembling from both the adrenaline rush and isometric stiffness, we congratulated ourselves on dodging the bullet. The A/C joyously slapped me on the shoulder. He'd just become my greatest fan. I don't know whether one would consider our survival *miraculous*, but I can say with certainty that it qualified as an "E-ticket" thrill ride. Before we were done, we had some choice words for the ground and approach control folks. As luck (?) would have it, because we had brought in so much cargo and had so little remaining fuel on board, our low takeoff weight allowed us to get airborne even with the modified runway length. My recollection: after the A/C's official report on this incident, none of our DC-6 aircraft ever attempted another landing on the CRB metal-mat surface. After extended maintenance time for water extraction, cleaning, lubing, and final safety inspections of landing gear, brake systems, and fuselage, we left this forsaken place for Da Nang Air Base. Upon refueling, we continued our flight plan to Atsugi.

After reflecting on the ground units' desperation for our life-sustaining supplies, I reconciled, without excusing, their actions. I gave thanks I was not living in the trenches where the *real* fighting took place.

Napalm Anyone?

Aware only that I had been a Naval Aviator in Vietnam, someone once asked me whether I had ever dropped napalm. That got me thinking: of all the flying jobs in a combat zone, mine was perhaps the least psychologically challenging. Although the work I did was indirectly just as deadly as dropping bombs, after talking to POW pilots and infantry veterans with more direct and horrific war involvement, my post-war adjustments seem almost insignificant.

My performance grades during basic flight training gave me a full choice between helicopter, multi-engine, or the jet pipeline. Many of my classmates that went Jet or Helo ended up dead, or worse—a prisoner of war. I'm both sensitive to and appreciative of my Vietnam brethren. Today I'm even thankful the CRB folks lied to us so we would deliver those much-needed supplies.

Summation

Remembering those questions my nine-year-old self asked Lockheed's *finest*, did I intuitively know something was wrong with the metal-mat runway? I took some risk executing the short-field landing procedure. A 7000-foot runway length, combined with plummeting rainfall, did not call for STOL measures—yet I availed myself of them without consulting the A/C or even consciously thinking about it. Why? The next chapter addresses those good, probative queries, as well as the "BIG Tough Questions" from the agnostic venue. In the meantime, let's see what you come up with on your own.

CHAPTER TWELVE

The ABCs of Miracles
Not What You Thought

♥   ♥   ♥

Cubic Bay, Philippines, was crowded with anchored ships from the Sixth Fleet. It was either a large-class cruiser or destroyer that filled the cockpit window as our fully loaded, four-engine transport inched its way through 150 feet of altitude—having just completed its takeoff run from NAS Cubi Point, Philippines. Then, without warning, life, as we *previously* knew it, ceased to exist.

We now enter a very interesting world of delight and conjecture. An imposing and paradoxical undertaking, trying to define the miraculous is to reach the pinnacle of subjectivity. Examining this subject may be both titillating and insightful; it's not for the timid, however. I supplement the details of my personal adventure with Spiritual perspectives perhaps quite different from anything you've read or heard about before. Consider setting all preconceptions aside. *Do not attempt to adjust the vertical. Do not attempt to adjust the horizontal.* Sit back and observe, as you are transported into the "Outer Limits" for an up-close-and-personal exposé on the conditions for, and the purposes of...*MIRACLES*.

As the direct recipient of several extraordinary life-saving experiences, I can testify directly on this subject. Because the Escondido intervention was so profound and purposeful, memories of my puzzling Southeast Asia encounters have refreshed themselves with new meaning. Even my most intimate friends and family members do not know of some of these escapes from what originally appeared to be certain death.

Defining the Miraculous

As judicious left-brainers benefit from a bit of structure before jumping into esoteric voids, these preliminary and very arbitrary definitions may be useful.

❶ **Level-two miracle:** heartfelt-prayer manifestations, or altered-state (meditative) focus, which heighten, sometimes extraordinarily, sensory perception/ESP.

❷ **Level-one miracle** — the "Big Kahuna": the very rare circumstance when an energy force or cosmic-based influence (depending on one's belief) manifests—without conscious, *knowing* invitation—for the purpose of overriding the freewill or behavioristic actions of a Human Being.

Celestial considerations for what I am calling a **level-one** takeover or interruption are neither what most folks would expect, nor prefer. Also true for prayer or attunements, Souls — by universal agreement — very reluctantly interfere with human free choice. For Sci-fi fans, the Soul's position is very similar to Star Trek's *noninterference* credo, or the late Isaac Asimov's "Prime Directive."

The Seeds are Planted

Extraordinary wartime experiences planted the seeds for the floodgate of inspirational insight and emotion downloaded after the Escondido Intervention: October of 1996 (30-day spiritual odyssey). The "white knuckle" military events in this writing all occurred in the late 1960s, and doubly reinforce the empowerment principles previously presented herein. After reading them all, decide if any Force or Being was at work behind the scenes. Were my crew and I just extremely lucky, or was something *otherworldly* going on?

Note: With the aid of self-hypnosis, I've paraphrased significant crewmate conversations with all the exacting detail I could muster. Recollection of the *effect* of these experiences is much clearer, and perhaps more significant.

I do not include a glossary of military flight jargon: any aviation term you have difficulty with will not significantly affect your understanding of the teaching at hand. Requiring non-aviators to stop their reading flow in order to check a separate glossary of terms did not seem beneficial. I do (where I think appropriate) include clarifying synonyms in parentheses. Lack of military, or aviation terminology will not inhibit your understanding the significant role Spiritual guidance — or intuition — plays in our everyday lives.

U.S. Military Tour of Duty

Amid my several-year tour during the Vietnam War, I trained as a US Navy pilot, Celestial Navigator, and Courier with top-secret clearances. In September 1963 I began twenty grueling months as a Naval Aviation Cadet (NAVCAD). The US Navy temporarily activated this special, limited, accelerated division prior to the anticipated troop buildup in Vietnam. NAVCAD and MARCAD (Marine Aviation Candidate) flight training was identical to the AOC (Aviation Officer Candidate) program depicted in the movie, "An Officer and a Gentlemen," starring Richard Gere and Debra Winger. Although Navy and Marine aviators receive identical flight training, the treatment between AOC and NAVCAD/MARCAD applicants differed significantly. The NAVCAD/MARCAD boot-camp harassment you partially witnessed in the movie, although lessened, continued for the total length of the 18- to 20-month program. The entire carrot—Wings *and* Commission—awaited our full completion. Although younger and lacking a full college education (two years vs. four), NAVCAD/MARCAD aviators achieved higher completion percentages than did their AOC counterparts. Obviously the all-or-nothing concept provided additional incentive.

In memory of my great friend
Joe "wrong-way" Cangilose

I received my commission (as Ensign) and coveted "Wings of Gold" in May 1965. After attending an eight-week Celestial Navigation school in Corpus Christi, Texas, and completing jungle/POW survival training at Whidbey Island, I accepted orders to VR-21, in Barbers Point, Hawaii. Yes, an assignment in *paradise* sounded pretty sweet to me, too. But because the Vietnam War rapidly escalated by the time of my arrival (fall 1965), I averaged only 5 to 6 days per month at home base for my three-and-a-half year tour of duty. With Beau Coup (a lot of) flying hours every month, I spent almost as much layover time in our staging sites of boring Agana,

Guam (good thing I knew poker), and lively Atsugi, Japan, as I did in Hawaii. I felt very fortunate to get assigned to transport duty, however. I wanted the combination of multi-engine experience and the many flying hours that would hold me in good stead, should I later apply for an airline job.

The C-118—Low, Slow, but Reliable

DC-6b

The Navy didn't put its heaviest budget investment into transport equipment. So, while the USAF flew the new, sleek, high-performance C-141 "Starlifter" jet transport, we inherited the USAF cast-off — the DC-6b "Liftmaster," briefly introduced in the last chapter. Cruising at a true air speed of 274 knots, the Douglas manufactured C-118/R-6D (Air Force/Navy designation) was a relatively slow, four-engine, partially pressurized, non-turbo-charged, propeller-driven, reciprocating-engine aircraft. Although breaking no sound barriers, I was impressed with its work ethic. Empty, the C-118b weighed a tad over 55,000 pounds. At maximum takeoff weight, the allowable almost doubled to 107,000 pounds. Fully loaded, it grudgingly climbed to approximately 10- to 12-thousand feet— eventually topping out at 18- to 19-thousand after sufficient fuel burn. Although the DC-6b had a rated service ceiling of 25,000 ft., we rarely climbed above 19k. With a full fuel load, this aircraft had a 4100 nautical mile range. We used to joke about our *birds* with "four *turning*" and "none *burning*," as we differentiated ourselves from the jet transports of the day. Engineered and manufactured too late to help the WWII war effort, the R-6D saw action in Korea. Throughout the 50s, prior to introduction of the Boeing 707, the DC-6 and DC-7 were mainstays of the airline fleet. The C-118 is powered by very reliable Pratt & Whitney® R-2800 power plants (engines). The 18-cylinder, twin-row, radial-piston engines rate at 2500 horse power.

Though designed to take the heavy airframe flexing that accompanies low-altitude, all-weather-condition flying, airport approach planning was essential as the DC-6 did not immediately respond to large corrections. Piloting a C-118 felt like driving one of those old *fishtailing* station wagons. Flown properly, however, it was a safe and reliable airplane, and I enjoyed flying it. [*Of the 665 DC-6s built during the 1940s and early 50s, almost 100 still fly the friendly skies.*]

The Rigors of Training

As you can imagine, any US Military flight-training program proves extensive and thorough. Virtually every type of conceivable emergency situation is dissected and procedurally practiced—both in a simulator and with live aircraft—until proficiency is assured. The key word here is *conceivable*. Some of the challenges I describe had no charted procedure or emergency solution—at that time—listed in the "Natops" (Naval Aviation Training Operation Procedures) manual, nor were they ever discussed in our squadron's training classes. As far as I could determine, no flight crewmember had ever reported any similar situations during the entire history of our flight squadron. Except for one or possibly two events, nothing resulted from our survival that could benefit future trainees. In fact, one phenomenon was so bizarre and *out-there* that our experience was totally disbelieved by all squadron personnel, except, of course, my flight crew who somehow lived through it. It makes a good book title, however.

One purpose of the technical part of my story telling: to test subconscious memory recall. To more accurately reconstruct these terrifyingly odd events, I went back in time, aided by an *Alpha-State* hypnotic regression. Those with direct flying experience may have a better feel for how spectacularly life threatening were these events.

Flight Characteristics

During VR-21 flight instruction, we often practiced **one**-engine-out (failure) procedures. Fairly straightforward, the failure of one engine was less critical (we still had three), *unless* lost during a maximum-allowable-weight takeoff, hot day, instrument conditions, etc. Even the squadron hotshots considered that combo a little hairy. We practiced the undesirable combinations and rare scenarios, until proficient.

Then we practiced **two**-engine-out procedures, with all possible variables and combinations. Dual engine failures on opposite sides of the aircraft were easier to handle, as the plane could normally be trimmed without problematic or asymmetrical thrust differentials to worry about. Two engines out on the same side of the aircraft were a lot trickier and much more dangerous. The plane tenaciously tried to skid or spin around on its vertical axis, requiring strenuous opposite-rudder control. Simultaneously the one-powered wing fought the pilot through rotation of its horizontal axis (trying to invert). Any horizontal-axis rotation required strenuous opposite-aileron control.

If this most-undesirable condition occurred during takeoff, both pilots vigorously applied opposing-rudder and -aileron controls until establishing sufficient altitude (if possible) and desired trim.

"Trim" (in the DC-6)—a mechanical process where the pilot dialed in (sets) slight adjustments—both compensated for and balanced out individual aerodynamic flying characteristics. Even with normal flight, trim settings deviated slightly from one identical type of aircraft to another. Trim settings also helped the pilot adjust for crosswind and other flying conditions of the moment. Once proper trim was set, fuel economy maximized and neither the pilot nor the mechanical auto-pilot needed to make arduous corrections to the flight controls in order to maintain balanced flight.

Two-engine-out crisis situations and rollover/stall potentialities eased with reduced power on the two remaining engines. At cruising altitude this combination proved not nearly as critical. With two engines, the DC-6 normally maintained straight and level flight at lower altitudes—conditional on either a light cargo load or dumping excess fuel. I had not heard of anyone in our squadron ever losing two engines on the same flight leg, but we practiced and practiced until we handled the two-engine-out procedure satisfactorily.

Believe it or not, we actually even discussed and practiced flying with **three** engines out. The DC-6b couldn't maintain altitude with only one engine, even under the lightest circumstances. But with sufficient altitude initially available, optimum procedures provided an extended glide range (minimum rate of decent) and the opportunity to set up for an emergency landing. Once again, we practiced and practiced until we milked every mile out of that almost-impossible scenario.

Practicing two- and three-engine-out procedures gave us much more confidence dealing with just a single-engine failure. Suddenly that basic emergency condition felt like a walk in the park. As a young, somewhat-cocky, ego-driven pilot, I used to fantasize and even hope for a real, in-flight engine failure just so I could master the live experience. In another example of *be careful what you wish for*, I was to be *gifted* this request—in spades!

I was a left-seat-qualified second pilot (2P) for all these *miraculous* adventures. My military rank was either Lieutenant Junior-Grade or full Lieutenant, depending on the chronological order of the reported events.

Now that you know the technical setup, fasten your seat belts and extinguish all closed minds. *We are off to see the wizard!*

Miracle Candidate #1: "How Did You Know?"

At the Cubi Point Naval Base, in the 1960s, the airstrip was tucked alongside steep mountains. Departing from the normal-duty runway, mountains were located ahead and on the right—requiring reciprocating-engine (prop) aircraft to begin an immediate left-hand turn after liftoff. Flight crews were then instructed to continue their climb-out over a normally unencumbered Subic Bay.

During a slowly climbing, 15- to 20-degree turn, we followed the assigned departure route. At maximum allowable weight, this was a hot, humid, high-noon, water-injected takeoff. Although pleased to be airborne and on our way to our layover destination in Atsugi, Japan, this was not to be a routine flight.

Crew of Ten. Two pilots in this crew were left-seat qualified. As fortune had it, this was my turn in the saddle. We normally flew with double crews to relieve one another on long flights. As continuous 15-24-hour flight duty sessions were the norm, rest was essential. We carried a complement of three pilots, two aircraft mechanics, two cargo handlers, and two radio-instrumentation personnel. During takeoffs and landings the designated flight engineer sat on a fold-down bench between the left-seat and right-seat pilots—practically rubbing shoulders with us. The engineer's in-flight job, among other monitoring duties, was to keep a keen eye on the engine instruments, trim the propellers—congruently matching their revolutions per minute (rpm's)—and upon reaching cruising altitude, lean the fuel mixture. Most importantly, the flight mechanic/engineer ensured that pilots did not over-boost (red line) the engines on takeoff, climb out, or when reversing the props during landing.

This particular Cubi Point departure proved tricky because many ships from the Sixth Fleet—out of Italy—happened to be anchored in Subic Bay. Recalling this incident, two or three cruisers/destroyers and assorted tenders harbored in that Bay. It was, of course, imperative that aircraft avoid these massive ships—complete with conning (radar) towers and tall whip antennas—during climb out. These and related precautions were discussed in the preflight briefing with Cubi flight operations. Already airborne, we were well past any anticipatory planning.

On hot, maximum-weight takeoffs, we always used water injection to maximize horsepower. This reduced takeoff-roll distance and helped cool the engine cylinders. Water injection was supplied through special lines with boosted pressure. The fluid originated from a separate storage tank on the fuselage, near the wing-joint, and four electric toggle switches located above the flight engineer's head controlled the injection. Naturally, this takeoff required all the power we could generate. Using water injection—listed on the takeoff checklist—was standard procedure during summer months in the South Pacific Rim.

Our Pratt & Whitney® powerplants performed perfectly during the preflight check, takeoff roll, and initial climb-out. In the cockpit, during that 20-degree, left-hand turn, at one-hundred-fifty feet, I had already given the verbal *gear-up* order, combined with a *thumbs-up* signal.

Suddenly, without warning, all four engines...quit. They reacted as if someone had just pulled back the throttle levers, or switched off the electric current-producing magnetos. [*Crudely stated, a magneto serves a function similar to the ignition switch in your car.*] This was *not* one of the practiced **one**-engine-out, **two**-engines-out, or **three**-engines-out scenarios. Void of procedures or checklists, I'm sure we all had the same thought: the *fat lady* just finished singing.

"How could all four engines fail simultaneously," you ask? Excellent question, but we had sufficient time to consider only that we were in *deep, deep, doo-doo*. Training had not—could not provide any rabbits for this brand of hat. After this little adventure—assuming we survived, we would have an additional offering for the Training Command's suggestion box. In the meantime, CJ, my mental critic, kicked in with: "I *told* you to take the jet pipeline, Dummy! Now look at the fine mess [*no ejection seats*] you've gotten us into!"

Freeze Frame. [*For a more detailed examination of this event, let us slow the passage of linear time. The most critical phase of what I describe happened in the span of 10 to 15 seconds.*] I quickly scanned the instruments to confirm my worst fears and verified what my other senses already told me—*yes*...rapidly losing power on all four engines. I looked quickly at Lou, our flight mechanic, white with stunned disbelief, as were we all. Then, I did something that horrified both the engineer and the copilot even more—if that was possible.

Reconstructed from witnessed accounts: without thinking or *conscious* action, my right hand moved to the overhead instrument cluster. Both the engineer and copilot (the senior officer and A/C for this trip) gasped "NO!" as I turned off all four of the power-producing injectors.

I continue now with my own recollections: Within three or four seconds, the life-sustaining engines began to come back on line.

Except for some initial *very loud* backfiring, all was returning to apparent normal operation. Still airborne—but just barely—Lou was ready to goose (over boost) our Pratt & Whitney's for all they were worth. In total agreement to not leave anything in the bag, I yelled "shove-em (the throttle levers) to the wall, Louie!"

[*With a clear, smooth Subic Bay, we would have now been in pretty good shape. I could let the plane settle a little by dropping the nose—very slightly—in order to pick up some valuable airspeed via bounce-back. This aerodynamic "ground-effect" principle is quite similar to the draft a cyclist or racecar driver uses to save energy and increase speed. Not to have that luxury, however; we'd lost about half of our one-hundred-fifty feet of altitude.*]

While temporarily void of power and maneuverability, we settled toward a menacingly large destroyer; a floating arsenal anchored dead ahead. With no tomorrow (in the *physical* realm) if we didn't rapidly regain that precious seventy-five-feet, plus a little more for insurance, I did all I could to keep our slothful old bird from stalling. Meanwhile, the copilot yelled "Watch that radar tower!" [*the cruiser's tallest, center-positioned instrumentation stack*] and "Watch your airspeed!" I spent another micro-second with a caustic notion to rejoin with, "Gee...can I get you anything *else* Sir, while I'm here?"

We hadn't yet retracted the flaps, still positioned at the 15- to 20-degree takeoff setting designed to create a higher angle-of-attack for the wing. [*This angle reduces the speed at which the plane can become safely airborne. Actually the horizontally moving airfoils (wing and rear stabilizer) create the lift. The rigidly attached fuselage of the aircraft, along with any inhabitants, has no choice but to accompany the movement.*] Even though this partial flap setting created extra air drag, we didn't dare touch it at this altitude and speed, lest we lose what precious lift remained. Our current angle of attack could stall the wing immediately if we even breathed on the flap setting. Providing us additional incentive, the stall-warning horn vibrated on the edge of its squawk mode.

I mentally tried to command an altitude increase to our 107,000-pound aircraft, while transfixed on that many-ton ship threatening to become *our* destroyer. When we initially lost power, I leveled the wings—both to save altitude, and to prepare for a forced ditching. The ditching option no longer appeared viable. The Sixth Fleet armada densely crowded the bay. Without return of power, we were guaranteed to strike one of the ships—probably that very large and getting LARGER vessel...DEAD AHEAD.

Even with full power restored, we were not out of the woods. So close to the massive vessel that both the copilot and I saw shipboard sailors running in panic, it appeared, barring a miracle, we would shear off their massive radar and antenna platform before crashing our remaining wreckage into the bay.

With vein, muscle, and sinew stretched beyond human capability, I somehow finessed the controls to keep our staggering Douglas from failing, but without sacrificing any life-extending altitude. *Adrenaline rage and poise made strange bedfellows.* Fortunately our four R-2800s now roared like the king of beasts. If I dropped the nose of the plane just slightly, I *knew* I could instantly pick up the required airspeed to guarantee stall prevention. To do that would mean a temporary loss of altitude, which we could ill afford. The utter helplessness of this paradoxical dilemma had me on the very edge of overload.

Slowly—too slowly—an opportunity to regain lost innocence was revealed to me. I made a silent plea to any force or presence that might be listening: "Might I *please* have a second chance at redemption?" It's true—there are no atheists in fox holes *or* in four-engine-out situations.

In the last available seconds, I judged sufficient elevation to risk giving back a miniscule portion—just enough for a shallow, left bank. This adjustment did the trick, as we *barely* missed the radar platform by some scant few feet. After miraculously getting past the cruiser/destroyer, I immediately re-leveled the wings to continue our acute climb-out. Three hundred…four hundred…five hundred feet…we gradually ascended out of harm's way.

After passing through fifteen-hundred feet, and while still holding our collective breaths, hoping against hope that whatever caused the power failure would not return, we assessed the malfunction. Way too heavy to land without a substantial weight reduction, we needed to decide whether dumping fuel—in order to return to Cubi Point—was an option. If we *did* have some kind of ongoing fuel contamination, we certainly wished to avoid a long, over-water flight to Vietnam—our scheduled destination. [*With a rearward crewmember reporting an undercarriage impact, it was later determined we clipped one or more of the ship's radar-tower whip antennas.*

No one had yet mentioned my action with the water injectors. We were recovering from the extreme adrenaline surge and probably suffering a degree of post-traumatic shock. In any given emergency situation, pilots and flight personnel are trained to flawlessly execute their respective procedures. Any feelings of terror or panic are routinely stuffed until the crisis is over. Now the enormity of the near-fatal event began to hit us. As we continued our climb-out, I switched on the autopilot. My knees were knocking and my legs felt like rubber. Lou, our recovering engineer, had been looking at me strangely for the past few moments. He finally spoke and asked me one short but emphatic question: "How did you know?" After clarifying what he meant, I responded, "Didn't we turn those injectors off during the climb-out checklist?" I had absolutely no recollection of having done so, but both Louie and the A/C verified my terrifyingly independent action.

After some quiet processing time, we collectively concluded our problem had not been fuel-tank contamination or any direct form of engine trouble. Certain enough of our analysis to tell the Control Tower we would continue our flight plan, they instructed us to switch communications to Departure Control. I made a strong mental note to never again fantasize about emergency situations—such as *engine* failures. This had been a major ego-humbling ordeal I had no desire to repeat. Impervious to my repentant bravado, more thrills and chills awaited us—a few months hence.

Aftermath

Upon arriving at Da Nang Air Base, our embarrassed first-class petty officer and chief mechanic/engineer confirmed the cause of our frightening mechanical malfunction. During aircraft servicing in Cubi Point, some green (untrained) airman deuce (E-2) inadvertently put oil into our water-injection tank. With access panels clearly marked, and different-size nozzle requirements (like the old leaded vs. unleaded auto-fuel nozzles), this mistake was a whopper. Flight-crew mechanics are ultimately responsible for supervising anyone that works on their assigned aircraft. Lou, his assistant, and the rest of our crew all learned a valuable lesson that day. We quickly put all recriminations aside, however…typical of a close-knit harmonious crew. We could not afford the expense of holding grudges. Our mutual butts were continually on the line—especially in the combat zones. The first survivalist rule: "get *clear* or be *dead!*"

Insisting I had a lucky horseshoe permanently inserted in my rear end, and that *my* flight crew was therefore immune to injury, Lou always attempted to get assignments with me from that day forward. It was either this, or his appreciation for my not berating him for his supervisory oversight. Lou never failed to ask me the same question every time we began a new WEST-PAC trip: "How did you know?"

As a consequence of our continued good fortune, and his powerfully Spiritual while also superstitious perspective on life, Lou named me "SoulMan." A moniker enhanced, no doubt, by my continued insistence that I had no recollection of turning off those water-injection switches—something Lou said he never would have thought to recommend in that situation.

The senior operations officer later wrote a new procedure for the squadron crew training manual. Water-injection contamination scenarios were discussed during all future aircraft familiarization classes. Once I thought about it, my unconscious toggle-switch action—which most certainly helped save our lives—began to trouble me. My agnostic (mostly atheistic) belief-system did not want to consider some of the possibilities trying to push their way into my consciousness.

With a few self-created distractions, I stuffed those nagging feelings (professional pilots are real good at this) and just wore the "Lucky Lieutenant" label. I didn't care much for that other tag. I felt fortunate when Lou's *handle* failed to catch on with the pilot group; a failure probably due to their general discomfort with Spiritual matters and paranormal events.

I should clarify one more (small) item for the analytical types possibly hung up on a detail like: "If the water-injection tank was contaminated, why did the injectors work perfectly on takeoff and fail only on climb out? Secondly, how were the engines able to quickly return to full power when the cylinders were so clogged with oil that they were totally shutting down?" I asked Lou these same questions. For the inquiring *mechanical* minds, here it is in a nutshell.

As Lou explained it, oil and water do not readily mix. Clean water still remained in the long water lines from the wing-mounted reservoir to the engines. Since the lines came from the bottom of the previously half-full water tank, the concentration of oil added to the top of the water tank took a while before it got thick enough to load up the spark plugs—thus preventing normal cylinder-head detonation. When the water-injection switches were turned off, fresh fuel, acting like a cleaning solvent, almost immediately washed out the cylinder heads. Since we hadn't disturbed the control levers during the crisis, aircraft fuel still pumped into the engine cylinders via the respective engine-driven fuel pump. The mechanical fuel pumps remained operational because of the windmilling Hamilton Standard® propellers. The decelerating, non-powered props temporarily turned their respective non-firing engine cylinders; the reciprocal of normal operation. The instant oil flow ceased, incoming fuel flushed the loose sediment and debris out the exhaust valves and manifolds. The still-hot magneto then ignited the fresh, non-contaminated fuel, and normal combustion resumed. This entire power failure scenario transpired during the longest ☉ 5 to 8 seconds of our lives. Luck (or Guidance) was with us, as there were no fires on restart. The combination of detonating backfire and the expelled—still volatile—residual fuel/oil mixture that saturated the engine cowlings (metal-jacketed covering that houses a power plant) could have easily resulted in one or more engine fires.

Lou's adrenaline-filled adventures were not concluded either. To his chagrin, he would participate in more wild rides with *Lieutenant Lucky*—aka "SoulMan."

Storm Catchers

Unlike the modern jets of today that cruise between 30 to 40 thousand feet, the DC-6 can't climb high enough to top potentially treacherous weather conditions. Forty thousand feet is sufficient to get over most T-cells (thunderstorms). Modern jet transports of today normally use advanced ground and airborne radar to avoid weather systems or "super-cells" they can't fly over. With a full cargo and fuel load, we maintained 10 to 12 thousand feet for several hours until light enough to climb to our customary maximum 18 to 19 thousand. Lower altitudes are more fuel-efficient for reciprocating engine aircraft—unlike jet engines that horribly waste fuel at lower altitudes. Our crews banked a lot of instrument flying time bouncing through storm cells and assorted weather fronts. The C-118 had a fairly good radar system. When it worked, we *occasionally* avoided the nastiest part of a thunder-bumper.

As you likely know, thunderstorms are electrically charged—some quite heavily. Lightning primarily discharges to ground, but it's not unusually rare for in-flight aircraft to take some hits. In three and a half years of military flying, my aircraft were struck three times. Yes, these are *skivvy-* (underwear) changing experiences—especially when hit at night. This was my fate on two of those three occasions.

Damage from the entry point is not the major problem. The exit site sustains the lion's share of any rupture. The C-118 extended protective static wicks from all trailing-edge surfaces, which included the ailerons, rudder, horizontal and vertical stabilizers (tail section), and even the radar and various antenna shielding. Engineered to deflect or absorb the majority of any lighting discharge, static wicks are 6- to 18-inch plastic, rope-like items made from tightly wound filament fibers. They provide a cleaner, less-damaging egress point for huge bursts of voltage. The theory is sound, but in reality they fall a little short of perfection. The static wicks *do* help deflect the high-energy bursts. And they are neatly removed by the discharge—as advertised. The problem: adjunctive components attached to the static wicks might also choose to depart the aircraft. Not wishing to get too technical, let's call this fuselage appendage material simply "WING," "RUDDER," and various "STABILIZERS."

In fairness, I don't recall our squadron ever losing a crew member, or an aircraft, to a lightning strike. Perhaps I should work on my static-wick *appreciation* skills. "Three strikes and I *are* still here!" Most would judge this an acceptable trade-off.

Pandemonium Over the Pacific

My most challenging lightning hit came one stormy night, halfway through a long—normally boring—10-hour trip between Japan and the small island of Midway. I had the duty leg in the Captain's chair, with one of the mechanics occupying the copilot's seat. The navigator's station—always a FUN job during rough storms—was just behind us, on the starboard (right) side. To maintain night vision, we had the aft (rear) curtains drawn almost completely shut. This kept light from the foyer and navigation table from entering the flight deck. While on watch, with fully dilated pupils, the brightest, most-piercing white light you can possibly imagine hit squarely on the nose of our aircraft.

Non-aviators might conclude temporary night blindness no more than a minor inconvenience for crews flying on "*look Ma, no hands*" autopilot. We could just wait a few until our vision readjusted, right? But noooo...not that easy.

The avionics instruments are shielded from any permanent damage, but the energy surge overloaded the electrical system. This interruption tripped the alternator relays and popped several instrumentation circuit breakers—exactly what the aircraft's protective circuitry was engineered to do. This domino effect tumbled (knocked off line) all the electrically driven flight instruments, rendering them temporarily unusable. The autopilot's safety feature shuts it off should any of its relied-upon instruments fail. Along with our temporary night blindness and loss of auto-pilot, we were minus all our electric flight instruments—most importantly the artificial-horizon gyro. So, flying over water, at night, with no method to reference straight and level flight, in the center of a raging storm, I tried to cover my abject terror. The caustic edge of my personality thought to itself: "Well, Lt. *Lucky*...how's the trip so far? Are we having FUN yet?"

My cockpit companion, now fully energized, definitely saw no humor in the situation. I *strongly* suggested he get those alternators and circuit breakers back on line, ASAP. He responded by grabbing the red-lensed flashlight attached to the copilot's bulkhead (wall). Through strained and tearful eyes, our young Petty Officer was barely able to turn around in his seat to begin a mostly Braille-type system of resetting the popped breakers. Meanwhile, I was plenty busy.

We had been trained to fly with total electrical failures — even those occurring at night — using static atmospheric instruments as emergency backup. These instruments were crude and difficult to read during *normal* conditions, let alone during a furious storm and night blindness. Even the Navy's most sadistically creative simulator instructors never chose to present such a scenario. Pilots would have mocked it as designed purely for torturous and punitive purposes. [*Since many Navy simulator instructors were washed-out flight cadets, aviators sometimes encountered trainers determined to prove they still had the **right stuff**.*] In smooth air, static instruments prove fairly reliable and sufficiently usable. Purely atmospheric, the only electrical they required is battery-supplied lighting.

Smooth flying conditions were *not* the order of the day — or night, in this case — so static instruments were next to worthless. After loosening his harness to get to the circuit breaker panel, our E-5 found it difficult to stay in his seat. With all his lurching about, he slammed into my right shoulder a couple of times — apologizing profusely. Dealing with a bona fide emergency, he lost none of his military bearing. I had no doubt he would expeditiously follow my explicit orders and "yes sir/sorry sir" me right down to the drink (watery grave) while continuing to do his very best. No debating or second-guessing this superior's (my) orders! [*I gained more respect for the Navy's no-fraternization (with-subordinates) policy after this experience.*]

Reflection. God, I loved the crew camaraderie. I normally enjoyed my leadership responsibility as well. Because of my frequency of crisis participation, I would later reflect on the intimacy and oneness that are part and parcel of any military unit — especially during wartime conditions. They are undoubtedly a main reason why war buddies stand the test of time.

The Moment of Truth

Simultaneous to the mechanic's efforts, I grabbed the pilot-side flashlight and began holding it between my clenched teeth. Although we had instrument lighting, my partial blindness required additional illumination. Continuously repeating a manual mechanical slave (realignment) of the artificial horizon gyro, I included this vital reference in my rapid scan of the static instruments. The horizon instrument's mechanical pull rod provided a temporary spin to its internal gyro. Used during preflight preparations to mechanically boost the gyro's speed, cautious pilots also used the pull rod to double check electric slave function *during* flight. This ensured the trusted gauge was still on-line. My Rube Goldberg, smoke-and-mirrors manipulations were unreliable, at best. We desperately needed our artificial horizon gyro back on line.

I watched our airspeed very closely. This gave me delayed but reliable information about nose attitude. If the airspeed began to decrease, I knew the nose of the aircraft had risen above level horizon. The correction called for easing the steering yoke forward, very slightly, being *extremely* careful not to overcompensate. Over controlling could send the aircraft and its occupants into a screaming dive. On the other adjustment end, stalling the plane in these conditions *also* meant certain death—since the reference points needed to make a recovery were absent.

[*Note: It is very easy to get disoriented in these conditions, as apparently did happen to John F. Kennedy, Jr. Without the solid reference points provided by instruments, or a visual horizon, it's very difficult—if not impossible—by touch or feel alone, to know whether you are straight and level, or in a seventy-five degree bank.*]

Even with all the hours of simulator time working with the most determined ground-training personnel, I was never presented a more difficult flying situation. *This was pilot hell!* Wringing wet from stressful perspiration, I thought how orgasmic the Navy's DC-6/7 simulator instructors would be to hear about our *juicy* emergency-flight situation. Before they could learn of it, however, we needed to survive. Blessedly, after what seemed an eternity on battery/flashlight illumination and wildly bouncing, static flight instruments, the mechanic got the main alternator and power back on line. I felt reborn! As I sang aloud a line from an old classic, "I was blind...but now I see," I temporarily set aside my atheistic beliefs, and felt—in my heart—that, **yes**, Grace *is* truly amazing.

Back in Business! So occupied with the job at hand, I failed to notice the entire flight crew was up. Hanging on to various pieces of hardware and equipment located behind the flight deck, they strained to see what the heck was going on. Included in the mix: the A/C for this trip, another Three-Striper (Full Commander).

Although this *Midway-thriller* does not reside on my subjective top-three list, in retrospect, perhaps it should. I realize today that no amount of flying skill, alone, could have pulled this off. I define the paranormal or extra-sensory perception areas as a **level-two** miracle. You decide where this experience fits. At the time, I found my ego-dominant self most happy to accept all the accolades and the continuation of my "Lucky Lieutenant" image. This story significantly segues to Miracle Candidate #2. I wanted you to fully sense the challenge and general crew stress from a blinding electrical storm. Combine the preceding conditions with ultra-secret, super-deadly cargo, and you're ready to appreciate the fascination and horror present during our next "Twilight Zone" episode.

A Boredom and Terror Cocktail, Please!

Since our squadron flew most transport missions with a double-crew complement, we normally got some rest during a flight assignment. The *country-club* design of our ex Air Force birds came with four privacy-curtained racks (beds) located rearward from the foyer and navigator's station, about eight feet behind the cockpit. One set of bunk beds resided on the port side and another set on the starboard. This arrangement allowed pilots and navigators to extend their flight-duty day up to twenty-four hours, versus eight hours of flight time (in 24) — the limit imposed by single-crew regulation. So, while I'd been up to my ass in alligators during the lightning strike episode, the A/C and the 3P (third pilot) had been racked out — at least until the fireworks commenced. As the sleeping area lay directly in line with the engine propellers, noise and vibration were a given. "Sleep," especially in rough weather, comprised hanging on while trying to get some semblance of rest. Cockpit crews wished to be as alert as possible for their respective turn at the helm. The rest of the crew, who had very few duties during flight, preferred the cooler, quieter, aft section — with fold-down canvas benches and reclining seats.

Transport aviation is often described as, "Long moments of boredom mixed with short moments of sheer terror!" Feeling any leftover psychological hypothermia after fighting for your life during the lightening-strike episode? If you like, I'll help you warm up over some St. Elmo's fire. This next story should toast your marshmallows.

Pensacola, Florida: T-34 – Primary Trainer (first solo); T-28b for next phase of training, included advanced acrobatic, instrument, cross-country, airfield procedures, formation flying (both two — and four-plane divisions), and field carrier-landing practice (VT-5 squadron). Single engine carrier qualification was achieved solo (no instructor on board) — USS Shangri-la.

Corpus Christie, Texas: Advance training in S2-F. Multi-engine phase included advanced cross-country, instrumentation, emergency procedures, and multi-engine carrier qualification—USS Bon Homme Richard.

Fleet Assignment: After completing jungle survival/simulated POW training, and an additional eight-week Celestial Navigation school, I was assigned to my FIRST CHOICE—VR-21 transport squadron based out of Barber's Point, Hawaii, utilizing the Douglas Aircraft Mfg. C-118b/DC-6b equipment.

CHAPTER THIRTEEN

Great Balls of Fire and Little Green Men

♥　　　♥　　　♥

Miracle Candidate #2. As far as I know, secrecy is no longer an issue for any of what you read in this chapter. US participation in the Vietnam War concluded in the early 1970s. The Pentagon has released period war secrets of a much higher level than anything I'm recounting. I've been neither instructed nor ordered to be silent about any of these events once the Nam war concluded. If I'm wrong about the secrecy issues, I hope those of you enlightened — or at least entertained — will kindly help out with my legal defense fund.

The load we least wanted to carry was the MK-4 chemical bomb. [*I may not have the correct weapon designation number, but my memory rings crystal clear regarding our experience.*] I hauled these babies only two or three times during my Navy career — more than enough, even for *my* ignorant bravado. These 4500-pound metal-caged monsters made us all nervous. Automatic cancellation of landing clearance (anywhere) should one of the monstrosities leak chemicals during flight, did nothing to ease our trepidation. With the bomb carriage open, we could see all the wires, tubes, meters, canisters, electrical switches, and relays in its assembly. Although we used secretive, Red-Label transfer areas for its loading and unloading, I was amazed so little effort went into camouflaging these behemoths of destructive power.

I choose not to recall where we delivered the devices, but more relevant was the mega level of non-communicated vulnerability we all felt. We repeatedly asked, "What do we do if a chemical canister leaks during flight?" The special couriers, who stayed with the weapons only until air transport was arranged, always had the same response. They closed their briefcase, handed us the top-secret manifest, and then — with a wry grin — turned and walked away. I'm confident these ultra-secret weapons couriers were in-training for future positions as the infamous *"Men in Black"* we were destined to meet. All we knew for sure: any bomb springing a leak during flight would place us in *deep doo-doo* — again.

For this particular trip we would carry two units, the maximum C-118 complement. I was pleased to have my compatriot Lou with us for this *adventure,* as we expected bad weather (T-cells) during our long, over-water section. I wanted our most thorough engineer in the cockpit during my flight leg.

Lou learned a lot from his near-fatal supervisory mistake in Cubi Point. Determined never to repeat that lapse in judgment, he was now the most-focused, least-complacent flight mechanic in our squadron. Having joined the instructional team, Lou trained all new arrivals in possible life-saving information. Because of that one incident others might refer to as a *bad* mistake, many future lives would potentially be saved. Every time he told the *near-crash* story to a rapturously attentive audience, he irrevocably influenced belief-systems and behaviors.

All renewed confidence aside, I sensed the normally gregarious Lou was as disappointed as I about our load assignment. He worried about the foul weather through which we must fly our electronically activated weapons. To measure any chemical discharge from the MK-4s, we carried a Geiger-like, leak-test meter. Test-gauge warning instruments did not reassure personnel trapped high above ground in metal cylinders. Because our load was classified Top Secret, the only circulated manifest accompanied the cargo. This paperwork rested in a special pouch along with a loaded .38 revolver. Normally the third pilot acted as aircraft cargo courier, and he made our reservations at the destination airfield's "Red-Label" area; a generic tag for any *north-forty* transfer point used to load and unload hot or toxic cargo. Other than the obvious implication inherent in requesting the use of a Red Label area, airport operations personnel were oftentimes kept in the dark regarding the true nature of transiting cargo. And they knew better than to ask. [*This procedural knowledge proved critical to saving our lives during Miracle Candidate #3.*]

Before departure, the cargo guys received plenty of extra supervision—even from the radio operators—ensuring our MK-4 *nasties* were double- and even triple-tied down. They were heavy cages. If one of them broke loose during a rough flight, it was *"all she wrote and goodnight Irene."*

Preflight completed, we commenced takeoff—climbing to our assigned cruising altitude without incident. Scheduled for the second leg, but too restless to sleep, I hung around the foyer shooting the breeze with the cockpit crew. Expecting a lot of electrical activity that night, we were understandably on edge. Chaperoning a potentially lethal combination of human- and nature-created energy would make even the saltiest of sailors cry for their mother. Now well after sunset, we saw only a small crescent of reddish orange sunlight reflecting through the broken stratus clouds ahead of us.

Harmless energy?

After leveling off at our initial cruising altitude, we noticed some innocuous static electricity formations called "St. Elmo's Fire" building up on the plane's metal exterior. This uncommon but not overly rare phenomenon was always entertaining. Like they had a mind of their own, while enjoying a great game, small golf- or baseball-sized spheres of charged energy rolled around on the outside metal surfaces. St. Elmo's rolling patterns were often repetitive and somewhat predictable. We amused ourselves on these long flights by guessing how many seconds a particular charge would take to complete its roll. From the nose, out the entire leading edge of the wing, St. Elmo then dropped underneath to eventually reappear at the opposite wing tip—having run the entire underneath surface—all before returning to the nose again. After numerous repetitions of its predictable pattern, the orbital energy balls would spontaneously reverse direction.

Telekinesis

On *this* particular night, the dancing movement of our brightly concentrated spheres of static energy seemed purposeful. When the energy appeared to be responding to my mental focus, I worried that psychological pressure from the MK-4 presence was getting to me. Either that or I was suddenly able to *completely* predict St. Elmo's change of direction. I tested this wild theory by mentally willing the rolling balls of fire to stop and reverse direction. I focused for several moments without saying anything to anyone. Each time, St Elmo seemed to respond to my mental instructions. Or, perhaps I responded to *its* commands? I speculated how any display of so-called *static* energy could be under the control of a person. Was this an example of telekinesis? If so, how was it possible? [*Because this experiment was turning weird, and I wished to avoid having my mental faculties scrutinized (something I later volunteered for), I've kept knowledge of these curious fireball manipulations to myself – until now.*]

Soon after ceasing my mental shenanigans, our frolicking batch of St. Elmo crossed a static wick and discharged harmlessly into the dark abyss and inky blackness of night. At least those static wicks served a safe purpose with old St. Elmo. After a half-hour of this jovial but eerie merriment, preoccupied with trying to make sense out of my aberrant discovery, I almost forgot about our hazardous cargo.

Calm before the Storm

Due to come on duty in 3½ hours, I made a final check of our sleeping giants before turning in. The leak-test meter needle had not moved. No surprise, as we stationed a cargo handler directly along side each bomb—watching and listening for any irregularities. All was quiet. The major weather cells looked like they might miss us. "Perhaps this flight will be uneventful after all," I reassured the rearward crewmembers. Since the nose of the first MK-4 sat directly behind my lower bunk, just a few feet from my sleeping position, I left the hatch (door) open. I could keep an eye on our weapons of mass destruction while I rested. Not alone in my mother-hen routine, all crewmembers nervously double checked tie-down chains and radiation readings, reassuring themselves that life – as they knew it – would continue a little while longer.

The flight droned on uneventfully. Shortly after the duty crew completed its post-fuel-burn climb, I was awakened. Now at eighteen thousand feet, it was time for Lou and me to take over. I overheard the navigator brief his replacement on course changes needed to dodge approaching T-cells. Surprisingly, I'd rested quite well—even dozing off for part of my rack time. But instead of sugar plums, dancing fireballs punctuated my drowsy slumber. As I slowly rose to a sitting position, I looked back at our ordnance to see that all was quiet. I chastised myself about being a wimp, fearing these spare-parts cages. I was a US Naval Officer, by God! It was about time I conquered all fears and bravely did my job. Feeling a renewed confidence, I glanced forward to see the primary navigator slaving over the LORAN (long range navigational aid) screen trying to get an update on our location, prior to shift change. The Loran was not cooperating due to increased electrical activity. Celestial sextant readings were unavailable because of cloud cover. The navigator dimmed his table lights, attempting to scope some reliable triangular readings. The only other illumination was the red lighting from the cockpit instruments, which I could see through the partially opened curtains.

A New Reality

Half awake, with legs outstretched from the bottom bunk, I struggled to pull up my pants. Suddenly, I heard two blood-curdling screams and the words, "OH SHIT!" from the cockpit. None of my physical senses prepared me for what then followed. Alive in the cockpit danced a flashing, pulsating, sizzling, popping, absolutely brilliant yellow-white light. A sphere of fire, slightly smaller but a lot more menacing than a bowling ball, created a blinding light show. Concentrated, supercharged, and noisy, without doubt this was the most dangerous, malevolent looking force I'd ever seen. The previously harmless mass of static electricity now claimed a size and concentration larger than any of us had ever seen or possibly imagined. The worst part: it was now *up close and very personal!* Somehow this terrifying, conscious-acting energy had penetrated our aircraft and was spinning ominously between the traumatized cockpit crew. Pancaking their backs against respective side windows, they desperately tried to avoid the monster's wrath.

I could not accept what I was seeing! Aircraft infiltration by this energy type was believed impossible! Although an occasionally discussed topic, perhaps the reason we'd not received any reports about this phenomenon was because the witnesses are no longer with us...I thought belatedly.

Come to Papa. The FUN was not over. The pulsating fireball, after its brief, *spirited* visit to the cockpit, resumed its aft motion. Three crewmembers waited up front to start their shift. They quickly stepped aside, as the white-faced cockpit occupants turned rearward to follow the Grim Reaper's path.

The supercharged, multi-colored fireball hopped and rolled down the aisle directly toward me. Still sitting on the bunk, frozen in horror and amazement, I thought, "Maybe there is a God and this is my punishment for screwing around with Mother Nature." All that wonderful confidence from a moment ago—gone. Only halfway into my trousers, I reflexively grabbed the upper bunk railing and swung my torso straight up into the air, as the bouncing lightning ball fortuitously dipped. Missing me by a scant few inches, my emotions flooded with relief! Short-lived, however, the Guinness record for *abject terror* immediately replaced my reprieve. Our charging, thrashing, St. Elmo Monster, obviously angered by its temporary confinement, jumped up and discharged—with an ear-ringing, metal-twisting, heart-stomping explosion—directly into the nose of the first bomb! My throat filled with burning stomach bile, as the crew spit out a chorus of four-letter words. I saw my life in review...regretting failed accomplishments and repenting my less-than-exemplary human behavior.

After the sobering flashback, I finally realized the bomb had not detonated—*yet!* Reactive noises, sparks, and swirling smoke from the mass of metal, tubing, switches, and relays were exactly what we expected from a breached casing. Bringing new meaning to *snap, crackle, and pop,* contrasting energies continued with no apparent letup. With burning electrical and super-charged ozone singeing our collective nostrils, I sensed a herd-type (symbiotic) consciousness with my crew. Our synchronous belief: *we were better off with quick death from a bomb detonation.* Slow, torturous, chemical exposure, after ditching in a lonely black sea, supplied material for a Stephen King novel—assuming we even made it *that* far. Again, our explicit, in-flight orders: "A chemical leak or weapons discharge cancels all landing rights." "CJ," my critical-mind symbiont, caustically queried; "If we promise to come down in pieces, might that order be waived?"

After a few more sobering moments, the A/C motioned for me to inspect the damage. As Second-in-Command, I had been volunteered to determine whether we lived or died. Barely able to make my fingers work, I zipped up my pants, went aft, and nervously reached for the leak-test meter; stowed on the bulkhead adjacent to the final target for St. Elmo's wrath. I didn't hear any sounds coming from the instrument, but that was of no particular comfort. The plane was always noisy, even without residual harmonics. Considering the past few moments, staying hopeful was a stretch. As crewmates maintained a fearful distance, I saw the world through the eyes of a leper. Holding their collective breaths, they waited for the inspection results. I activated the sensitive test instrument and directed the Sniffer into the nooks and crannies of both bombs. My slow, methodical inspection covered every square inch.

After the longest wait of their lives, I gave my enthusiastic report: *"Not a peep—she's clean as a whistle!"* ☺ This messenger brought *good* news. Amidst deafening cheers, whooping, and hollering, we took a real breath for the first time in many minutes. Having temporarily suspended protocol, I got handshakes and hugs from everyone. At that moment—suspended in time—we ceased to be separated by rate or rank. We were a tight, cohesive, intimate, professional, and very appreciative group of dedicated men who just walked through Dante's Inferno and lived to celebrate it. Lou was the loudest now as he exclaimed, "I told you guys the Lieutenant was lucky...he's a *Soul* Man!"

Except for Lou and a few of the original crew that miraculously survived the Cubi-Point takeoff, very few squadron personnel openly categorized my water-injection shutoff action as paranormal or psychic. Now, *this* crew looked at me strangely. Clearly, Lou's spirited rhetoric was gaining converts. Considering what we'd just experienced, I couldn't be upset with him. Once again...I was very thankful to be alive.

I had some remaining concerns, which I shared quietly with the Aircraft Commander. We discussed the possibility of some as-yet-undetectable housing cracks. A remote chance also existed that the test meter, so close to the explosion, was on the fritz. His call, but I agreed with his decision to keep the negative scenarios between us. No need to worry the crew unnecessarily. All personnel would get checked out upon landing. We congruently decided reports of this incident were best left for later, lest some panicky operations officer deny us landing clearance. Our strict orders were to report leaks. As far as we knew, we had none.

After safely landing on hardpan (ground), we tendered our verbal incident report to the receiving courier. Listening impassively, he said nothing. Yes...*definitely* a "MIB" candidate. He used his backup test meter to recheck our findings. No evidence of a leak, relieved us of possession. I was never so happy to get rid of a cargo. Later, people in the know told me that weapons of this type are heavily shielded to protect them from unwanted or accidental energy surges. "It is a highly remote possibility for a static charge, or even a direct lightning hit, to break the shroud or breach any chemical-contained area," the experts decreed. I'd still like to see one of those *"ex-spurts"* stoically stand by and *observe* while St. Elmo performed its power-ball show. Betting odds would favor *any* witness coming out of their skins — just as we did. To pontificate theory — after the fact — is one thing; quite another to experience the real deal. In the ready-room of our temporary staging domicile, not one of the other flight crews gave our story any credence.

After safe delivery of worrisome cargo, it was standard crewmember procedure to make a beeline for our respective service clubs; there to get crocked on aged whiskey and wild women...or was it Wild Turkey and aged women? Regardless, the crew commonly engaged in festive tomfoolery to celebrate their avoidance of death.

When we returned to Barbers Point, investigators, including some non-squadron and very serious government types, dressed in — you guessed it — non-descript black, interviewed our entire crew. Incredibly, *still* no one believed us. Perhaps the special agency investigators did, but they remained tightlipped — as usual — and never gave us any feedback or assurances. Our local physics expert who doubled as the squadron's meteorologist told us that behavior of the St. Elmo phenomenon (as presented) was not possible, because it would discharge into the first metal it contacted. In other words, the squadron's unofficial position: we were either falsifying statements, or were all delusional. After mandatory examinations by the base flight surgeon, and several "would you rather burn the US flag or spit on the bible" type questions, they granted us a return-to-flight-duty status — *provided* we not speak further about the incident. Seems our reportage disturbed the other squadron crewmembers. Our response? "How about us? We found it *damn* well disturbing!" Some squadron pilots nervously chided us, suggesting we'd seen something akin to a UFO — complete with *"Little Green Men."*

At the time, I found it extremely frustrating to be disbelieved. I didn't possess the larger perspectives I enjoy today. I now know that *fear* was the reason everyone denied our testimony — not any lack of credibility on our parts. We reported the existence of a world-class Boogie Monster... one that strikes defenseless crews, without warning, in a small, metal straight jacket, thousands of feet above solid ground. Yes, I eventually forgave them for cracking jokes about Little Green Men. Lacking any rational explanation for our experience, this denial proved a necessary component to maintaining military discipline, effectiveness, and the fulfillment of assigned duties; duties that included the continued flying into electrical storms — with or without hazardous cargo — in order to deliver the goods. Squadron personnel fears may have been temporarily stuffed, but they were certainly not healed or released. To any brave but frightened military men or women — past or present — who read this, including my VR-21 squadron mates, I trust this Spiritual overview to help put mental and emotional monsters to permanent rest.

Collateral Duties

Do you still think life a series of random events? Note how my non-flying experience proved vital to surviving our *next* adrenalin-filled adventure (Miracle Candidate #3).

Although flying was our priority function, both officer and enlisted personnel performed additional responsibilities. During wartime, auxiliary functions were left primarily to administrative types specifically trained in those areas. Aviators who wished to make a career out of the Navy were well served by participating in as many collateral duty assignments as possible. They then received supplementary administrative fitness reports, which, if rendered satisfactory and above, proved indispensable for advancement. Not screwing up almost guaranteed an officer the first three (junior) grades. Promotion to Lt. Commander (0-4) and above required the demonstration of administrative ability, and perhaps just as important, political savvy. I surprised myself by discovering that, in spite of relationship-trust issues, I possessed fair-to-good organization and people skills. I got a little *gung-ho* with revising and upgrading procedures—until I ran into the proverbial brick wall.

I came up with a great plan to economize both time and money. The Department head, a full Commander (O-5), career officer, and someone I flew with occasionally and found unimaginative, pooh-poohed my concept. He could not cite any actual objections or flaws in my reorganization plan; but noting my obvious enthusiasm, he patiently explained that *"IT"* had always been done this *one* traditional Navy way and no precedent existed for creating a new plan to replace the old Navy Way. The logic of his argument escaping me, I responded with: "Let me ask you this, Sir; if we came up with a better mousetrap to utilize our personnel more effectively *and* save the taxpayers money, could it not become the *new* Navy way, SIR?" [*When pushing my luck with a superior, I always used two "sirs" per sentence.*] The Commander, with a stern scowl replacing his patient demeanor, rejoined with, "Are you trying to be a *wise-ass,* mister?"

Anchors Away

Not philosophically aligned with one-dimensional thinking, further resistance proved futile. My judgmental views were very black and white in those days. Sufficiently motivated, I could have discovered ways to be creative and still respect Navy (Blue) tradition. Lacking a more expansive realization, I dispensed with any more thoughts about making the Navy a permanent vocation.

Although I lacked some polish and maturity when not flying, my performance in the field was judged exemplary. Well respected for my flying skills and decision-making abilities, by late 1967 I acquired several times more than the required recommendations needed to be eligible for Aircraft Commander Training. Operations officially offered me an upgrade, but because I intended to forego a career in the Navy, I declined the promotion in order to maximize flight hours and improve my airline employment opportunities. I could—and eventually did—obtain an Aircraft Commander designation after joining the Reserves. Forgoing A/C training added the second ingredient to the fortuitous and lifesaving intervention described in Miracle Candidate #3. Now meet an additional cast-member.

Lone-Wolf Sailor

Late 1966 or early 1967, a young, recently promoted Commander named "Buckley," joined our squadron. Commander Buckley was an intense, hard-driving personality that most of the junior officers ill favored. A lone wolf, myself, I did not see him as intimidating. Looking past his surly exterior, I saw one of the Navy's most entertaining characters. He had so much individually expressed, "out there" personality, I was amazed he'd made it to full Commander. Subjectively speaking, although mavericks were occasionally recognized for their intuitive prowess on the battlefield, middle-grade promotional opportunities favored conformists that stayed under the radar and didn't make waves (pun intended). A blusterous, *take-no-prisoners* Commander in our squadron was going to be a lot of FUN. Here was a guy doing it *his* way, and surviving.

As Buckley came to us with an impressive history of varied flight experience, he was to be upgraded quickly. All aviators started as third pilots in order to gain experience with our particular aircraft, squadron procedures, staging satellites, and instrument approaches to airfields we transited—especially those in Vietnam. I flew one trip with Buckley back when he was a 3P. He impressed me then as an intense, but quick study. By late 1967, the Commander had sufficient experience and the required recommendations for the top spot.

On Buckley's very first departure from Barbers Point, as a brand new Aircraft Commander, the stalwart and proud three-striper ran his plane off the far end of the runway in an aborted takeoff attempt. The less-than-impressed Skipper of VR-21 noted the resulting giant cloud of smoke and dust rising from the distant tundra. We later pieced together what happened. Visually double-checking the aircraft from the cockpit windows, just prior to the takeoff run, either Buckley or the copilot saw something red attached to one of the landing-gear struts. A gear lock-down pin left in place would prevent the wheels from retracting after takeoff. When maintenance personnel moved or stored aircraft, they routinely inserted landing-gear pins (with red tags) into the struts. Ground crew then removed them prior to gate departure.

Rather than taxi all the way back to the hangar to check out the gear, Buckley did the more expedient thing by sending the chief mechanic outside to take a look-see. Since all engines were running and warmed up, he lowered the flaps to the full-down position to minimize prop wash. Thus the mechanic more easily opened the aft side door to make his way to the gear struts. The red marking turned out to be some non-standard paint strip.

Inspection completed, the tower announced that Buckley's plane must depart immediately, or make way for other aircraft piling up behind. In their rush to get going, they made a critical error. Changing any one of the final takeoff settings required, by procedure, a redo of the entire takeoff checklist. They did *not* do so and everyone overlooked the flap setting, still at *full flaps!* This position, correct for an approach and landing, allows the lowest possible airspeed without wing stall. The correct *departure* setting was 15 to 20 degrees.

Not realizing the full-flap setting was preventing sufficient liftoff speed, they used up precious concrete. Already past the safe-abort marker, Buckley reversed engines and applied maximum braking. The flight crew was lucky to escape without physical injury when—as could be expected—the aircraft bounced into the dirt, weeds, and other foliage off the end of the duty runway. The plane was not critically damaged, but the cockpit crew egos definitely took a hit. In addition to flight-crew embarrassment, aircraft accidents and incidents create a pile of paperwork. The final report included negative notations in the flight jackets of the entire cockpit crew. The Commanding Officer ordered all responsible personnel to fully retake their respective training programs. Back to A/C school went the new laughingstock of VR-21. From this point forward, our proud officer was known as "FLAPS" Buckley. Junior officers never dared call him "flaps" to his face, but senior officers, many who resented his independent aloofness, did so gleefully.

This serious, intense, man, now on a mission to never make another mistake, double- and triple-checked everything. With mandatory redundancy a real pain in the backside for anyone who flew with him, Commander Buckley became even *less* popular with crewmembers—officers and enlisted alike. Flight personnel did everything they could to avoid flying with him...especially those who were not top-drawer. Buckley insisted on the same professionalism and intense focus on the job that he brought forth. Anyone with a mediocre performance level had better call in sick if they got assigned to his crew. *Hell hath no fury* like Buckley riding anyone he felt not up to the highest knowledge and skill level. It should not surprise you that I actually liked, respected, and got along—as well as anyone— with this intense loner. While definitely not relaxing, being on his crew wasn't boring either. Commander Buckley had a way of attracting other independent types that took pride in their work. His challenge: creating an atmosphere of *team* participation out of a collection of talented and determined misfits.

Unfriendly Fire

For the years I flew in and out of designated combat zones, the only weapons fire I encountered was from small, semi-automatics. We sometimes were shot at during final approach and touchdown at the various bases throughout South Vietnam. We learned that a few US airbase employees, sympathetic to the Viet Cong (VC), sneaked out at night to the end of active runways and took potshots at approaching aircraft. With 100 percent security impossible when hiring civilian workers, a constant cat-and-mouse went on between base security and the secretive perpetrators. Fortunately for us, it was difficult to do serious damage firing at a moving target from long range with just a pistol. Leaded shielding underneath our seats provided an extra precaution. A couple of crews were hit in the windshield. Good fortune and our normal transit of the more secure routes and airfields favored us with no squadron fatalities—knock on wood.

In the late 1960s, US forces were not universally effective stopping enemy supply lines. The VC became more aggressive in their excursions south of the DMZ, and big, slow-moving aircraft like ours made especially attractive targets; so we were understandably nervous when inside any reported problem areas.

Miracle Candidate #3—"Checklist Blues."

The preceding preparatory background set the stage for the next miracle candidate. As I drop us right into the scene, I invite you to try to feel this experience, just as we did that early morning of January 30, 1968. Vietnam veterans "in country" will recognize this date.

At approximately one or two in the morning, we prepared for departure from Tan Son Nhut Air Base after completing half of a very long duty day. I was more than ready to get out of Saigon. We were #1 in line and had received clearance for immediate takeoff. Commander Buckley was in the left seat. I was flying copilot on this leg. Buckley requested the takeoff checklist to be done *again,* his post-accident routine. Although everything on the field was quiet, and I was not one who normally succumbed to nervous anxiety, I felt a sudden and unexplained urgency to get airborne. Even with the strictly adhered-to rules of protocol and military order, it took all my patience to follow, without censure or comment, the Commander's directive. The tower pushed us to go and I was *sure* we were set. I felt the continued mounting of that inner pressure, as I slowly, agonizingly, repeated the checklist. I then grabbed the radio mike to transmit to the tower that we were rolling into runway position, when Buckley announced: "Tell them to let our other plane go around us. I want to recheck the engines." I noted the roll of Lou's eyes, as our salty, now Chief (E-7) mechanic, sat in the engineer's seat for takeoff. He, too, wanted to haul butt out of harm's way.

Another of our squadron's aircraft just happened to be there at the same time. After notified of our further delay, they quickly came around to begin their takeoff roll in what had been *our* position. Under full power, their C-118 advanced about 200 yards when all hell broke loose. While squadron plane 2 continued its fortuitous escape, enemy explosives began raining down on the perimeter. The mortar firing positions were located in the distant jungle foliage—out beyond our end of the airfield.

The VC strategically chose the time of month. With no moon, other than the firelight of battle, it was pitch black. Clearly the VC had prepared for a major battle; the shelling systematically moved in our direction. Even a Maytag® Repair Person never experienced the loneliness we felt at that moment. The runway apron, upon which we sat, was way out on the least-secure corner of the airfield. As we watched our replacement successfully climb out ahead of the oncoming danger, Buckley was now more than ready to follow their lead.

Believing we could outrun the mortars, *if* we departed immediately, we again requested departure clearance. Control-tower personnel refused to release us. They immediately closed the runway to normal traffic, waving off and diverting all incoming planes, allowing launching of aircraft vital to the counterattack. We then tried *begging*—to no avail. The tower ordered us to shut down right where we were and to take cover. We reluctantly complied, quickly exiting the aircraft. Just then a mortar shell hit a fuel-storage area almost 200 yards to the side of our position. The VC now had our range; the fuel shack was about the same distance from the estimated mortar launch point as were we.

The only cover at our barren location was a deep trench running perpendicular and adjacent to the end of the duty runway. The Commander ordered all personnel to take cover in the ditch, which seemed prudent at the time. He attempted to encourage the crew through his vehement prediction that "the helos will get the bastards!" Fully armed attack helicopters began their search, scouting just ahead of the scrambling jets that would soon be strafing in the blind with chemical napalm explosives. Meanwhile, the burning fuel shack lit up our position like a Christmas tree. Our shiny, aluminum-skinned aircraft was a sitting duck for the continued mortar attack. Like a moth drawn to light, small weapons fire advanced toward us as well. To make matters worse, we discovered a six-inch diameter fuel line running the entire length of our ditch protection—originating from the burning shack!

No rocket scientists were needed to survey our situation and evaluate our chances. Evident that we were once again—say it with me please—in *deep doo-doo*, I advised Buckley of my concerns about becoming the VC's target of opportunity. They seemed a larger force than originally believed, and therefore might make it to our location. Buckley returned to the aircraft radio more motivated to get takeoff clearance, but his second effort also failed. Ground control granted only the promise they would send a marine transport unit, when available. In the meantime, they advised us to continue "lying low."

Fearful of losing another aircraft, Buckley wanted to believe the incessant VC would be repelled in time, or the marine transport would save the day. "It's not possible for the most secure air base in Vietnam, this far south of the DMZ, to be overrun by an inferior military force," he screamed above the clamor. I did not share the Commander's confidence (or denial), as my inner alarm bell rang even louder—"danger, danger, Will Robinson!"

Suddenly, right in the middle of this stress-filled crisis, I experienced a reassuring calmness. As strange as this may seem, my highly stimulated "Larry" personality felt itself slipping softly into the background. At the time, I only briefly sensed some presence—beyond my conscious awareness—taking the lead. The internal reassurances were so strong and purposeful, I unconsciously went with the flow. From this moment forward, concerning our outcome, I both participated in and *witnessed* my own actions.

Through the din of battle I observed myself shouting to the Commander, "I've got an idea how to get departure clearance. I'll be right back after checking it out." I could not hear his verbal response, but his body language said anything was worth a try. He seemed to finally comprehend the seriousness of our situation. Lou, *definitely* understanding our dire circumstances, asked how he could help. I instructed him to stay put and try to calm the terrified crew: "I *will* get us out of here!" This confidence came from someplace other than Larry's anxious presence, I assure you.

I sprinted (I was a little lighter and faster in those days) for the closest area where I thought I might find a field phone. I still had no idea what I was going to do, or say. With no close structures, I ran several hundred yards to the nearest barracks area. Upon arrival, I almost got shot in my tracks by a frightened marine sentry. In the darkness, telling friend from foe proved next to impossible.

After harnessing his .45 Colt, the sentry took me to a ground telephone line and helped me ring the tower. Later, I questioned how we even got through to them during this extremely hectic period [*I no longer wonder.*] Almost immediately, I talked to the duty operations commander for Tan Son Nhut Air Base. At this undesirable hour he was not the most senior or experienced ground officer in the command, undoubtedly in our favor with what came next.

Still not knowing what I was going to say, I quickly identified myself. Even as a somewhat placid observer, my human personality self was not prepared for what came out of my mouth next: "Sir! Because the enemy is surely listening and we didn't want to become an even greater target, we felt it prudent to not say this over an unsecured airway. It's my duty to inform you that our shiny and very visible C-118 Bravo at the end of the field is carrying extremely hot, Red-Label cargo. If it should be hit by those encroaching mortar shells, the resulting blast will kill not only our crew, but likely take out (level) at least three fourths of the entire field. What are your instructions...SIR?"

The junior field Commander hesitated a few, agonizingly long seconds. I pictured him deciding if I was running a bluff, or whether our cargo was as advertised. Operations had to quickly assess the opposing risk factors. He surely knew that non-manifested, Red-Label cargo did, in fact, pass through secretly. And no way existed for him to quickly verify my story—one way or the other. These rational factors occurred to me much later, though. I was not *thinking* at this point—only cooperating with what I now believe were Guiding influences. After a torturous few moments, he answered: "You are cleared for *immediate* takeoff. Call us when ready to roll and we'll hold up traffic." "*Yes Sir...right away Sir!*"

I hustled my deceitful butt back to our ditched crew and announced our departure authorization. Coincidentally, Commander Buckley had just gotten a tower update, which confirmed our clearance. He gave me a questioning look as I scrambled (huffing and puffing) into the right seat. Lou—hot on my heels—hit the jump seat. We did the fastest engine start and takeoff checklist on record, wasting not one second lest our precious departure clearance be revoked. Still concerned about encroaching mortar fire, I silently prayed the tower chief would not ask for cargo confirmation. My prayers were answered as he soberly announced, "You are cleared for immediate takeoff—contact departure control when airborne." After a tense, mortar-dodging takeoff run, we switched radio frequencies and very thankfully continued our climb out.

As we carried on to Japan with our load of barbed wire, extra-soft toilet paper, and other non-essentials for the Commanding Admiral in Atsugi, we learned the Cong overran three quarters of the entire field before finally being driven back [*equal to my feigned blast radius, you'll note*]. In just 15 more minutes, our trench position was totally beset by enemy troops. With one .38 revolver among our entire crew, no one—including the A/C—doubted we would've been *maggot* food without that takeoff clearance. Commander Buckley gave me the only "well done" anyone had ever heard him grant. He then asked, "How *did* you get that clearance?" "Please don't demand an answer to that question Commander. Trust me when I say you are much better off *not* knowing." My serious look and tone did the trick. No follow-up order for details came from the always-inquisitive Buckley. I gave Lou a little eyewink, and he gently squeezed my left shoulder in an affectionate "thank you Lieutenant" gesture.

Tan Son Nhut Air Base - Saigon - Jan. 30, 1968

R. THOMPSON

Party Time

The squadron was all a-buzz about our close call with the beginning of the infamous Tet Offensive. At a special reception, we feasted and accepted congratulations from the Skipper and his senior staff. I let the Commander take all the credit for our narrow escape. After all, he had been the responsible A/C. I stayed in the background to (hopefully) not attract uncomfortable questions. Our Barbers Point Naval Base newspaper published a front-page spread with a proud Buckley front-and-center, entitled "The HERO Returns." I was genuinely pleased he'd lost the dunce ("flaps") image.

Nov. '69 class w/Western Airlines, awaits

OK, to be *perfectly* candid, I was a *little* bummed over having to be the silent hero. But I was more afraid of getting into additional hot water with the CO. The Navy doesn't pass out medals for running bluffs on operations officers. Ego would have to be content with my poker skills and the *incidental* fact that we were all still alive. Besides, in the back of my mind I remembered that I really didn't have wherewithal, gumption, or the sensed timing to have pulled off this little maneuver, all by myself. As I mulled over the *how* of that Saigon performance, atheistic rigidity prevented me from realizing what did.

In the next chapter I will attempt to summarize our examination of the miraculous.

CHAPTER FOURTEEN

Miracles—a Conclusion

♥   ♥   ♥

Evaluation—**It's Your Turn.** So, what do you think of the three primary miracle candidates? Now that you've read them all, consider which one (or ones) subjectively qualifies as a **level-one** miracle, per the listed definition.

Determining how much *paranormal* intervention you require prior to labeling an event or circumstance "miraculous," is of course arbitrary and generally unimportant. Subjectively speaking, a miracle is a miracle—you define it by *your* beliefs and associated feelings, not by any arbitrary standards. Discerning levels offered herein help stimulate creative imaginings and show the degree to which *all* life is a miracle. It is suggested you not be dissuaded or distracted by the special circumstances rendered in my experiences. Most were byproducts of wartime conditions—a non-required venue for extraordinary, life-extending events and circumstances.

Even though subtle in their action, most miracles prove dramatic in their effect. Example: think for a moment about how rarely motorists learn of delicate influences that delay them just enough to miss dying in a fatal auto crash. Why do some miraculous encounters seem more spectacular or theatrically staged, when compared to others? What determines why one group of persons are born and raised in opulent affluence, while others come aboard as slaves in impoverished, fly-ridden rice patties? From good/bad First Reality dualism, it's no stretch at all to create a myriad of reward-and-punishment scenarios. Upon Second Reality LOCATION, your empowering and more reflective answers progressively shift into levels of expansive *inclusion,* rather than limiting *exclusion.* More Earth logistics to come.

Good Luck, or Divine Intervention?

The Forces that Guide us generally understate Spiritual stimulus. Once in a great while an intervention takes place that—when directly experienced—even the most ardent critics don't ignore. By the way, if it's intended that you receive some particular insight from this portion of the guidebook, you will. Although no *cosmic* rule prevents having FUN as we grow and awaken, my purpose particularly prods you toward searching your own subconscious memory. You, too, have experienced extraordinary, unexplained phenomena—but, do you remember? Discoveries in this realm can very compellingly facilitate feelings of universal connectedness and empowerment. *Once cosmic union takes place, beneficiaries report all feelings of loneliness and isolation leave them forever*—certainly true from my experience.

After much contemplation, I choose not—at this time—to reveal if my apparent brushes with death were *confirmed* as actualized **level-one** miracles. Analyzing the miraculous is such a personal issue, I've decided to let you determine significance for yourself. *Verification* would mean very little to those who interpret life's events solely from a five-sensory, materialistic view. Conversely, seeing the world through *multi-sensory* glasses renders verification moot. Intuitives already possess a sense, or *higher knowing,* of these happenings. For the wonderfully skeptical, inquiring minds, highly motivated to know, you'll find a way to confirm that which you seek when no longer needing *outer* authorities to tell you what to believe.

Intuition—NOT a Five-Sensory Limitation

In past periods I required substantive confirmation to authenticate even my *own* visions and insights. Afraid to trust any esoteric or Spiritually-based Guidance, I disavowed my intuitive gifts; deferring instead to empirical evidence.

From the materialistic view, intuitively derived wisdom may seem less tangible or real than the more commonly accepted scientific, analytical, five-sensory observations. Like most left-hemisphere-dominated persons, I used to believe intuitive perceptivity too imaginary, wispy, airy-fairy, and lacking in structured reliability. Today, with the advent of Holographic Psychology, we have the best of both worlds. HP gives us the formatted structure to test the personal import of intuitively delivered theories and revelations. Productive use of strong, intuitive touches (visceral input) is becoming commonplace. Additionally, HP provides *psychic* right-brainers a method to convert their *knowingness* into practical use in the grounded, here-and-now world. As a Soul, you joyfully co-exist in a multifarious, unlimited realm of existence. As humans, our destiny includes significant awareness of this intimate symbiosis.

ALL Input...Subjectively Interpreted

As the years unfolded, I came to believe my crewmates and I literally had a Guardian Angel on our collective shoulders. Hair-raising threats not withstanding, it wasn't our time to go. For me, events such as these no longer reside in the *mysterious-ways* category, but in the (significant) parallel-path, life-lesson-plan category. Our lifetime of experience—up to that point—prepared us to be both messengers and co-facilitators of new, creative beginnings; including that dark January night in Saigon. Those who die in war affect world curriculum just as equally. *Humanity shares only ONE lifeboat.*

Today, I reference strong intuitive motivations as a symbiotic relationship with Spiritual Guidance. Holographic Psychology refers to this as our "Spiritual DNA" component. During those inevitable moments when you may feel a little powerless or despairing, perhaps the unifying testaments in this book can help you find your way back to the light. It's time for us to take our rightful and intended place as fully empowered co-creators. Additionally, we can have a heck of a lot of FUN in the process.

The difference for me now—as compared to my past awareness— is that I am certain no badness exists in *not* making a productive change or breakthrough. Although smallness and transitory suffering often follow the *not trying,* as Eternal Beings we truly have forever to master the experiential process. I no longer fear any cosmic beasts lying in wait, should I not awaken. Remember: *nothing in either human or cosmic life experience can ever damage your true Being (Soul).* Releasing my mental/emotional fear of death, increasingly fills me with appreciation for each moment of life.

Many have been taught to believe a person's Soul can be damaged or possessed by negative human behavior or beliefs—whether originated from within, or without. Many religious practitioners, even some fringe metaphysical teachers, preach this as truth. Through guilt and feelings of inadequacy, we experience difficulty reconciling human negative thoughts and feelings with the omnipotent and omniscient forces of the Eternal. There's tremendous challenge in shaking the core belief that impure thoughts and actions are either caused by, or do damage to, our Celestial connection. First Reality (perspective) quite logically determines that if one distorts the *human* world by thought, feeling, and action, the same must be true for the cosmic realm. No wonder we find it so easy to buy into a judgmental, wrathful God.

The good news: we are fully capable of shaking off non-serving cultural directives—which attempt to make us over in another's image—replacing them with more empowering perspectives. As you witnessed, I've not always taken the high road. I walked my share of *burning coals* before achieving meaningful realizations. Having your feet held to the fire does wonders for self-actualizing.

The reality of the presented perspectives is fully testable. I encourage you to freely investigate and decide what *you* believe to be true. But before you do, ask yourself these questions. What is the common denominator between the three miracle candidates? What inner personality trait helped provide us both sanctity and sanity during these ordeals? Was there a relationship between my reactive evaluation(s) and resulting experiences? If so...what? Can you respond based on consequences of *personal belief*, rather than externally decreed, culturally-defined issues of right and wrong? Revered Science of Mind facilitator (teacher of teachers), Dr. Harry Morgan Moses, posed this powerfully reflective question at the end of one of his classes: "Do *contrary* beliefs (differing opinions) have safe passage through your consciousness? "If no...forgiveness work is indicated," was his recommendation. If YES...welcome to an early stage of Third Reality.

Summation. Let me begin by...concluding (a classic oxymoron). During specific meditative attunements held to clarify the "Choice vs. Divine Guidance" question, some information came through on miracles. Guidance startled my human self by revealing that *expressed negativity, or the prevention thereof, is not the parameter for Divine intervention.* Observed from documented historical record, great atrocities are often *not* prevented in spite of Herculean efforts. What appears to be a miraculous extension of life can bestow to one who seems—from the judgmental human perspective—much less deserving.

Consider the continued good fortune of Adolph Hitler: On several occasions during WWII, inside attempts on his life were mysteriously thwarted. In one instance, a quality-made bomb—planted on his personal airplane—failed to detonate during flight. In another botched assassination attempt, an uninformed intermediary moved a secretly placed attaché case, containing killing explosives, to a precise location (within the Bunker) that protected Hitler from the main blast.

Afterwards, under Hitler's continued leadership, the torturous loss of life continued — both from acts of war *and* genocide.

If we define miracles as extraordinary bestowments granted solely to the good and deserving, we miss the higher purposes and meanings to Celestial interventions. How about all those courageous Vietnamese solders who died trying to take the airfield in Saigon? Obviously ordered by superiors to partake in a likely suicide mission, does the fact they were neither victorious nor miraculously saved on that collective *dark-night-of-the-Soul* mean they were "evil ones" and therefore less deserving? Ponder your answers as we continue.

Channeled Message

The power attunements I engaged in to clarify this subject resulted in the following message from Spiritual Guidance: *The determination for what many humans consider "the miraculous" is a complex calculation — even from a Soul or Eternal-Forces point of view. It will not be understandable to ones who view all pain and/or death as negative. To gain understanding in this area, with just the analytical mind, is to venture through an endless quagmire of intellectual inquiry. To approximate an understanding, one must enter a meditative attunement moving beyond human conscious awareness, into the Eternal realm. This is where one can feel there is no badness or loss associated with physical death. Physical death is a transition to an expanded consciousness — not any final ending to life. The events you refer to as the Holocaust were the result of choices made by many millions of fearful and selfishly absorbed humans. As much as you wish to more easily assess blame, you must prod beyond the face of one man, or one organization, to find truth.*

I find this last sentence even more significant in the aftermath of the September 11, 2001, attack on the New York World Trade Center.

A Human's Role in Actualizing Miracles

Exploring your participation in miracles may have more significance from a *universal* perspective, viewing all life and Creation as ONE. If we are truly *not* separate from the forces of the Eternal, then human *experiential life is a temporary holographic projection* — hence the *subjective reality*. The *objective* universe, which stands both in and beyond space and time, is always with us even when we don't accurately interpret it. This is true regardless what label or definition we wish to give it. In other words, we are making it (experiential meaning) all up. This is the great message within the *Conversations with God* dialogue, wonderfully facilitated by Neale Donald Walsch.

The paranormal or psychic-power experience—such as Ruth's graveyard miracle, or the airborne, lightning-strike episode—are representative of heart potential expanded beyond five-sensory limitation. Combining action of heart and head, we can consciously transcend space and time for an instant or more. We can *all* demonstrate psychic ability or extra-sensory perception when directing more focus toward multi-sensory existence. Simultaneous integration (heart and head) is a potential only recently demonstrated by more than the occasional mystic. To understand more, and live more abundantly, begin holistically practicing altered state (subconscious-accessing awareness) processes where you can affect mindfulness that serves.

The attunement exercises already given you, plus the empowering cosmic-connection visualization presented later, will help expand your awareness. Discovering the truth of your magnificence, you awaken to an unprecedented empowerment—one you will never again be denied. You don't have to have your conscious mind tricked by placebos, or be susceptible to the negative thinking, feeling, or actions of others. Once aware of even a portion of your awesome power and potential, outside subjective opinion ceases as a significant threat, and victimization is eliminated.

The Real Deal

What I refer to as **level-one** miracle is perhaps a slightly different initiation from our **level-two** variety. There appear to be instances when Souls, Guides, Angels, the Collective, God—whatever we wish to call the Eternal Forces—seem to act on their own to override the freewill or conditioned behavior of individualistic Human Beings. Purposeful and dramatic interventions *seem* rare, but this may be a perceptual limitation. To answer the *why* of **level-one** phenomena, I present a somewhat nebulous explanation (my opinion) from intuitive Guidance. Could this ambiguity have been intended? More likely, I just don't fully "get it" yet, as my cosmic questioning centered on the Escondido intervention.

Because of some complex interweaving of human energy patterns intended to play out within the realm of space and time, certain Soul-intended archetypal and experiential interactions would be adversely affected if that particular human action were allowed to proceed.

Spiritually speaking, if true we are Eternal Beings impervious to space and time limitations, the above seems a dualistic, contradictory explanation. I have to remind myself to move beyond intellectualizing titillating concepts, lest my imaginings outpace experiential levels. Subjective but practical interpretation of the Escondido Intervention, combined with purposefully revisiting my Vietnam experiences, motivated me to reevaluate my life. This, in turn, resulted in everything you read herein. For me, participation in the miraculous *has* been a wake-up call to my awareness of the expanded cosmic reality and the here-and-now actualization of liberating empowerment. As a facilitator of new arenas of human choice, I fulfill my lifetime contract—one that I chose with you. At this point I'm less concerned with the *why* of existence. Instead, I practice psychologically sound replacement; allowing me to live joyously and abundantly in the moment—regardless of the environmental playing field. If this be your objective as well, let's continue the practical achievement of peace, harmony, joy, goodness, wholeness, creativity, and love.

I see physical life as a grand metaphorical theater, with all of us playing improvisational roles. When it meets my personal criteria for a belief-system upgrade, I most certainly take advantage of wisdom that crosses my path.

The Akashic Library

The more powerful inputs I get from attunements (directed contemplation) are like enjoying a dialogue with my deepest Soul-Self. Deeply felt meditations often result in what I call the "gooseflesh syndrome." Some sects of metaphysics refer to regions of expanded consciousness as the door to the Akashic memory records. If you'll recall, "Akashic" refers to a symbolic, esoteric archive purportedly containing every piece of knowledge, experience, and creativity ever manifested within and without space and time. Consider Celestial or Akashic memories as something innate within you, rather than any *separate* information source. Cultural beliefs in dualistic separation allowed us to be manipulated, divided, and conquered—time and time again. The Source of wisdom that Gurus and Mystics plug themselves into is the same universal energy we all use. To avail ourselves of it, however, we must expand our focus beyond our grounded, left-brain hardware.

Unlike many Eastern disciplines, bashing the ego (Beta-consciousness) mind, or disavowing physical comfort and technological achievement to receive multi-sensory input, is not necessary. Consider making your own direct (sacred) connection to the Collective via Earth's fear-healing lessons and Spiritual DNA activation. Look at your current-life syllabus as a simple, condensed synopsis of the ancient wisdom—after filtered through actualized human interaction. The Divine plan is for metaphysical concepts to connect with you—not from an impractical esoteric void, but from good old Terra Firma.

To break those master-slave belief-system shackles, we transition from worshipping *outside* sources of wisdom and power. Our co-facilitation herein further exemplifies the grand synchronicities of life. This—like many forms of Guidance appearing to you—is an intended catalyst for your own Spiritual odyssey.

Personal Reflections on My "Miracle" Experiences

If I had not actually experienced these life-extending events, I might have placed them in the science fiction, fantasy, or *coincidental* category. In fact…not until after the Escondido event and the odyssey awakening that followed did I deeply revisit the Vietnam encounters.

Based on the arbitrary definitions from the previous chapter, can any experience be subjectively categorized as a **level-one** miracle? Although a given that my crewmates were extremely thankful to be spared, from the Soul perspective our lives were no more important or valuable than others' (not extended). These are very complex areas of human understanding, as mentioned by Guidance. But consider that we are *all* uniquely special. "Special" does not mean "better," however. *The Little Soul of the Sun* (CD), by Neale Donald Walsch, is a powerful and endearing explanation of this…and what we're doing here on Earth.

Having joyfully participated in those power-packed, post-Escondido days and nights, definitive answers to my lifelong questions began appearing. Understanding my actualizing potential, it was important I ask myself: "Where were these thoughts, feelings, and resulting revelations *prior* to my understanding? Was I deluding (imagining) myself, creating them from a desperate need to know? Or did they preexist in the collective ether, awaiting my remembrance and acceptance?"

With neutral observation, your answers—like mine—reflect a perceptual choice. Decide what view serves you. Or, *do nothing and abdicate your right to unfettered liberation—opting, by default, for a skeptic's need of empirical proof.*

Helping you make your connection, or gain confidence in associations you've already made, prove central to my purpose—one revealed to me during my Spiritual odyssey. "What if you're wrong," you ask? Then I'm having a heck of a lot of FUN with my fantasy! How's *yours* working out?

Celestial Fire

The St. Elmo's fireball experience, although spectacular and fear evoking, apparently did not place us in mortal danger. For me, the gift of that dramatic event is the realization of the unlimited manifestations, potency, and even sentience inherent in all energy—most importantly the creation of life itself. You'll recall the St. Elmo fireball—*before* and *after* entering the aircraft—seemed purposeful in its movements. In the raging energy's direct path lay an abundance of metal hardware. This included the metal decking the fireball was gingerly bouncing off of. Energy consciousness may seem like a wacky theory, but explain how a static charge failed to disperse through the first, second, or even third piece of metallic material it directly contacted? Is it possible this unprecedented display of concentrated energy intentionally directed itself toward the bomb? Was its true purpose to deactivate a portion of the mechanism, and therefore take the weapon out of action? Did this intervention result in saving lives from future acts of war? Logically, these questions may seem way out there. But this rationale is something to think about, is it not? My curious, analytical self would enjoy knowing if our reported encounter resulted in a change of plan for the weapon's use. My intuitive Self rests content with just the synchronous *thought* of such a deliberate and willful design.

Bottom Line. How we *label* or categorize experience is not the important theme of this chapter. Consider the greater significance within the gifts of synchronicity, grace, all-inclusive Guidance, and the Heavenly connections usually interpreted as *coincidence*. Remember: ***Divinely bequeathed gifts are a constant, although precursors are often in the form of temporary challenge.*** Because of an intense focus on the material world, we often miss indicators of Celestial comforting, protection, and subtle guidance. For many, just the *acceptance* of Divine manifestation brings solace...especially during times of hardship.

Take a quiet moment now to feel a special blessing from the ones who Guide you. Close your eyes, take some cleansing breaths, and...*Choose to embrace the ever-present cosmic forces. Allow our loving Spirit to penetrate your awareness with well-deserved peace, harmony, joy, and goodness. Make a gentle releasing. Feel our presence in your core of*

Being...as we guide you...as we love you. **Know in your heart that you have never, will never, be alone.**

The next chapter takes a closer, more intimate look at Spiritual influences, along with *anecdotal proof of the existence of a Collective Force from which we manifest.* We both test and enhance skeptical analyses in the remaining portions of this manual.

CHAPTER FIFTEEN

Spirit Guides, Angels, Ghosts
& Ground-Based Spirits

♥   ♥   ♥

For the benefit of human consumption I continue to present awakening realizations and celebrations in a sequential, horizontal (linear), time frame. While reading this *very* subjective chapter, it is suggested you expand your imaginings beyond literal interpretation. My primary intent is to stimulate your thinking, feeling, and childlike joyousness regarding the grand synchronicities of life. May the FUN be with you!

I still remember the first time I was introduced to the idea that humans have Spiritual Guides or Angels sending love energy and supportive enlightenment as we deal with our tough Earth curriculum. On first perusal, my Spiritually skeptical, fearful, and subconsciously manifested "Caustic James" (CJ) mental critic courageously exhibited a mock dialogue with the Source of all Creation. CJ envisioned a plea for Celestial assistance thusly.

Imagine a Celestial Board of Governors—that determines all Spirit-Guide assignments—indignantly responding to my request: "Sorry Stevens, there's no allotment of omnipotent masters available to someone at your dense level of self-absorbed consciousness; you need to *season* yourself first. Come back and see us after sacrificing ten or more years cave-meditating with selfless monks and gifting away all your earthly possessions."

Another potential response scenario: "You want what? Don't make us laugh, Stevens! How could you possibly deserve full-time Spirit masters at *your* beck and call? You arrogantly think we have Eternal Beings lying around with nothing to do after investing hundreds of incarnations mastering Earth life? Surely you jest! What great, loving things have *you* been doing lately? OK...maybe you've earned a few good karma points and this is why we've agreed to talk to you, but you're still manipulating for love. We suggest you hang out with a Sister Agnes, Mother Teresa, or Saint Francis type for a few years—truly selfless givers can always use additional assistance—then resubmit your request after mastering *unconditional* love."

The *best*-case response my Caustic-James self could imagine: "OK, Stevens...we are feeling gracious at this moment. We can let you have one junior Spirit guide on temporary loan. He has successfully completed Spirit-Guide 101 School, but he's been creating elsewhere in the Universe and doesn't know much about Earth. Although you'll need to show him the ropes, he's a quick study—certainly faster than you—and possesses an abundance of unconditional love and support. You have a fair supply of compassion and sensitivity for children and animals—especially dogs—but are deplorably *weak* in the *loving-all-humans* category. If you were a canine, you'd already be finished with Earth school and be outa there. While we grant some kudos for your nice animal-rescue work, you and your human brethren/sistern would be better served if you had more faith in what we're doing up here regarding *human* lesson plans. Anyway, Larry, meet your Spirit-Guide-in-training—Jimmy Farquar, Jr. Now, the two of you can get out of here; we have important work to do with the *truly* enlightened. DISMISSED!"

As you can see, I struggled with some worthiness issues when the concept of Spiritual "Guiding Ones" entered my world. In addition to having a little FUN with our shared insecurities, my purpose is to show the behind-the-scenes mental critic, which most of us struggle with from time to time, is *not* our enemy. Some may see CJ as irrefutable evidence of schizophrenia or personality disorder. Our choice of perspectives is the great gift of human free will.

Today, CJ is semi-retired, relaxing on a peaceful, sun-soaked beach with a cool Piña Colada and very few worries or cares. Because I finally *acknowledged* my insecurities, rather than continue to escape and evade, I now use CJ as an effective mirror or biofeedback mechanism. Acknowledging and "de-monstering" our human shadow is of paramount importance in our quest for healing, self-empowerment, and acquiring those *warm and fuzzy* inner feelings. We can bob and weave to resist our mental critic, creating even *more* stress and inner turmoil, or we can face the reality that most—if not all—of us have at least the occasional pressure period when we fear we're losing it. During times of inner chaos, we more likely lower our emotional barricades, coincidentally discovering our specially designed, perfectly attuned, self-diagnostic. Or we can completely ignore the mental critic, or psyche, while continuing to do the same thing—again and again—expecting a different result. Carl Jung said: "A habit pattern repeats itself with monotonous regularity." Once aware of a non-serving pattern, one is empowered to practice replacement.

In times of crisis I suggest you ask yourself the two questions so beautifully formatted by Raphael Cushnir in his award-winning book *Unconditional Bliss.* ❶ "What is happening right now (referring to all your conflicted thoughts and painful feelings)?" ❷ "Can I (for the moment) *be* with it?" *What we resist…persists.*

Instead of continuing to live with fear that *acknowledging* a closet-based ego persona would somehow diminish me, I learned to reinterpret my relationship with CJ. The key here: who or what is in charge? If the mental background faultfinder starts running the show, then psychosis becomes a definite possibility. Enjoy some actual dialog from my diagnostic friend CJ in an upcoming segment.

Evidence of Soul-Guide Contact

September 11, 1999, at 5:00 PM PST, in Los Angeles, California, I had taken a break from writing to watch the US Open tennis competition. Afterwards, I went back to thinking about material for this chapter. [*In a subsequent review, I was stunned by not recalling that this very connecting event occurred on Sept 11th. It has even more significance for me now.*

The show "Pensacola" came on TV, as I had not yet turned off the set. As a former Naval Aviator, this show always evokes in me nostalgic feelings and wonderfully recalled memories. The September 11th episode provided an extra emotional twist. One of the regular series characters with the handle "Spoon" was experiencing an emotional crisis over the impending loss of his father to an insidious tissue-eating disease. The program showed many touching moments as Spoon dealt with the same decisions and emotional feelings I previously described with my own father's death from cancer.

In the show's final sequence, Spoon enthusiastically aced a practice bombing run and thereby redeemed himself for his previous below-standard flight performances. Upon landing and being congratulated by his wing mates, he received word from the hospital that his father passed away. Prodded by that touching scene, I immediately began boo-hooing in earnest. I visualized his father's energy and Spirit, as it rode with Spoon to assist him in his critically needed precision flight check. I deeply empathized with the story line, vividly recalling what the loss of a father means to a son. Intimate memories of my great hugs with Dad—especially during his final days—came flowing back. Almost able to smell my father's scent, I verbally reached out to say how much I missed him and those special embraces. With tears streaming down my face and arms wrapped around myself entering a fuller remembrance of Dad's physical presence, the phone rang. Startled and angry by this interruption, my reverie felt violated.

Twilight-Zone Ahead

Surprised to get a Nevada call from my good friend and investment partner, Irving, I just spoke to him the day before and no remaining business required follow-up. As an opening greeting, Irv asked me how my day was going. Spontaneously I blurted out I was weeping. That disturbed my dear friend until I assured him these were joyful tears, occasioned by the Pensacola episode and fond memories of my father. Irv then told me the reason he called. After coming home only to unload a new TV, Irv was immediately returning to Las Vegas. On the way out, he glanced at his digital answering machine. The caller-ID feature flashed that *Larry* (with my number) had attempted a call within the past few minutes. Although anxious to get back to the New Year's party (Jewish holiday) at his daughter's house, Irv felt an unusual compulsion to return my call immediately. Amazed to hear I had not even attempted a call since we last spoke, my compassionate, loving, agnostic-based friend was bereft of any logical explanation. What rationale could explain a previously clear machine suddenly registering a phantom call? I'm quite certain had we not enjoyed an impeccably trusting relationship, Irving would've concluded my having fun at his expense.

That vibrant and very welcome glow of cosmic *joy juice,* I've previously described, descended over me. I knew without doubt that Spiritual Forces—including my father's essence—were reaching out. While reaffirming their ongoing union and love, they further illustrated for all who may read these words that *no one is ever lost to us.* It's intended this shared visitation help others regain a sense of comfort and connection to loved ones—on both sides of the veil.

What are the results or consequences of having our lives suddenly and tragically ended—such as with September 11, 2001? Do we continue to have awareness and options? If so, which part of us? Is there still an "I" with which to reflect or perceive? I will attempt to address these highly subjective areas.

Ghosts and Ground-Based Spirits

Consider, again, the intangible nature of this subject. To get much from this portion you'll need to *feel* the material, not just logically conclude its meaning. Based on both corporal and visceral input, this represents — in a metaphorical sense — my current understanding.

As stated previously, Souls complete the creation of their respective human personality matrix prior to human birth. The matrix contains the general blueprint and internal motivations (Spiritual DNA) for a particular incarnation. As a new birth approaches, and the host Soul intensifies its focus on Earth energies, its specially selected cosmic support team steps to the background. As a collective Guiding Force, it lovingly manifests a lifetime of subtle influence. Our Earth-voyage *suitcases* are over-packed with the gifts, talents, and abilities needed to effectively actualize Soul-desired creativity and respond to all challenge. The motivation to persevere with our uniquely individualistic objectives, as well as the universal goal of releasing temporary patterns of mental and emotional fear, provides an enhanced appreciation for *all* life — including the self/Self. It's possible to *not* follow the Soul-preferred lesson plan, stay stuck, and go to physical transition with an intensely negative focus — if that be one's choice [*assuming a human subject has awakened to a level where true choice becomes available*]. We are allowed to manage our opportunities even if we decide to live an entire incarnation believing in dualistic exclusivity or another symbolic form of isolation resulting in joyless existence.

"Why is it that some (over a lifetime) are so apparently shifting perceptions and quality of life, while others seem to endlessly repeat their initially learned behaviors right up to the moment of transition?" If you've asked this question, congratulations! Old-school metaphysics generally answers; "it's a freewill choice." But as you've learned, where is free will without a reflective capability and *perceptual* choice? Note how potential answer(s) change, depending on WHO or WHAT is asking. The first two levels simply contend "shift happens; we can never know the reasons why," or other limiting explanation. Assuming for a moment there are subject-object *comparative* benefits accruing to the dualistic-based observer, what's the view like from all-inclusive Third Reality? As you witness and ponder, recall what I said about the variance between *admiring* a picturesque mountain, and climbing it. Anytime you feel frustrated with the *not* knowing, be assured that *all pathways lead to an experiential realization of the symbiotic kinship humanity congruently enjoys with all Creation.* **Variety of expression need not be questioned by the Manufacturer (Oneness).**

You're Grounded! Universal respect for free will is not limited to physical life. Reflective freedom allows Spirit to open to the reality of the synergistic continuum on its own—*without* commandments. When the veil of amnesia lifts at transition (physical death), omni-sensory awareness of the expanded (universal) realm naturally replaces an individual's extreme five-sensory focus. In the more common passing, we quickly shed the cloak of our intense human personality and begin the celebration of Spirit and renewal—rejoicing with all Souls for creating and participating in yet another generation of human evolution.

For some personalities, the Earth adventure is not quite finished at physical death. In rare cases, a few isolated projections of Spirit remain grounded in the Earth's denser frequencies. This is mostly due to an extreme, Earth-based focus at the time of death. So consumed with self-absorbed negativity at their end of physical functioning, some individuals ignore or disavow the loving energies that surround them. Most of these affected Spirit personalities feel such intense unworthiness that they refuse to turn toward the warm, benevolent light provided as a beacon for their ascension. In some cases, the events of a sudden, tragic departure result in temporary confusion and a refusal to accept physical death. Distorted Spirits can self-create a suspended form of purgatory, believing they need to finish some remaining Earth business before entering the loving glow of celebratory Oneness. This indistinct, ground-based energy is smaller than the Soul awareness. [*Post-life Spirits are a remnant of the Soul-created human personality. Beyond the linear (material) equation there is no pre- or post-life—just life, itself.*] With compassionate understanding, Souls infuse temporarily confused Spirit energy with Universal love. Supportive encouragement continues until the benevolent and ever-present encircling forces can be felt and accepted.

All this happens in the blink of an eye from the Soul's perspective, but Spirit releasement can occasionally take weeks, months, or in extremely rare cases, years of our Earth time. Vibrational energies of ground-based Spirits, a frequency slightly higher than Earth's physical realm, vibrate slowly enough that light bodies can sometimes be seen, heard, or felt by physical sensing. Spirits or "Ghosts" can be encountered in bizarre ways. The most common scientific type of detection records a significant drop in the temperature of isolated air pockets, called "cold spots," combined with abnormal geomagnetic and/or electromagnetic levels—which may or may not be present.

Prolonged negative focus after death is rare; normally limited to personalities who *combine* the following characteristics, which, you'll note, all contain a strong identification with First Reality.

- **Create few or no openings to multi-sensory perspectives during a lifetime.**

- **Remain rigidly atheistic in their beliefs—holding no possibility of any so-called afterlife.**

- **Die in a sudden, possibly violent and traumatic manner (murder or war, for example) having strong feelings of isolation and unworthiness.**

- **Lack the opportunity to prepare for physical death and Spiritual transition.**

Even in this extreme mishmash example, the loving/healing Soul energies eventually facilitate the release of all Earth-bound Spirit personalities. To help balance the grounded Spirit's Celestial energy, special angelic Beings temporarily sequester and administer to transitional ones. Upon renewal, revitalized entities rejoin their collective Soul mates for a joyous reunion and festive celebration.

Some may choose to see restorative segregation as the biblical prophesy of Purgatory. Rather than something decreed by God or the Eternal Forces, as post-death punishment, consider Celestial treatment a natural consequence of an overly fearful and victim-based life orientation. This follows the corollary established on Earth, does it not? Good to know we benefit from group hugs on *both* sides of the veil.

For my left-brained, five-sensory brethren—and others expressing from more rigid, material-world perspectives—the preceding explanation probably reads like a plot from a Dean Koontz novel. For my intuitive, omni-sensory, right-brained friends possessing a more metaphysical stance, this overview may connect some *inner-core* dots. For those desiring more scientifically based information on this subject, contact the International Association for Research, Regression & Therapies (I.A.R.R.T.) in Riverside, California: 951-784-1570; www.IARRT.org. Also check out the books by former I.A.R.R.T. researcher, Dr. Edith Fiori. Dr. Fiori made a career of studying, counseling, and facilitating the release of ground-based Spirits. Take from this subject that which personally serves you. As usual, you are free to **believe it—or not.**

Soul Perspective on Human Biological Duplication (Cloning)

Genetic engineering is another technical advancement from our continued expansion of intellect and focus on the material world. Through genomic study, gene splicing, and other DNA manipulations, we now virtually duplicate living organisms—including those as complex as mammals. Do you remember baa...baa...Dolly? As we come closer to *human* biological duplication and science-fiction achievements, we debate issues of medical necessity versus moral consequence. Leading-edge research moves beyond the question of *can* it be done, to *should* it be done. Might this emotional, ethical issue facilitate a paradigm shift in conscious awareness where *Spirituality*—often depicted as fantasized surrendering—cornerstones scientific study? Behold the Holographic Universe!

Immediate scientific (and commercial) interest answers the increasing demand for replacement organs, skin, and other genetically matched tissue. With transplant techniques perfected, the capitalistic market concerns itself with where to obtain those replacement parts. I predict biological cloning debate results in further shifts of perceptive awareness. We will be increasingly pressured to decide whether biological DNA, although irrevocably intertwined, exists subordinate to the cosmic component; or whether a distinction is relevant at all. At first blush, human biological duplication may seem an appalling consideration—easily dismissed until a loved one prepares to depart the physical realm *without* the benefit of said technology.

The Great Debate

Look for a further blending of science and Spirituality as humanity anxiously...then *urgently* deliberates this volatile subject. We shall be prodded, first, to expand our definition of "Human Being." Then, as Third Reality becomes more commonplace, we'll realize the inherent limitation of *any* Earthly label.

Are humans simply the top of the animalistic food chain? Or mind-body-Spirit creations? Succumbing to old, culturally-based fears and beliefs that we somehow tamper with forbidden areas, many expect punishment by God—or the devil—if we meddle with biological gifts from Creation. Even when dismissing the threat of cosmic retaliation, it's wise to consider manipulation consequences.

Researchers have engaged various forms of biological engineering for some time. Many foods we currently eat are hybrids or manipulated offshoots of nature's originals. Insect-resistant plants, flowers, and vegetables are just a few modification examples science made to the *original;* in order to serve us — or not — depending on one's perspective. When it comes to living organisms, I generally appreciate what nature has developed over millions of years. As an example: With consumer demand for immediate, symptom-treating benefits, do we pause (test) sufficiently to consider potential side effects from human-made pharmaceuticals?

It's fair to note that only a few domestic feline or canine breeders offer *authentic* species types that date back over 500 years. The vast majority of the American®SM and International Kennel Club's®SM "pure" breed designations combine crossbred constructs; the ever popular Golden Retriever and my beloved Doberman Pinscher, serve as examples. So, I do appreciate *some* human-created mixings. Consider any difference between prudent animal crossbreeding, as a modified form of natural selection, and genotypic or phenotypic manipulation. We certainly learned indiscriminate inbreeding magnifies weaknesses. In the wild, inherent barriers between species generally ensure the continuation of nature's balance. A dog cannot naturally impregnate cats, pigs, sheep, or hyenas, as an example. However, many — if not all — of our current farm animals live as slightly altered cousins of the original. Society will undoubtedly continue to debate the difference between assisted natural selection and manipulations to the actual building blocks of a species. Not respecting the natural order can potentially make everything *mad* — not just cows. Might we benefit from urging prudent and continued testing for the *downside* of human and animal duplication? How often have we dived, helter-skelter, into a proffered panacea (Phen-Phen) only to discover a dagger in our heart?

Test-tube babies and other forms of human engineering, although not generally considered human biological duplication, aid many hopeful parents who might not otherwise conceive. The majority of us, after initial concern, accepted these science-derived alternatives to natural conception. Manipulations continue in ever-increasing numbers, no longer encumbered by the front-page publicity a particular process originally engendered. Very few persons today suggest test-tube-conceived babies arrive without Souls or live as less human.

After constant exposure to so many types of human-created manipulations, we give them little thought. So why do we feel such trepidation regarding Human biological duplication? Besides the threat of negative side effects, might our concern include common cultural and/or religious beliefs asserting humans separate and apart from the contemporaneous ingredients of life? Certain [enslaving?] pervading beliefs insist we are *exclusive* and therefore made of different "stuff" than that which permeates all other creations.

Consider that species limitations include certain physical barriers *not* intended to imply philosophical, psychological, or Spiritual (essence) separation. If not yet awakened to synergistic and symbiotic relationships of *all* matter, what we define herein as *inclusivity*, then it's logical to conclude a vast difference between past creations and the choices we currently face. In its own way, science unknowingly perpetuates this "exclusive" belief. Until quite recently, science chose to exist in a vacuum separate from any Spiritual or holistic partnership. Newtonian Science, in particular, grew from the belief that any cosmic union, such as Dr. Carl Jung's suggestion of a great Collective Unconscious, or the more-recent quantum-theory experiments, would taint results obtained by strict interpretation of the scientific method. But another cosmologist (like Stephen Hawking) always comes along to help bridge the gaps in our compartmentalized imagination.

If we continue to look at physical life as just five-sensory, biological creations, we are destined to miss the great synchronistic interweaving of all cosmic energy—including our continued omni-sensory evolution.

Leading-edge scientific researchers like Fred Alan Wolf and F. David Peat; eminent thinker, Einstein protégé, and quantum physicist—the late David Bohm; neurophysiologist Karl Pribram; physicist Gary Zukav, and astrophysicist Stephen Hawking, personify just a few of the modern emissaries visualizing a holographic universe. Courageous thinkers are discovering answers to the mysteries of life unresolved by conventional scientific and theological interpretation.

Another Minority Group?

Another area of future societal concern has to do with our attitudes toward, and treatment of, human biological clones. How will duplicate material be harvested and used? How many envision a new sub-human class of tissue? How will we treat people who received a cloned organ? Will these medical marvels and those that facilitate them hide in closets, fearful of discovery? Will fear-based perceptions result in new rounds of prejudice, loathing, and abuse? Or shall we rise to a new level of appreciation for the miracles of life?

"Space—Above and Beyond," (the TV series occasionally found on cable networks including the SCI-FI channel) explores this impending social relationship of natural births vs. duplicates. This wonderfully creative show, mirroring our societal concerns about "tanks" (laboratory created identicals), boldly demonstrates, again and again, that—along with atheism—bigotry fails to exist in foxholes.

With background perspectives and corresponding challenges now delineated, you are likely interested in what Souls have to say on this subject, are you not? When I found myself curious about the Soul perspective, I entered some specific attunements and asked for clarity on human biological duplication. The following *italicized* paragraph summarizes what came through.

Scientific engineering can duplicate the biology (DNA) of living matter, but that, by itself, does not animate life. Everything created on Earth exists in concert with the Forces of the Eternal. Humans co-create utilizing the infinite Source of all energy. The "energy" (the best word humanity has to describe the awesome power of Creation) from Source maintains the physical reality, time, space, and all life in the Universe. If the specific energy — wielded by Souls that maintain this reality — were to be withdrawn, physical Earth life would cease to manifest.

My interpretation of the preceding: we—as co-creators—choose to construct beautiful, cooperative, but unique castles, as monuments to our free expression; *or* make the human species extinct. The operative word: *how*. Whether we use it *constructively, or destructively,* it's all the same energy.

If you wish to go deeper, consider the following ethical questions. Would a Human Personality Matrix inure to a mechanically duplicated biology? If so…how and from whence would it originate? Might an *adjunctive* Soul creation come out of a human's ability to biologically clone?

As I've presented, Spiritual DNA determines the human blueprint and directed motivations during a lifetime. Souls—*not* being separate—easily adjust to new human choices and conditions. But if humanity selects biological duplication technology, *and* eventually replicates a complete human body, will Souls embrace this newly provided vessel? Will the Celestial Forces infuse new animation of life with the required Spiritual DNA? If so, genetic engineers can then speculate why cloned duplicates possess *differing* personalities; even when cylinder-grown "tanks" possess identical DNA.

Who's on First?

If you examine the latest findings from some of the more open-minded quantum physics researchers, you'll discover the amazing synergism between the observer and the observed conscious-acting sub-atomic particles. Imagine the scientists' surprise when the very basic substances permeating all life in the Universe exhibit different behavior for different observing researchers! Could the building blocks of the Universe be alive and consciously aware? Quantum physics studies as early as 1982 set the scientific community on its proverbial buttocks. Researchers observed subatomic particles instantly responding to one other, whether ten meters apart or ten billion kilometers distant! Clearly impossible with speed of light limitations! With an all-inclusive holographic perspective that transcends or warps space-time, this particle response becomes more discernible. Taking ourselves out of the sealed (Newtonian) box allows discoveries of an awakened imagination.

Turning to historical record, how were our courageous messengers of new thought and observation received? Fortunately we give the Galileos of today a bit more latitude. [*NOTE: Readers wanting more on the new cosmic-quantum partnership, read* The Holographic Universe, *by Michael Talbot.*]

Consider that Human Beings expressing *exclusivity*—thereby limiting their focus to the five-sensory, left-brained, physical world—will not *directly* participate in duplicating or stimulating awakening Spiritual DNA. But all expressions serve their intended purpose. We—as Souls—always guide exploratory, love-based uses of energy. Whether rooted in fear (greed-based selfishness) or love, Souls never condemn humanity for their selections [*only humans condemn themselves*]. For me to truly get this in core-mindfulness, I had to develop a new-paradigm envisioning of traditional areas of badness—like pain and expressed negativity.

The concluding portion of my (reassuring) specific attunement emphasized no threat of usurping Creation's plan for life on Earth. *Other than the usual, temporarily painful consequences* [psychological, physiological] *and side effects from scientific experimentation trials, humans have nothing substantial to fear from cloning technology.* **There is absolutely nothing that humans can invent beyond the divergent scope of possible patterns already known and provided for by**

Creation itself. Apparently, according to Guiding Souls, both benefit *and* challenge are intrinsic to technological advancement. It's our choice to accept and get past perceptions of lack and limitation.

Rather than charging ahead willy-nilly, questioning the future consequences of experimental change certainly serves us. In the words made famous by Ross Perot, "Measure twice and cut once."

Psychological Cloning

Let's get to the core of our *real* cloning issue. The problem creating most of our relationship stress: the conscious, or unconscious, attempt to *psychologically* manipulate our friends, family, and relations. We design these control efforts to replicate, or *clone,* the belief system of our significant other(s), so as to more comfortably align with our own. We distortedly believe coerced validations make us more secure and less anxious. Attempting to instill one's belief system within another emerges directly from our own emotional fear and worthiness issues.

Ignorance of our not *directly* relating to people, events, or environmental circumstances exacerbates this controlling-of-others process. Our *evaluation* of psychological and philosophical dynamics determines quality of life—or lack thereof. *Self-image perspectives and associated habit patterns—**not** the external environment—determine our level of security and comfort.* Example: Parents so fearful their children will fail, or fall prey to some pain-pit, try to force their offspring to be and do what fits the parents' comfort level, irrespective of the child's needs, desires, and Spiritually-provided motivations (calling). To achieve a frustratingly elusive comfort zone, we often try to manipulate (fix) our spouses in similar ways. Next time you're frustrated, remember the mantra: *"Go within, or go without."*

Biological Duplication—Bottom Line. Grand-finale (Third Reality)
Question: If all life is of the same *stuff* from Source, how can *anything*—regardless how it comes into being—be artificial? From everything you've been awakening to, do you still believe Self/self limited to the body? If you mentally countered with "Which body?" move to the head of the class. You're at least *thinking* vertically and therefore outside the dualistic box.

Consider—if you will—that nothing is "solid," "artificial," or "*super*-natural." Every manifested person and thing—that science ever measured—has been found active at some level or frequency. In projective theory, then, even the core of a Black Hole releases energy.

Note: I wrote the previous paragraph years before the more recent "channeled" research—spearheaded by cosmologist extraordinaire, Stephen Hawking—revealed black holes, in fact, leak radiation. So, if something dense and *solid* as a black hole evolves, how can *anything* be fixed or stagnant? *All creations intrinsically transform.* And this is not "super" natural—just *natural* we're coming to realize. The differences between *natural* and *artificial* deal with human perceptions—the categorizing, charting, labeling, metaphorical philosophizing, analyzing, and symbolic conjecturing. WE ARE MAKING IT ALL UP...as intended!

Souls that temporarily express through human bodies are the same Souls that would express through cloned bodies. Regardless how the seeds of procreation manifest, the end result is a Human Being—no difference from the Soul perspective. In spite of advancing technology, no possibility exists for diluting a Human Being's one-of-a-kind personality. Souls choose each temporarily expressing, independent ray of the ONE Collective Consciousness (within a body). We—experiential humans—represent and enjoy a more intense and focused expression of Creation. As the *cloned* product of Source, nothing stops us from manifesting our passionate, heart-felt dreams and ambitions—except ourselves. Yes, experimentation and change invite consequences. But even a turtle must stick out its neck to get anywhere.

The next two chapters explore out-of-body (OBE), Soul-travel processes and how to use these latent abilities to enhance quality of life in the *here and now*. But first...the Souls tell us *their* version of Adam and Eve.

CHAPTER SIXTEEN

The History of Creation–Soul Style

♥　　♥　　♥

The Awakening. The following "Soul-Speak" awakening-emergence story, presented with a linear *beginning* and *after*, represents an abrupt celebration solely for human orientation. In realms without space-time boundaries, timekeeping is irrelevant. Regarding the channeled, *italicized* dialogue: *who* or *what* is speaking is intentionally left to your imagination. By focusing on symbolism, rather than literal fact, what may seem whimsical can sometimes morph into transformative remembrances.

Once upon a time, long, long ago, a collective of angelic, light-body energy Beings came into awareness. This is as close as we can come to describing Beings, such as ourselves, and the dawning of awareness, in Earth words. **Who** *we are will be more comprehensible than* **what** *we are.*

Celestial Beings or "Souls" are aware of their great intimate connection to one another. We exist without secrets or divisible barriers. In synergistic continuity, we, as omnipotent free-flowing entities, are able to instantly incorporate ourselves within every individually expressing ray of the Collective. Souls subsist in a perpetual state of joy, peace, harmony, goodness, creativity, and love.

Upon awakening, original Souls manifested wonderful imaginings by focusing on specific expressions – or multiple creations – with just the energy of thought.

Since Souls exist in realms not limited to space and time, **all** *are "original." Although WE, and therefore YOU, are uniquely special, no Soul is newer, older, better, or wiser than another. As Spiritual Beings, we experience the wonder of tapping into one, magically united mind as a foundation for individualistic creativity.*

The Dawning

The Souls awakened in a magnificent arena. Nothing on Earth compares exactly, but imagine one of your most lavish gathering places. Your human selves might call this grand palace "extravagantly majestic," with nothing meaningless or wasted [If you've been there, visualize a place similar to the grand reception area of the Hearst Castle; San Simeon, California].

All Beings in this awakened gathering were fully in the moment, partaking of unlimited gifts. Souls felt deserving of gifts, and relished in the opening and sharing of their "presents." Additionally, their host had prepared a sumptuous [Kundalini] *Energy Feast as celebration of their arrival. The Source of this — and all Creation that had always been — was the benevolent cosmic force you call* **"God."** *Souls feel an intimate, loving, very direct integration with God. In the absence of separation from this everlasting force, Souls exist without differentiation.*

Howdy to you, too!

Creation officially welcomed all Souls. Although the Souls sensed an automatic knowing of God, as themselves, they simultaneously thought: *"How is it that we came into Being?"*

God, the Force that had always been, answered: *"I created you to be my companions for a grand adventure. I, too, have everything I can conceive of, upon imagining that which I desire. I exist with no needs or wants, except to partake of this beautiful existence with other Beings of, but not as, myself. I intend the beauty of existence and creation to be shared. You have all the abilities I possess. You need only open to them and create anew, as have I."*

Souls were overjoyed with their actualization and the prospect of a shared, but individualistically formulated focus. They, including you ones temporarily expressing as Human Beings, wished to give birth to new, magnificent castles as a way to please themselves and express love for that which provided all.

Souls knew then what they prefer humanity to understand now. They, and therefore you, are never separate, or alone. The creative forces of God pervade every particle of your essence and can never be divided or damaged. It seems that Souls understood the omnipotent and omniscient gift from God. The creative *torch* was passed, and we — as Souls — went forth to create anew.

Souls Create the Space-time Continuum

And so it was, as integrated Souls imagined a place with the appearance of differentiated Space, Form, and Time. Souls had existed for eons in joyous celebration and now desired a specific experience of intense individuality. Their wish to give birth to material reality did not come from any human-like sense of boredom, or lack, but out of a loving interest in emulating the gift of Creation.

Souls began manipulating Celestial energy forces constantly available from Source. As Souls changed the form of energy, great cosmic gases developed. In experimenting with condensing and squeezing those gases, "Quanta Matter" was created. With quanta matter further differentiated, Souls seeded Earth with water, hydrocarbons, proteins, amino acids and other organics, via massive, ice-laden comet asteroids. All this was experientially new to Souls. Foregoing a predetermined or exacting blueprint, Souls understood the experiences they wished, and kept those objectives in Celestial focus. Again, there was/is no sense of *waiting* for time to pass, as the Soul Realm is never limited to linear equations.

Another way of looking at the Celestial realm: *all* time exists simultaneously, simply by imagining it. A very complex and difficult concept for us humans to quantify—we see ourselves expressing exclusively within the material world during normal conscious awareness. We are culturally indoctrinated to relate to linear concepts of *before*, *present*, and *after* (horizontal realm). There is no "before" or "after" in the vertical realm—there just IS.

The impressions from my attunements: not all Souls primarily focus on the "Physical Space and Time" project. Spiritual Beings select particular or multiple areas of creative construction. Since there is no separation, all Souls intimately support the physical universe— especially the gloriously created life forms of Earth. *Human scientific discovery [reductionism] revealed much of your physical history in what it calls "Natural Selection;" but denotes an incomplete explanation for your Beingness. If you were to blend scientific discovery with intuitively provided mystical realities—the love-based portions of which could be termed* **"Involutionary Creationism"**—*you ones would approximate an even greater truth of your intelligent design and magnificent emergence.*

Souls Create Natural Selection

After vibrational frequency adjustments to the planet's energy matrix and essential magnetic grid, the powerful Earth gases eventually cooled and solidified. *Design involution led to form evolution.* Souls became more proficient in manipulating and maintaining life-sustaining energies, and physical life began to evolve—eventually thrive. Although—from the Soul perspective—it all took place in an instant, sufficient cooling of condensing gases required billions of Earth years to form a mantle crust. Then, development of the necessary elements for sustaining the emergence of living organisms took additional billions of years. The Soul's plan included all this for the physical realm of existence.

Today's Creations

Souls continually celebrate their handiwork. Wielding and maintaining the undifferentiated forces of God, we continually create new expressions of life. That life, a solidified form of universally permeating energy, continues to evolve through Spiritually selected encoding. Life (independently and collectively) expresses, flourishes, and recycles itself—as intended. As varietal forms of physical life climb the evolutionary ladder in complexity, substance, and ongoing cycles of renewal...nothing is wasted. To both create and maintain the material reality, the ever-expanding Universe—including the Earth Magnetic Grid—is subtly adjusted and modulated. This multi-dimensional [holographic] focus presents us with an entirely new, more-expanded reality. We fully integrate our consciousness into the continually adjusted Source power, and thereby sustain intensities beyond any previous experience. "Integration," an incomplete description, as the energy of Creation is never held separate.

You as a Soul

We can approximate, within the limitation of Earth words, a symbolic description of the Eternal realms that may be helpful. Let us say that in the Soul Realm, existence comprises a very broad band of simultaneously expressing vibrations. Using Earth radio waves, as an example, imagine a thousand radios playing at once—all tuned to different frequencies. Remove human pain and confusion from this barrage of input, and assume an ability to simultaneously integrate all broadcasts. With infinite discrimination (unbounded contemplation), ones can approximate a portion of the Soul awareness.

Imagine you—as a Soul—enter another room where competing radio frequencies are nonexistent...leaving just one high-definition monitor with fully interactive programming. Dialing in the desired frequency and fully immersing yourself in the selected channel, you simulate the focus used to create a human personality matrix—complete with talents and abilities needed to fulfill any chosen mission. Souls do not predetermine exacting lifetime performance scripts, but for mutual benefit, infuse influential motivations [callings] within their interdependent human symbiont. Souls see all possible human-choice patterns and are troubled by none of them. Souls rejoice more, however, when humans emphasize the larger, love-based expressions.

Atlantis & Lemuria

The earliest human colonies were located in what you named Lemuria and Atlantis. [Reminder: focus on symbolism, rather than literal fact.] Because of higher frequency resonance, the original, pioneering humans were light-body manifestations. Evolving circumstances modified that density in direct proportion to increases in the intensity of the human experience. Major shifts occurred during what much of humanity refers to as the "Garden of Eden" period.

When Souls opted for lower vibration, allowing a more grounded and intense experience, it was agreed they would step to the background and let their human counterparts participate in an independent-feeling, freewill type of illusion. The forces of the Eternal would henceforth wait to be invited forward into awareness by individually expressing humans. Souls understood the possibility of a shift in focus from love-based expression to more varied and self-absorbed manifestations. They did not judge the potentiality of negative choice as *bad* or *wrong*. Souls clearly saw all possible patterns of human choice. Although Souls (I am told) do not specify which paths humans take, this is not a limitation. All past, present, and future events play themselves out **simultaneously** in an expanded realm that includes but is not limited to space and time. Until Human Beings walk their respective pathways, the Spiritual (visceral) cannot claim the experiential (cognitive).

Liberating license was exactly intended. The feeling of freedom to choose was, and is, the ultimate gift that Souls — wielding the forces of the Eternal — could confirm on their creation. This bestowment represents the same gift Souls received from God — the Source of all Creation. The symbiotic piggyback with humanity allows a temporary illusion of separateness. We — as Souls — rejoice in our varietal acquaintance with human feelings of individualism and expressed uniqueness.

Subjective Experience Associated with Differences

As Earth time unfolded, early humans began separating themselves from one another in various ways, such as exhibiting those diverse talents and abilities that the Souls placed within the respective human matrix. An example: some were prodded to experiment with various implements indigenous to the area. Through motivated experimentation and practice, those ones eventually learned to create crude ornamentations from colorful seashells, rocks, sticks, and other distinctive objects. Developed craftsmanship took many hours of diligent practice. The final product became a unique adornment for its artisan. Others wishing decorative embellishments, but lacking the crafting skills to produce them, created the first dilemma for independently expressing humans. Suddenly there was this *one*, uniquely crafted necklace, and many who desired it.

The new choices, exclusively human, were beyond anything in the Soul's experience. The Spiritual realm expresses no concept of lack, or scarcity. When Souls desire something, we instantly enter the full experience of that which we seek, simply by imagining it.

The new breed of human was free to focus on the realm, or realms, of its choice [a provided potential]. *Those maintaining an inner type of focus still sensed their connection to the forces of the Eternal. They felt the love subtly pouring into their hearts and wished to share all with other humans, as they continued to feel irrevocably joined. The more love-based members of the ever-expanding and varietal species of humans learned to barter their various talents and abilities through a developing exchange system. Natural supply and demand—along with patience, acceptance, and cooperation—decided value. Compassionate, fair-minded co-ops provided for the rare, impaired one.*

Advent of Fear, Greed, and Selfishness

Those exclusively fixated on the physical environment began to feel *different from* and eventually uncomfortable with the inner-oriented grouping. This led to a detachment and eventual withdrawal from the heart-focused humans and a new alignment with those more outwardly focused. Both factions believed the other side significantly changed. Being more fearful and self-conscious, the more forceful, intense members of the selfish clan began controlling the decisions of others. They forcibly took what they wanted, often with little or no trading involved. Ones demonstrating unbearable debauchery were eventually confronted. The losers of these intimidating, often violent altercations were forced to leave the security of the enclave—if able— or stay and become slaves to the dominant ones. As weaker persons continued submitting to authority, they exhibited increased feelings of lack and unworthiness. Never before had humans felt self-conscious, defensive, or unworthy.

Master-Slave Relationship

Thus began the authoritative, First Reality master-slave creation—a continuing major factor in throngs of humanity feeling separated, alone, and unworthy. Our story continues.

Compassionate ones tried to reach out to the others, but were met with great resistance. The now untrustworthy, self-absorbed grouping decreed expressed differences between humans as undesirable—even bad—and they turned away from offers of cooperation and friendship. The fearful ones continued using force to take what they wished, believing in their distorted perception they had nothing of value to exchange. This led to more conflict and great physical, mental, and emotional struggles. Overseeing Souls continued sending forth their loving energies at the more subtle levels previously established. But negative, suffering, material-based individuals no longer heard the soft, loving voice of the Eternal. Distortedly concluding their connection to the origins of life lost, a dark cloak of emotional sadness descended over those no longer sensing an Eternal bond.

The fearful busily reacted to the environmental conditions they, themselves, inadvertently created. In time, negative stress generated by conflict became so strong and out of proportion that a great upheaval began. This disturbance proved powerful enough to directly affect geology and other ecological elements. With more and more humans turning away from their tremendously powerful synergistic connection to all life, the turmoil escalated. The more Spiritually focused—still aware of the higher realities—ardently tried to assure the desperate that developing imbalances were false illusions. But only their own, like-minded assemblage understood the guardians. Meanwhile, the miserable, negatively expressing and self-absorbed submitted to a pecking order of domination and destruction. Torrential fear engulfed every waking moment, as distorted psyches produced nightmares and fitful sleep.

Under the continual stress of energy in opposition, the emotional friction became too great to sustain form. Colliding atoms and the unstable energy matrix created geological disruptions through volcanoes, earthquakes, and unrelenting wind and rainstorms. This phenomenon, never before seen in Eden, represented what you humans metaphorically call the "forbidden fruit exchange." Tumultuous emotions escalated. Souls did not interfere, as these upheavals were human creations. Souls could see that humanity was embarking on a grand adventure. Although an extended period of strife and dissension, Souls knew Human Beings would eventually reawaken to congruency and love-based realization; the war-beaten pathways of fear and selfishness would come full circle.

Humanity would learn, through developed inventiveness and accomplished solidarity, what Souls came into consciousness already knowing. For millennia, human ingenuity and creativity has continued its passionate advance. Arising from the ashes of destructive, fear-based creation, humans—in stages—rediscover that only the minions of love and creativity are real.

Reflective Overview

After my own left-hemisphere analysis of this mythical, allegorical representation, I realized what I originally perceived as *fantasized embellishment* was an initial, fear-based reaction to the deeper meaning contained within the story. Fixating on and then creating resistances in life because perceptual details conflict with a current belief-system, create dogma. For the moment, let us focus on the underlying message as it relates to our ongoing human process. We could potentially conclude that we humans are not now, nor have we ever been, victims. Furthermore, temporary negative challenge is not a punishment from God, negative karma, or because of some *fallen angel* running amuck.

The Souls did not see anything *wrong* or *bad* in any human choice because they understood then, what they wish us to comprehend now. Behind challenge and adversity lies an experiential awakening, awaiting actualization. Expansive self-realization gradually brings humanity's conscious awareness back to Creation, having mastered the Earth pathway. The desire or need for lesson repetition, always an individual matter, is like taking a group hike through a grand forest to your home castle on the other side. You have choice in how to get there. You can beeline for home using the paved expressway, complete with chauffeur-driven, climate-controlled limousine service. Or you can meander through the woodland with your backpack and experience the complete package of symbolic geology: including streams, flora, fauna...virtually every nook and cranny of Earth experience. Regardless which path we take, all trails lead to our home castle.

Unchained from reactive mind limitation and right/wrong, good/bad definitions (First Reality), a person gains the humanistically empowering sense of self (I AM) and expanded patterns of freewill choice and consequence (Second Reality - cause and effect). With the transcendent paradigm, We celebrate our core, transpersonal Self, reawakening to Oneness—the ALL THERE IS of Third Reality.

A Modern-Day Quintessential Mystic

As we return to the here and now, let me more adequately introduce you to the human developer of Holographic Psychology and our reality-levels model. As a foundational explanation for the bizarre nature of both ordinary and extraordinary experience, I use concepts formulated by the esteemed Dr. James Paxton Pottenger.

After many intimately shared dialogues, I became curious about Dr. Pottenger's background and how he came upon his empowering principles. This amazingly synchronous biography includes some early history on Science of Mind and other metaphysical organizations.

Rendezvous with Destiny

In the late 1940s, Martha Pottenger's youngest son, James, was a senior at the University of Arizona. One evening, James was returning home with his girlfriend from a "Cinco de Mayo" celebration in Nogales, Mexico. As they proceeded north on the dark, desolate, two-lane, state highway, a southbound motorist drifted into their lane. Horn honking failed to alert the other driver to the imminent danger. At the last possible second, James attempted to save their lives by veering to the right shoulder. Overshooting the road surface, the car crashed into a ditch and rolled over. Fade to black.

The police reported that both James and his passenger were thrown from the car. Although his inebriated companion escaped with only minor injuries, James suffered serious head trauma. Unconscious, barely alive, and on his way to the nearest emergency facility, paramedics determined James had expired. They delivered his body to the morgue for the medical examiner's official pronouncement of death. Upon arrival, handling personnel noted movement under the covering sheet. With the weakest signs of life, James was again in route to a Tucson hospital. Continuing his tenuous hold on the material realm, attending physicians worried that even if James regained consciousness, probable brain damage would render him permanently incapacitated.

In Another Reality

Eventually, James became semi-conscious. He walked, talked, performed basic functions, but had no realization of who he was or even what planet he was on. Arizona specialists had no remedy for his walking-coma state. Because James possessed little sense of his current reality, he felt no limitation. He seemed to interact with a different, more expanded world—one without Earth's physical laws and barriers. Martha Pottenger, fortunately a woman of means, hired full-time bodyguards to accompany her *ozone-headed* son. Because he firmly believed he could fly, James attempted to leap from roofs, windows, and tall buildings. Most of us can only imagine what a parental nightmare it must have been to care for a strong, physically mature son who had no concept of material limitation. Other than his terrestrial body functions, James appeared to be joyously frolicking in an "elsewhere" area. Examining experts found James hopelessly schizophrenic and delusional. They advised Martha to institutionalize him at once.

Surreal Homecoming

James' mother brought him back to his hometown of Chicago, Illinois, for a consult with one of the country's top neurosurgeons — Dr. Loyal Davis (1896 –1982). One would be hard pressed to find a brain specialist with more prestigious credentials: Chair, Department of Surgery, Northwestern University, Evanston, Illinois (thirty-one years); Chief of Surgery, Passavant Memorial Hospital; Chair, Board of Regents, American College of Surgeons (president during 1962 and 63); Founder, American Board of Neurosurgery; Editor-in-Chief, *Journal of American College of Surgeons*, 1938 –1982. Incidentally, he was also Nancy Reagan's adoptive father. Yes, indeed...*very* impressive credentials. If ever there was one Human Being in the field of conventional neurology that could bring sanity to her beloved James, Martha believed Loyal Davis was that person.

A Mother's Faith

After an exhaustive examination, Dr. Davis voiced his reluctant agreement with the Arizona physicians. The physical brain had healed from its injury, and with no evident tumor, remaining clots, swelling, or evolving physiology, well-wishers need not expect any change to James' condition. Once again, a renowned specialist told Martha her son needed to be medicated and institutionalized; probably for the rest of his less than natural life.

Mrs. Pottenger listened attentively to this foremost expert. After Dr. Davis finished with his definitive diagnosis, the spirited mother of the future Dr. James P. Pottenger turned to the world-renown neurosurgeon and said: "With all due respect, sir...you're wrong. My James is destined for great things in this world and I will prove it to you and all those other one-dimensional naysayers!" Martha Pottenger, a strong, independent person in her own right, was having none of it. If she had to travel to every corner of the globe, she was determined to find a cure for her son.

I sat transfixed as James related this amazing, *second-coming* narrative. How could an intelligent, coherent, rationally thinking person evolve from such an inauspicious beginning? This is the place where infomercial telemarketers say, "But wait...there's more!" Where most people would surrender to the inevitable, our purposeful, still-optimistic matriarch was just getting warmed up.

In her study and travels, Martha Pottenger had been introduced to various metaphysical practices, including "faith" cures. Now that a conventional solution had been ruled out, she turned toward Spiritual Science for transformational healing. After consulting with several top metaphysicians who explained the power of collective petition, she believed her best hope rested with a unified prayer group. Once Martha made her final determination, she relentlessly pursued the top religious and Spiritual leaders in North America. She used every influential method she could think of to mobilize a giant conglomerate of cottage groups. She employed them to focus on one, single purpose...bring her sleepwalking son back to full consciousness!

Martha's recruitment included, among others: Mary Baker Eddy's Christian Science organization in Boston, Massachusetts; Unity Church, originated by Charles and Myrtle Fillmore of Lee's Summit, Missouri; the Divine Science organization founded by the Brooks sisters from Denver, Colorado; and what would turn out to be the most helpful of all...Science of Mind Founder Dr. Ernest Holmes, of Los Angeles, California. Martha impressed Dr. Holmes with her love and unwavering determination, and he was intrigued by James' fate.

Ernest Takes the Reins

In discussions Dr. Holmes would later have with James, he revealed Martha's motivation was most impressively *not* a product of a mother's fear, but a resolute and faithful knowing that her son would awaken. The SOM Founder agreed to help. He coordinated the combined efforts of the unified groups previously enlisted. Ernest added his entire congregation and Science of Mind staff to the mix. James touched the hearts of all those who learned of his ordeal.

Approximately nine months after the accident, and after the top medical experts in the country definitively concluded her insane son would never amount to anything, James awoke.

A New James...A New Quest

Still without past recollections, James remembered nothing of his childhood or the environmental events leading up to his rebirth. Those clustered around him seemed somehow familiar, but James had no direct knowledge of his friends, schoolmates, or family members. His newly awakened personality was also different. Being a child of privilege, he was generally thought arrogantly aggressive, aloof, and self-absorbed. Still quite charismatic, intelligent, and inquisitive, the new model seemed more sensitive, caring, and tolerant toward others. [*Metaphysicians call this type of dramatic personality change—with a normal psyche (no pathology) but no recoverable recollection of past events—a "Soul swap" or "walk-in."*]

Although lacking memory of how he'd obtained a formal education, James intuitively knew things. In an effort to resolve those larger-perspective questions no one would or could answer, our impending protégé went back to school. James devoured all the philosophy, psychology, and theology courses he could get, and at Pepperdine University in Malibu, California, he earned his first advanced business degree (MBA). James had a new and especially strong interest in the workings of the mind and in the variances of human behavior. While pursuing a career in private education, James, always the voracious student, added anthropology and linguistics to the mix. Our fledgling human-potential pioneer felt an unexplained motivation to research unexplored areas of consciousness, and humanity's link to the Transcendent.

James meets the Holmes Boys

Not until the middle to late fifties did James Pottenger personally met Ernest and Fenwick Holmes. With Fenwick the intellectual brother of the charismatic, crowd-pleasing Ernest, the three bonded instantly. So much so that James was invited to guest at Ernest's home during the thirty-month period he attended seminary training. James became so enamored with Ernest, Fenwick, and their unifying, all-inclusive Science of Mind philosophy that he decided to become a Religious Science minister.

Ordination

Dr. Pottenger continued to share his astonishing and previously private history with me. He described a mentoring epiphany—what Zen Buddhists call "Satori"—with Fenwick, and especially Ernest. James and Ernest would often discuss the oneness of life and existence until the wee hours of the morning. 1958–60 were especially joyous years for James. Whenever the spirited seminary student quizzically disclosed some contrasting challenge with an instructor, Ernest would reassuringly say: "Just get your certification, James; *then* you can teach concepts your own way."

In 1960, the same year the Los Angeles Founders Church of Religious Science was dedicated, the previously insane and written-off James P. Pottenger was ordained. Also in 1960 (April), Ernest, the beloved teacher, motivator, and energy healer, made his glorious transition. Although saddened by the passing of his great friend, mentor, and father figure, James felt he'd found a home in Science of Mind principles.

The Question of Oneness

One day—shortly after Ernest's passing—James looked out from his Malibu ocean-home vista and asked this probing question: "Since you, *water*, are out *there*—all wet—and I am standing *here*, dry on the beach, how can it be that you and I are One?"

This unifying concept of Oneness, or Universal Mind, provides the foundational principle of Science of Mind. Integrative questioning and the development of testable humanistic applications practical for the here-and-now material world have been the overriding motivation of this theologian turned human-potential researcher. Dr. Pottenger has invested the last 40 plus years bringing forth a teaching combining the science of matter, mind, and Spirit. Holographic Psychology (HP), along with the open-ended Science of Spirit, culminates his tenacious search. Focused on *self*-realization and *self*-salvation, this facilitation embodies the maximum in personal growth possibilities.

Third Reality and Science of Spirit...Revealed

As a new Religious Science minister in the celebratory company of the aging founder, James Pottenger witnessed a quantum shift in Science of Mind realization...one that transcended (while still including) the humanistically oriented Science of Mind principles then in publication.

The empowering new theory that James, Ernest, Fenwick, and other select Science of Mind practitioners began exploring during those last few precious weeks of Dr. Holmes' physical life, is now available in a testable format. As you've learned, Holographic Psychology™ labels it "Transcendent Awareness," or "Third Reality." From directed mindfulness—which top neurologists said would *never* manifest—comes an unprecedented tool to assist our ongoing development. The components of HP are not just intellectual concepts. They represent an inclusive and allowing heart structure that helps individuals more fully grasp the overriding role that *belief, imagination,* and *intent* play in quality-of-life experience. Upon incorporation of the reflective core of HP (LOCATION of Comprehension), victimhood is eliminated, and mastery of the Earth pathway — assured.

Spiritual DNA and the Human Personality Matrix

As principle researcher, Dr. Pottenger postulated the theory that a psychologically manifested *Spiritual DNA* component is part of our human personality matrix. He's also credited with the modern discovery of the aforementioned **Location of Comprehension** to assist us in our reflective awakening. LOC's observer view of evolutionary behavior provides us the structure to discern the level of understanding we currently express. We learn that thoughts and actions can positively influence and enhance quality of life *without* any required change to one's external environment. The Pottenger model allows us to see our life, our world, our creative options, *and* ourselves, from a multi-dimensional and therefore more cooperative viewpoint. Not present in LOC is the need to label any belief or modality "wrong" or "bad." When fully realized, *Location* is the gateway to allowing for *all* of life's expressions — not just those a dualistic, separatist orientation prefers.

Our next chapter puts inclusivity to the test, as we journey to what most refer to as "a *past* place and time."

Progress Check

We've just completed another four-thousand-year-old evolutionary cycle. The *practice* of medicine chronicles humanity's progress.

I HAVE AN EARACHE!

- 2000 BC... **Here...eat this root.**
- 1000 AD...That root is heathen, say this prayer.
- 1850 AD... That prayer is superstition, drink this potion.
- 1920 AD... That potion is snake oil, swallow this pill.
- 1950 AD... That pill is ineffective, inject this antibiotic.
- 2000 AD...Antibiotics are artificial, leading to monstrous bacterial mutations.

Here...EAT THIS ROOT!

CHAPTER SEVENTEEN

Past-Life Regression to the Sioux Nation
A Second Reality Therapy Tool

♥　　♥　　♥

Touchdown. With an obscure awareness, I can both sense and vaguely see my mostly bare torso. Great tension lies within me as I begin an urgent search—but for what? Aware of villagers milling around, I'm restricted to narrow, tunnel-like vision. As the peripheral blinders fall away, it hits me! I am the designated Spiritual leader for this peaceful Lakota Sioux tribe of about two-hundred Souls. We live in a small, fairly hidden and normally tranquil valley with gentle, sloping hills on all sides, with grasses green and lush. The gloriously brilliant sun warms the ambient temperature, but I shiver uncontrollably.

A great sense of foreboding tells me something horrific is about to happen. In spite of Larry's strained effort to awaken from his amnesiac fog, I feel my heart swell with respect and admiration for this intimate tribal grouping. At this very moment, however, I must force myself to make eye contact. I fear I have betrayed my family in a way possibly fatal to all of us. Then…it all comes to me in a rush.

I awake to full recall of events leading to this day. The General of the "Blue Coats" wants revenge, as he suffers immensely from losing some of his own family members. Accused Indian defectors—known to us but not *of* us—quite cleverly masquerade, as they are enemies of our people as well. The furious general demands the scalps of those responsible for the heinous crime, and exclusively focuses on our peaceful tribe.

Two Moons Prior

When I first received notice of the renegade attack, I immediately went to the white Chief with offers of assistance. Several Indian scouts and civilian traders demonstrated great courage coming to my defense. They stood their ground and shared their collective belief that we were not the responsible party—in spite of the cleverly planted evidence. The General begrudgingly gave me *two moons* to bring him the criminals that his demented mind believed we harbored.

After a way-too-brief reconnaissance mission, I returned pleading for more time. Exhausting all our resources, we had not located the *evil* ones. My diplomatic ability had never failed me before in my many negotiations with the white man. My unassailable skills were now moot, however. Over the objections of his remaining white advisors, the General would have his demanded scalps—any scalps—at first light tomorrow, or we all would pay. With the fire of hatred in his eyes he ordered my dismissal: "The blood will be on *your* hands! No more *savages* in this valley!" he declared. He allowed me to leave the fort to consider his *humane* compromise proposal. Either present the demanded human sacrifices to satisfy the General's blood lust—and the balance of our tribe could leave—or we *all* die early next morning.

With a defeat never known in my still young life, I returned to our village. I could not accept that such a horrific slaughter could actually happen. The Spirit Gods who guide and protect us would never allow the senseless murder of the innocent. I must have faith. That's it! This is a test of my faith in the Great Spirit. I felt so ashamed that I let dread and panic overpower my great love for the Creator of All There Is. This was a sign: although our favorite domicile, it was time to leave this tranquil valley. We must not fear renewing our nomadic lifestyle. We had gotten fat, lazy, and no longer wished to migrate. The Spirits were speaking—I would listen.

Dawn came and went. With the sun well above the horizon, I felt my confidence soar. What a glorious day—one of the best of the season! When I then noticed over one thousand armed soldiers approaching all sides of this very vulnerable—no defense/no retreat—but beautiful and plentiful valley, I abandoned all hope.

Moment of Reckoning

The other Chieftains immediately understood this a day of retribution. Innocence was no longer of consequence. The blue-coated despots advance purposefully, with death in every movement. The tribal members look to me without even a tinge of recrimination. Their respect for me, a feeling I do not have for myself at this moment, is still complete. I love them more than words could say. I was and would always be—even beyond death—their Shaman.

Now in full emotional, mental, and Spiritual contact with all tribal members—including beloved children and animals—I released my guilt for not granting them time to prepare for transition. At this very instant we were a *herd* consciousness...in full telepathic communication.

This *is* to be a glorious moment after all! We are going home, but not just victims of a horrible slaughter, or martyrs of principle. Given the opportunity to create the beginning of a great awakening for all humankind, we shall depart Mother Earth as teachers of forgiveness and love. We share heartfelt communion with our Spirit Gods. They have not forsaken us.

We would not fight today. This event would likely shift the belief systems of many thousands of persons in their *current* lifetime, and residually affect future generations, as well. We resolve to show the conquering revengeful ones what we've learned from centuries of living in harmony with nature and one another. We intend to demonstrate that love, not fear, is our master.

Past-Life Regression...Goal Achieving or Tension Relieving?

Regardless how entertaining they may be, my intention is to use my trials, tribulations, and stories as a logical and inspirational path to the respective principle under discussion. I want to be your motivational guide, not just a reporter of events. If this writing fails to serve you, my reader, in a *practical* way, then I've not met my objective and prior promise.

When first learning of Past-Life Regression Therapy, *Caustic James* went on overload. *"If you can't take the heat, get out of the kitchen! Humans found yet **another** way to escape life's realities. No longer limited to alcohol, drugs, sex, food, shopping, gambling, working, and basic compulsive addictions, they can opt to go somewhere more exciting, less stressful/painful, etc. Parlor tricks...you people are funny!"*

CJ, my mostly retired mental critic, manifested in the past as part of my confused, subconscious-mind patterns. Apparently housing some fearful past-life memories, CJ seemed to be protecting my conscious mind from something it perceived too much to cope with. Succumbing to this inner terror inadvertently blocked me from expanded levels of empowering awareness. Sarcastic humor has always been CJ's cover for fear, partially offset by a courageous intellect. CJ waited to learn—just like my *complete* human personality—that **the past does not have to equal the future**.

While surfing the I.A.R.R.T. database (International Association for Regression Research and Therapies—Riverside California), I came across a Florida-based psychologist; Dr. Brian Weiss. Dr Weiss is also a past-life-subject author and one of several facilitators reporting quick healing results from this therapeutic modality. Intuitively I questioned whether my background mind-chatter might, in-fact, be responding to a subconscious fear. I overrode CJ's trepidation in order to take a closer look.

Back to the Future

A past life—as a tribal member in the Sioux Nation—had been revealed to me by multiple metaphysical sources whose paths I crossed during my 30-day Spiritual odyssey. Certainly no *feel-good* revelation, Akashic accounts exposed only that the past-life personality in question had helplessly watched his entire family be slaughtered. Without the import and context of how this historical event unveiled, one would be hard pressed to understand how a rational left-brainer like myself could even consider such a bizarre, sensationalistic tale. With all my exhaustive personal-growth work, I still experienced unexplained feelings of unworthiness, along with some lingering fear of rejection. Relentlessly diligent, I could not find any remaining current-life wounds that would benefit from counseling or therapy. My openings to Advanced Second and early Third Reality were just beginning, with ability to go direct to Collective Source for clarity and realization not yet realized. I believed there might be an untried therapy (for me) to help release the final vestiges of my disabling unworthiness.

The driving need to emotionally heal—leading to more self-acceptance and love—combined with my increased faith in a regression-therapy process, finally convinced me to take action. I sensed this part of where I was Guided. My fear and pain of *not* healing (therefore continuing to attract negative partners, or sabotage positive ones) had now become stronger than my fear of facing all demons. Much like Bruce—the dysfunctional man from Colorado you read about in Chapter Four—I, too, felt like I wallowed in a deep pit, and was now determined to put the FUN back into life. [*Note: The upcoming regression event took place only four days prior to my mountaintop Samadhi realization in Malibu.*] Once I decided to use regression therapy, my challenge was to find the right facilitator. A cool, detached, traditional therapist would not work for me. My gut sensing suggested I would not trust or feel safe and loved (dropping mental and emotional barriers) in a clinical environment. I wanted an *intuitive* therapist—someone who could join me in the alpha state, gently point out appropriate choices for healing, and let me do the rest. This particular past-life trauma felt like it connected to my deepest wound. Did a highly intuitive facilitator with regression skills exist? Something positive and loving deep inside of me said, *"Get this remaining pattern healed and everything you've dreamed of for this lifetime will open to you."*

Past-Life Facilitator, Terry Nash

When I saw her it was love at first sight. She was warm, loving, accepting, patient, fun, lighthearted, and nurturing. I felt a warm, comfortable attraction—as though I already knew her. I sensed all this even before being introduced to her. Terry Nash was one of two facilitators (along with Janet Cunningham, Ph.D. from Florida) that teamed up for a post-I.A.R.R.T. conference workshop on the "Interlife." Metaphysicians generally define the Interlife as one's Spiritual existence between physical lives. This subject area captivated me after I read James Redfield's books symbolically illustrating the evolutionary process of Soul, and more specifically, psychologist Dr. Michael Newton's fascinating Interlife reference work, called *Journey of Souls*. As I watched Terry interact with seminar participants, I sensed she was the one I could trust for my leap into the fear pit. Little did I know what a perfect magician she would be. [Note: Subsequent to our fateful meeting, Dr. Terry Nash earned her Ph.D. in Creation Spirituality. Facilitations, such as the following, were most certainly leading her toward that goal. Way to go Terry!]

The workshop concluded...I stood by as the crowd thinned. After detailing my specific need, Terry readily agreed to help. To my increased delight I learned that—in addition to practicing conventional therapy—she was an educated intuitive providing consulting for Spiritual matters. "How cool is that!" I thought.

Terry's office in Ventura, California, was ideally situated just 35 minutes from my same-day Woodland Hills appointment with Ron Scolastico. I had a strong inner motivation to complete this potentially transformational session prior to the Scolastico retreat scheduled the following week. Terry's office space was very cozy, intimate, and safe. I wished to record the session, as the tapes from my readings with Dr. Scolastico proved invaluable. [*Note: Bettye Binder, Ph.D., past president of I.A.R.R.T. — formerly known as APRT (Association for Past-Life Research & Therapies) — and one of the most knowledgeable past-life educators on planet Earth—also worked with me during this odyssey period. The Egyptian Rejuvenation Sanctuary and Sarcophagus (next chapter) came to me during a past-life session facilitated by Dr. Binder.]*

As our mutual efforts failed to produce a working device, my session with Terry was unrecorded — by any *mechanical* means anyway. This process was going to be very interactive; post-flight analysis was not my priority. Not embarking on some historically oriented regression experiment, I had no interest in metaphysical clipboard note-taking, or in charting the position of celestial bodies. Likely to be quite busy slaying demons and releasing subconscious worthiness baggage, I planned to take the express train home without ever needing a return visit.

Confidence engendered on the drive up from Woodland Hills evaporated as I neared Terry's office — my heart suddenly lodged in my throat. The torturous emotional fear within me for so long, felt almost comfortable. Did I really want to upset the applecart?

I slipped into some familiar altered-state dialogue with CJ, to help me face my inner turmoil and release a little pressure. *"Hey buddy, it's not too late to hit the pause button — take more time to think this whole thing over. Don't go crack-brained on me — haste makes waste. Maybe talk to one of those hard-science folks where you can go slow and **prove** your experience? How about it, Bucko?*

The more hopeful, positive part of my personality countered with, "Thanks for sharing, CJ. Regarding *haste*, I've been living with emotional pain for over forty years — just in *this* lifetime. I know what your problem is. Terry — our facilitator — has talents and abilities new to you. You're afraid you won't be able to defend yourself. Furthermore, I love you but I'm getting real tired of your depressing negativity. Your extreme cautiousness served me well in the past, but now I need you as an important observer. So, kindly sit down and shut up! Perhaps *you* might learn something, as well."

Live or let Die

While trying to muster at least the pretense of courage [*CJ* — *"damn the torpedoes, full speed ahead!"*], I greeted and hugged Terry. After just finishing the very penetrating, insightful reading with Ron, I had been lucid dreaming while driving to Ventura [*clearly not recommended for motoring safety*]. So, already in Alpha and uncharacteristically emotional, I told Terry more about what I hoped to accomplish. After sharing my intense feelings, and while debating whether I should lie down, sit up, which pillows to use, and should I..."what the *&%$?2x4!?"...I suddenly stood right in the middle of a Sioux tribal village, ready to do battle! I could just barely hear CJ's weak, terrified voice in the distant background: *"How'd she do that? She back-doored me!"*

Just like leaving the platform and beginning a steep climb up the ramp of a giant roller coaster, it was too late for escapes. I was now committed to the process. I had a flash thought about finding a source of white light for protection, but lost that idea in the action. I was no longer comfortable with brilliant white lights anyway, as you'll recall. "Okay Stevens," I said to myself, "deal with it—this real-feeling experience is just an illusion!" [CJ— *"Oh yea? Ask yourself why it looks and feels so familiar, **Buddy**. I've been here before, so you are on your own. I hope they have some quality Sioux Indian 'weed' handy. I'm gonna need it!"*]

Now grounded in my past-life body, "Larry" stepped into the background, allowing the Indian personality to take the initial lead. [NOTE: *As we continue with the action, the present-tense dialogue represents a blending of the two personas*].

Death Chant

Facing outward, we form a circle and link our arms together. With total peace in our hearts and clarity in our minds, we begin to chant our beloved Spirit-home song—our final creation before departing for the *Happy Hunting Ground*.

Approaching rapidly, soldiers readied themselves to kill *savages*. They were *not* prepared to slaughter pacifists holding hands and singing instead of running and screaming. Many decorated, courageously proud men-at-arms refuse the General's orders to "kill all men, women, and children!" Still trying to appeal to their Commander, staff officers witnessed their troops running from the impending massacre. The General fired not at us, but shot his own men in the back as they fled the genocidal nightmare.

The General's rage is relentless. Battalion members keep advancing—mostly on foot, as their horses refuse to participate. Contrasting the soldier's torment, the love-based energy of understanding, compassion, and forgiveness emanate from my Sioux family. Demonstrating how our small tribe from the Dakotas—and many other American Indians as well—had mastered life on Earth, we deliver the message loudly and clearly.

As the combined energy force vibrates to a level never before experienced from our chanting, dancing, and rituals, I feel myself slip slightly outside of my body. With soldiers shooting wildly—most intentionally missing—the remaining bullets find their mark and tear into us; bodies begin to fall. We close our circle automatically, as if unconsciously guided. Through stunned inaccuracy, many soldiers waste so many rounds they run out of ammunition. Others, out of shock and horror, cannot make their hands work intricately enough to reload their weapons. At this point, the remaining garrison lies just a few feet from our enclave. With blood-white faces showing deep woundedness and numbed hatred for their genocidal action, pitifully disgraced soldiers draw their swords to finish the slaughter.

Amazingly, I am the last member standing. His soldiers refusing to make the final thrust, the General screams in a sick, tormented voice. I am reconciled, even eager, to join my fallen comrades. So close I could smell his dank odor, feel his despoiled character and failing body, this shell of a man stops dead in his tracks and says: "Death is too good for either of us. Suffer now as I suffer. I pray you have a long, miserable, tormented life!"

And Then? The defeated General turns and slowly rides away— his life energy depleted. Remnants of the surviving regiment keep their distance from this previously respected warrior. Our collective merchants of death never look back…eventually disappearing over the rise of a distant hill.

The Grim Reaper of Grief—no longer denied—began its purposeful descent. With mind and flesh too weak to resist the encroaching darkness, the blue-coated one would soon have his *final resolution*.

Aftermath

The enormity of what just happened hit me like a herd of buffalo. Why am I still here? I don't want to be alive. The calm and purpose I felt while linked to my tribe—gone; human emotions of fear and grief take over. A tidal wave of nausea began its trespass just as I thought, "I'm here because some of my people are still alive—they need me!" A few surviving animals, also grief stricken, are still about. My remaining purpose must be to find survivors, band them together in safety. Love for my tribe outweighs the will to die, but I doubt my strength to do what's required.

I begin the gruesome process of tearing through the tight pile of broken, bleeding bodies. Frantically, I search for survivors. The Spirit

Gods will guide me. Through wracking sobs of an intensity I'd never known, and stinging tears so fluid I could barely see, I desperately look for signs of physical life. Halfway through the grotesque rummaging, when impossible to continue, I crawl to the river's edge and collapse. Cold water revives me enough for reality to push aside the denial. What if there are no survivors? No one appears to be moving; I hear no sounds from the mass of flesh that used to be my wonderfully animated loved ones. How could I survive with absolutely no one to care for...no wounded to tend? How could I numb the exploding pain if entirely alone with my loss?

Struggling to abate the stark terror, I climb to my feet; fully prepared to race back to continue the frenzied search. Suddenly, a large black shape I barely notice out of the corner of one eye, gives me a huge blind-sided blow to the head. I stagger, fall to my knees, but quickly recover to assume a defensive position. Okay...if someone wants a fight, they'll get one. Peace and passivity be damned! No more dishonorable hit-and-run tactics; whoever returned better have more than a saber. I shouted at the vaguely discernible force: "You wanted a savage? Okay, you've got one! I'll take that sword and shove it where the Sun God don't shine!" While facing the dark, cloudy, imperceptible mass, a chill penetrates every fiber of my Being. I now recognize it. Not a returning soldier, or even my preference...the Commanding General...this inky, black, nebulous entity was my own personal demon. *This* was the monster from the id, nipping — sometimes ferociously — at Larry for all his years, up to and including October 31, 1996.

I then realized that I (Larry) was intended to be there with this old fear pattern, to see and experience its moment of inception. For my current (1996) psyche, this twisted creation, this still-active, self-sabotaging unworthiness, directed my subtle manipulations and attempts to control the product of love. For years I followed this false prophet, this internal fear-based program requiring Larry to feign perfection to trap love — if that be the only way to possess the elusive elixir. Lastly...hopelessly...when Larry did actually find a love to match his ideological intensity, sensitivity, and deep longing, he invariably torpedoed any vibrant, honest, non-dysfunctional relationship. Motivated solely by underlying feelings of lack and unworthiness, Larry turned again to dark, old-paradigm, patterns of rescuing and controlling. Should Larry inadvertently heal (fix) another's woundedness, the dysfunctional reasoning went, the privileged individual will *surely* adore him, as he will have finally *earned* love.

This is the fear that I—Shaman Chief of a small tribe in the Dakota Sioux Nation—yielded to, three agonizing days after the slaughter. With intense grief, hate for myself and all others (especially the Gods), combined with the reactive belief I could never heal the pain, I succumbed to indirect suicide.

This ending may be the experiential truth of a past-life event, but a new ending was to be written in the *now*. Both Larry and I [*Collective Consciousness—Universal Mind*] were getting a second chance to defeat (transform) this old nemesis. After all the workshops, counseling, and personal work to conquer his feelings of lack, combined with healing all consciously known childhood and other traumatic current-life experiences, here "it" hid in a remote corner of the past, terrified of discovery. Facing it squarely, like Larry and I were doing now, the opaque monster knew it had no chance of survival. Our blended personalities saw its weakness. It previously got to me (Lakota Chief) from my ignorance and fear. The last time around I lacked the life experience to recognize it for what it was—a soft, nebulous cloud *without* fangs. A mere wisp of smoke and a distorted mirror were its only weapons. Never real, it had *always* been a malignant perception of my subconscious mind. Yes, it gave me a good wallop back when I lost my whole family, and before I recognized what Larry knows today.

A New Choice

"Okay, you were able to blindside me on our previous go 'round, while I lay defenseless. Now I'm facing you, fair and square; let's see what you've got." I was back with all the tools and wisdom gathered by Larry. "Come on…take your best shot! I'll even lower my arms and turn my cheek."

At that point, a wonderful awareness came over our blended personalities—a truly unprecedented (for me) personal experience. With great relief, the *monster from the id* dissolved into our mutual arms. Vaporizing before our eyes, we lived no longer under its spell. How could we have feared this illusion? Fear now thanked us—yes, *thanked us* for acknowledging and setting both it and the new ME, free. With joyous tears pouring down my previously bereaved face, I felt the exhaustive burden lift. Instantly the now-benevolent cloud turned into a white feather—the final feather of a wounded dove I no longer needed to fix or rescue. An almost hysterical sense of release, peace, and love descended over me. I saw FEAR (**F**alse **E**vidence **A**ppearing **R**eal) in a brand new light. *Emotional anxiety had wanted to be my friend all along!* Flooded with amazement at this insight, I realized mental and emotional fears had *always* been diagnostic tools aiding me in my healing and reawakening.

Breakthrough realizations came with releasing this depressive burden. Upon reflection, empowering awareness resulted from taking responsibility for my thinking, feeling, and four levels of action.

❶ **Acknowledge and be fully present with the respective thoughts and feelings.**

❷ **Absolutely refuse to accept any more poor-me illusions and outcomes.**

❸ **Gather and direct a support team.**

❹ **Practice the desired replacement.**

This result sure beat *sympathy* and going to codependency meetings. No more *"you did me wrong"* song for this kid. I felt blessed — as never before — for the confidence swelling within me. [*Unleashed empowerment led to Third Reality (Samadhi) realization. Using inner attunements, I would henceforth go* **direct** *for break-through communions.*]

Back at the Ranch

While all the action took place, Terry intuitively knew where to give me a gentle prod and when to get out of the way. I intuitively took on several roles and did my own cross talk — as written here — while reliving this *dramatic* but no-longer *traumatic* past life. I was happy in allowing this old memory to eternally *rest in peace*. I brought home (to 1996) a new, friendly tool. I would now go forth courageously *looking* for other lingering emotional fears needing benevolent releasing, resulting in even more love inflow. I finally felt deserving of love, because from this point forward, I achieve empowerment through *self*-fixing, rather that external blaming, manipulating, and controlling. Emotional fear, when and if it should present itself, will henceforth be my ally.

Wow...what a realization breakthrough! As we become balanced, all-inclusive, female/male integrated examples, we transform the WORLD! I rapidly realized the higher truth: regardless what society does, *I can be free and joyous all on my own!*

Rewriting the Script

I had another very emotional, special finish to my session with Terry. On this second Sioux Nation go-'round, instead of making physical death after several days of post-genocidal agony, Terry helped me *"grow up"* the Medicine Chief persona. In this therapeutically empowering scenario, my old Indian personality matured to a ripe old age. He not only completely healed—after defeating and befriending the minions of emotional fear—but went on to become a revered Spiritual healer and teacher. A Shaman of great wisdom, he made physical death in his eighties.

When Terry asked me to picture my aged Sioux self, without any conscious thought (I was still in Alpha) I immediately pictured a portrait I purchased years before from the artist—Wendy's former husband and my niece's father—Paul Surber. After placing this particular painting in a storage closet, I completely forgot about it until that very moment. This now *prominently displayed* painting *is* of an eighty-year-old Sioux Indian, although I did not know this at the time of my regression experience.

Sioux Medicine Chief by Paul Surber

Paul Surber—Indian Historian and Artist Extraordinaire

Paul told me the original sketch of the aged, but self-assured Sioux Indian, found by *chance* (yeah, right!) in some off-the-beaten-path antique book store, was so intriguing he decided to paint it even though it was not a Crow or Blackfoot—his specialty. He also confirmed (I had not previously known this, either) the circle grouping and toning as the "Death Chant" formation, indigenous to the Sioux, particularly the Lakotas. The discovery of gold, often through illegal prospecting and trespass, instigated open season on *savage* Indians unwilling to surrender land guaranteed to them by treaty. My regression experience amazed Paul—an historical enthusiast and collector of rare Indian artifacts. He confirmed Death Chants did occasionally take place *exactly* as I envisioned.

Being in the NOW

But that (past) was then, and this is now. I give thanks we have Second Reality therapies like past-life regression, re-birthing and various power-breathing exercises, Neural Linguistics, hypnotherapy, energy balancing, and *altered-state* processes that allow Spirit (the Collective) to come through and assist our healing and Spiritually Guided awakening. I don't know about you, but I've got the self-inflicted *suffering* part of life pretty well understood and mastered. I'm now more than ready for classes in FUN and LOVE.

As Terry facilitated my glorious return to the present, I gave thanks to all those Beings — both human and Celestial — important to this monumental undertaking. These breakthroughs we all can make, with just a few simple understandings. With the use of desire, courage, and faith — located alongside the full force of emotional fear, pain, and forgiveness — healing and blessed release awaits. Decisive action can then reveal multiple enlightening disclosures.

Fear as Friend?

As I hope you've learned, emotional fear need not be permanently avoided or stuffed. A friend-in-waiting, it continually works, either behind the scenes or front and center, as a self-diagnostic. We need not crouch in dark corners, demonstrating mental-emotional cessation and fetal-like paralysis. When you demonstrate a readiness (intention) for positive change, Guidance provides a continual parade of facilitative opportunities. I now know — with certainty — there are no victims. *We are all heroes and heroines poised for actualized greatness.* Throughout our lives a continual string of human co-facilitators bless us. Noticing their opportunistic arrival requires we keep our head up and pay attention.

Past-Lives — Real or Memorex®?

About two and a half months later (early 1997), as I reentered and wrote some preliminary remembrances from the Sioux Nation lifetime, I received even more detail and clarity. Despite my vivid experience and beneficial results, some friends and acquaintances asked: "How do you know your past-life scenario is real? Can you prove your regression experience was not some fantasy of an over-active imagination, wounded psyche, or another logical cause?" Can you guess whether these friends are primarily left or right brainers? By now...an easy guess.

My associates suggested this regression a construct compiled from the conscious, subconscious, super-conscious, unconscious, non-conscious...basically a psychological mind trick to give me what I wanted. They claimed proof of their theory in the rewrite where I changed the original outcome with the therapist's help. I prudently considered these well-conceived questions. New, more intuitive openings did not prevent my logical mind from functioning. Determined to never again live that stubborn, fully skeptical, frozen-hearted condition, an integrated, left/right-brain meditative attunement process provided me some answers to those probative questions.

Facilitated in either very deep Alpha or Theta awareness, a degree of conscious thought probably blended with the subconscious during this regression. Also possible—subjectively speaking—that my Higher Self assisted the inner psychological dynamic (rewrite ending) for a more expansive, broad-based healing. The new, more-empowered ending helped me expansively appreciate emotional fear and feelings of worthlessness as not only distorted perceptions, but directed diagnostics for focusing our feelings toward forgiveness, healing, and beneficial replacements.

Had I remained challenged by *is-it-real* skepticism, I could, I suppose, enlist the services of a Dr. Michael Newton or a Dr. Brian Weiss—submitting myself to a deeper regression process (theta super-consciousness). Potentially rendering purer, historically correct remembrances of particular lifetimes, still no guarantees exist even at the hands of those experts. Altered-state work largely depends on one's intent (attitude), underlying beliefs, and level of consciousness.

Because it serves me, I accept the *spin* ending as a concert between intuitive-therapist Terry—prodding me toward the revised finish—and inner Guidance answering my request for *healing*...not historical research. Here is my best gut-instinct analysis, filtered through my current belief system. Confronting the shadow beast provided a means for purging my worthiness issues. As a Soul-directed exercise, the silhouetted beast symbolized both my human shadow *and* the negative patterns remaining (unresolved) after a traumatic physical death. Although the fullness (detail and flavor) of the regression felt like an historical past-life experience, consider the rewrite ending a further answer to my preflight prayer. If only a metaphor for one's unlimited potential, how big a prize do you need before adding it to your *plus* column? Might self-healings clear the path for graduate courses in experiential life?

The next series of logical questions: Whose past life are we experiencing? Just because I experienced this transformational event as my own, how can it be proven mine? And why is exclusiveness important? These questions reside at the core of these teachings. Even the most experienced past-life educators, like Dr. Brian Weiss, author of *Many Lives Many Masters*, or Bettye Binder, former president of the Association for Past-Life Research and Therapies, cannot *empirically* answer the "whose is it" question. But *you* are acquiring the tools to answer these and *all* questions, yourself. Keep recalling the fundamental power of belief, as I explain further.

I have talked to experienced regression counselors who report sessions where the same historical figure manifests through different subjects. One hypnotherapist at the Philosophical Library in Escondido, California, told me of several different regression subjects manifesting Cleopatra. Now even if we believe in specific Soul lineage (reincarnation), it seems unlikely all subjects could have been Cleopatra—*unless* we have the ability to plug into *all* past-life experiences simultaneously (transcendent awareness). Can you feel the synergistic power suggested by this all-inclusive Akashic connection? Perhaps synergy and symbiotic inclusivity are what Dr. Carl Jung meant when describing the Collective Unconscious.

"Once an individual awakens to Third Reality, past *anything*—including lifetimes—become moot," says Dr. Pottenger. At fully actualized third-level awareness, being present with all past and present creations—material *or* cosmic—ones expand beyond space/time differentiations (dualism) and linear time components.

Using what physicist Dr. Gary Zukav calls multi-sensory perception: by continually practicing expansion of consciousness we eventually access the realm or realms of memory, awareness, and the totality of human/Soul experience. That level of entry serves us both now and in the so-called "beyond." Complete healing of all thoughts and feelings of unworthiness, or lack, clears us to *fully* use Universal Mind. If we open to believing nothing in life is separate—including all past human experience—we enter the Heaven-on-Earth cosmic-union world foretold by past mystics and confirmed by present-day researchers. Consider how ongoing emotional *suffering requires a past orientation*. What if you lived *only* in the present moment? How would that focus change your life experience?

The Akashic Records

An existing Celestial library of all recorded human events and experience is exactly what the renowned trance medium Edgar Cayce suggested, and for some metaphysical researchers, conclusively proved. Note that Spiritual mediums such as Edgar Cayce, Ron Scolastico, Lee Carroll, Harold Klemp (Eckankar), and others are employed to assist a *particular* client or grouping. The original purpose or intention was not for Cayce's therapeutic readings to be disseminated to the general public. We mislead ourselves with generalized forecasts made by Mediums, Clairvoyants, and Mystics — especially when soliciting predictions for the *future*. This is like asking an all-there-is Force to describe all-there-is-*not*. Intuitively delivered prophecy might be helpful or tension relieving for the *subject* person, even if the foretold events fail to occur. As far as exhaustive research has been able to determine, Cayce's ten-thousand or so medical readings were *always* diagnostically appropriate for the respective client.

A More Practical Question. Very subjective and entertaining theories — for sure. But what difference does it make if my regression experience was a *real* past life, construct, or symbolic illusion? **Bottom line:** if it therapeutically works, why not use it? Most psychologists and psychiatrists practicing regression therapy use the mantra "If not relevant, don't sweat it." They use it because they get good, fast, often permanent, end product. *Why* it works is not a therapist's focus. The greatest strength when using self-help, or making beneficial judgments: our *own* thoughts, intuitive feelings, and most valuable of all, *practical, testable results*. The same question (are they real?) could be asked about all subjective feelings — like love for example. Can you *prove* you've been in love? The *fact* that you've experienced the effects (emotional, Spiritual and physiological) of love provides proof enough for you, although it may not pass muster with the *scientific* community.

I test my theories by asking myself: "Does what I've just experienced *feel* like truth? Does it uplift and empower me? Do I now feel better about myself, and as a result, better about others and life itself?" If I can say yes to these questions, then it (the process) is *truth* for me. If it looks, walks, and quacks like a duck, I'm calling it a duck while the research gang checks the DNA. I don't really care whether it was *my* past life. I accept that once an experience resides in the Collective, it belongs to all of us equally. The big point here: *separation is an intended illusion.* We live under a temporary experience of individuality and separateness for the intensity this unique perspective brings to the human-life process. The Sioux Nation life helped me overcome my fear (distrust) of intimacy. New insights expand beyond the previously limiting mental or emotional fears — they no longer have a strangle hold on me. I am grateful for life-transforming gifts. Gifts that can be realized by all, *without* needing to first walk a bed of hot coals. But if you want to, you're free to stay stuck in that five-sensory, First Reality imperative, *"Is it real?"*

What the Professionals say

Some psychologists believe that, as a tool, past-life therapy retrieves healing images directly from the psyche. These experts tell us regression clients are often not in a past life. The "psyche" theory could explain why different people often fixate on the same historical figure (like Cleopatra), rather than experience something more individually intimate. Additionally, neurosis-based psychological squeezing can block the healing available from Source energy — similar to the hindering effect on creative expression when writers or artists focus on impending deadlines and other pressures. Opening to a belief in universal inclusivity — the synchronistic wholeness of life — greatly simplifies the larger answer. Assuming only **one** innate and Collective Source, any method can affect the healing replacement by allowing ones to open to it and then integrate themselves with it. *If your orientation releases your distorted notions of fear, unworthiness, and lack — replacing undesirables with empowering feelings of connection, unlimited love, power, and potency — then you're on the fast track to clarity and more expansive truths.* Again, most regression therapists don't care *how* the modality is held or perceived. Their **bottom line**, after "cause no harm": simply whether the client benefits from the facilitation.

Mind Power and Placebo Effects

Before concluding regression exploration a valid therapy option, let's prudently include at least a rudimentary examination of the Placebo Effect and general power of the mind. You often hear speculation on what percent of our brain we typically use. The common range: five to fifteen percent. These same theorists also tell us our brain power is unlimited. Even as a youngster, I continually asked about this apparent contradiction. How does one measure a percentage of infinity?

Brain vs. Mind

If you will, consider that although certainly needed for Earth life, brain *hardware* is mostly moot regarding our cosmic connection. Our real power comes through our Soul-mind (software) link to the Universe. The human brain, unquestionably a phenomenal physical organ, serves us extremely well on Earth. While taking care of all our autonomic bodily functions and animal-type reflexes, gray matter enables us to perform complex cognitive deductions and remember billions of bits of information. This includes the ability to tap into a huge genetic-DNA-provided, learned-behavior potential. Typically, our brain can house as much recallable information as contained in five Encyclopedia *sets*. Even so, science cannot *precisely* determine where our brain stores memories. We know from numerous animal studies that large portions of the brain can be surgically removed and, assuming the body remains functional, the subject can still demonstrate a complex, previously memorized task. In holographic photography, any part of the original image can be used to reproduce whole, three-dimensional laser pictures. Could human memory be another expression of this innate holographic profile?

A Human Being normally requires a healthy functioning brain to access mind consciousness. Eventually the brain dies—consciousness does not. Consider the Soul-mind a property that differentiates Human Beings from the pure animal form (herd consciousness); one which contains our Spiritual DNA and personality matrix. Telekinesis, telepathy, remote viewing, and all the so-called psychic areas are some of the peripheral (physical manipulation) talents demonstrated by persons downloading expanded portions of the Collective Mind.

Super-Sized Athletes

At their high level of participation, top sports champions understand physical talent, preparation, and conditioning not the only determinants of performance. Many use guided-visualization techniques to calm and focus themselves during intense challenge. They learn to fully sense a future circumstance and intended result, before it becomes a reality. Some psychologists report teammates (commonly) entering an intuitive group-mind state known as *super-beta consciousness* during emotionally charged competition. Teams can temporarily manifest congruency of thought and physical coordination similar to a flock of birds, or school of fish. For solo competitors, the mental process involves expanded sensing, or "zone" euphoria. Expanded sensations potentially transcend anxiety, pain, and even previous physical or psychological limitations. Athletes with equal talent, but without the focused mental-mind discipline, experience more fear of failing. They don't perform nearly as well as their psychologically prepared competitors, especially true during times of extreme stress. Actor's, or writer's, block illustrates another example of fear squeezing out creative inflow.

I especially enjoy watching Tiger Woods scramble with his "B" golf game — when he fully demonstrates his psychological preparation and discipline. How many times have we seen Woods mentally will the golf ball into the hole during a crucial, do-or-die situation? Television commentators acknowledge with admiration and awe his telekinetic-like ability. Normally dormant and not scientifically provable, how can an exclusive, five-sensory science *ever* prove multi-sensory abilities? To attempt such is a non sequitur. I suspect Tiger's competitors respect and fear his psychological strength, perhaps even more than his physical talent.

Fantastic new technologies enhance our ability to zone-in. HEART MATH (www.heartmathresources.com) has developed multi-sensory Freeze-Framer software that's an incredible aid in helping athletes, business professionals, and especially our hyper-active (ADHD) children, calm and center themselves — leading to improved memory recall and performance. Unless you *prefer* drug regimens, consider how a deficiency in heart-focus relates to stress.

For those believing the HEART too sentimental for high-stress work and other competitive environments (as a professional pilot, I used to assume this), I quote from page #78 of David & Bruce McArthur's outstanding book, *The Intelligent Heart*: "The heart energy actually *enhances* the intellectual capacity of an individual. It assists us in moving beyond limiting emotional patterns to view a situation accurately. There is a well-known nerve pathway from the head to the heart through the autonomic nervous system. But there is also a nerve pathway from the heart to the brain. The result of the activation of the heart energy is the stimulation of the neurocortex of the brain, which is the source of our higher reasoning capacities. *The brain works better when heart is engaged.*"

Brain-Mind as One

Now that I hopefully have you thinking about your conscious awareness in an expanded-mind concept, rather than the perspective of being confined to a deteriorating physical organ, forget any separating theories or axioms. We are much more than the sum of our human parts, as we — for the moment — coexist (mind, body, Spirit) in a sea of unlimited power, potency, creativity, and love. Unless functioning as dedicated biology researcher or other subdividing reductionist, what our brain does — versus our mind — is not relevant to everyday existence. While here on Earth, we rise to our fullest potential with the symbiotic cooperation of the *totality* of what Creation provides — actualized, or not, by human free will.

Many examples exist of certain focused individuals facilitating their own recovery from cancer — and other terminal illnesses — by first believing and then visualizing their own cure. Some have achieved self-healing even after doctors definitively state there is nothing left in medicine to assist them. I could list specific examples, but I believe you are familiar with the *spontaneous remission* phenomena. If not, get on the Internet and you'll quickly find relevant search examples. Many drugs approved by the FDA score only slightly higher than the respective placebo test groups. In double-blind studies, the placebo group members — as well as the researchers — freely speculate which class they're in. Imagine the placebo results if the facilitators and their respective subjects were *convinced* of being in the chosen grouping! For years, family practitioners have given in to pressure from their patients to prescribe antibiotics for colds and flu, although a scientific certainty that antibiotics do not cure or otherwise affect viruses. Convinced an injection or pill *will* heal them, many persons actually do get better. They thus prove (mislead themselves) the medicinal therapy worked. This result demonstrates the power of accepted mental suggestion — the *placebo effect*.

A few psychologically astute doctors have *suggested* to terminal patients — when no conventional treatment remained — they obtained a new, powerful, unreleased drug, which was "the" cure for their disease. Upon taking the saline injections and colored sugar pills, patients especially open to suggestion have then been observed going into complete remission. Later, inadvertently reading that the experimental drug turned out to be a failure, these same ones often return to previous states of dis-ease. In the vast majority of the monitored terminal cases, belief (acceptance) in the bad news resulted in the quick return to ill health and — shortly thereafter — death. Because wholeness *preexists* our acceptance of it, we have the innate ability to access an existing cosmic powerhouse of rebalancing energy. If you believe in this potential, *and* can set clear and accepting intentions, add "Mega-Placebo" to your tool kit. [*This manual presents the healing power of belief and prayer prominently in chapters 4, 11, 16 (Meet a Modern-Day Quintessential Mystic), and 19.*]

My final consideration (validation of past lives) has to allow the possibility of the placebo-mind effect in healing my own unworthiness. Did I release, heal, and replace because of the past-life review, or was I pre-sold on the *location* of my continued self-sabotage (in a past Sioux Nation lifetime), and simply validated my belief?

When accepting any extremely vivid past-life causal, the mind is sufficiently powerful to implement current-moment emotional healing—similar to the spontaneous remissions in cancer patients. So, is anything *real* or is it *all* Memorex? Ask yourself what difference it makes whether the egg or the chicken came first? Simply rejoice in the understanding that here on Earth, just like the mind/brain symbiosis, one does not exist without the other. Appreciate the power and potency available to all through Spirit connection, continually stimulated by life experience and resulting levels of expanded awareness. Enjoy the variety of Second Reality tools creatively discovered to assist healing/replacing undesirable fears and negative beliefs. Celebrate a return to the love, peace, joy and happiness intended for you. Interactive processes serve us quite well until we awaken to advanced levels of Second Reality, and eventually Third Reality consciousness where they're no longer needed. We experience the direct conduit to omni-sensory, Source potential in the transcendent (heart). Evidenced by a plethora of self-help systems developed in just the last 50 years, we live in a time of unprecedented transformation!

How would you like to exit the human amnesia to see first-hand who you *really* are and how and why you are here on Earth? In the next chapter I facilitate some temporary ether antidote. It's time you met your own Soul—*up close and personal.*

Sioux Medicine Chief by Paul Surber

CHAPTER EIGHTEEN

Seeing and Experiencing Beyond the Veil

♥   ♥   ♥

Some people who meditate regularly achieve deep alpha or theta levels of consciousness and report *out-of-body* (OBE) experiences. Others sense a vibrant existence just beyond the veil of our more common beta-mind awareness. Those new to meditation, or attunements, can quickly learn to feel peaceful, loving, resonant, even *cosmic* types of experiences if open and desirous of making the connection. In fact, this synchronistic union is achieved quite naturally when we enhance and deepen our human relationships. Some challenges may also accompany our search for bliss, however.

A fear of Earth negativity may present the subconscious mind motivation to remain in cosmic orbit. Some report a reluctance to return to the material world reality after extensive altered-state meditations, as they subsequently find Earth life too conflicting...too confining. Some advanced Eastern Guru meditators use assistants to remind them to eat, clean, and groom themselves. Long, deep, continual altered-state work (depending on the subject's intent) may lessen one's sensitivity toward the physical, such as reducing awareness of hunger, heat, and cold. Without motivation to do otherwise, metabolism and circulation can gradually slow down— similar to animal hibernation—even when one is not meditating. Using advanced Hindu disciplines, some Yogis demonstrate complete mind-over-body mastery. Select masters have learned to control every biological system in their body—some to the degree that life signs are undetectable without advanced diagnostic technology.

Kuda Bux
When just entering adolescence and full of those pesky unanswered questions, I came across an extensive article in a major news magazine about one of the first Yogi Masters to break vows of silence.

He had come west to demonstrate his remarkable abilities *and* to deliver what he believed an important self-empowerment message. Already known in Europe as the "Man with the X-Ray Eyes," his adopted Western name was Kuda Bux (1905-Feb 5, 1981). Khuda Bakhsh (birth name), the Pakistani mystic, became a legend in 1939 when he performed a spectacular fire-walking demonstration for the University of London's Council for Psychical Research. In 1945, Kuda—who hailed from Kashmir, Pakistan—submitted himself to a battery of scientific tests administered by a major East Coast research university. Kuda began his demonstration by displaying complete mental control over all the autonomic systems in his body. While being x-rayed, he repeatedly stopped and restarted his pulse and heart muscle. This was incredible enough, but the best was yet to come. The most profound display, one that greatly stimulated my desire to understand the great mysteries of the Universe, was his ability to see his environmental surroundings *without* the use of his physical eyes. [*Later, both the governments of the USSR and US (Central Intelligence Agency and Defense Intelligence Agency) experimented with parapsychology—telekinesis, telepathy, and remote viewing. The US program operated under code name Stargate.*]

I still recall the university contingent assuring themselves that Kuda Bux used no form of misdirection, magical illusion, or masked deception. [*Illusionists in the industry still conjecture whether he used trickery*]. First, the researchers covered Kuda's eye sockets with globs of thick flour dough. They held the gooey mixture in place with large cotton balls and surgical tape. Next, they tightly covered his entire head (except for a small nostril and mouth opening) with a dense turban wrap of multiple blindfolds. Kuda Bux then climbed on a bicycle and blithely negotiated heavy New York City traffic, including Times Square, eventually coming to rest without mishap. To further convince the still skeptical investigators, he placed himself behind a solid door-like partition. Then, amazingly, with only his bare hand extended around the barrier, he read from randomly selected books. Kuda Bux explained that once he entered an expanded state of consciousness, he could define his surroundings with any part of his skin surface exposed to the neighboring environment.

Apocrypha

Although Kuda Bux did not explain the skin-exposure requirement, the more mystical portions of the original Greek and Latin bibles refer to a related ability. The Vulgate and Septuagint versions—generally excluded from the Jewish canons of the Old Testament and *all* versions of the New Testament—describe an ability called "apocrypha." Apocrypha is the capacity to see physical reality through the use of tactile perception only. Most dictionaries of today define apocrypha as "a sham," or "of doubtful and disingenuous origin." Consider how the current definition may have arisen from the same philosophical (and political) shift which dawned the greatly demystified New Testament. Today more advanced techniques and visualization vehicles assist us, however. Subconscious Analysis and Reprogramming (S.A.R.), Neurolinguistics (NLP), and Holographic Psychology, provide some of the more aggressive examples.

Assuming Kuda's visual field process did involve a multi-sensory facilitation, and that he could read the environment from beyond the limitation of his physical eyes, was skin exposure a *self-imposed* limitation created to psychologically keep in phase with the material reality? Or a necessary natural-law bridge to the energy forces that animate all life? The skeptic in me can not entirely rule out the possibility that Kuda Bux employed another ESP talent—such as telepathy, or very clever deception—in his blind-reading demonstration. Blind persons develop a decisively enhanced level of perceptiveness with their remaining senses. A few have even achieved a level of awareness approaching our Kashmir mystic's alleged mastery.

Kuda Bux did explain the *process* that led to his x-ray sensing ability. He invested many years relentlessly meditating by candlelight on a portrait of a loved one (a deceased sister, perhaps). He focused on every minute detail until he saw that beloved face as clearly with his eyes closed as when they were open. He eventually became *one* with that image, and perhaps fully integrated with the essence of his sister's energy field. Sri Bakhsh then shifted focus toward other persons and objects until (with his eyes closed) he could see them, too. His theory: with rare exception *Human Beings are **conditioned** to believe they can see reality only with their physical eyes.* Kuda Bux told the researchers he came west to teach that visual acuity is in the mind— not in any physical organ—and that we must look beyond the physical senses to find the higher truth of life and human existence. Kuda, like most Yogis, believed the world's suffering populace handicapped by such an extreme focus on materialism. He later proved his theory with a most practical demonstration.

Ironically, the captivating Yogi Master eventually lost the use of his organic eyes to glaucoma. During his senior years, Kuda's Poker and Hearts buddies (reportedly) used to playfully pester him to put on a blindfold so he could at least read his *own* cards.

I question whether any university reductionistic researchers comprehended the true significance Kuda Bux's message, any more than *worshipers* understood the potentially liberating messages of Buddha and Jesus. Many psychics, mentalists, and magicians tried, with varying degrees of success, to duplicate Kuda's talent. Lacking any multi-sensory *"third eye"* capability, many cleverly manufactured convincing simulations — suggesting Kuda Bux did the same. In fact, mentalists like Kuda, Mesmer (the father of hypnosis), Romark, and the remarkable Joe Dunninger, provided mentoring inspiration to the plethora of mentalists and stage hypnotists entertaining us today. Since today's magicians and mentalists spend so much time focusing on clever illusion/deception methods, few consider the possibility of a latent ESP talent — even if subconsciously manifesting it. For the vast majority of these gifted but rigidly skeptical performers, they label something not fathomable just another gimmick they haven't figured out yet.

Harbinger or Huckster?

So...was Kuda's apocryphal demonstration a true example of a subconsciously based *third-eye,* or an elaborately staged hoax that fooled top scientists — both here and abroad? More importantly, can you believe *yourself* capable of developing a multi-sensory focus? Using it then to expand your subjective awareness of relationships and life in general?

Journalists who interviewed Kuda Bux in his later years claim Kuda became cynical and disheartened — believing his basic empowerment message had fallen on deaf ears. I'm confident Kuda's Soul-Self knows his omni-sensory demonstrations — impossible to completely prove or disprove in a five-sensory laboratory — helped many to look toward the limitless Universe for their dreams and ambitions. He taught us to continually question in our quest to understand the great mysteries of life. I exist as proof that his message was heard. Regardless of Kuda Bux's true inner motivations, character, and abilities, he left us an impressive empowerment legacy. For that alone, I salute him.

Looking back, I realize how examining that documented article on the Kashmir mystic resulted in a major Spiritual DNA activation moment for my young, inquisitive self. That I could so easily remember exacting details from a 45- to 50-year-old article shows me how significantly that informational encounter influenced my future motivations. I needed just a few small details: the year the East Coast research examination took place, correct spelling of the mystic's name (I recalled his last name as "BOX" because he definitely didn't live in one!), home city, and his birth year—all obtained from an Internet search. If you probe your memory, it's quite likely you'll recall some early defining moments.

Incidentally, I also remember the university researchers concluding no scientifically determinable explanations for Kuda Bux's extra-sensory talent. Armchair skeptics (also lacking alternative explanations for his clinically demonstrated abilities) believed the Yogi Master broke vows of silence simply to make a buck in the lucrative Western market.

Until suddenly prompted, prior to writing this segment, I made no attempt to follow Kuda Bux's career after reading (in my youth) the 1945 university research project. It's no stretch to conclude legitimate demonstrations of this nature being well beyond the capability of the human brain. Consider that Kuda's talent may have exemplified omni-sensory ability—an awareness achievable only through an expanded state of consciousness using the power of the Collective (Universal) Mind.

Pitfalls

Returning our focus to potential pitfalls using meditative attunements to escape the harshness of human existence, consider how one's motivation determines outcome. If we use meditation and altered states of consciousness to escape the world's harshness, what is our incentive to return? By using the enhanced awareness and life-management tools obtained from reflective contemplation, we learn to fully engage physical life while expanding our connection with the Eternal. Maximizing experiential life on Earth is the Soul's preference for us; best achieved by courageously forging ahead with all the creativity and fear-busting passion we can muster. And, after reading this far, you know the benefits of moving forward without blaming, fetal cowering, or trying to escape Earth materiality. This is who we are and why we are here.

Bottom Line. *You don't need to live your entire existence on a mountaintop, kiss anyone's feet, swallow hallucinogenic root juice, or spend years contemplating your belly button in a cave with monks, to discover your life's purpose.* "How else can we take a peek beyond the amnesic veil," you say? Glad you asked!

Life after Life

Dr. Raymond Moody, researcher and author of the landmark book *Life after Life*, interviewed hundreds of persons who recovered from clinical death—complete heart stoppage and cessation of all electrically monitored brain activity. The vast majority of *returnees* share stories about warm lights, tunnels, and the presence of lovingly supportive Celestial Beings. The resurrected decedents, after enjoying their otherworld love-fest, generally report being transformed by the experience. From personal experience I can attest how *fear* of physical death helps one to more fully appreciate living. Many bring self-empowering messages from *the other side,* as they call it, combined with a new purpose to their remaining life. Most would share many of the insights you're reading in this manual.

In contrast, persons who died from traumatic events, like terror-fraught suicide, report a much-less pleasant transition experience. Many of these tormented returnees report being sequestered away from the main Spiritual population in some dark, quiet, holding area while being administered to.

The Physical Reality—Manifested Vibrational Energy

I include this section for those who've not personally experienced a cosmic OBE, hopefully to provide you a sense of the expanded Universe and multiple realms of existence. We are not generally aware of these realms while grounded in lower-frequency bodies and preoccupied with beta-mind consciousness. *All existence can be thought of as various manifestations of vibrational energy.*

Human Beings (*all* manifested life for that matter) are created from condensed energies of sentient light and—on Earth—sound vibration. An elaborate, esoteric-based, hermetic-chemical process reduces frequencies to a level resulting in our physical presence. A rock, which most consider solid, also possesses a vibrational frequency—albeit much slower than the human frequency. When scientists studied rock particles under powerful electron microscopes, well before the subatomic-particle studies of quantum mechanics, they directly witnessed rapid atomic-energy movement within the heaviest elements. In theory, then, even the densest substance in the known Universe, the core of a black hole, comprises some slight movement—even with a magnetic energy pull so powerful that it traps and holds light.

The larger truth: *nothing*—even Black Holes (according to more recent findings by Stephen Hawking)—is fixed or solid. We are temporary forms of embodied energy and, as we learned with Albert Einstein's General Theory of Relativity, energy—once manifested—can never be destroyed. Energy simply changes form, just as we do. Even our belief in *solid* is therefore subjective.

So, for my magnificent atheistic and agnostic friends, does the concept of *Eternal energy* help you to at least consider the possibility of an immortal Collective Consciousness...Universal Mind...the Great Link? For the many with less-esoteric belief systems, *vibrational energy*—not an exact description, but the best human phrase we have for cosmic DNA—represents the **Higher Power** in their lives. Opening to a belief in an energy type of human origination widens the door to Third Reality. As we simultaneously balance and integrate left- and right-brain hemispheres, we automatically maximize our Earth life potential.

"Cosmic" Contact—Visualization Exercise

I recommend you practice the previously provided (Chapter Two) relaxation technique for thirty days, as preparation for this next big step. That said, feel free to read about your next paradigm shift *now*.

Let's say you've become more open and desirous of intensifying your intuitive feelings. You yearn for an intimate personal connection to the cosmic forces that guide you during your lifetime. When ready, I shall be your facilitator for this majestic, potentially transformational love venture.

Caution! Again, I *strongly* suggest rereading the relaxation technique in Chapter Two, to ensure you are current on all precautions and preparations—prior to beginning this new exercise. Pay special attention to the *expectations* segment. You will have the experience intended for you at this time. During other times, you will experience what is intended for you during *those* particular efforts. Do not try to compare your encounter—especially when trying this with others—to anyone else's description. All events are unique and special, even when ones do not feel anything especially profound or transformational. The sudden *Epiphany* type of shift comes less frequently, but several small openings are cumulative and just as significant. So regardless of your short-term results, release your need for immediate gratification. Stay the course, keep practicing, and know that you can *not* do it wrong. The Eternal Forces always know when you invite them forward into your conscious awareness. Look for unusual coincidences in your human pathway. Certain people, events, and circumstances (this book) come into your view in response to your prayers and the continuation of your Spiritual DNA lesson plan.

To better assist your connection, I suggest (for personal use) you record my guiding facilitation on a cassette tape, to then follow without distractions. Be sure you phrase the instructions in the first person, "YOU." You can order inductive relaxation tapes (*for educational purposes only*) from my website; **www.soulmanlarry.com.** These include the basic relaxation, Holographic Fear-Blasting Technique, the Egyptian Sarcophagus Rejuvenation (coming up), and both **phase-one** and **phase-two** of this Celestial contact exercise.

Inductive relaxation is best achieved with a quiet, secure environment. Enjoy this gift of love from the Souls who Guide you. Once again, do not pressure yourself with preconceived expectations, fear of results, or thoughts and feelings that you are not worthy of cosmic connection. Perform the Holographic Fear Blasting Technique to release stress or expectations. Lovingly trust and invite your Guiding Souls forward, rather than demand or plead for their presence. As you repeatedly practice getting out of your head and into your heart, I assure you a deepening connection. Be gentle with yourself by providing time to adjust to higher-frequency sensibilities. The more you focus on special heart-opening memories, or triggers, the more profound and connecting your experience (both now and later). You will not be alone during this or any other attunement to Soul and the Forces of the Eternal. **Reminder:** I offer the following as an **educational program only** — not therapy. Are you ready?

After making all preparations and a final visit to the restroom, put yourself into that deep relaxation state in which you've been instructed. Take a deep, clearing breath…hold it…and rele-e-e-ase. Feel, sense, or imagine a deeper universal connection. As the ribbons of multi-colored light take their turn entering your Crown Chakra, picture an elevator within your mind. Step into that personal lifting device and observe yourself carried higher and higher to an infinite level of cosmic existence. Picture, feel, sense, or imagine (pick ones that apply) your energy quanta and sub-atomic particles as they temporarily scatter and merge with those of all other animate and inanimate creations. Picture yourself as ONE with this cosmic cradle of love-based soup. You still have a light sense of self, but with human preoccupation no longer at the forefront of your consciousness. Right now you are equal, congruent portions of mind, body, and spirit—the *trifecta* of Creation.

Connection – Phase One

From this perspective, take yourself to your most serene, tranquil location. Use the place that provided relaxing sanctuary during previous attunements and meditations: a babbling brook, a misty waterfall, an ocean bluff with seagulls quietly squawking in the distance, or a beautiful 360-degree panoramic view from a mountaintop that looks down on a combination of these described vistas. From a mountaintop's warm, grassy knoll (as an example), you experience a swirling, gentle breeze bringing invigorating ions and transformational scents from all those previously listed, specially energizing places. See yourself sitting comfortably upright on a smooth granite rock, warmed by the perfect rays of a life-giving sun. Look out over your selected vista, fully immersed in the experience of *oneness* with that selected environment.

As you scan the outer boundaries of your special place, you see a soft, warm, billowy, dense fog bank coming your way. Completely surrounding you in a 360-degree arc, this fog bank closes its circle as it advances closer and closer. Nothing to fear, no storm hidden in or behind the veil, you sense a knowing-loving consciousness, with form and purpose in its approach. Finally, the opaque bank of cloudiness arrives. Incredibly, it communicates with you. As you hoped, from its orderly and purposeful advance, it's alive! Your heart races and your eyes well with tears, as you realize the enormity of this visit. This is the answer to your lifetime of prayer, to no longer feel separate and alone on Earth – proof of the existence of your beloved home world and *all* who unconditionally love and support you. You are *not* lost, you are *not* an alien, but a revered member of this benevolent grouping.

These loving Beings came to you – at your request – by pushing back the amnesic veil you experience as an opaque fog bank. They now speak to you directly.

We are here in this time, as we embrace you…as we love you. As you wonderfully continue your chosen Earth incarnation, we have come in response to your heart-filled desire to more directly experience our [your] collective existence. Please know, beloved Spirit, that all the thoughts and feelings you've had about isolation and separateness are just confused thoughts and feelings – not truths. Feel our presence now as you are ONE with the all-inclusive Divine Aura. Because you set a clear and purposeful intent, your request to penetrate the veil is granted. And now, dear one, lean forward and insert your outstretched arms directly into our veiled bank of warm, pulsating, rejuvenating energy.

Responding to the invitation, you throw your head back in response to the connection. A goose-bump-producing shiver goes through you. You feel so much joy that all emotions open and flow freely—totally without censure or barriers. A floodgate opens and years of pent-up doubt and overdue tears course out of you, fueled by self-forgiveness and acceptance of your Divine nature. You now *know* it's true, you were not alone in the past—you will never be alone in the future, and you are certainly not alone now. Loving Beings—standing in perfection—unconditionally love and celebrate your human life, even with your perceived imperfections and shortcomings of thought and deed. Take this moment to emotionally rejoice in their embrace. [*Leave space here on your tape for serene musical background and quiet interaction with your beloved Soul-mates*].

After some very intimate moments spent in loving connection with your Guiding Ones, the cosmic veil withdraws to whence it came. You are left with the remembrance and knowledge that you can revisit this intimate reunion anytime you desire, simply by inviting the connection. Count yourself back down the floors of the elevator as you return to your starting place. Give yourself a quiet moment to reflect on your experience. End of **phase one.**

For those who achieved a deep, meditative state and may be temporarily feeling a little overwhelmed and out-of-sorts, take time to regain your equilibrium before trying to stand or race off anywhere. You may choose to remain in an altered state for further contemplation and receiving additional messages from the Souls that Guide you. In a few moments, have some water and a small snack to help ground you. Here's a visualization that can help. In a sitting position, close your eyes and put your feet flat on the floor. Coming out of the bottoms of your feet, picture, feel, sense, or imagine several tendrils or tree roots aggressively burrowing themselves downward into the bowels of the Earth. Once you feel grounded, release the imagined stem hooks.

For initial **phase-one** facilitations, I purposefully suggest you stop to fully experience *this* particular portion (arms only) of cosmic contact. The objective: to achieve a level of comfort while softly interacting with a conscious form of Divine energy. With practice, you will learn to trust your connection and completely surrender your human self (entire body) to the collective cosmic forces. You may picture, feel, sense, or imagine the form of these benevolent energies any way that suits you. For best results, delay the impulse for instant gratification; first integrate with partial body contact *before* moving on to **phase two.** Take whatever days, weeks, or months you personally require to accomplish a tranquil connection, knowing that what you have right *now* is a gift beyond compare. *Know* this to be true, even if your contact seemed more a relaxed imagining (the more common initial experience). After several successful **phase-one** inductive processes—feeling comfortable, worthy, and in balance—you may more fully penetrate the energy flux.

Again, do not expect profound connections right away. Most likely your initial experience will be less penetrating—a normal beginning, so be patient. Those besieged with grandiose expectations, stemming from unworthy thoughts and feelings, often quit. If not quickly experiencing earthquakes, lightning-bolts, levitation, or other gravity-defying sensations, they chastise themselves for having been so gullible to even consider a belief in Guiding Entities (Universal Energy, et al). Concluding the absence of immediate fireworks as evidence you are alone and unloved—besides feeling damn lousy— illustrates distorted reasoning and another round of suffering, feedback-loop curriculum looking to happen.

Yo-Yo Effect

It's very human to expect a steady, straight-line rise in intensity of contact with each attempt; leading then to subjective analysis of the measured improvement or setback. We reprimand ourselves (when a later attunement is not as strongly felt) for inefficiency, or worry that Guiding Souls have withdrawn from us—even more common after first experiencing a particularly strong or transformational sensation. Fears of cosmic abandonment, combined with a desperate need to reestablish previous intensities, cause many to force-mode future connections. This squeezing can snowball into a self-fulfilling prophecy, as our human selves temporarily close off our intuitive perception of the loving Celestial embrace. Rather than *enhancing* one's openings to the omni-sensory transcendent Source, affected ones stress themselves into *ground-hugging* overload. If this should happen to you, know this psychological condition to be *temporary* and totally self-created. This overload in no way relates to reward or punishment for your daily activities, choices, or attunement technique(s).

A correction that has worked well for me: courageously face the fear of abandonment and unworthiness. Give those fears a voice. Use the Holographic Fear-Blasting Technique to release temporarily expressing negative thoughts and feelings. Once again, accepting the *fact* that Guiding Souls are always with you, whether or not your human self feels them at the moment, frees you from expectations and self judgment. *Cosmic love is all-inclusive and unconditional.* Your relationship with the Forces of the Eternal *never* diminishes — regardless of your behavior. Created by those very Forces, you can never be separate from them—except in the recesses of a fearful (feeling unworthy) mind. I support you in preparing for each attunement as you've been shown. Then allow the experience to visit you — just *let* it happen, rather than trying to make it happen. Cosmic contact exists at a higher vibrational frequency than our goal-oriented, force-mode patterns. The following visualization may further assist you to acknowledge your connection.

Rejuvenation — Egyptian Style

In past lifetimes of Earth — ancient Egypt for example — most persons walking the Earth lived an extremely harsh existence, usually in human servitude. Working with mostly barren land, eking out even a basic survival existence took a tremendous toll on the citizens of the day. Obtaining and maintaining food, water, clothing, and shelter consumed most of their waking moments. The combination of tremendously harsh conditions, without having yet awakened to concepts of inner power, was extremely draining to the mind, body, and emotions of these original survivalists. Much like today, life was made more bearable through Spiritual Rejuvenation Sanctuaries. Each center, an oasis of pure love energy where exhausted individuals replenished their vigor, also provided visitors an education on the higher purposes of human existence. Governmental officials minimally interfered, as shelters benefited the overall production quotas brutally demanded by slave masters and ruling hierarchy. Nevertheless, benevolent priests exercised caution (avoiding the Pharaoh's wrath) when suggesting *all* persons had an intrinsic right to salvation, joyousness, and the afterlife.

It took great effort — mostly on foot — to travel the vast distances to an oasis retreat. As a result, *and* based on custom, normally only the patriarch made the trek. The rest of the family awaited the shared wisdom, energy, and love brought back to the family enclave.

From the time an individual entered the open-air sanctuary of alabaster columns and billowy, muti-colored, silk-like coverings — which kept the burning sun at bay — one felt an instant loving acceptance and resurgence of both body and Spirit. Loving priests, with no agenda except sharing life-sustaining energies, readily embraced weary travelers. The havens' fresh, cool, bubbling reservoirs of crystal clear water finally quenched throats dry from continuous existence on bare, parched land. In addition to meeting the immediate survival needs, the loving facilitation of the Benevolent Ones uplifted the traveler's spirits.

The wise and Divinely Guided clerics knew when to just listen, as ones emotionally vented their tremendous burdens of fear and despair. Miraculously—one by one—the honored guests felt a great sense of unexplained power and potency flow within them. The priests used the momentum from these Angelic openings to heal and inspire appreciation for the true, underlying magnificence of every Human Being.

The highlight of each trip occurred when travelers were each given their turn in a marbleized, cloth-lined resting chamber that supported them on all sides with soft pillows and cool, translucent coverings. Priests stepped forward to surround the climactically participating occupant(s), individually bathing in the luxury of the rejuvenation sarcophagus. The loving facilitators collectively radiated their tremendous healing energies—well beyond anything the honored recipients had ever experienced. Knowing this but a small sample of the perfect energy animating all life, the omnipotent feeling of power, potency, honor, and connection awesomely transformed the wearied. Revitalized beneficiaries now understood their urgent desire to reach a rejuvenation center—not only for healing and basic survival, but to discover the preexisting inner potential and power needed to pursue life's higher purposes.

Those entering rejuvenation centers left buoyant with a renewed sense of purpose, awakening to the realization they—as a Soul—had *chosen* the often-difficult Earth curriculum as a shared pathway to greatness. Returning to their abodes, the grateful recipients shared the uplifting, inspirational messages of hope and purposefulness with their beloved family and friends. They rejoiced, understanding their bodies might be held in bondage, but their minds and Spirit reigned free. Visits to a rejuvenation shelter showed life on Earth much more than animalistic survival. New awakenings enabled ones to approach daily toils with a newly found sense of purpose. Despair was replaced with an awareness of the symbiotic relationship and synchronistic connection to all life. Their newly energized faith produced an inner strength lacking during previous periods where they saw themselves only as fodder for slave masters.

Processing

While reading the preceding narration, did you slip into an altered-state or lucid-dream experience? Did you feel yourself joining the group in the rejuvenation center? If you answered "yes" to either question, rejoice! You are definitely getting the hang of it. Some feel a great familiarity with that special place, even *knowing* (until their skeptical, analytical self takes over) they experienced a life in ancient Egypt. The rest of you...be patient with yourselves. Your luminous, beyond-body, Soul-travel ability just takes a little more time and practice to achieve. With input from the lower vibratory physical senses so intense, we must learn to refocus on the expanded, omni-sensory realm. This is why I continually suggest that lacking a high degree of metaphysical experience usually requires thirty days of diligent practice (with the relaxation technique) as precursor to the cosmic connection exercise. From my own experience with human preoccupation, I understand how we prefer instant-gratification shortcuts, even when the greased-lightning expressway does not lead to our desired destination. When all else fails, be ready for the less-traveled toll road and the process of building a solid foundation on the basics. Every champion learned to intern—walking before running—in his or her quest for greatness.

Input Clarification

Do not be dissuaded if not clearly visualizing or if sensing little or no color when doing these attunements. I rarely experience visual clarity or color. When I say "visualize," I refer to the mind's eye, or *third eye,* as known in metaphysics. For me, a heightened attunement experience includes a harmonized, sensing/feeling/knowing sensation, combined with hazy visualizations. When I wish to see more detail, like a face, I mentally project a high-intensity halogen spotlight on the subject. If intended that you see a face clearly, this process may help. For those experiencing difficulty getting enhanced sensations (in any form), focus on *imagining* what is suggested in the cosmic-contact exercise. With practice, your impressions get stronger and more defined. Cosmic union does not depend on powerful out-of-body sensations. Souls know when we invite a closer connection and are always there regardless what we sense or feel. Release the need to perform perfectly [*suggestion primarily for me*]. With routine repetition, your present communication method gets wondrous results—even without refinements. Just because I present loosely structured guidelines, don't get hung up on technique. Have a *knowing* (not *blind*) faith, and while practicing, *accept* that you're already joined. OK, let's continue.

Phase-Two Visualization — Cloud Integration

Sufficient practice with **phase-one** of the cosmic-cloud contact, expressing loving openness, readies you for transport to your *cosmic* healing chamber. At the normal **phase-one** point of tingling sensation, with your arms outstretched into the void, ask for *full* immersion into the benevolent opaque cloud bank. As it encircles you, immediately see, feel, sense, or imagine an additional ribbon of gold light entering the top of your head (crown chakra), spreading through every cell of your body. Focusing on the golden light, you receive a continual flow — ribbon after ribbon — of every basic color of the rainbow. These colored ribbons of light continue, in turn, spreading their unified energy — as did the golden threads — until you sense their combined omnipotent presence within you. This rainbow of light is your transportation system to the Celestial Palace where your vibrational rejuvenation awaits.

Surrender to the intense pull of this Divine energy. Happily and emotionally turn your attention to a long tunnel whence the energy rainbow originates. Linked to a *beyond-space-and-time* locality in response to your heartfelt request for Celestial unification and healing, you feel completely comfortable temporarily leaving your human body. The Souls who Guide you during your Earth incarnation preserve and protect your human vessel. In reality, no separation exists between you as a human personality and you as Soul. You simply expand your consciousness to simultaneously experience *multiple* realms of existence. Releasing any lingering reservations immediately transports you down the protected tunnel to your Celestial destination. Not in ancient Egypt, you have returned to your shimmering, Crystal Paradise, home world.

Your Celestial Home World

Upon arrival, you immediately notice a brilliant gathering of festive beings joyously dancing and singing. At first unsure how they will respond to you, you are drawn to them like a bee to honey. Greeted lovingly by intimate Souls, you immediately recognize them all and feel the most exquisite joy. This Celestial garden is your palace of origin. Universal energy surrounds you; the same energy that you — as a Soul — used to finalize the creation of your human personality matrix — just prior to birth. As a Human Being, your wondrous life journey has taken you deep within a hidden forest. With your intense focus on the flora and fauna of Earth, you temporarily forgot your home world and all your Celestial friends. Having also benefited from Earthly journeys, your Soul mates rejoice in your terrestrial exploits.

During your celebration of Spirit and adventure, suddenly it dawns on you: this intimate cluster of Souls helped create the other, unique matrix personalities your human self so intimately intertwines with on Earth. Incredibly, you're honoring the very Souls that manifested not only *your* human self, but your friends, workmates, family, and extended family members! You feel blessed beyond expression. It's true! Feelings of separation and loneliness, whether for human companionship, or the Divine, involved a fear-based distortion. Expressed individuality and uniqueness are part of your chosen human adventure. These same Beings celebrate you *daily* by walking in your Earthly heart. You will remember this—especially during times of extreme challenge. This grand, brilliantly intimate foyer is where you return upon completion of your present Earth incarnation.

With ancient history, memory recall, and home-world interweaving not your main purpose for this visit, you commemorate your current achievements *and* review the balance of your master plan (blueprint) for Earth life. There is much rejoicing for the fine accomplishments already mastered, and a loving reminder of issues and patterns still awaiting experiential manifestation. You realize this gifted creation is not an *assignment*, as these same Souls love and support you regardless of any further attainments. You—as a Soul— wrote the curriculum for your prevailing lifetime and you wish to continue pursuing the remaining creations and experiences as originally orchestrated. In the glorious light of the temporarily suspended amnesic veil, you see this truth. Included with your current clarity: you need only heal and release lingering patterns of human fear and unworthiness to partake of both *this* and Earth realms simultaneously.

Your objectives in living an Earth existence:

- **Creative mastery in the physical arena.**
- **Inner peace, harmony, joy, goodness, acceptance, appreciation and love, by continually awakening to more and more expansive levels of consciousness.**

Celestial-Fire Restoration

With your renewed awareness and motivation for continued experiential life, you slip into your specially prepared rejuvenation chamber. You joyfully await the group caress from your beloved Soul mates. In this multi-layered energy field, with no sensation of marble and silkiness (as in ancient Egypt), you undergo a suspended love cocoon made from a concentrated form of that energy rainbow that transported you here. In the beautiful backdrop of sparkling chandeliers of light, your Soul mates bathe you in the full power of Creation, itself. The cosmic group hug seems almost overwhelming — even for your Soul Self. Still in contact with your earthly body, human emotions purge in a torrent of healing release. The full blast of Kundalini energy feels infinitely more powerful than your human counterpart could ever sustain without a buffer. You — as Soul — simultaneously dispense just the right portion of healing and forgiving presence to your human vessel. Totally rejuvenated and in tune with the full purpose of your incarnation, your self/Self reinforces the intuitive belief that *you exist in a completely integrated cosmic wholeness*. Not — as previously believed — separate, divisible segments upon which your human self chose to focus. Take a quiet, peaceful moment to enjoy this cosmic love bath. [*Allow extra time on your facilitation tape for relaxed contemplation.*]

Back to Earth

Feeling rejuvenated and complete, you enthusiastically return through the pulsating, rainbow-colored tunnel. Your energized self reunites with your resting human body. You bring memory of this transformational cosmic experience with you, because you — as a human personality — invite it into your conscious awareness. Congratulate ✿ yourself on your enhanced discernment. Your continued mental and emotional healing, and inspirational enlightenment and openings to love, will intensify. The empowering Celestial love bath serves as a holistic replacement for old, self-diminishing thoughts and feelings. You feel your self-absorption and previous preoccupation with fear-based judgmental perceptions fading away. As forgiveness and releasement flow through your invigorated human awareness, you open to a *billowy burst* of peace, joy, goodness, appreciation, and love — just as you experienced in the Celestial Fire Palace. You feel overjoyed at discovering your true magnificence.

- **You feel determined...to revisit your celebratory home world for needed rejuvenation.**

- **You feel determined...to remember your true, empowered Self.**

You give thanks to the Souls who love you, guide you, and are always with you. You bring a whole new attitude to the table about human challenge. There has *always* been a sumptuous feast before you, even when your human self fasted. Yes, you reaffirm that Earth is a tough school. But, as part of the design team, you imbued your human self with all the talent and courage to master the entire lesson plan. In addition, you feel an ever-increasing desire to support your Soul mates to accomplish their respective Earth curriculum. *Enjoy this Soul-gifted process of healing and inclusivity.* **You deserve it!**

Why We Chose Extra-Challenging Lives

For those who come away from the cosmic contact experience with heads spinning and the feeling that your whole world just turned upside down...congratulations! No...you don't need an exorcism. You are processing and recalibrating your center Core of Being (matrix), adjusting your beliefs about what currently serves you — and the world in general. Some of you (especially left-brainers) may feel that *pyramid-inverting* sensation.

To add to *why* we — as Souls — would choose such difficult, potentially painful Earth lives, I reprinted a section from Dr. Ron Scolastico's book, *Reflections* (available as a FREE e-book download: ronscolastico.com). You received a partial answer in "Justice and Revenge," the concluding portion of my Sioux Nation past-life experience, and from various other segments of this teaching. Understanding the answer to this particular question is *critical* for making core openings to believing in our willful planning for a lifetime on Earth. Self-Realization replaces any residual feelings of victimization. For this and other Soul-Guided reasons, I'm prodded to further clarify the liberating concept of Soul choice. The [bracketed] items are my own comments.

Quotations taken from *Reflections,* pages 240–243, "Healing the Hurt Inner Child," with permission from the author — Dr. Ron Scolastico.

> QUESTION TO THE GUIDES: **You have said in other teachings that prior to all births, each person's Soul chooses its respective human personality's biological parents and associated geographical environment. What are the**

considerations—from the Soul's perspective—for a one to choose potentially painful and traumatic environmental experiences, such as where he or she is very likely to be a victim of child abuse?

VERBATIM ANSWER: *This is a very difficult area for you ones to understand, for you have created within yourselves such a fear of pain that you have made suffering and pain seem horrible and terrible. With such an attitude toward pain, it is almost impossible for some humans to understand why a Soul would choose to project a child into a family that most certainly will inflict pain upon that child.*

*So, for those who would be convinced that pain is **only** horrible and terrible, we can not be of much service. We can only suggest that you gently work* [with yourselves] *each day to try to realize that pain is temporary. Pain cannot destroy you. You have the forces of God itself to draw upon to heal pain. And, if you are courageous and confident enough, eventually you will heal all pain. Not because you are terrified of it and wish to eliminate it, but because you finally realize that it can not damage you—your **true** Being.*

For those of you more willing to believe that pain is not horrible—although certainly undesirable—we would need to describe in the following manner the way that a Soul might choose an abusive family for its human personality creation.

*Imagine that you are an Eternal Soul, standing before your present physical birth. You have the capacity to look about at **all** Human Beings. As you prepare to project a portion of yourself as a new Human Being into physical form, you have the freedom—in coordination with other Souls—to choose any father and mother on the face of the Earth.*

As you prepare to make this Soul choice, there are many patterns and energies that will generally turn your attention in certain directions; toward certain countries, a certain race, a certain social structure, and so forth. But, you are free to choose what pleases you. And, you have the vision to know what is the most beneficial for the new child that you will project into Earth. So, you must assume that the choice of your human family is a choice that is made in vast wisdom, understanding, and love.

Imagine that you as a Soul are now making the family selection choice. You look about Earth and you see a potential father and mother who are presently alive in human form, and, in past lifetimes of Earth, have been deeply loved by you. Perhaps they were your own children in a past lifetime. And, let us say that you see them presently struggling in a large city of the United States—perhaps Baltimore. They are of a racial grouping that is being mistreated and intimidated, one that has great pain and suffering, in general. In this current lifetime, the male one is an alcoholic and has uncontrolled sexual desires. The female one is simple, perhaps not so intelligent, and she is constantly being beaten by the male one.

Now, you as a Soul, looking at these two who were so beloved by you in past lifetimes, can see these patterns of challenge that they are presently manifesting, but you are not frightened by them.

[For those oriented toward a transcendent, non-dualistic (Third Reality) perspective, where **all** expressions exist in the *now*, see this representation as Creation's desire to experience ALL THAT IS NOT...fear, in order to intensify ALL THAT IS...love.]

You understand that the negative patterns are temporary. You realize that even if these two fail to heal their negative patterns in their present lifetime, they will not be damaged in their Being [Soul]. You are fully aware that one human life is an instant in eternity, and, in so many lifetimes, these two were your beloved ones. So, without the distortion of the human element of negativity, you truly love this male one and this female one, and you deeply understand their fear, their pain, and their human suffering.

Thus, you as a Soul would say, in essence; "I have been so deeply loved in the past by these two, particularly by this male one, that if I go forth to these two as a female child, then perhaps the male one might be touched so deeply in his heart with love for me that he might heal his present fears that cause so much pain and turmoil in his current life." [Example of Spiritual DNA stimulation—what HP researchers call "preexisting potential."] *You would know full well that if he does **not** heal, then your childhood is likely to be very painful. But, you understand clearly that you have had even more painful childhoods in past lifetimes, and none of them have damaged your Being. But, to address the pain that you see you might suffer as a female child in this family, you bring forth an extra amount of courage and strength to weave into your new female personality. You bring various capacities and abilities to heal yourself, if there is abuse of you by the fathering one. You bring forth determination, stamina, and persistence, so that you can succeed in your life, even if your childhood is quite negative.*

Then, when you are born as a female child, each one in the family begins to determine which patterns will affect you as they make their personal choices. Let us say that the father is not touched by you deeply enough to heal his fears and negativity. He continues his alcoholism and his uncontrolled sexual desire and you are eventually abused sexually by the father. As a result, as you grow, you fall into your fears — your pain and suffering — and you forget the great healing capacities that you as a Soul placed into your personality. You do not use them. Instead, you curse your father and hate him. Your life is terrible from your point of view. Then, you die, seeing only badness in your father and your life because it was painful.

This [worst-case scenario] result does not change the fact that the intention of your Soul in choosing your particular family was rooted in goodness and love. Even the pain and suffering of your life does not diminish the love that still joins you to the father that abused you.

At this point in time, there is not enough depth to human words to bring a fully satisfactory understanding of the Soul's choice of a challenging family. But, this example may help you to feel the love that would lead a Soul to make such a choice.

As the Guiding Ones stated, YOU, as Soul, chose the early environmental circumstances of your current lifetime. Considering this Second Reality perspective can lead to tremendous healing, releasement, and potential replacement of all debilitating thoughts and feelings. A clear pathway allows one to transcend and abolish feelings of victimization—regardless of current circumstances. Additionally, be assured the greater the personal challenge in your life, the greater the gifts, talents, and abilities you possess to overcome and eventually thrive in peace, harmony, goodness, joy and love—just as Soul intended. Feel free to continue to see yourself as an angry, vengeful, persecuted victim. Neither bad nor wrong, this less desirable choice measures **small** compared to your true potential for creating magnificent pathways on Earth.

Test both these perspectives in your daily life. Live one or two days imagining or pretending your everyday existence if you released all the anger, pain, and past feelings of victimization. Don't tell anyone what you're doing—just notice the effect you have on others, as well as yourself. During this test period, continually ask the question: "What would LOVE *do* and *be* now?" After the one-to two-day test period, go back to your angry, frustrated, vengeful, self-pitying personality. How does that work for you, in comparison? Distancing yourself from others by pushing love out of your life in a futile attempt to exact some begrudging revenge or retribution for past wrongdoing—real or imagined: is this worth the price of self-inflicted pain and suffering? The choice that best serves you (in today's world) should now be obvious. The past is over, unless you insist on playing the repetitive role of Phil Connors in *Ground Hog Day*. Upon making your choice, there's just one more thing to do. Continually *practice* your chosen replacement until it becomes the new habit. Self-*actualization* must follow self-realization to manifest permanent change. From the very beginning of our journey together, you've not needed to take anything herein on blind faith. All concepts and principles under discussion are fully testable. In our next chapter, we release our need for scapegoats and claim our true power. Time for you to suit up, step up, and accept your Soul-assigned title: "Spiritual Warrior."

CHAPTER NINETEEN

Forgiveness, Gratitude, Devils,
Deep Blue Sea

♥   ♥   ♥

For many millennia, humanity has been given (and accepted) the proffered choice of either God or the Devil to explain the negativity in the world. When Christianity (as an example) was in its infancy, opposing persuasions (mostly pagans) resulted from the proviso that ones not only accept an omnipotent, monistic Creator (God), but a *sole* deity also responsible for world-wide suffering, torture, murder, and mayhem. Consider that in past times of Earth, many thought it illogical or unacceptable to have a benevolent, omnipotent, loving God also manifest punishment and abject cruelty.

As First Reality perspectives were almost universal in past times of Earth, some unseen, external power (monotheistic) or powers (polytheistic) had to be *causing* everything. Yet, progressive thinkers considered these two opposing expressions (creation-destruction) mutually exclusive and beyond the purview of any *one*, Supreme Being. Since all suffering and/or joy caused by *outer* causal factors typified the predominant belief, the idea of just one omnipotent force, failed to rouse new-order endorsements. While early Christians struggled to differentiate themselves, the old guard quoted from the Old Testament, where a wrathful god takes responsibility for ALL Earth creations. Speaking through the mouth of prophet Isaiah, God says: "I form the light *and* create the darkness. I make peace *and* create evil; I, the LORD, do all these things."

Pick a god...any god

You may also recall from history that societies endorsing heathen or polytheistic beliefs normally worshipped and made simultaneous conciliatory sacrifices to several deities. Each god specialized in a particular segment of Earth life. Submitting and showing respect to less than all gods was believed to be suicidal. To appease potentially angry deities, savvy pagans ensured all their bases were covered. This was true even during the vast span of Spiritually astute ancient Egypt, except for one courageously dissenting Pharaoh. That sole exception to polytheism proved very unpopular with citizenry and especially with the many priests suddenly without gainful employment. Monotheistic pronouncements were short-lived, however, resulting in not only the demise of the Pharaoh Amenhotep (who renamed himself Ikhnaton), but wholesale destruction to most of the many obelisks his regime constructed. Ikhnaton honored his professed *one,* true master of the Universe by paying exclusive homage to the Sun God, Aton.

The Marketing of Christianity

Over the years, monotheism gained progressive favor with the elite. The masses kept their options open, however. "Why trust all your *stones* to one basket?" was the Pagan rallying cry. For a one-true-god concept to fly, the sales job needed to be competitive and intense. Early Christians found explaining suffering and disease difficult—especially when applied to the innocent. "If only *one* God Force, it must be responsible for the barbaric treatment and general mayhem," continued the incontrovertible logic.

In response to many years of human expression languishing under the import of this serious question of faith, Christian orthodoxy came forth with a brilliant answer to God's apparent impotence with the introduction of two major concepts: ❶ "Original Sin" (the Western version of karmic debt), and ❷ the "devil" incarnate, Lucifer/Satan. The invention, or reinvention, of these two very creative artifacts framed the door to hell for those continuing to disbelieve. Satan—now an alleged fallen angel—was redefined along with a supporting cast of lesser demons.

Bring on the Devil!

References to Satan—Hebrew for "obstructer," or "accuser"—can be found in the Old Testament. Satanic Beings, originally insignificant Celestial errand boys, were ostensibly sent to Earth to check up on the loyalty of God's subjects. Singularly, this was also its original function as "diablos" (the devil), when it first appeared in the book of Job. One of the first modern devils historically appeared in Persia, sometime before the sixth century, BC. His name was Ahriman, described by the prophet Zoroaster (Zarathustra) as the evil Prince of Darkness engaged in the battle to control the world against Onnazd—the Prince of Light and Goodness. Since the Jews had been under Persian domination for almost two centuries, historians surmise that Ahriman somewhat influenced the formation, or resurrection, of both the Jewish Satan *and* the Christian devil. Judaism had mostly forgotten about Satan until the Christian hierarchy began the devil's resurrection.

The Lucifer creation further exemplifies early, Roman inventiveness. Lucifer's original Latin meaning: *"bringer of light," or "illuminator."* Today Lucifer rings synonymous for a defrocked archangel, or "Satan." In original Moslem texts, a "jinn" represents a lower echelon Spirit that may appear in either human or animal form—both good and evil. In evil mode, jinns manifest as "shaitans," adversarial persons or animals. Since "shaitan" expresses the root word for Satan, Moslem definitions may have influenced the New Testament's upgrading of Satan.

The Christian devil, with which we are most familiar in today's literature and art, appears often but is ill defined in *early* versions of the New Testament: Greek, Latin, and Aramaic. After many centuries of debate, the Roman Catholic Church settled on a fairly unified picture of Satan's history and function.

These many years of confusion and argument seemed to have kept the devil from significantly appearing in Christian art until the seventh or eighth century. In the Christian world, the real heyday for the "evil lord" began in the second millennia, crediting the Devil with virtually every bad event or happenstance on the face of the Earth. If you guessed this the zenith of dualistic, reactive, First Reality expression, you would be correct.

Now blaming Original Sin and a devil for all the *bad* in the world, Christianity effectively reassigned the causative factors for the ills of the planet. Selling a purely benevolent god-force—even if somewhat emasculated—met less resistance. Loyalty was attained through assurances the devil could only wreak havoc, including the seizing of individual or group Souls, on those of impure thought and deed—defined by the ruling hierarchy. Outer-fixated (orthodox) religions, now promising sanctuary and safe passage for the faithful, gained a foothold in the masses.

With Satan firmly entrenched as scapegoat, early Christian and other piggybacking theocracies were no longer pressured by the previously unanswerable: "If God is omnipotent, omniscient, loving, and the Creator of all there is, why are the weak and innocent being preyed upon?"

Much later, when moral codes and other restrictions seemed harsh to many Catholics—especially the well-to-do—the church redefined penance and began offering more easily obtained confessionals as a way to *permanently* cleanse one's Soul. This, of course, had the added benefit of filling the church's coffers. Bishop Martin Luther, aghast at the ease with which the wealthy could buy salvation, vehemently protested. Excommunicated from the Catholic Church, Martin Luther founded his own religious sect—Lutheranism.

I do not profess expertise on demonic possession, or even religious practice, but I am pretty good at reading motivations. If we want others to believe in our dualistically exclusive and *separate* god-force and the respective doctrine, we need to create a good "fall guy" or *heavy* to blame for the badness in the world, do we not? If this independently operating Lucifer force is strong enough to cause all the havoc around the world (since the beginning of time), seemingly indifferent to the power of God, we damn well better be bowing, scraping, worshipping, *and* sacrificing—until the cows come home—to escape its wrath!

Caustic and cosmic humor aside, why is it so difficult for us to release this need for an outer causal factor to explain human negativity? Hopefully we have evolved sufficiently to start taking personal responsibility, which includes the acknowledgment that—in a cause and effect Second Reality—*the negativity currently being manifested in the world is the direct result of past and present human thinking, feeling, and action—motivated by self-absorbed fear and greed.* Within Third (transcendent) Reality, that same "fact" shifts to: there never was any negativity—just an inclusive understanding that, at less-expansive levels of awareness, a lack of perfection (for any expression) *appears* to exist. The *fact* that ones cannot see or imagine even the *possibility* of perfection existing within what's generally considered a cruel act, proves only a limitation in the observer's level of accepting consciousness.

We are not stuck with good-vs.-evil as our only interpretive option. In addition to HP principle, the wonderful technologies supplied by Colin Tipping (Mr. Radical Forgiveness), and the "Two-Question" formula of *Unconditional Bliss* author, Raphael Cushnir, add to your more expansive and inclusive options.

We are free to believe some minion of supernatural evil responsible for Earth badness. And that this powerfully malevolent force is inescapable, unless a conditionally loving God chooses to rescue us by delivering the faithful to the Celestial conveyer belt to Heaven. For those who've read all the self-directed, self-actualized principles and facilitations in this guidebook, and still feel this vulnerable, you might benefit from reviewing the various healing and empowerment tools presented herein. Then take some positive ACTION toward advanced degrees in liberation and FUN. Rather than staying frozen in complacent uncertainty, consider the option of acting on *something*, even if not your best choice.

During times of reactive stress, I take a time-out moment and ask myself three insightful questions.

- **Can I be (for the moment) with all my current thoughts and feelings, without judgment or editing?**
- **Do the choices I've made in the past serve me now?**
- **What would love do at this very moment?**

Revenge in Perspective

When broaching the subject of revenge (Chapter Eight), I was not suggesting we cease exacting some form of direct, societal consequence from the perpetrators of violent crime. Perhaps punitive assignments could include the currently imposed physical detention combined with comprehensive behavior modification and the opportunity for productive work. Efforts at restitution from non-hardcore prisoners can psychologically benefit both perpetrator and victim. Our current penal system—by itself—focusing on vengeance and temporarily removing perpetrators from circulation, does not offer much deterrent to future crime. The majority of criminals eventually get released. Without adequate replacement behavior (self-image improvement), parolees often strike back at what they perceive to be an uncaring, vindictive society—thus escalating the cycle. Striving to create more than programmed automatons in the prison system, or in our educational classrooms, serves us individually and collectively.

A Different Way

Although not the focus of this communication, experiments in restorative justice seem to offer some hope for positive change. I salute the efforts of caring practitioners looking for *practical* solutions to the current epidemic of crime and incarceration. The key, as I see it: *positive action from all parties*—not just slick metaphor and crocodile tears. When victim and offender fail to heal, release, and replace non-serving thoughts and feelings, society stays stuck in a repetitive feedback loop.

The populace requires cooperative laws and rules (structure) to function efficiently. We need those GO lights. The main message of "Revenge and Justice," and this is **very important**: *we do **not** need to be held hostage for the rest of our lives because of the negative acts of others.* To do so allows the violence to repeat (psychologically) over and over—sometimes for the rest of our *unnatural* lives. Temporarily satisfying retribution does not make us whole. The illusionary power of revenge typifies ego-mind distortions.

Power of Forgiveness—a Stage Process

Releasing hate for perpetrators of heinous acts overcomes our belief that forgiving the offending person(s) would—by inference—condone their behavior. Are forgiveness and responsibility mutually exclusive? Do we fear *personal* forgiveness would say to the criminal—and society—"past atrocities were not really so bad, let's cut the *'perps'* some slack"? That extremely liberal alignment could feel like *giving* power away through forgiveness, rather than recovering it. Consider, however, that holding on to anguish—intending to punish the offender—allows the wrongful acts of another to psychologically violate us, again and again, in the *present*.

How does your perspective change when you see forgiveness as something you bestow primarily to reclaim your personal power and well-being? An offender receiving solace from your shift in psychological interpretation could (at this level) be considered secondary, or even irrelevant. True self-healing (personal salvation) expresses a monistic, all-inclusive actualization from openings made to the Infinite Inner, not a prize we win from an outer-located, Cracker Jack® box. Consider also how your choices affect the planet's energy.

Avoiding the psychological deprivation that occasions our preoccupation with revenge/justice requires a more expanded view of forgiveness. Beyond never having to accept acts or behavior you loathe (personal boundaries), you have another reflective empowerment option: change you mind about the *significance* of the previously offending behavior. Rather than the *pain* and *badness* of extreme challenge remaining stagnantly synonymous, awakening to higher vibratory meanings (purpose) reveals and opens the door to Third Reality and joyous Earth mastery. Review Third Reality (transcendent) forgiveness—what Colin Tipping calls "Radical Forgiveness"—in chapter Five.

But from a Second Reality (ESR) perspective, the key to liberating, *first-stage* forgiveness: psychologically place the behavior and the respective person into different categories. This more traditional orientation provides you an initial safe haven to heal imbalances and regain your sense of personal power—without renouncing the perpetrator's responsibility. Forgiving yourself, or another, without differentiating one's behavior from the person violates all First- and most ESR sensibilities. This could result in even greater feelings of powerlessness. Second Reality relationships focus on behavior—rather than the reactive attacking, belittling, or judging of personalities. This humanistic contrast makes a great difference to the psyche of a young mind. A corrective parent could say: "You are an intelligent and normally responsible and caring person, Jimmy, and I love you with every fiber of my Being. But you dropped the ball today. Per our previously agreed-to understanding, you are grounded for this [specific] infraction."

Culturally-Based Powerlessness

With great sensitivity for the ongoing pain of many, I dive—once again—into the controversial snake pit. Carefully consider the following psychological dynamics.

Assume for a minute (then cancel-cancel this thought) that you or your cultural grouping have been the victim(s) of murder, mayhem, and a multitude of unspeakable criminal acts during past times of Earth. Ask yourself this: How will focusing on suffering, powerlessness, victimization, and moral indignation for the atrocities committed in the *past*—so as to *never* forget—prevent your psychological entrapment in relative impotence? When we hold on to hate, righteous fury, and moral superiority, might we reinforce powerlessness? Allowing past criminal behavior to control and manipulate your prospects for liberation in the present—a freewill choice?—or conditioned-brain response to old programming? Subconscious-mind dynamics prove very subtle, especially with historically reenacted atrocities.

Astute terrorists wish to create inner conflict via conscious or unconscious self-sabotage. The *eloquent* Watergate conspirator and Nixon Chief of Staff, H.R. Haldeman, believed: "Get them by the balls, and their hearts and minds will follow." And the classic by George Carlin: "If you can't beat them, arrange to have them beaten."

Intent powerfully persuades, whether used constructively or destructively. "The very existence of flame throwers proves that some time, somewhere, someone said to themselves: *You know, I want to set those people over there on fire...but I'm just not close enough to get the job done.*" [Another quote from George Carlin]

Human Beings are more than just survivors. As co-creators we co-facilitate our mutual healing, empowerment, and complete liberation from emotional fear and the negative acts of others.

This is Earth Mastery

I support your absolute *refusal* to let outside circumstances—past or present—over which you have no control, dictate the finality, or course, of your life. Recovery processes challenge us to create a new, positive focus—realizing the preciousness of life. Instead of taking life for granted, dedicate yourself to living in the moment by exercising special choices and communications before it's too late to share them directly.

Law of *Choice* and Effect

Earlier passages in this book mentioned how the Universe has a way of providing us what we need, often not what our human selves prefer. I have tested this "law of attraction" theory in my own life and continually observe it with others. Just like the pull from opposite poles of a magnet, *what we fear (believe) we actually draw unto ourselves.* In his classic book *Think and Grow Rich*, Napoleon Hill said, "What you fear comes upon you," and, "Whatever the mind of man [and women] can conceive and believe, he [she] can achieve." In *Sermon on the Mount*, a book based on the assumed teachings of Jesus, we read, "As a man [or woman] thinketh, so is he [she]."

I'm sure you've known people consistently negative in their expressions and attitude. Even in apparent good fortune, they look for and expect the worst. They actually do seem to experience a lot of challenging (*bad,* if you insist) happenstance in their lives. Negatively expressing individuals often create the very circumstances they dread—a form of prayer. Our emotional fears can be disguised in a blanket of other negative emotions such as anger, jealousy, envy, etc. In First Reality consciousness where we have the big ego investment, fear is not cool and therefore rarely acknowledged. Regardless of our denials, until we heal and awaken to a higher reality, the Universe provides unlimited opportunities to practice dealing with fear-based expressions. Personal responsibility (thoughts/feelings/actions) lights the way out of those dark, depressive, self-made storm clouds.

Are Ya Talkin' to Me?

When crouching in numbed darkness trying to avoid problems, we inadvertently ask (pray to) the Universe for a *more* challenging agenda to help reconcile troubling issues and our current belief in lack. What a breakthrough realization this was for me—when it finally kicked in. The amount of practice we need prior to an awakening is an individual matter.

As you continue with me now, this choice remarkably indicates your consciousness shift already taking place. Congratulations! By mastering old-paradigm, *victimhood* classes, you're more likely ready for less-reactive creations. Ask not what life can do for you—ask what you can do for your life. Second Reality makes the prospect for a more enjoyable life—even *with* the challenge areas—a lot more viable, does it not?

Drop the Barriers—Express Love Now

I've learned to tell friends and family how I feel about them *now*. We never know how much time we have left with the special ones in our life. Of course we can forgive ourselves for not doing so until *after* they've transitioned; and yes, from the Spiritual perspective it no longer poses an issue when we, ourselves, pass. In the *now* world, not holding back is darned well important! "Tell them how you feel before it's too late!" is what hospice caregivers hear, again and again, from departing patients. Consider dropping the requirement(s) that family members and friends make changes, see the light, or apologize for their alleged wrongdoing. They don't have to change for you to love them, nor do you have to like or accept their behavior. Without surrendering self-determined boundaries against what you consider inexcusable behavior, forgive the troubling persons. Courageous acts of forgiveness release you from psychological holds. When you learn to fully forgive, love, and respect yourself, you'll no longer be a punching bag, a psychological clone, or one standing on street corners holding a *will-jump-through-hoops-for-love* sign.

Third Reality and Radical Forgiveness

To reclaim personal power by separating behavior from the person may seem to contradict transcendent principles. At the transpersonal levels—advanced Second and beyond—we no longer visualize ourselves as *ever* a victim. Instead, we see only special facilitators provided to assist us with important parts of our life's curriculum. Mastering essential, humanistically based lessons places one's awareness in a category similar to the Gibson family's achievement.

In the next chapter I face my biggest challenge as I consolidate and summarize our journey together. I'm reminded there is never a *final* or closing chapter for Eternal Beings. For us, my beloved Soul mates, life is forever ongoing and expanding.

CONCLUSION

♥　　♥　　♥

Now that you've made it this far, and almost done with the reading portion of our mutual lesson, think about the following questions. Ask yourself how your original responses (prior to our journey together) differed from your current answers.

What determines why some individuals grow up in privileged circumstances while others live in impoverished conditions like those found in Somalia, Rwanda, Ethiopia, Afghanistan, Iraq, North Korea, and a host of others? Why do some newborns find themselves in loving families while others are born into such dysfunction, they will likely suffer horrendous abuse—even torture? Although I address these questions from various reality levels *and* a dialogue from the Soul perspective, here's further clarification.

If we take the First Reality inventory of karmic debt, immortal (Original) sin, God/the devil's will, and other dualistic, victim-creating scenarios off the table, what's left? From a humanistic perspective, we either exist as some accidental crapshoot artifact that washed up on the Earth beach—to eat or be eaten—*or* we voluntarily participate in an omni-coordinated, all-inclusive, *Celestial* project. In my own rational study, combined with visceral contemplations, the answer falls into three segments:

❶ **Unconditionally loving connection and support (from the cosmos);**

❷ **Creatively experiential variety (manifesting on Earth);**

❸ **Collective Soul choice that values every life experience equally.**

All experience is special—none superior. Note: This Conclusion overview transcends, without denigrating, the more limited, linear (within space and time) *reincarnation* explanation for our ongoing evolution.

Considering the perspective that we—as Spiritual Beings—choose to be here, our collective energies create and maintain the physical

Universe. We do this because we can, and for the sheer joy of a denser, more intense experience. As Souls we do not look at pain as the negative our human counterpart generally views it. We know pain to be temporary and *no* human experience, no matter how vile or tortuous, ever damages our true Being. From a Soul perspective, then, a simple life in a challenging third-world country expresses as much value as one lived on Wall Street. Holographic Psychology's all-inclusive principles support this view. While the human value of any experience is being subjectively determined, a transcendent orientation sees no better or worse assignments. Although Souls — wielding the forces of the Eternal — create and maintain the Universe, physical space and time does not limit their creative undertakings. Souls freely and simultaneously participate in the full range of human experience. From this viewpoint, what Larry experiences, or what *you* experience, represents an independent manifestation of the *One* Collective Consciousness. Consider this: we — as Spiritual Beings — *do* live in Somalia, Rwanda, Ethiopia, Afghanistan, Iraq, and North Korea, *as well as* in our current abode. Human feelings of separation or lack of Oneness illustrate distorted appearances that persons temporarily *accept* as truth — not truth itself. *Experience always validates belief.* Our life choices vibrationally magnify and *directly* affect life forms throughout the planet — **believe it or not.**

The filtering benefit of our (agreed-upon) *amnesia* generally shields us from potential schizophrenic (psi) input and its corresponding confusion. Without selective, Spiritual-DNA-provided filtering, our human selves could not experience dualistic, material-realm illusions and still maintain sanity. For some, the filters do break down. Contamination (non-sifted junk from the Collective) can occasionally result in the psyche fearfully escaping into multiple personality disorder, bi-polar, out-of-body past lives, and other forms of mental corruption. Smaller doses can manifest as unexplained mood swings and panic attacks. With a fortified, protective program in place, we can more freely give attention to our specific and very unique curriculum. Opinion: It is ill advised to practice ego bashing as a way to enlightenment. We need our left-hemisphere steering wheel to successfully navigate the material pathway (intended illusion). Location (of comprehension) and insightful balance, together, lead to mastery of the Earth adventure.

Even with minimum survival needs (food, water, and shelter) met, the average Westerner finds it difficult to conceptualize a happy, fulfilled life in any harsh locale. Accustomed to technological conveniences, the *haves* suffer greatly when denied air-conditioning or pain medication (as examples). Consider, however, that *home is where the heart is.* Once we—as humans—come full circle, realigned and fully aware of our transcendent nature, the synchronistic continuity of all life (Oneness) becomes obvious.

Graduation

I trust that openly sharing my fears, challenges, and the results of my choices motivates you to make your own quantum leap. If you truly want quality of life and relationships—as I did—you can have them. As a fellow traveler walking life's mysterious, often difficult pathway (with more questions than answers), I began my quest on shaky legs—well short of brazen courage. To be safe, I cowardly chained up all my psychologically created *weapons of mass destruction* before the scary trek to my first mountaintop. I feared what I would do if denied Dr. King's liberating "Thank God Almighty, I'm free at last!" The one great gift at my side: the determination to continue the search, even when the rare vista of insightful illumination was at first denied me.

You would not be reading these words if it were not intended for you to make these same openings and connections. You would do yourself a disservice by requiring your breakthroughs to be as dramatic as some of mine. Comparing "dramas" is subjective folly. Maybe my extra-rigid skepticism and stubbornness were somehow factored in, leading to more definitive reassurances. Perhaps Spirit saves the *heavy artillery* for the more self-absorbed. That would be ME—in earlier days, certainly. This I *do* know, however: If a rough-and-ready, procedure-programmed, ex-military *jarhead* can get there, you've got it made in the shade! The feelings you experience—when liberated—will be just as significant. So, get out of your head and *into your heart.* In your attunements, focus on what opens you emotionally. Use the illustrative stories spread throughout this book; even better, draw on your own emotional experiences. Face your fear of the pain of rejection or abandonment. Dismiss any thoughts that you are not worthy of cosmic connection or human love. Everything works itself out, as intended. Believe in yourself and the Universal Collective. Practicing your relaxation meditation and the Cosmic Connection Process will lift you into deeper and deeper couplings with the Eternal Forces. Use the Holographic *Fear-Dancing* Technique, Cushnir's *Two-Question* formula, and Tipping's *Radical Forgiveness* technology (see my website), to get past all resistances. **The best preparation for both human *and* cosmic union:** heal, release, reframe and replace underlying worthiness issues that manifest as rigid righteousness or unquestioning skepticism.

We have reached the point where I, as a Spiritual counselor, human potential researcher, and *heart-shift* facilitator, am supposed to wrap this all up with a pretty bow on it. It's expected I tie all remaining loose ends together with a *grandiose* conclusion, leaving no doubt as to the accuracy of any postulated theory, while simultaneously leaving you breathless in the wake of my sage finale. Well...sorry. Keeping with my less-orthodox *think-for-yourself* presentation style, you'll likely not experience any of the above. You are quite free to interpret this closing segment any way you wish. In spite of having slipped into some preachy prose from time to time, psychological cloning has never been my objective. In the main, I have attempted to stimulate your own Spiritual DNA actualization, not remake you in my image [Aaaaarrrrgh! What a terrifying thought!]. As for being *breathless*, I find a little deep breathing balances that right out.

Illusion of Lack and Limitation

I realize I have used — perhaps overused — the term "Spiritual DNA" to describe innate motivation to remember the expanded truth about ourselves. Consider its import, however. Without some intuitive prodding from beneath our conscious awareness, how could we overcome early behavioristic programming and associated illusions of not being or having enough (what Toltecs call the "parasite")? First Reality looks at the average income levels of India (as an example), and reactively believes it *factual* evidence of poverty. From Second Reality: lack, limitation and poverty are states of mind — just as is wealth. Neither are environmental conditions or "facts."

Consider how our *collective* belief in poverty (anywhere in the world) creates the conditioned illusion. If abundance (wholeness) preexists our acceptance of it, then poverty is the lie we temporarily accept in lieu of the greater truth. What enabling energy do I send when I provide you a daily fish? — "you poor thing...living in poverty." Remember how the Universe always mirrors (manifests) our beliefs. How does the energy level and associated belief change when I offer (not demand) to show you how to catch your own fish? A benefactor's (personified) belief represented by this second example: "You are experiencing a *temporary* financial condition, which you are empowered to change." Can you see how a well-intentioned charitable organization might actually add to the stated impoverishment it purports to alleviate? A misguided heart can (and often does) enable status quo, as our world will always validate our belief about it.

I'm not suggesting no real suffering occurs, or that we should be insensitive to the plight of others just because life on Earth is full of illusions and multiple levels of potential experience. Only that our collective acceptance of lack, limitation, and scarcity (there's not enough) *contributes* to the suffering condition *throughout the world*. As we reflect, not just react, we can shift our energy to ACCEPTANCE, ALLOWANCE, and COOPERATION, rather than competition over the few (alleged) scraps on the table. *What we do to and for others, we do to and for ourselves.*

Hopefully I've conveyed the message that during our entire experiential lives, as one door closes, several more open. Opportunities, themselves, are never lost. If not acted upon, they simply pass on to another who *is* ready to embrace them. Based on your own inner psychological dynamics, self-experience and level of comprehension, *you* determine the meaning of this message and whether to act upon the opportunities presented.

I hope I have met—from your perspective—my non-burdensome responsibility for the promises I made at the beginning of our journey together. If not, please write or e-mail me (www.soulmanlarry.com) and I will try to include that area of interest in my heart-to-heart website section, or in future book releases. I would also appreciate feedback from you on ways this manual benefits your life. Were you simply entertained, or were you able to feel some deep transformational shifts of awareness or *light-bulb* moments? I would also be pleased to receive true stories about any extraordinary events you directly witnessed. Submissions with permission to publish may be selected for future inspirational offerings.

This has been quite a journey and I am truly amazed at the scope of material covered. I had no idea that a simple sit-down to write a short research paper on human free will vs. Divine influences would give birth to such immense inspirations and unlimited implications. Within these pages, I've done my best to pass on the gifts and insights that benefited me personally in my search for a purposeful and joyous life. Six years spent preparing this FUN-book most certainly became the creative pinnacle of my life. I never before allowed myself to be so consumed with a project without a stated goal and the associated plan foremost in my mind. I compare this writing to again being a carefree child...with the amnesic veil partially lifted. Although I see only the tip of the sensed *love*-berg, I feel responsibly blessed to report such infinite wonders just beyond normal conscious awareness.

Whether a probative life-guide to begin the 21st Century, or an amusing autobiography for my family and friends, the personal import of my writing experience remains the same. I trust those intended to read and benefit shall somehow find their way to it. Although I stand ready to passionately share my continuing message, especially in venues where more intimate exchanges are possible, future events need not and should not be under my direct control if this communication is to be *self*-empowering.

Almost finished with this transcendent message of hope, clarity, and limitless, preexisting potential, I'm now thinking about for whom it has been written. From what I understand, professional writers don't even begin to write without knowing their intended audience. I did not wish to analyze potential readers in advance. I felt a strong urging to stay in the directed flow — as much as possible — while my compartmentalized self worked on the foundational structure from behind the scenes. I was motivated to make the principles a practical precursor for the opportunities presented. Our assorted backgrounds, differing stages of actualized awareness, and personal beliefs prove quite diverse. Now out of the main flow of the collective ether, I review my writing with a more analytical eye. We have moved around a lot in presenting principles from various points of view and levels of consciousness. This metaphorical following of the *bouncing ball* serves us well if we sincerely wish to understand life and relationships from multiple perspectives. A sound structure for charting progress and identifying courageous leaping-off points has been provided.

My brother-in-law offered the opinion: "You wrote a Spiritual book for agnostics!" After thinking about it, I agree. This love offering exists for all who question, doubt, and experience frustration over efforts to understand the greater purpose and meaning to life. I wish to assist those yearning for a substantive connection to that which exists beyond ego-mind orientation, while not making the ego or any portion of our life experience less real or significant. If unsatisfied with uncompromising dogma and fear-based teachings, you've likely found a home here and you can continue your developmental experience through Heart-to-Heart and Soul Talk News, found on my website: **www.soulmanlarry.com.**

If your motivations parallel mine, you hunger to touch the true liberating message(s) of the great mystics and masters, not just the translations brought forth by opportunistic, male-dominated spin merchants—past or present (opinion, of course). Derived from my own, undifferentiated, all-inclusive search for clarity, truth, and more expansive options, this book exemplifies and expresses what I, myself, have relentlessly searched for. Clarity and truth are, of course, highly personal. You decide whether my *spin* rests more in line with your inner core of Being.

When writing this message it was not my intent to exclude anyone. As a practical matter, however, this guidebook will primarily interest those motivated toward independent self realization— especially ones who taste a portion of the power and potency of inner deliverance. Totally closed persons, regardless of labels, don't generally question their life or their world. They pretty much etch their opinions in stone.

Liberation is enhanced by:

❶ Using contemplative attunements or meditation to develop a reflective (witnessing) capability;

❷ Self-actualizing preexisting potential by practicing reframing and replacement of non-serving thoughts, feelings, beliefs, and actions;

❸ Acknowledging and allowing for the perfection within *every* expression and manifestation...regardless of appearance.

Rigid groupings express little or no desire to rock the boat through the questioning of authorities firmly established in their world. Although this may clearly not serve you, there's nothing inherently *wrong* or *bad* in closed orientations, and *zilch* that requires cloned fixing—unless you believe otherwise. Once comprehensive shifts occur, only we—as individuals—determine whether our current, inner beliefs (and external authorities) serve us. We change the world by changing *ourselves*.

Shortly I review the stages of consciousness that strictly determine our quality of life. Only an intellectual outline (except for those awakened to a particular level), as I've emphasized, a great difference exists between academic understanding of concept and core shifts of actualized realization. After making inner, *ah-Ha*, belief-linked breakthroughs and related understandings that bring meaning to our world, we begin the empowerment process and harmonized self-sufficiency. Accepting all interpretation prior to LOC, as being totally subjective, dramatically expands our view of so-called empirical observation. Practical benefit: understanding all language as metaphor and all beliefs...opinion, greatly reduces, if not totally eliminates personal victimization, conflict, and inner stress. We can then release our often-desperate need to make the choices and beliefs of others wrong. When psychologically liberated, no outside circumstance, event, or person can ever threaten our well-being. We can then, to the degree we deem practicable, appreciate the totality of purpose and contribution from *all* forms of inventiveness. Liberation of thought and feeling normally results in more patience and understanding for the smaller, negative types of choices made by others.

With newly manifested and expanded realizations, we see how all expressions help facilitate our experiencing and awakening. A threefold partnership determines the timing for shifting to an expanded level of consciousness:

❶ **Spiritual-DNA motivation.**

❷ **Guidance from the Collective, which provides imagination.**

❸ **Human choice (free will).**

Free will assumes ones have realized the level at which true choice-making becomes an option. The final determining factors for achieving mental, emotional, and Spiritual breakthroughs: *passion and intensity of purpose.*

A Larger Life through Three-Reality Eyes

We rarely squabble over or misinterpret the defining of five-sensory physical objects—rocks, doors, hammers, apples, and neckties, for example. More significant to life transformation are substantive areas likely to involve human emotion; i.e. happiness, love, joy, peace, harmony, fear, anger, and general vulnerability. Religious interpretation, philosophy, social/political ideology, and negotiating all forms of our interpersonal and inter-species relationships—including moral issues of right and wrong—provide topics of much greater debate and general wrangling. Inner psychological dynamics—manifesting as reality levels—directly determine quality of life.

First Reality:

- We see the outer world *causing* our interpretive thoughts and feelings.
- Not comprehending how underlying, psychologically-based beliefs completely determine one's level of life experience, ensures the reactive knee-jerk.

- We *think* we make our own decisions, but behavioristic conditioning fuels our Pavlovian responses to environmental stimuli.

In contrast, consider the empowering benefits associated with your shift to Early Second Reality.

Shifting into ESR:
- Change of inner perspective awakens you to unprecedented differences in your quality of life.
- You stop draining your life-sustaining energies and begin to release the need to control and manipulate the outer environment.
- You now allow and encourage a process of mental and emotional cleansing of psychologically limiting thoughts, feelings, and those pesky worthiness issues.
- By taking that one, fateful, on-ramp to the road less traveled, the birth of personal responsibility and true choice-making begins.
- Enjoy the enthusiasm generated by your breakthroughs, without trying to psychologically clone others in your new-found image.
- View destiny and fate as a fluid partnership between Spiritual DNA and human personality choice-making, rather than an etched-in-stone decree.
- Begin letting go of victim-like beliefs in *any* exclusive, outer cause; thus leaving behind insecure and ineffective interactions (need for outer validation).
- Release the compulsive need to "be there" for others according to their self-absorbed, First Reality view of support. Yes, by holding the line you'll take some disparaging heat. Note: If you cannot, as yet, feel and respond accordingly to the energy differential between needing to be accepted, and your Spiritual (Soul mate) contract, you are still manipulating for love and acceptance. Do you enable loved ones with addictive drugs (to feed their habit) because they'll hate and reject you if you don't?

Uniqueness vs. Superiority
Diverse inclusiveness — the gift of varietal difference — is something to which I've tried to stay true while writing this manual. I attempt to point out options and potential consequences — not declare persons bad, wrong, or ignorant should they choose to ignore my conclusions or list of options. Being special (which *all* of us are) is not being better (which *none* of us are).

In ESR, we credit the *separate* book, tape, affirmation, mantra, technique, instructional course or workshop, Guru, Minister, Religion, or Supreme Being for our inner shifts of awareness. As ones continue to worship the predicate/noun, "I believe in _____," many have at least exchanged unadulterated victimhood for the adulation of New Thought representations of hope. In spite of stage limitation, ESR embodies a huge change from one's suffering past. Evolving toward Second Reality for hundreds of thousands of years, the self-empowerment process has begun in earnest. Only in the last 50 to 60 years have any real appreciable numbers of Human Beings opened themselves to humanistic shifts in inner power and potency. This paradigm resulted in the Self-Help industry—something quite rare before the middle of the twentieth century.

Shifting Into Advanced Second Reality (ASR)

- Realize it's never the guru, Spiritual Guide, process, religion, book, or God that *directly* changes your experience, but your psychological/mystical interpretation (evaluation) of those inputs.
- You can now take full charge of our own inner psychological dynamics—including *self*-diagnosis and *self*-development.
- Tap into the multitude of self-help processes, facilitators, cosmic (guiding) entities, or Universal energies as *tools* to effect self-healing and inner replacement (change).
- Truly feel powerful, loving, and free—now fully up to speed in taking full-time personal responsibility for *all* your thoughts, feelings, and actions.
- Retire from the moralistic judging-of-others business and give up the need to rescue or fix other able-bodied persons; their pre-selected curriculum deserves loving, sounding-board support and noninterference.
- You remember your loved ones must work through their own challenges, in stages. They'll feel the *thrill of victory* processing their *own* bed of pre-selected hot coals.
- Exchange lower vibrational motivations (ego-driven emotions of superiority) for love-based feelings of sensitivity, compassion, and balanced understanding.
- Rejoice in your ongoing Earth life experience and awakening, while simultaneously making openings to the Collective Consciousness, or Universal Mind.
- Allow *coincidences* to take on new meaning. Fully appreciate the all-inclusive synchronicity of life. Accept that you are never alone.

- Sense "Guidance" as a Force *within* you, rather than something separate. Allow this upgraded perception (ASR) to reveal the door to Third Reality.

Early Third Reality

- Shift your realizations from an exclusive "I" focus to a "we" orientation—both in language and belief.
- Move into *conscious* transcendent realization: your place on Earth temporarily expresses an independent ray (Soul) of the one, Collective Consciousness.
- Know your *oneness* with the cosmic reality, feeling an even deeper intimacy and congruency.
- Know the intuitive touch of Spiritual Guiding Ones (or Angels) includes the vastness and synchronicity of Universal Mind—no longer separate or exclusive.
- Sense a synergistic continuum as your overriding universal cosmic residence; feel periods of intimate integration with this omnipotent love-based presence.
- Understand both human challenge and the *extraordinary* as the elaborate bookends of Spiritual DNA actualization.
- See the human pathway as assisting, nurturing, and awakening the individual—as it expands the Soul's experience.
- Fully sense how you, as a benevolent Soul, were and are part of the design team creating your personality matrix and selection of Earth curriculum.
- Transcend the ego mind with increasing regularity, but still appreciate a healthy psyche as necessary to master all realms of the Earth adventure.
- Be thankful for the awesome nature of INCLUSIVITY; cherish and value the *entirety* of human expression, no longer threatened or enslaved by any human belief or behavior.

Advanced Third Reality

Note: The following bullets are no longer suggestions; ones in ATR are fully aware of their dancing through the cosmos. I provide this information as a further example of potential in actualization.

- Enjoy total liberation, whether grounded in body or creatively skipping through the Universe.
- Congruent with Soul-Universal Mind, *separate* human free will is now moot.

- The illusion of separateness from the Collective has run its intended course, but without sense of self being lost or minimized.
- With no further issues of lack and unworthiness, individualistic human curriculum is fully completed.
- Enjoy Earth life with pure FUN and joyous festive celebration.
- As highly evolved energy, mentor/facilitate Spiritual DNA activation within others motivated to question, open, and integrate life *as* Creation itself.
- Live a continuous expression of Location, inc. Heaven on Earth.

Practice IS Perfect

From an empowerment perspective, consider that practice, itself, does *not* make perfect. Know, instead, that *perfection preexists — awaiting acceptance.* Rather than practice *causing* perfection, through practice we accept (in degrees) a higher and higher level of perfection. As perfection preexists, we more accurately practice *excellence.* Although repetitive action allows (facilitates) continued improvement, our BELIEF (vision) about our practice garners the lion's share of results. Top sports psychologists employ this powerfully adjusted awareness.

We benefit from repetition of reality-level structure in order to better comprehend our place in both human and Spiritual involution. Right-brainers simply feel their synchronistic association and resoundingly *know* the wonderful and unprecedented adventure in which they partake. Remember there are no better or worse levels of consciousness—they're just different. All levels serve their intended purpose in experiential life, and naturally overlap. Continuing your development practice, you'll realize a higher percentage of the expanded levels, while progressively outgrowing the lower and denser frequencies. Joyousness and quality of life magically parallel this frequency shift. To view this encapsulation as a way to negatively judge, or compare yourself or others, will not serve you, however. It's not my intent to establish comparisons or belittle any supposed weaknesses. Let's look at contrasts as distinctive, magical opportunities to peek into the continued involution/evolution of humankind. We benefit from understanding how behavior (current reality) and belief are irrevocably linked.

Even with the powerful tools you now have at hand, it's strongly suggested you not become preoccupied with drastically changing or compulsively *fixing* your individuality. Your Soul, standing in Divine perfection, chose your personality — a personality existing in total Oneness with Creation itself. You profit from releasing all thoughts and feelings of being anything less than magnificent. As Human Beings, we do fairly well *analyzing* and *judging* life. What can benefit us additionally at this time of Second Reality expression: to give, to the degree possible, unconditional acceptance and love—both to ourselves *and* others. Choose to identify and gently work with self-diminishing patterns. In this manner you combine a deep, kind, patient loving with the desire to vigorously learn, grow and awaken to your next area of co-creation.

Self-LOVE

Here's a way to internally love and rejoice throughout your lifetime— regardless of what you may be thinking, feeling, or doing. Take a quiet moment and say to yourself: *"The true nature of me, within this human self, is wonderful...is goodness...is beauty. I express with many talents and abilities that reflect the perfection of the Eternal Forces within my Soul. At the same time, I can have thoughts, feelings, choices, and experiences that can be confused and distorted—even fearful. At times when this should occur, I possess the wisdom and power to acknowledge, release, reframe, and replace non-serving thoughts and feelings."*

Do not think for a moment that if you do not achieve ultimate mastery of Earth life, including the highest possible levels of consciousness, your life is somehow diminished. This would not be truth. Humanity has been experientially evolving for hundreds of thousands of years—expressing almost exclusively in First Reality survival mode. Based on what we've awakened to in just the last fifty years, we're definitely on the fast track—in spite of our continued development of mass-destruction weapons. Forgive your perceived shortcomings and rejoice in your accomplishments, realizing that perfection *is* what you *currently* express—always open to further expansion and enlightenment. We are Eternal Beings. There is a plan, and we proceed according to that plan's many options. You identify with the portion of the three realities (Level) to which you have currently awakened. The rest of it may seem theoretical or even phantasmal. Have patience with yourself. Allow for the often-subtle realization of your inclusive, preexisting gifts, talents, and abilities.

"Defining" Love—a non Sequitur?

Consider how many things, perhaps *everything* in the nonphysical realm, cannot be proven scientifically or fully explained in human language. Take love, for example. I've seen and read many wonderful attempts to explain love—some quite divine. Until one's heart experiences love, the larger truth of love has not been revealed, however. *We must **feel** and **experience** love, not just contemplate or logically conclude it.* Perhaps heart-felt love, combined with its physical expression, is what keeps us — as Souls — creating and maintaining life on Earth. We must have *something* here in the physical reality in which our Soul-selves wish to creatively partake, or Creation would have confined its focus to the non-physical realms of existence — right?

Cosmic Shadow

My concluding promise to you was to discuss the ancient human fear of *cosmic shadow*. This umbrella of universal fear has culturally been with us for so long, some would call it genetic. Intuitive Guidance suggests that in addition to delineating the immense splendor, power, and potency from whence we come, my secondary purpose is to help facilitate the healing of mental and emotional fears that block us from love. Public challenge (not enemy) number one: the overriding fear there are cosmic beasts waiting to eat us — either during or at the end of our physical lives. So ingrained in our psyche, this belief's influence may seem inescapable.

If you are not separate from ALL THERE IS, what could consume you other than distorted imaginings? This is self-image psychology. Only through the illusion of dualistic separation can ones fantasize the fear of *boogie* entities. From Oneness, YOU are the thing that goes bump in the night. *Change your mind about being the effect (of anything), and accept you are the Alpha and the Omega — the cause of everything.* This will serve you until awakening to Third Reality where cause and effect coexists and you accept full presence in the NOW (all there is) Club.

Enlightened mystics and master teachers have always walked the path of human evolution, but linguistic limitations and present (of the day) mindsets produced many more worshipping followers than emancipated leaders. Slowly, with generation after generation pushing for personal liberty, creativity, and mutual cooperation, most humans develop a delicate respect for one another's sovereignty. Still, throughout the Earth, many of us continue to cower — subconsciously or otherwise — in fear of cosmic riffraff.

How many chickens, ducks, goats, and virgins do you suppose we've sacrificed, believing that no good — let alone bad — deed shall go unpunished during *this* lifetime, the hereafter, or both? Even some of our greatest intellectual minds expressing what they believed rational, secular beliefs — when push came to shove — fell back on some sacred form of cosmic shadow as the underlying explanation for expressed negativity in the world. Quite probably these 180-degree flip-flops represent fear of a final judgment day where imperfections will be harshly scrutinized. Seizing this conscious and unconscious belief, fledgling religions (including early Christianity) fearful of extinction and frantic to recruit and hold membership, brandished devils and demons to threaten punishment of the faithless—while promising Eternal bliss to worshipping disciples. The many millennia of barbaric treatment of the populace, by despotic and autocratic slave masters, makes this desperation quite understandable. Beginning with the most stouthearted and fearless slaves, men began organizing in an attempt to get more humane treatment. Women had their own way to covertly manipulate (behind the scenes) for survival, although in much of the world they continue to be chattel—up to and including the 21st century.

Notwithstanding the heartbreaking setback of women's rights perpetrated in parts of the world, some long-resistant countries now show signs of moving toward a more unified democratic system—so say pro-democratic watch groups. Freedom House's end-of-the-millennium report on the *State of the World* considered 85 nations free—44 percent of the world's total. Those inhabitants now enjoy a broad range of political rights and civil liberties. According to the parameters established by the International Freedom House, Israel is the lone country in the Middle East currently considered free, but there is a lot of change taking place. Electoral democracies exist [in varying degrees] in 119 countries, representing 58.2 percent of the world's population. Just 100 years earlier, not one nation offered universal voting rights to its people. So, in spite of global war horrors, acts of mass genocide, and the current weapons arsenal, the twentieth century exemplifies (should you choose to accept these statistics) the reining champion for empowering democratic principles.

Cultural Belief

With all the fear-based cultural beliefs in the world, it's a wonder any reasoning, thinking person remains open to even a questioning agnostic perspective. Could the human tenacity to uncover higher truths denote further evidence of an inner-motivating component? Having been one, I understand the rigid, unwavering denial of an Atheist. If the only choice offered was the enslaving dogma of debilitating, fear-based superstition, count me out as well. In subjective realities, of course, one person's superstition is another's religious faith. Opposite choices of *resigned abdication* (surrender of self) or *atheistic denial* (there's nothing *but* self) are neither bad nor wrong, but could they be small compared to the human potential for unlimited inner (blended) actualization? Personally, I choose to live as an empowered, love-based, co-creator, rather than a powerless supplicant. Life is a lot more FUN from the former. Empowering perspectives will mean nothing to those convinced the quality of salvation, a so-called "afterlife," lies in direct proportion to the level of unending suffering one endures in *this* life.

When we take the time to listen, Souls tell us our reluctance to move beyond fear of cosmic shadow portrays our human predisposition toward thinking ourselves undeserving and imperfect in the presence of a judgmental God (human shadow). *Unworthiness blocks our ability to value free will as the greatest bestowment of all.* With the power of Second Reality (self-responsibility), we build anew out of the ashes of the past—or not—depending on choices made from either destructive fear or constructive love. Believing in Divine love does not suggest there are no aftereffects associated with negative choice. Direct and indirect consequences exist both here/now *and* beyond (in linear terms). Let us see these corollaries from a heightened, Soul-like, *all-is-good* perspective, rather than wasting our creative energy making difference undesirable.

A More Empowering Perspective

Souls value *all* human experience, but especially rejoice when we conquer fear-based expressions—replacing them with the blessed healing power of inclusive forgiveness and love. We—as Souls—eventually experience the resolution of destructive patterns and the inherent congruency between human personality and Soul. Consider our tough Earth lessons a result of combined Soul and human choice, rather than karmic debt or *sins-of-the-father* decrees. A quantum perceptual shift regarding the true cause of Earth-bound negativity is critical; especially for ones wishing to release analogous feelings of victimization. Whether we use our Universal power constructively or destructively...it's the same power.

WE ARE SOUL (Collective Consciousness, God, et al.) temporarily projecting a portion of ourselves into a specifically created human body. Ascension requires a decision to release and replace non-serving beliefs in lack, scarcity, and unworthiness. Or we continue to look for scapegoats to blame or credit for quality of life, or lack thereof. When we point a judgmental finger at another, three fingers curl back toward ourselves.

A Daily Guide

Here is how I personally benefit from the principles presented in this manual.

- I put forth a maximum, allowing/accepting effort toward positive, purposeful expressions, rather than getting bogged down in resisting undesirables (what I don't want).
- I choose to believe that the Saddam Husseins, Timothy McVeighs and Osama bin Ladens of the world—in spite of their destructive actions—are part of my experiential process, as are the Nelson Mandelas and Mother Teresas.
- I strive to continually practice my sensitivity and newfound love of *all* life. This includes developing an expanded, *omni-sensory* perspective regarding the appearance of dark, negatively-expressing Human Beings.

Most find violent-acting persons the most difficult for whom to have any compassion. I do *not* suggest we embrace behavior we detest. But consider, again, that *there can never be terrorists without persons blindly reacting (giving power to) to the acts of terrorism.*

Finally getting past my feelings of victimization, and distorted need for revenge, opened the road to multi-view understanding. Some of our most significant Soul mates—*not* the ones we are on a mission to find—are those persons that push our respective emotional *buttons* the hardest. Challenging *hard cases* are the primary co-facilitators that help actualize preexisting potential. So before you cast only negative aspersions toward those whom you've had the most difficulty, consider this thought: challenging individuals not only list among your most significant teachers, they set the tone and focus for your Soul-designed Earth School curriculum—as intended.

Give an old enemy a hug. Enjoy the liberating presence of power and potency by freeing yourself of the fear of outer events and circumstances. Your shift, alone, goes a long way toward negating the corruptive dominance of the world's bullies. Recall the great Buddhist teaching about facing and releasing the fear of physical death, to fully value living in the present. Souls may appreciate *all* experience, but expressing only knee-jerk responses to the behavior of others does not liberate us in the NOW, nor is it much FUN.

Another important choice: decide whether you wish to be quality-of-life fodder for able-bodied persons convinced they have little or nothing to live for. A fine line resides between loving support (for better or for worse) and enabling codependency. If someone you love insists on turning toward the dark side, how far into that despairing pit are *you* willing to descend, just to stay in their supportive—albeit destructive—wake? Might being the example for *alternative* (holistic) choice serve them more than compliant commiseration?

Ruling Hierarchies

History reflects that any ruling hierarchy that ignores the masses also dooms itself. **We are a *world* society.** By showing fellow Human Beings how to feed and empower *themselves*, thereby developing a vested interest in life, you not only convert old enemies into business partners and friends, you continue to restore empowering balance, peace, and joyous glory in your own life. Simplistic—even controversial—especially when dealing with fear (both theirs and ours) and inflexible belief-systems, but changing the vibrational frequency of the planet does not require as many synchronous minds and hearts as most believe. If you can picture, sense, feel, or just imagine the significance of the *journey*, rather than final arrival point, move to the head of the class.

I seek to both absolve (de-fang) fear-based manifestations *and* remain sensitive to today's challenging issues, but without buying into them. I diligently strive to release remaining hate, anger, and negative emotions. I do this, *not* by stuffing or purposefully resisting fear, pain (I'm still working on this one), and negative images, but by acknowledging and working through the distorted appearances. This then allows for reunification with love and joy.

SNIOP Anyone?

This increasingly complex, five-sensory overload world constantly bombards us with an exponential rate of input—much of it quite negative. A smorgasbord of advertising media competes zealously to manipulate our buying decisions, most effectively by appealing to our mutual insecurities. Back when we were fleeing from Woolly Mammoths and other Mastodons, I doubt we stopped to notice the sweetness of our breath, or to check for underarm wetness. Let's pause and ask ourselves why we've allowed these relatively inconsequential—even natural—occurrences such a pivotal place in today's world. ***Turning off your TV set, not reading newspapers, or becoming a hermit will not prevent your experiencing negative input.*** Why? *Because we're all connected on the inner.* Realizing how you're empowered to filter and process all incoming data, regardless of its source, truly liberates and frees us from SNIOP (**S**usceptible to the **N**egative **I**nfluences of **O**ther **P**eople). Correctly placed internal anti-virus filters help ensure rain-free parades. Filtering requires a left-hemisphere, which we don't benefit from when bashing the ego mind.

Through attunements, I open to my Soul awareness of a cosmic plan that is completing itself, resulting in a unified Spiritual humanity. By continuing to heal non-serving patterns and regaining my trust in love, I know I am helping the planet's energy, as well.

What the majority call "perfection," is unnecessary in achieving a joyous, love-based existence. But consider doing what I do on a regular basis, just to see if you notice any differences in your life.

- Enjoy the benefits of taking a time-out moment before emotionally reacting to anything...excepting an immediate, life-or-death situation.
- Take personal responsibility for your own thoughts, feelings, and actions. Regardless how enlightened one becomes, the human personality subjectively processes data and expresses only *opinions*. "Facts," like beauty, are interpreted in the minds and hearts of the perceiver. This empowering, allowing level releases you from the disabling need to defend your views (definitions), while allowing coexistence with all other beliefs. Earthly liberation does not get any more powerful that this, my beloved friends. We can either cooperate with, or resist what is sure to persist.
- Through repetitive practice, become (in stages) a product of the teachings in this book with which you resonate.
- Reinforce your expanded awareness through habit-forming deed.
- Feel blessed to develop a grateful, accepting perspective on life that allows peace, harmony, joy, goodness, love, creativity, and FUN to be the primary expression and focus in your everyday life.

I do not intend to suggest even a hint of hopelessness over our remaining Earth challenges. To clean up old-paradigm messes and begin living in peaceful harmony, humanity is evolving with an abundance of intelligence, power, potency and compassion. I strive to avoid outer fixes for inner challenges, including attempted *cloning* of others. I'm learning to restrain myself from controlling and manipulating the conduct of mentally competent adults, unless absolutely necessary for self-defense or preventing immediate and potentially serious injury and loss of life.

If we absolutely must intervene, let us strive to do so by addressing only the current life-or-death *behavior*, rather than expressing judgment about the person or persons themselves. Perhaps our caring, non-judgmental crisis intervention can pave the way for therapeutic dialog and mentoring opportunities. Remember the importance of patience as you wait for questions or requests for assistance. Otherwise your restoration efforts will not only fall on deaf ears, they will likely be interpreted as criticizing interference. You can't have a heart-to-heart dialogue with those accepting *dark-side* influences, any more than you can have a rational conversation with ones under the influence of chemical substances. I continuously work on these and the following prime-directive behavioral principles.

- When personal restraint is difficult, especially when seeing the empowering choice so clearly, I try and remember how I got to where I am now.
- Focus on the understanding that—just like our *own* pathway—until ones awaken on their own, they've not yet completed their respective curricula.
- Rather than denying special ones their own confidence-building breakthroughs (rescuing and enabling can potentially magnify negative self-image), I strive to be a support system and mentor.

What many learn via examples demonstrated by human teachers like Stephen Hawking, Christopher Reeve, the conjoined Schappell Twins, and many other master messengers, is that *we are much more than our temporal human bodies*. We live in a new-age celebration of inner Spirit that opens us to the synergistic continuum. Our ongoing consciousness shift provides the potential for simultaneous left-right hemisphere awareness and Human-Soul integration of *all* realms of existence. Much of humanity is now poised on the threshold of a transformational shift in consciousness. Healing our own false feelings of lack and unworthiness opens us to the power of transmutable love. Simultaneous remembering renews Earth through automatic transference of balanced energy. This, ladies and gentlemen, is how we change the world. What an exciting and opportunity-filled time it is to live and love on Earth!

When Reality Sucks

Some reading these words may not currently feel personal or global greatness. Know those thoughts and feelings as *temporary* and not the truth of you, or the planet. No argument from me that Earth life can be, and often is, a tremendous hardship. Chronic pain, of any sort, can sap our will to continue. We can feel totally lost in self-absorbed depression. In those periods, finding the energy to survive just one more day seems overwhelming. I have a very dear friend engaged in a desperate struggle with hopeless despair as I write this. *Especially* for you and others feeling the same, I conclude with a message from those that love and guide us.

Dear beloveds. Know that you have been created by and are the direct product of perfect manifestations of love-light energy. There have been no mistakes with your assembly. At this very moment, boundless Celestial Beings are pouring their limitless love into your heart. Take a deep cleansing breath. Close your eyes for a moment...and reach out [past the veil] *to feel our Divine embrace. Our love for you is like a perfect mother's love. Open to us, now, and make a gentle releasing. As you receive your blessed caress from the Collective Forces that never leave your side,* **cry not...as the bell tolls for thee.**

As we bring our shared pilgrimage to a pause, it is sincerely hoped we bring you light in places where there is darkness; salvation where there is suffering; and LOVE where there is isolation and fear. YOU are the ultimate Creation, imbued with talent and ability to fashion a grand life regardless of temporary challenge(s). Continue to look inside yourself for the beacon of light pointing the way toward your continued journey.

THE END???

Once airborne...you're *free* to move about life's cabin.

"There is absolutely nothing that humans can invent that is beyond the divergent scope of possible patterns already known and provided for by Creation itself."

—The SoulMan

EPILOGUE

♥   ♥   ♥

Practical Game-Plan: Now is the time to ask yourself whether you will be served by making the personal commitment to—forevermore—take full personal responsibility for all your thoughts, feelings, and actions.

You have been given all the instructions needed to open your specialized suitcase of gifts and continue creating your own idyllic life—based in reverent idealism and love. My human self has faith that, at some level, I've helped you. My Soul Self absolutely knows we've helped one another—just as we agreed to do before this lifetime began. Thank you for staying the course and taking this journey with me. I'll be thinking of you often. No coincidence you hold this Spiritual synopsis in your hands, your *own loving Soul* was that special amigo that wanted you to have this gift of inspiration, faith, and belief in both your human and Eternal nature. Your Soul wishes you—as a human personality—to know not only your unique magnificence, but also your partnership role with the forces of the Eternal. You are invited to celebrate and festively rejoice, as your life is everlasting.

What happens to our human personality and Soul when we physically complete this lifetime on Earth?

Ah...the Eternal question. Before I unearthed a satisfactory answer to the grand finale, I had to first overcome another hurdle. If we are Spiritual beings, with omnipotent, omniscient Souls, why is so much negativity expressed in the world? Socrates, Plato, Aristotle, Spinoza, and in more modern times Whitman, Jung, Bohm, Einstein, transcendentalist Emerson, Holmes, and other great minds, debated the Eternal question. Although their individual answers vary, these giants present us one common thread...*Collective Oneness.*

The *not-knowing* feeling originally left me skeptical of all esoteric explanations. Orthodox religion seemed more like a fearful response to the not knowing, than any answer. I continually asked myself and others: "Doesn't theology pose a self-interest motivation promoting *blind-faith* axioms? Not only is the *Carrot and the Stick* technique a perfect method for controlling the flock, it keeps the tithing troughs open." In those early days I was very unilateral in my judgments. Effectively I believed as rigidly as any dogmatic doctrine.

Later, from a base of questioning skepticism (Secular Humanism) I began my personal search. You've read my stories. How one interprets these narratives is, of course, based on a currently expressed set of beliefs. At the time, each of my brushes with death seemed extraordinary — even supernatural. Not so today. Details from past experiences have not changed, but my *interpretation* of those events has dramatically shifted. Why? Realization expands in direct proportion to life experience and one's willingness to neutrally reflect (witness) on past circumstances.

Have you answered the question whether an underlying motivation or directional influence comes from beneath *your* conscious awareness? Something not explained through genealogy? For me, this question is now moot. As to when new concepts and revelations spring forth, consider the import of Spiritual DNA.

With maturity we experience less tunnel vision, do we not? Let's choose an ever-increasing RAM (random access memory) as our expanding-vision metaphor. We start our lives at 16K. By the time we complete our incarnation, we've upgraded ourselves to 512K, or more. At transition (linearly), our RAM memory (total life experience) gets added to the permanent hard drive (Soul, God, Collective, et al.). All is remembered...nothing is lost.

In answering the question about what happens to one's Soul, ask yourself the following: **Where is Soul?** Where is *any* idea, concept, or realization before it comes into one's conscious awareness? Was the Special, then General Theory of Relativity ($E=MC^2$) lost, and then found? Or did it preexist, awaiting recognition and acceptance? Remember the old joke about "good girls/boys go to heaven, but bad girls/boys go everywhere?" Very playfully and without any implied disrespect, let's pretend that "Soul" is that bad boy/girl — it's *everywhere*. Not limited by space and time, Soul does not go to and fro. It covers the gamut just by focusing on that which it seeks. Even though difficult for Human Beings to envision a realm without a before and an after — a beginning and an end — dualistic opposites hold court only in a linear, five-sensory world. To be judged by some dispensational afterlife determinate (God, as an example), you would have to be *separate* from God. Separation exemplifies an *appearance* consistent only with the awareness level that supports it. Consider *separation* not to be the higher truth.

My subjective answer, based on intuited information delivered to me from the Eternal Forces (whatever you wish to call them), is that we do not GO anywhere at physical death. The veil lifts and we simply awaken to what already is. Spiritual transition is a process by which we shift the spotlight from the physical *doing* of life, to the just *being*. There never was any separation; we co-created dualism as illusion—a dream for the experience. Only an amnesic-based tunnel vision temporarily prevents us from discerning our multifarious realities. Limited views are expandable, based one one's inner motivation and resultant actualization. Physical death, never an imperative for removing the blinders, represents the back door to Universal Awareness. Unconditional *love, gratitude,* and *acceptance* hold the master key to the front door of the Mansion. Mental and emotional fear, as well as our limiting five-sensory reductionist perspectives, have us staring through banquet windows with opera glasses, clipboard, and the scientific method, *watching* celebratory feasts instead of joyfully participating in them.

You might ask, "Why do we, as human personalities, resist awakening to our complete magnificence and unlimited potential— our Soul selves? What possible reasons exist for us to remain in the dark about our Universal presence?" What you ask now took my entire life to partially realize and this entire manuscript to partially answer. I appreciate the opportunity to condense a response, so we'll call it square. Behold the Holographic Universe!

Consider, again, that we—as independently expressing rays of the ONE Universal Mind—choose to be here. What a wondrous gift is this lifetime! Not an assignment from God, a sins-of-the-father consequence, debt repayment for a past-life transgressions, or any other victim-creating scenario; you—as a Soul—wished a specifically intensive curriculum. Your one-of-a-kind human personality matrix represents a most complex and magnificent conception—as does your human body. Not the *only* creation you (as a Spiritual Being) participate in, but I support you in visualizing it as the most glorious.

Souls see all pain as temporary. You—as pure Soul energy—did not intend emotional pain for your human counterpart. But you know that no act, no matter how vile, can ever damage one's true Being. Contrary to many religious teachings, Souls can never be damaged. With the $E=MC^2$ gift from dear Albert we share how mass and energy are interchangeable, and that energy can *never* be destroyed. Energy can and does change form, however.

If we, as humans, entertained full conscious awareness of everything we are—our complete power and magnificence—the pure potency of our human pathway would overly commingle with non-physical realities. Our human self could not then experience the intensity and differentiated uniqueness of an *individual* waterfall, a challenging hike up a *specific* mountain trail, the smell of a *particular* wild flower, or the joy of raising glorious offspring—sons and daughters that out of billions of options chose *you* to be their nurturing, trail-blazing parent. We could not stay focused on a unique, laser-beam directed life without specified amnesia and underlying influences to keep us on track. By adding *independent* life experience to the Universal Hard Drive, Soul/God continues to be enriched. Our unique independence does not equate *separation*, however.

So relax...you're already perfect and have nothing to do but live and love in the current moment. *There has been no mistake with your assembly.* Hardship—including tough lessons from childhood—provide particular sensitivities intended to be shared with others whose paths we cross. Rather than make mistakes, we learn, grow, and awaken to opportunities. When we know *all* experience, even the most painful, as part of our evolutionary and chosen process of awakening, we value all life equally. Dualistic opposites, while still appreciated, are moot when expressing from our transcendent selves...our collective Oneness. Forgiveness and grief (as examples) are intentionally relevant *only* when ones believe **separate** persons and circumstances (losses) require forgiving or grieving. If I have communicated one thing, it's that dualistic views are neither right nor wrong—only limited to the stage awareness that supports them.

ALOHA! I love the word **ALOHA**. This greeting means both hello and goodbye—both or neither. That's exactly how I feel now. This *SoulMan* is experiencing mixed emotions about concluding this shared message. Throughout the entire creative process, I've been energized with a strong euphoric feeling of Soul mate connection. I achieved this intimacy even while writing in joyful solitude (for a major part of the past six years). A part of me does not want to bring this written celebration of Spirit to an end, although I will be quite pleased to have it done and out there. We worked hard and stretched ourselves during this actualizing process. We've every reason to feel wonderful about what we've accomplished in life so far—even with the darker moments—while ever-hopeful regarding the future. In spite of all that, I was beginning to feel a little heavyhearted, and then ALOHA came to me...thank you beloved Spirit! Now more at peace with this place and time, I release my fear that our connection could ever be broken. This is not an ending, or a good-bye, but an **ALOOOHA**.

Communion

In this and all other moments, my glorious friends, the most loving and supportive Beings surround us. You may name them Angels, Spiritual Guides, Souls, the Collective, Infinite Inner, God, or the Eternal Forces. Regardless what you call benevolent expressions of light and pure love energy, open to them now. As you embrace this union, make a gentle releasing. Let your Celestial Guardians imbue you with the most exquisite love. Let their brilliance shine a beacon for your continued journey. Know in your heart that you *have never, will never, can never* be alone.

And remember...Ye *are* God!

I, LARRY JAMES STEVENS—Soul Person—sign off for now, in Love, Light, Laughter...and ALL GOOD.

Dance, like no one is watching...

Sing, like no one is listening...

Laugh, Joke, Play, like no one is judging...

And thereby enjoy your intended Earth Mastery

*This is **not the end**...the adventure continues.*

"All the love and abundance we could possibly imagine, both for us and those we care for, is here for the accepting. It requires courage, faith, and determination to

Prod Beneath the Surface

of our manifesting opportunities."

—The SoulMan

APPENDIX - GLOSSARY OF DEFINITIONS

♥ ♥ ♥

① **Holographic Psychology™ (HP).** *An all-inclusive study and delineated structure, explaining the human/Soul mind and the evolutionary process that brought us to this unprecedented threshold of remembering.* This term, coined by California's James P. Pottenger, Ph.D., and his research staff, represents the culmination of this brilliant man's lifetime of service to humanity in the study of human potential. As a psychological expansion, HP symbolizes the *trifecta* of a synergistic mind-body-spirit connection, a revolutionary understanding that each person subjectively determines his/her entire comprehension as part of their psychological dynamic. Self-image, an intrinsic portion of the process of human perception, evolves through three distinct reality levels. This awakening—once actualized—represents a quantum shift in realization. After a major consciousness expansion, a person's external, objective-world orientation changes to a subjective, internally based, multi-sensory realization. Awakening recipients suddenly realize the five physical senses—by themselves—fail to provide the true meaning and purpose to experiential life. What we witness, or sense externally, does not cause our anxiety, frustrations, or joy. *Our currently expressing habits and beliefs psychologically determine the meaning we ascribe to any sensed experience.* Interpretive language—all considered metaphor—mirrors a person's present reality and self-image.

Three distinct levels of comprehension embody individual dynamics, and comprise: ① Behavioral (first-level understanding), ② Humanistic (second-level understanding), and ③ Transpersonal (third-level understanding). All three levels directly relate to perspective, behavior, and the resulting quality of life—whether responding to human challenge or creative expression.

In First Reality's subject/object-language model we name person, place, or thing: "He, She, or It." In Second Reality's (I AM) process-language model of humanistic psychology, we have a self, I, ego, or person...actualizing potentials. With Third Reality's inclusion of transpersonal psychology, we recognize an "awareness of awareness," which is one's Eternal nature awakening to its unlimited Source. It is in Third Reality (WE ARE) that intellectual concepts of Oneness become a core reality. The complexity of each level of understanding—which includes and appreciates all *previously* awakened levels—provides a structure to understand our Divine and Eternal (absolute) Nature.

In the ancient past, humanity thought Third Reality, the transcendent level, accessible only in the afterlife, or in more recent periods, only if one disavowed the material realm by totally eliminating the ego mind. Holographic Psychology shows us how to simultaneously achieve both a deep esoteric connection *and* material mastery. Discovery of this expanded paradigm of inner psychological reality continues our evolutionary pathway. A Human Being's Spiritual DNA subconsciously (uniquely) prods him or her toward mastery of heart as well as head. The important question: Are we—as human personalities—reflectively listening?

Underlying Spiritual components lead many theistic researchers to subjectively conclude the Source of all existence a collective base innate in nature. Under this theory, Source has already supplied humanity the preexisting talents, gifts, and abilities to fully master life on Earth. Beliefs—including the activation of one's own creative abilities—manifest according to an individual's current level of understanding. Holographic Psychology comprises Universal laws discerned—in past times of Earth—by only a few gifted mystics. Rediscovery of these principles and our unlimited potential appropriately terminates membership in the classic *victimhood club*. Consciousness shifts deliver perspectives and choices of which beneficiaries have not previously been aware.

In Third Reality, a person knows with certainty that s/he is not a Human Being having Spiritual experiences, but a Spiritual Being having progressively enlightened (stage awareness) human experiences—involution begets evolution.

This awakening process of realization is called "FESTSTELLUNG" —a German word for simultaneous integration of both objective and subjective realizations. HP does not disavow the existence of an objective world, but simply explains that human interpretation of any objective reality expresses a subjective evaluation based on one's underlying precepts and presets. What we *believe* represents an indivisible absolute — that is, until we discover LOCATION of Comprehension and its observational adjudicating options.

One of the greatest benefits of Holographic Psychology: perhaps for the very first time we have a science, or theory, defining human behavior *without* throwing the baby out with the bath water. HP, an all-inclusive facilitation, fully embraces all elements of past human behavior, experience, and scientific study; *without* labeling behaviorism, humanism, or transpersonal perspectives as wrong, bad, or obsolete. The *totality* of experiential life — vital to our collective evolution — continually expands in complexity, as intended. Holographic perspectives provide an omni-directional look at human behavior, and life in general, with limitless concepts — both here and beyond space and time.

This view parallels recent discoveries in the observed behavior of sub-atomic particles. With much of this intellectually beyond me, quantum cosmologists — like Stephen Hawking — make fantastic calculations and observations well beyond the purview of any Newtonian precept or even Einstein's General Theory of the space-time continuum. Could it be that quantum particles are uniquely sentient and therefore respond (communicate) to their atomic counterparts like characters in some *Outer Limits* episode? If so, is this further evidence of our universal collectiveness?

Under the umbrella of "Unified Field Theory," England's premier physicist David Bohm (an Einstein protégé), the eminent scientific and artistic genius Walter Russell, *and* Albert Einstein, himself, all paved the way for the expanded presumption that we live in an ever-evolving holographic universe. They collectively advanced the theory that magnetic, gravitational, and electrical energy are all manifestations, or phases, of the same process. Carl Jung also predicted the quantum breakthroughs (realizations) that we enjoy today.

A Hologram is a three-dimensional projection, or view, created by reflected, multi-colored laser light. Holographic Psychology, as multi-dimensional perspective, recognizes all humans as something akin to manifested vibrations and frequencies of light and — on Earth — Sound energy. ECKists (students and practitioners of the metaphysical science of Eckankar) will note the similarity to their own envisioning of Spirit. This new, all-inclusively derived field views life and human potential from an expanded, reflective, and refractive perspective labeled the THREE REALITIES of consciousness.

Bottom line. *Mastering the intuitive realizations facilitated by this science represents a quantum leap in human understanding, while eliminating boundaries that have been enslaving humans for many thousands of years.*

② **Spiritual DNA.** *The human-life blueprint created by higher-source intelligence.* Spiritual DNA is a function of involuted teleology. In collaboration with its genetic-based partner, Spiritual DNA determines general Earth themes, patterns, and curricula for the respective individual. Plato named these patterns "Forms and Ideas." Dr. Carl Jung called them "archetypes" or the "Collective Unconscious." Emerson said these governing patterns were a product of the "Over-Soul," and some modern quantum physicists use "Intelligence and Design" to describe Higher Source Intelligence. The level of motivation with which the respective person functions (encoded within one's human personality matrix) is not predestination, however. We can, through human free will, modify— positively or negatively—the blueprint, as we go along. Unfolding life lessons actualize certain trigger points and switch on conscious awareness *light bulbs*. The stronger, core-shaking *ah-Ha's* can represent actualizing quantum shifts. Facilitated (according to Dr. Pottenger's research) by our individually expressing Spiritual DNA component, strong internal conversions change a belief system as ones suddenly awaken to previously unknown levels of understanding.

In Volume One of *The Holmes Papers* (DeVorss), containing transcribed recordings of Ernest's Tuesday free-flow sessions (late 1950s), Dr. Holmes states: "There is in you and me a unique presentation of this [Spiritual DNA] that by the very nature of the process of our evolution we should finally spring, fully orbed, into our Divine nature and *consciously* participate with it."

What comes to me intuitively: we are guided—never forced—to follow our Soul's preference. If, however, we humans get too far afield on the negative side of the ledger, we generally create a lot of pain and suffering for ourselves that may not have been part of the original game plan.

Nothing conventionally scientific in the above—just reporting what's coming to me from the expanded realms. One advantage of not being a scientific, five-sensory reductionist: I don't hold back any of the good and *juicy* parts from you!

③ **Self-image.** *An individual's subconscious mental image that validates his or her belief system.* An essential part of the decision-making process, self-image forms the basis of an individual's self-acceptance, or state of being, projected to the world. Those living in First Reality comprehension cannot recognize or appreciate the significant role self-image plays in their everyday experience. Chapter Two covers self-image in detail.

④ **Subjectiveness.** *Communication based on our current level of understanding.* The assumed knowledge of an individual's conscious awareness, as separate from the object world, is where we, as Human Beings, interpret data with the resources available to us at the time. What we believe to be true is true for us *individually,* not necessarily authentic for someone else—same world, same facts, but different interpretations. That's why belief is subjective. Awareness of pre-conditioned bias, part of a reflective Second Reality or "observer" awakening, cannot be understood by First Reality's reactive mind.

⑤ **Truth.** *What we feel in the very core of our being.* Expressed from a transcendent perspective, what the Toltec teachings call "Dream Mastery," or "Mastery of Love," the Soul-mind perceives truth as functional wisdom converted to a system of values fathomable within a Human Being. Experienced as an inner knowingness of what works, *Soul-mind truth resonates deep within the individual.* For brain-mind humans, subjective (relative) truth always expands—unless one is closed to expansion. This closure, a common state of First Reality consciousness, ties ego self-image directly to personal beliefs. In First Reality, we exist in the black-and-white, right-or-wrong, judgmental world. Those expressing from the first level consider being right more important than being free or being loved. They must defend—at all cost—that which they believe objective truth, or risk being made *wrong* or *bad.* Being *wrong* results in a major hit to the ego, which runs the show in First Reality.

⑥ **Dualism.** *A belief in the division of body, mind, Spirit, and the environment.* Dualism exists until one awakens to the reality that s/he, rather than external factors, psychologically evaluates and creates her/his world view. In other words, one's conscious awareness functions separately from the understanding that gives meaning to his or her actuality—until it doesn't. "God's will," used as a term to differentiate or separate human consciousness from the Eternal Forces, denotes a dualistic expression. The cornerstone of dualistic principle: *Cause and Effect.* Dualism has more meaning and significance after one explores: ❶ our human history of suffering and victimization; and ❷ transcendent realms not limited by space and time (Third Reality).

⑦ **SELF vs. self.** *Our Soul or Universal-Mind existence (Big Self) vs. our human personality matrix* and our view of the operating system we believe solely determines our choices and behavior (little self). Upon reflection, we awaken to advanced levels of comprehension (Self) and discover — in stages — all dualistically oriented perceptions as temporary, but intended, illusions.

⑧ **Attunement.** *An altered-state process of directed meditation or subconscious contemplation.* In most metaphysical arenas, attunement is synonymous for conventional meditation. Here, we use attunement as a vehicle to bypass some portions of the conscious mind, for the purpose of obtaining clarity of thought with a *specific* objective. Some see attunements as a process of opening oneself to the Akashic, or cosmic, Library. Other labels include Universal Mind, Collective Unconscious, Source, God, or Higher Intuitive Self. For me, attunements compare to remote viewing. With an all-inclusive format, attunements can be both divinely connecting *and* goal achieving. As a directed form of meditative contemplation, I demonstrate how attunements can be used as a natural-law bridge to the Eternal Forces.

⑨ **Location of Comprehension (LOC).** *An emancipating principle that represents the apex of Holographic Psychology.* The few human-potential researchers and Spiritual facilitators that know of it consider Location of Comprehension the definitive quantum leap in human psychological evolution. This paradigm shift in understanding begins to arise in Second Reality awareness. LOC provides freedom to referee (what Dr. Wayne Dyer calls "witnessing") one's own thoughts, feelings, and actions, while enjoying — for the first time — true and complete options in the decision-making process. Until an individual shifts into *observer view*, his/her mindset generally limits itself to automatic, predetermined responses to both environmental and internal stimuli. Fully opening to second-stage comprehension, ones become aware they are totally responsible for their feelings — wonderful, terrible, or indifferent. Practicing reflective Location eliminates all forms of victimization. LOC provides individuals a way to determine, regardless of environment, his or her own quality of life — based on the philosophical and psychological dynamics within one's self-image. Internalized habits and beliefs determine our responses to contextual communication (language). Current Science-of-Spirit research suggests an inherent human capacity for realizing a Collective Source, existing—for the most part—beyond our consciousness awareness. Synchronous with the individually-expressing self/Self, this congruent association with the Collective Source provides the preexisting potential for replacement (change). A most-challenging paradigm, LOC collides with behavioristic beliefs that one learns while functioning in first-level understanding—a "formal" education is such an example. *LOCATION is the master key to authentic inner power and omni-sensory perception.*

⑩ **Chakra.** Stated very simply, *Chakra* is an Eastern delineation of various energy power points located in the human body. The seven (some cultures describe more) chakra vortices center on a horizontal axis (parallel to the spine), running from top to bottom. In Hinduism, each wheel-spinning chakra point—focused on certain emotional, mental, and physiological states of Being—represents a different deity or Spiritual influence. Some parallels exist between chakras and the "Chi" energy flow patterns used by holistic Chinese medical practitioners for over five thousand years. Western empirical science has not been able to definitely pinpoint these energy centers. Leading-edge quantum physics (multi-sensory) researchers, noting the unpredictable interactions of sub-atomic particles, are opening to the concept of a holographic universe with a complex interweaving of conscious-acting Prana energy and quanta matter.

SOULMAN'S TRUISTIC QUOTATIONS

♥   ♥   ♥

NOTE: Permission to use up to three quotations per article, review, or book chapter, is hereby granted; conditional on author credit given with each quotation used, and website URL listed at least once per book, review, or article: www.soulmanlarry.com).

"Humanity shares only *one* lifeboat."

"Life's not about earning our place...it's about learning our space."

"It's the quality of allowing perception, not the quantity of resisting deception, that's the benchmark of an authentic life."

"One need not walk a MILE in another person's shoes, when just a few feet will do."

On Remaining Humble: "A pinched nerve running amuck through the rib cage reminds me that my human self is not, nor will it ever be, so wise or *advanced* as to be anymore than an instant away from assuming the fetal position and crying for my mommy."

"To blame ourselves for past behaviors, or things not yet accomplished, is like blaming an acorn for not as yet being an oak tree."

"Expanded perception, often in the guise of confusion, is evidence of a rising consciousness."

OR: "Enlightenment arises after a monumental healing and releasing experience, often heralded by a period of confusion."

On Oneness: "Variety of expression is not second-guessed by its Manufacturer."

"Once airborne, you are free to move about life's cabin."

"YOU are that thing that goes bump in the night."

"Activity does not guarantee accomplishment."

"Adrenaline rage, and poise, make strange bedfellows."

On Questions: "Until we can frame the question, we are unlikely to understand (or even hear) the answer resting within."

"Beneficial change does not require torturous circumstances... unless we insist."

Ask yourself: "Is the sandbox I'm creating, the one I wish to play in?"

"If you want to *do* and *experience* differently, you must *believe* differently."

"We are not on Earth to scrimp and survive...but to blossom and thrive."

"YOU, like the rest of us, have been driving nails with a rock. Wouldn't you rather have a hammer?"

"Ask not what life can do for you...ask what you can do for your life."

"Until we prod beneath the surface of our manifesting opportunities, it's unlikely we'll awaken to the larger intimacy, cosmic connection, and expansive insights (meaning-making) that reveal our true nature."

"Change your mind about being the *effect* (of anything), and accept you are the Alpha and the Omega — the *cause* of everything."

"Let us rejoice my beloveds! This IS the change we've prayed for. Let us look past the surface ugliness and see the beauty within...a beauty that has *always* been, awaiting only our remembrance and acceptance. Welcome home!"

"To *not* embrace life fully and completely is like being invited to a magnificent feast containing a multitude of delectable delights, but having only lettuce."

"We can choose to take the blinders off and smell the roses (just BE), rather than stomp all over the foliage on the way to the next goal line."

"What I encapsulate, here, is a condensed appreciation for the empowering difference between dictatorial *commandments* from God, and the preexisting potential so generously *gifted by* God."

"Let your life choices be based on consequences of belief, rather than subjective issues of culturally-defined right and wrong."

"Expressed negativity, or the prevention thereof, is *not* the parameter for Divine intervention."

"Divinely bequeathed gifts are a constant, although precursors are often in the form of temporary challenge."

"Love—much like meditation—is not something we give, receive, or do; but rather, something we allow to be visited upon us."

"Happiness is not so much about *having* the best of everything, but in making and accepting the best of everything."

When All Engines Fail: "Pushing through the sensory overload, one thought dominated: *Pilot skills – alone – are not going to save us.*"

"Our world—for all practical purposes—is a subjective reality based purely on mirrored projections of our own beliefs, habit patterns, and self-image."

"The Universe gives us what we need to complete our life's curriculum. What our pleasure-seeking, pain-avoiding selves ask for, or want, is generally not the same."

"Simultaneous integration of both heart and head afford the maximum in empowerment options and awakening potential. THIS is the way of a Spiritual Warrior."

"Terrorist or other negative activities, unless you choose to make them so, do *not* determine your security and quality of life."

"God does not give exclusives—question everything!" This will make a good chapter title.

"Victimization is a state of mind and heart...not the result of the human condition."

"All the love and abundance we could possibly imagine, both for us and those we care for, is here for the taking. It requires courage, faith, and determination to *prod beneath the surface* of our manifesting opportunities."

"When you learn to fully forgive, love, and respect yourself, you'll no longer be a punching bag, a psychological clone, or one standing on street corners holding a ***will-jump-through-hoops-for-love*** sign."

"All pathways eventually lead to an experiential realization of the true symbiotic kinship that humanity inherently enjoys."

"There is absolutely nothing that humans can invent that is beyond the divergent scope of possible patterns already known and provided for by Creation itself."

"Only through turning within can we truly be liberated from without. There can no be enlightenment or liberation without core responsibility for our thoughts and feelings."

Angel Author and "LOVE Master"...Leo Politi

I'm progressively reminded how very short our Earth lives are. Special remembrances not only take on greater meaning for me today, but I clearly see how pivotal moments (such as this) can dramatically change the course of human events.

Having never suffered dis-ease or dis-ability, children's book author and artist, Leo Politi, made his peaceful transition in 1996. Not knowing of his passing, I showed up at the front door of his Bunker Hill residence a few months later with healed heart in-hand, finally ready to declare my life-long love and appreciation: I'd not had contact with the Politi family since 1976.

Leo continued actively inspiring his and many others' hearts to sing...right to the very end. If you enjoy sharing inspirational, Soul-connecting stories with the little ones in your charge, contact any children's-department librarian.

The LOVE of in-laws

My *father-in-love*, children's-book author/artist, Leo Politi, featured multi-ethnic children and the opportunity to remember what life was like before we began to artificially separate ourselves based on distorted notion that *uniqueness* (difference) equates *badness* (prejudice). His main character: the zestful, unassuming "Little Pancho"...a hero child of peace, harmony, joy, goodness, curiosity, and inclusive love...appeared first in 1938.

Almost every day, Leo drove from his home on Edgeware Road in Los Angeles, California, to the nearby Mexican Cultural Center and trade section known as "Olivera Street." There, through the eyes and hearts of playful and trusting children, he witnessed who and what we truly are...and can be again if we choose all-inclusive, connecting *light* over deprecating, debilitating, and separating darkness.

In 1969, Leo's daughter, Suzanne, invited me home to meet her uncommon family. While ready with my cleverly constructed, *sure-to-please* answers to standard parental interrogation questions, our disarming and credulous artist obviously had other intentions. Within minutes of introductions he had me down on the hardwood entry floor, gleefully playing with his impressive collection of antique, wind-up toys! In retrospect, perhaps this *was* a test...one to determine if Suzanne's *warrior-suitor* had any "play" left in him.

Thereafter, I lived in awe of Leo's willingness to immediately and unconditionally embrace a serious pursuer of his daughter's affection...without even a *hint* of reservation. In the years I knew Leo, I never once saw him criticize any event, action, or person.

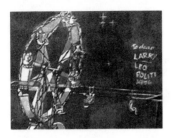

Leo wished only to accept, allow, love, and play. His daughter had brought me home—clearly all it took for him to welcome me with loving, appreciative arms.

Magic of Believing

I recall, now, how I then wished to believe in myself as much as did trusting Leo. I've invested a lifetime emulating, to the best of my often struggling and resisting ability, Leo's demonstration of natural, inclusive love. Although Suzanne (cut from the same *angelic* cloth) and I chose individual paths after celebrating five glorious years together, my *acceptance* practice continues.

Due largely to the shining examples of the entire Politi family (Father/Mother/Son/Daughter—to whom my book is dedicated), you can add me to the Leo Politi list of idealists who believe in the potential for a heart-based Heaven on Earth. I witnessed this Love Master of play and life, as one who did not grant fear-based expressions access to his consciousness or heart.

Leo Politi lives on in his inspirational stories and illustrations (Scribner's Publishing), and now in the 2005 biography offering: *Leo Politi - Artist of the Angels*, by Ann Stalcup (www.annstalcup.com); Silver Moon Press, Publisher.

Those who gift themselves the experience of Leo's hopeful and connecting message, or visit his "Blessing of the Animals" mural creation at Olivera Street in Downtown "City of Angels," will likely awaken to the deeper and larger truth of their own magnificence.

"Blessing of the Animals" mural — Olivera Street, Los Angeles, CA

"The search for truth is more precious than its possession."

—Albert Einstein

"We depend upon others to inform us, but wisdom can never be taught—we must first experience, and then decide the truth for ourselves."

— Outer Limits

"Be the change that you want to see in the world."

— Mahatma Gandhi

Mail Order Form

Internet (PayPal) orders for quickest service: www.soulmanlarry.com

Postal Orders: Soul Talk Unlimited. PO Box 6611, Pahrump, NV 89041

Email: orders@soulmanlarry.com

Please send *Celestial Fire* to:

Email address: _____

Name: _____

Address: _____

City: _____ **State:** _____ **Zip:** _____

Telephone (order troubleshooting only): (_____ **)** _____

Quantity of Books @ 24.95 ea. _____ **Sub Total:** _____

Please add 6.75% sales tax on all orders shipped to Nevada: _____

Add $5.95 for Priority Mail Shipping/Handling (1 or 2 books): _____

TOTAL of Order .... _____

Mail Order Form

Internet (PayPal) orders for quickest service: www.soulmanlarry.com

Postal Orders: Soul Talk Unlimited. PO Box 6611, Pahrump, NV 89041

Email: orders@soulmanlarry.com

Please send *Celestial Fire* to:

Email address: _____

Name: _____

Address: _____

City: _____ **State:** _____ **Zip:** _____

Telephone (order troubleshooting only): (   ) _____

Quantity of Books @ 24.95 ea. _____ **Sub Total:** _____

Please add 6.75% sales tax on all orders shipped to Nevada: _____

Add $5.95 for Priority Mail Shipping/Handling (1 or 2 books): _____

TOTAL of Order .... _____